MW00824535

The Limits of Coexistence

The Limits of Coexistence

IDENTITY POLITICS IN ISRAEL

Rebecca L. Torstrick

Ann Arbor

THE UNIVERSITY OF MICHIGAN PRESS

To my friends in Acre

who continue to believe in

the value of democratic coexistence

and who work to make it

a reality in our lifetime

Copyright © by the University of Michigan 2000
All rights reserved
Published in the United States of America by
The University of Michigan Press
Manufactured in the United States of America
∞ Printed on acid-free paper

2003   2002   2001   2000   4   3   2   1

A CIP catalog record for this book is available from the British Library.

Library of Congress Cataloging-in-Publication Data

Torstrick, Rebecca L., 1954–
    The limits of coexistence : identity politics in Israel / Rebecca L.
Torstrick.
        p.   cm.
    Includes bibliographical references and index.
    ISBN 0-472-11124-8 (cloth : alk. paper)
    1. Acre (Israel) — Ethnic relations.   2. Acre (Israel) — Politics and
government.   3. Palestinian Arabs — Israel — Acre — Politics and
government.   4. Jews — Israel — Acre — Politics and government.   I. Title.

DS110.A3 .T67   2000
956.94′5 — dc21   00-037739

Contents

Illustrations

Tables

Preface

I owe a great debt to my friends and informants in Acre, who let this foreigner into their lives. Without their cooperation, this book would not have been possible. I want to especially recognize Jonathan Schechter, the municipal archivist, who helped me by translating and interpreting records in the archives, introducing me to local officials, and providing insights into local happenings. He continues to keep me informed about life in Acre. Harry Frey, former director of Project Van Leer, put me to work when I arrived in Acre; he continues to be a most perceptive informant and dear friend. Shaul Feldman, Mohammed Assadi, Oren Rechman, and Violette Zuckerman (formerly of Project Van Leer) and activist residents of the Wolfson neighborhood (especially Muhammad Fahili and Herzl Nehama) helped educate me about life in a mixed neighborhood. Their hospitality made my entrance into Acre much easier; I learned (and continue to learn) much from our conversations and discussions. Bernard Dichter, now deceased, graciously allowed me the run of his library on Acre, a product of his great love of the city and his interest in its history. Sharon and Eli Hadasi, Basma and Salibah Watfa, Levy Ovdaiyev, David Berg, Ruti Gur, and Naim Sabbagh were the friends who kept me grounded during my stays in Acre and Israel. Thanks are also due to all of the other informants, who must remain nameless, who helped me to better understand life in Acre.

I met Elektra Spathopoulos when she came to interview me for an article she was writing about Acre. As foreigners, we shared a number of feelings and experiences; as the wife of a Palestinian, Elektra had experienced a side of Israel that I had not. In our numerous discussions, her keen insights into Israeli society (both Jewish and Palestinian) both challenged and supported my own ideas about life and politics in Israel. She worked with me supervising interviews in the Wolfson neighborhood and translated the Arab interviews into English over the next few years. She, her husband, Shouki Samour, and his parents helped me to understand better what it means to be a Palestinian in Israel.

I have benefited greatly from discussions with a number of colleagues or their thoughtful critiques of earlier versions of part or all of this manuscript—Smadar Lavie, Virginia Dominguez, Ted Swedenburg, Rahel Wasserfall, Madelaine Adelman, Charlotte Frisbie, Nina Glick Schiller, Tania Forte, Joel Peters, Oren Rechman, John Bowen, Robert

Canfield, Peter Heath, Henry Berger, Jean Ensminger, Patty Jo Watson, Pedro Cavalcanti, and Art Wirth as well as the two anonymous readers for the University of Michigan Press. They all provided much needed encouragement at different points during the writing process. I also want to acknowledge Erik Cohen, who made available to me his own field journals and copies of interviews he had conducted in Acre twenty years previously. Nancy and Ken Dickinson provided me with a home to return to and a sounding board for my ideas. Barbara and Amos Shamir connected me with people in Israel and helped when I simply could not make sense of Hebrew. My dear friend Solon Chervitz, now deceased, listened to numerous brilliant ideas and provided moral support as I grappled with doing justice to life in Israel in my writing. I know that for both Barbara and Solon it was often difficult to hear what I had to say, but they both encouraged me to remain true to my material. Many thanks to Ardeth Abrams for drawing my maps. I particularly want to thank Susan Whitlock, my editor, for her unflagging support and patience in guiding me through this process.

My field research in 1987–89 was sponsored in Israel by the Department of Sociology and Social Anthropology of the Hebrew University and supported by grants from the Lady Davis Fellowship Trust, Sigma Xi, and the National Science Foundation (BNS 88–07901). My 1998 visit was funded through a summer faculty fellowship and grant-in-aid from my institution, Indiana University-South Bend, as well as an International Projects and Activities Grant from the President's Council on International Programs of Indiana University. I am grateful to my department and colleagues for their support as I worked to complete this book.

An earlier version of parts of chapter 1 and chapter 3 originally appeared in " 'Educating for Democracy' in Israel: Combating or Perpetuating Racism?" *Identities: Global Studies in Culture and Power* 1, no. 4 (1995): 367–90, reprinted here with the kind permission of Gordon and Breach Publishers.

Finally, I want to thank my life partner Jeff and our daughter Maia for their support and patience. Maia endured ten weeks of living in a world where she could not understand much of what was happening around her. Her ability to cope and adapt served as a reminder to me of the tremendous flexibility of which we humans are capable. Jeff was editor and statistical consultant for this work. More importantly, he held our life together throughout the revision process.

Note on transliteration. Arabic transliteration is according to the guidelines of the *International Journal of Middle East Studies.* Hebrew transliteration is according to the guidelines found in the *Chicago Manual of Style,* 14th edition. English translations from Hebrew sources used in the book are the work of the author.

Introduction

Doing Research: Identity in the Field

This book is based on data collected primarily through participant observation during three separate periods of field research in Israel in 1985,
1987–89, and 1990; an additional visit in the summer of 1998 allowed me
to update my earlier work. My visit in 1985 coincided with the end, in
late June, of Israel's formal occupation of Lebanon (although Israeli
soldiers remain in the "security zone," a three- to twelve-mile strip of
territory north of the Galilee border). My return trip from 1987 to 1989
coincided with the outbreak of the *intifada* in the West Bank and Gaza
Strip. My visits in 1990 and 1998 occurred during periods of immigration
of people from the former Soviet Union to Israel, also a process that
continues. War, the Palestinians, and immigration have been three staple elements of Israeli life since the founding of the state; all three, in
different ways, produce, reinforce, and break boundaries.

I first visited Israel during the summer of 1985, when I made a
preliminary visit to choose a field site, develop academic contacts, and
enrich my understanding of Israeli society. Prior to beginning my work in
Israel, I traveled in Greece and Egypt. I can still remember the feeling of
relief and familiarity that swept over me as the plane came in to land over
Tel Aviv. After the dust, noise, and sprawl of Cairo, Israel felt Western,
like coming home. It was a feeling that was not to last. As I noted in my
field journal a week later, "Tel Aviv disturbs me more than Athens or
Cairo because I feel like I should be at ease (am at home) and yet I'm
not." For two weeks, I toured the country. I took an Israeli packaged tour
to Masada and the Dead Sea, I traveled with friends by car through the
Galilee and Golan, I explored the Old City of Jerusalem, and toured
Christian sites near Jerusalem with an Arab guide. Jewish guides presented a unified narrative of a benevolent and progressive Israeli state
that, through its triumphant return to the Promised Land, had realized its
stewardship of that land to the benefit of both Jewish and Arab residents.
In my travels alone or with an Arab guide, however, the fractures in this
narrative kept surfacing. "Sites" were of two types only — biblical and
modern Israeli; the thousands of years of lived experience between these
two time periods were simply made to vanish. Arab guides provided

information about where dividing lines had been, whether an area was Arab or Jewish, and why soldiers guard the Tomb of Rachel (to protect the Jewish women who go there to pray). They continuously reminded us that we were traveling in the West Bank, not in Israel, as the Israeli guides would have it.

I returned to Israel on 28 July 1987 to begin intensive field research. My primary method of data collection in Acre was participant observation. Because my unit of analysis was a residential community of forty thousand people, I focused my research efforts on three arenas that I believed were critical for understanding how boundaries are created and ruptured—the schools, public rituals and community events, and a mixed residential neighborhood.[1] In addition to my research in these areas, I interviewed local public officials, attended local council meetings, spoke with shopkeepers, and listened and observed in many different settings in the city—standing in line at banks, at the post office, at the tax collection office; waiting and traveling on buses. I pored over material from the municipal archives on housing, municipal elections, municipal celebrations, welfare and educational services, the Custodian for Absentee Property, and relations with the Arab sector of the city. The Bernard Dichter Library provided me with travelers' accounts, pamphlets, academic research reports, student seminar papers, and journal articles on Acre. Dr. Erik Cohen provided me with Hebrew transcripts of 170 interviews he conducted in Acre during 1968–69. I traveled to other Arab villages and Jewish settlements in the Galilee; went to weddings, christenings, brits, and family gatherings; and observed or participated in demonstrations in Jerusalem, Tel Aviv, Haifa, and Acre. Wherever I found myself, I tried to pay attention to, absorb, and understand what people were saying and doing. I place these focused observations within a larger historical and sociological understanding of Acre in particular, and Israeli society in general, that I developed through archival and library research as well as interviews and observations. My data, therefore, are both qualitative and quantitative.

Acre is the real name of the town where I conducted my field research. In a country as small as Israel, it would be difficult to disguise the identity of the community. In addition, it would be impossible to provide a historical setting for this work while preserving the community's anonymity. The events described in this work were also real. I have changed people's names or created composites from many different individuals whom I interviewed in order to preserve the anonymity of the town's residents, except for public officials, whose deeds and words were reported widely in the local or national press.

In a strong sense the way to process what one lives through in the field is normatively laid out in advance by peers, profes-

sors, monographs, articles, and books. In addition, one carefully grooms a persona, an identity which conforms to the expectations, but becomes the persona necessary to engage in
certain experiences needed to craft the expected texts. Our
documentations are forms of how we know. If inquiry does not
conform to books one has read, the fear (perhaps the terrible
reality), is that one's experiences will not be relevant for the
texts one will write. (Rose 1989, 28)

It is popular in anthropological writing today for the researcher to
appear quite prominently in the text. This turn toward reflexivity is
supposed to overcome the limitations of earlier forms of ethnography in
which real people's lives and feelings were reduced to facts and figures,
ciphers on a page. There is the danger however, as Erika Friedl notes,
that what is produced is "travelographies filled with trivialities and reve-
lations about the researcher's personal life that add yet another layer of
'text' without necessarily furthering insights into what moves the people
with whom the researcher interacts in seemingly continuous soul-search
mode" (1997, xvii). I have chosen not to cast myself as an actor within
my text. Nevertheless, I am very aware that *who* I am will figure in how
various readers will interpret *what* it is I have to say.

As a non-Jew, non-Palestinian who chose to study Israel, I found my
own identity played with and played upon by the people I was supposedly
studying until it was no longer clear where the boundaries of otherness
lay. I felt much like Trinh T. Minh-ha's insider anthropologist: "She is this
Inappropriate Other/Same who moves about with always at least two/four
gestures: that of affirming 'I am like you' while persisting in her difference; and that of reminding 'I am different' while unsettling every definition of otherness arrived at" (1991, 74). The persona that I groomed in
advance of my fieldwork could not cope with the reality of my field
experiences—the disorienting process of moving within Israeli society,
between Jewish and Palestinian society, and between the working-class,
Mizraḥi world of Acre and the elite, Ashkenazi world of Jerusalem and
Tel Aviv.

I was, at one level, clearly and unequivocally an outsider for Israelis.
I am the child of a Baptist-converted-to-Catholic mother and a father who
should have been raised Protestant but was baptized Catholic. During my
twenties, I began the process of an Orthodox conversion to Judaism
(while considering marriage to a Jewish man), only to realize what such a
conversion would have meant in terms of my own identity. In considering
conversion, I apprehended for the first time that I would be required to
leave behind pieces of my life that I saw as important in my self-
construction. My ethnic heritage is English, Scottish, French, Dutch,
Cherokee, and Swiss. I am the firstborn of a coal miner's daughter, whose

grandfather fought to bring the union into the mines, and a grocer's son, whose grandparents were merchants, artisans, tavern keepers, and farmers. My roots lie in Kentucky, in the Appalachian hills of the Southeast and the cobbled streets of a river city, although I have since acquired a midwestern and urban layer to my identity.

The process by which I was/was not absorbed into Israeli society, those experiences of my own identity in Israel, provided me with the insights I needed to structure my experiences and write my text. Virginia Dominguez, another categorical outsider, noted that as time passed Israelis told her she "felt Jewish" as they attempted to appropriate her otherness (1989, 179). In most cases, people I met for the first time automatically assumed I was Jewish — a function of my name (Rebecca), my physical appearance (dark hair and eyes), and my place of residence in the United States (St. Louis has a thriving Jewish community) and because it is unusual for a researcher not to be Jewish. Because I had tried to live an Orthodox Jewish lifestyle for a year and had studied Israeli society for three years prior to my fieldwork, I did not give off immediate, obvious signs of "foreignness." My non-Jewishness, once revealed, was not problematic for my Jewish friends and informants. The solution was simple: I would find a nice Jewish boy, convert, get married, and stay. As happened with Dominguez, they assumed that somewhere I must have a connection or tie to Israel and Jewishness — I must have Jewish ancestry. Yet, over the course of my stay, my "otherness" became distressingly apparent to those same friends and informants because I did not share their emotional connections to and defense of the Israeli state.

I found myself chafing at Jewish attempts to absorb my voice and rework my identity. As a non-Jewish resident of Acre, I resembled more closely the Palestinian residents of the community — a minority member. Israeli Palestinians also assumed that I was Jewish upon first meeting me, but they had a way of carefully checking their assumption. Eventually in the conversation some remark would be made along the lines of "didn't I want to stay in Israel because of my special connection to the land?" My response, "what special connection?" would begin the process of establishing that in fact I was not Jewish. In most cases, this produced a dramatic reversal in our conversation: someone who was previously "not interested in politics" would suddenly begin expounding on the subject. For Israeli Palestinians, I was a connection to the outside world, someone who could tell their side of the story. Even here, however, my "otherness" did not fade away. As a citizen of a wealthy First World country that is an ally and benefactor of the Israeli state, I was keenly aware that I had access to resources and power that they lacked. I could speak in contexts in which they needed to remain silent.

My position in Acre, therefore, was one of ambivalence and ambiguity. Different people tried to take over my voice and my understanding to present their realities and truths, but the "they" were not unitary subjects (Palestinians, Israeli nationalists, Mizraḥim, Ashkenazi intellectuals, educators, worried parents) and the "truth" they proclaimed was varied and multiplex. In crossing and recrossing the boundary lines, I was more exposed to "the heterogeneous reality we all live today, in postmodern times — a reality, therefore, that is not a mere crossing from one borderline to the other or that is not merely double, but a reality that involves the crossing of an indeterminate number of borderlines, one that remains multiple in its hyphenation" (Trinh 1991, 107). It is this reality, in all its messy complexity, that I have tried to convey in this work.

That who I am matters in my research was even more forcefully brought home to me by the comments of one of the reviewers of my manuscript. This person, as a Jew, wanted to know not so much *who* I was but *why* I chose this topic and this locus of study. What, he or she asked, was my quest? At one level, I am used to explaining to people why, or rather how, I came to do research in Israel. I had already developed an interest in how nations "created" cultures through years of international folk dancing. I knew some governments encouraged folk traditions while others actively quashed them. My master's studies in organizational behavior and workplace democracy further piqued my interest in how larger organizational structures intersected individuals' personal identities. In choosing graduate programs, I wanted to work with a particular individual who was a Middle Eastern specialist and who was willing to work with me only if I also studied the Middle East. Israel was the country I knew best as I began my graduate study due to interactions with Zionist friends from my undergraduate years. Looking at how nationalism affected local ethnic and personal identities seemed the logical next step. In other words, my Israeli project represents the intersection of a number of different pieces of my life.

Or does it? Like my Israeli informants, I construct narratives that bring my life into a coherent focus. Yet I want to resist constructing a master narrative that explains it all and neatly ties up the loose ends. I honestly do not know what my quest was in going to Israel, but I do know that I learned a great deal about Israelis, myself, and my own society during the time I spent there. It is a place that breaks hearts.

Finally, while there were discussions during my graduate training about doing field research in a police state, the reality was more difficult than I anticipated. Americans do not generally think of Israel as a police state, but the General Security Services (Shabak) is ever present behind the scenes of Israeli life. While Israeli Palestinians are more likely to fall under its gaze, the Shabak also keeps track of left-wing Jewish political movements (such as Matzpen or Women in Black). Since I am not Jewish, I assumed I was more likely to be watched. When I broached my concern with academic friends in Jerusalem, they laughed. My project and person were not "important" enough to interest the Shabak, I was told. I chose to proceed as if they might be, however. This meant that I had to make choices about what questions I would ask and whether I would write down people's answers or other information I learned in the course of conversations. In effect, I disciplined my research—possibly more than I needed to, but I did not want to risk harming any of the people who were assisting me. In hiring interviewers for the Wolfson project, I learned that I had to hire people who were trusted for the Arabic interviews. They needed to be seen as non-state affiliated and nonpolitical.[2] I was never directly questioned by the Shabak (although I know of at least one researcher who was). Conducting research in a climate of fear is never easy; it takes a toll on the researcher, who must decide what can and cannot be asked or recorded and who may or may not be approached for information.

CHAPTER 1

Prelude to a Discourse on Identity

The Place and the Problem

Listen, we have a big problem here. I've already been breaking
my head over it for years. For me, the intifadah did not change
the major thing that awaits us. With regard to what's happening in the West Bank, the solution is already on the horizon.
Whether we want it or not, whether we bend our backs or walk
erect, the solution is there. The Palestinian state will come in
the end. Remaining then will be the difficult and complex and
most dangerous question of the Israeli Arabs. And no one is
really conscious of that, not Peace Now, or the Jewish liberals
in Israel, or the intellectuals who are willing to meet any Arab
in Paris but not here. (quoted in Grossman 1993, 128)

Thus, Sami Michael, a Jewish-Arab-Iraqi (and now Israeli) writer,
summed up in 1993 the major problem that he saw facing Israeli society
in the future. Michael is not alone in his assessment. Women peace
activists had raised the same question earlier in 1990 at a conference in
Haifa: "Why am I angry? Because we need to think clearly about another problem. We have to think that after two states for two nations we
must live with our Palestinian citizens, and our next struggle will be
equal rights for all the citizens of Israel" (quoted in Emmett 1996, 76).
Sociologist Sami Smooha, also Iraqi born, has said that the true test for
the structure of Israeli society will not be what happens with the Palestinians in the territories (the West Bank and Gaza Strip) or with those
Palestinians outside of Israel and the territories but how Israel deals with
its own Palestinian citizens. He sees the latter situation as having the
potential to change the fabric of Israeli life.[1]

As intellectuals and politicians have groped for solutions, Israeli
Jews who live in the country's mixed Arab-Jewish cities have confronted
the need to share their space and resources with their fellow Palestinian
citizens.[2] Since the lifting of military rule in 1951, the Arab and Jewish
residents of Acre,[3] a town of forty-five thousand inhabitants located on
the coast north of Haifa, have worked with each other, done business
with each other, and lived together in the same neighborhoods and
buildings. In over forty years of living together, they have forged an

uneasy status quo in which the Jewish residents of the town hold the dominant position. This relationship withstood the disruptions of three Arab-Israeli wars, but beginning in the 1980s both Jewish and Arab residents experienced increased levels of tension in their dealings with one another. Acts of intercommunal intolerance and violence began to increase, culminating in an openly confrontational local election campaign in early 1989 and the murder of a local Arab youth by a Jewish man in May 1989. These latter two events threatened to rupture the coexistence that had come to be seen as the city's trademark. Local residents (both Jewish and Palestinian) attributed these problems to the influence of the Palestinian uprising (*intifada*) against Israeli occupation of the West Bank and Gaza Strip, which began in December 1987.

Such local explanations at first appeared to make a certain sense. Israeli Jews were involved in violent clashes with Palestinians in the territories. It was not unreasonable to think that such a conflict might also spread to Acre. It was common sense. As Clifford Geertz suggests, however, common sense is not simply "matter-of-fact apprehension of reality" or "immediate deliverances of experience" but rather an organized body of thought that is historically constructed, that is, in fact a set of "deliberated reflections" upon experience (1983, 75). Why did the Palestinian and Jewish residents of Acre believe that an uprising would take place there? There was little in their immediate experiences that might lead them to believe that the city was ripe for revolution. Acre was far removed from the conflicts occurring in the West Bank and Gaza Strip. Its Palestinian residents were not under military occupation; they are Israeli citizens, with all the rights that such status entails. Palestinian families could be found living in almost every residential quarter of the city. Some Palestinian and Jewish children attended the same kindergartens and played together on neighborhood playgrounds. Palestinian and Jewish residents shared the same medical clinics and doctors, purchased services from each other, and may even have worked together in one of the local industries. Peaceful coexistence had been a valued component of Palestinian-Jewish relations in the city for both municipal officials and some residents themselves. In fact, Acre received a national prize for tolerance in 1986. No major incidents of intercommunal violence had occurred in Acre since the discovery in 1969 of a terrorist cell in the Old City. Even then, the members of the group carried out their sabotage activities not in Acre but in Haifa, a large, predominantly Jewish city about ten kilometers to the south.

During those first two years of the *intifada,* more than 600 Palestinians in the territories were killed by Israeli soldiers, police, security agents, and settlers; more than 39,000 people were wounded; 40,000 were jailed for various "security" offenses; 363 homes were demolished or sealed; and 60 activists were deported. On the Israeli side during the same period, 43 Israelis were killed, while the wounded included 2,438 civilians and 1,635 soldiers.[4] Besides demonstrating and confronting Israeli army patrols, Palestinians had participated in work and tax strikes, economic boycotts of Israeli products, and other strategies of noncooperation with Israeli forces. The Israeli army had utilized administrative detention, curfews, searches, school and university closures, and deportations in addition to rubber and plastic bullets, wooden clubs and beatings, tear-gas grenades, water cannons, and a gravel-throwing vehicle. There was little congruence between life in the occupied territories and life in the city of Acre. Why then was it common sense for the residents of Acre to expect an uprising?

Underlying their common sense explanations were notions about the boundaries of different identities, about what it means to be Israeli or Palestinian, to be Jewish or Arab. Israeli is equated with Jew, Palestinian with Arab, and in popular culture it is taken for granted that Jews and Arabs hate each other. This simple equation masks a number of contradictions. Some Israelis are Palestinians, some Jews are Arabs, many Jews throughout the world are not Israelis, and not all Arabs are Palestinians. Some Israeli Jews oppose the existence of the Israeli state, while some Palestinian Arabs have officially recognized the existence of that same state. Some Israeli Jews (Ashkenazim) have greater access to power and resources than other Israeli Jews (Mizraḥim). Some Palestinian Arabs (in Israel or abroad) enjoy higher living standards than other Palestinian Arabs (in the refugee camps of Gaza or Lebanon). While some Jews and Arabs, Israelis and Palestinians do indeed hate one another, others seek simply to coexist. As one Palestinian worker explained in Rosemary Sayigh's study of Palestinians living in refugee camps in Lebanon, "We know that Israel exists, we don't want to throw the Jews into the sea. We don't want to die, we want to live. We want to live, and we want others (i.e. Israelis) to live. But we don't want others to live, and us to die" (1979, 190).

How Israeli and Palestinian national identities came into being and the struggles for control over their content are not the subject of this work. Both have been well documented in a series of other works (on Israeli nationalism [Zionism], see Avineri 1981; Avishai 1985; Liebman and Don-Yehiya 1983; and Eisenstadt 1985; on Palestinian nationalism, see Said 1979, 1985; Muslih 1988; Sayigh 1979; Quandt et al. 1973; and Miller 1985). As national identities, however, they provide a series of shorthand codes that reduce the complexity of people's identities to "friend-foe" dichotomies that provide clear and absolute rules for guiding action and interaction. While a number of studies of nationalism have concentrated on the importance of print and broadcast media in "narrating the nation" and relaying the national message (see, e.g., Anderson 1991; Bhabha 1990; and Kapferer 1988), national identities are not simply products of such "indirect social relationships" (Calhoun 1991). Rather than assume that nationalism has thoroughly permeated local relations, I have tried in this case study to illuminate under what circumstances local residents came to accept and use the national identity categories and prescriptions for action.

Connolly states that in late modern times the state is most secure when it appears to be accountable to an electorate that can replace its leaders and change its policies through open elections: "the ideal of democracy sets the terms for state legitimacy" (1991, 201). Democratic states constantly tinker with policy formulations in order to find those configurations that resonate most with their constituents. Policies that are resisted at the local level serve to increase resentment against the state and destabilize state control. Israeli state elites may try to transmit particular versions of identities through government policies and the mass media, but policies are carried out in Acre by local teachers, municipal officials, and government employees who themselves have direct social ties with local residents. The state's efforts to control social categories at the local level will succeed if enough local officeholders and residents perceive such policies as sufficiently legitimate and useful to their own needs and interests. Those individuals in the local community who resist the state's efforts may find themselves marginalized and stigmatized, further confounding their efforts to renegotiate the social categories and change government policies. In this study, I analyze how state policy efforts in the areas of education and housing are implemented in Acre as well as a local electoral contest (influenced by national political struggles) in order to gauge how effective the Israeli state has been in transmitting its notions of social identities and appropriate forms of relationships.

If people's identities were subsumed in bounded and cohesive categories, then it would not be surprising to see intercommunal conflict break out in Acre between its Palestinian and Jewish residents because they would understand each other only in terms of their categorical identities (as Israelis and Palestinians). Identity is better understood, however, as what Ferguson terms "mobile subjectivities," by which she means an identity "too concrete and dirty to claim innocence, too much in-process to claim closure, too interdependent to claim fixed boundaries" (1993, 161).[5] Such identities are sites of "interdependence and strife between incipient formations/presentations of self and intersubjectively constituted modes of identification" (Connolly 1991, 175).

People in Acre can draw upon many facets of their identities in resist-ing the state's messages and constructing meaningful relations with people who may themselves maintain a complex life at odds with state Zionism. Through the routine interactions of everyday life, Acre's resi-dents do construct their own local categories of identity and acceptable social behaviors. Local experience, while not always entirely trusted, still provides the basis for framing different models of Arab-Jewish relations. These local narratives are often counterposed to the national-ist narrative of enmity.

This does not mean, however, that national categories of identity and the narratives about them are resisted and subverted at the local level. As Connolly notes, there is a mutually reinforcing bond between personal and collective identities. A collective identity "recapitulates the contingent, conflicted character of personal identity; it also inflates tendencies in the latter to dogmatize its configuration when confronted by disruptive contingencies" (1991, 204). Modern states first garner the generalized resentment of their citizens at the deleterious effects of modern economic life. The state then serves as the vehicle through which the population is reassured about the benefits and durability of that life, and finally, it serves as the instrument of action against those elements most threatening to the collective identity. By constructing various "evil" others, the state can demonstrate its power to discipline and punish, paper over its defects, and transform cracks in the estab-lished identity into threats against which a need for collective unity can be invoked (206–9). In this work, I explore how effective the Israeli state has been in its efforts to control the process of creating identities in Acre.

The processes at work in Acre today have their roots in the late nine-teenth century, when Jewish leaders in Europe, influenced by the cur-rent of nationalism then sweeping the continent, decided that the only way to end the persecution of their people was to regain a homeland. The adherents of Zionism, the belief that the Jewish nation required a state of its own, consciously worked to bring about the rebirth of Jewish sovereignty in the ancestral Jewish homeland — Palestine — then part of the Ottoman Empire.[6] As early as 1897, Zionist writers on Palestine described the indigenous Arab population in general ("natives of the land") or sectorial terms ("urbanites," "*fellahin,*" "bedouins," or "Chris-tians"), thus as lacking a collective, national identity (Shapira 1992, 44). To have recognized the existence in Palestine of a viable Arab national movement would have undermined the legitimacy of establishing a Jew-ish national state in the region.

During the prestate period, the Jewish community of Palestine was pluralistic, divided into a number of different factions, each of which had its own goals and priorities. Political parties, labor movements, and economic, religious, and ethnic associations proliferated. Each subgroup received from the Jewish Agency an allocation of resources — immigration certificates, land for settlement, jobs, money, and political — that was based on its political strength. The glue that held the different factions together was their mutual interest in founding a Jewish state. If the Jewish people had a state of their own, they would no longer be subject to persecution, discrimination, and violence in the diaspora (exile). The Palestinian community during this period was also divided into factions, each loyal to different families or political parties. The tie that united these factions was their opposition to Zionist plans to found a Jewish state in Palestine.

The unfolding of the Zionist vision after 1918, as Ottoman was superseded by British rule under a mandate from the League of Nations (1922–48), is well documented.[7] Although the indigenous Palestinian inhabitants of the land struggled to retain their rights in the face of Zionist incursions throughout the early part of the twentieth century, by the end of the British Mandate over Palestine the United Nations had voted to partition the country into two states, one Palestinian and one Jewish. The Jewish state of Israel was declared on 15 May 1948. During that year and the next, war raged throughout Palestine. When the final cease-fire was called, 25 percent of what would have been the Palestinian state's territory had been conquered and annexed to the Jewish state (Akenson 1992, 232). What land remained was annexed by Jordan (the West Bank) and Egypt (the Gaza Strip). A Palestinian state never came into being. It was *al-Nakbah,* "the catastrophe."

With statehood, the parties of the Labor movement, under the leadership of David Ben-Gurion, emerged as victors in the struggle for control of the new polity. The pluralism of the prestate period could no longer be tolerated. The new leaders of the state believed that the country had to be integrated so that the entire Jewish population would unite to support the state and its institutions. In order to successfully carry out the twin missions of *kibbutz ha'galuyōt* (the ingathering of the exiles) and *mizūg ha'galuyōt* (the absorption of the exiles), one unified state structure had to be developed. State building required the suppression of difference in the interests of national unity.

Ben-Gurion and the other Labor leaders consciously strove to establish their particular model of society as the *only* possible social order. While still at war in 1949, the new Israeli state opened its borders to Jewish immigration, and by 1951 the country's population had doubled. Many of the new immigrants came from North Africa or the Middle East. To veteran Israelis, most of whom came from Eastern Europe, these new immigrants were culturally foreign creatures. These people bore little resemblance to their ideal Israeli and would require extensive modification to reach that ideal. These immigrants, who lacked any ideological awareness of or attraction to socialist Zionism, threatened the integrity of the state that the Labor parties were attempting to build because their votes could upset the political balance. In addition to these immigrants, a significant Palestinian population remained within Israel's borders at the time of the final cease-fire. These people who had been the enemy now had to be integrated somehow within the new state.

In solving these dilemmas, the early leaders of the state produced a paradox: while attempting to subsume different groups within a single social order, they also simultaneously imposed distance between themselves and those groups by stressing the otherness of those they ruled.[8] In denying pluralism, Israeli government officials in fact established differing patterns of relationships with various groups and in the process spawned new categories of identity (Ashkenazi, Mizraḥi, Israeli, Israeli Arab, Palestinian) with both intended and unintended consequences. In establishing the superiority, typicality, or universality of some identities in terms of the inferiority, atypicality, or particularity of others, Israeli state elites generated a hierarchy of belonging in which some groups are more Israeli than others.

Once these categories of identity were established, Israel's political leaders enshrined their approach/avoidance relationship with each of the potentially threatening populations by means of particular institutional arrangements. The indigenous Palestinians comprise 20 percent of the total population of Israel. While they were allowed to become citizens, they were distanced from the center of power because the Israeli state was a *Jewish* state and Israeli national identity incorporated explicit Jewish symbols and referents. Government officials categorized and labeled them by religion (Muslims, Christians, Druze), region (Galilee Arabs, Triangle Arabs, Negev Bedouin), and family connections, or *hamula* (Haberer 1985, 148). In official and popular culture, they ceased being Palestinians and were re-created as Israeli Arabs or Arab citizens of Israel. Expressing Palestinian identity by displaying the flag, singing nationalist songs, or reciting nationalist poetry was illegal in Israel until only very recently. Self-identification as Palestinians, Israeli Palestinians, or Palestinian citizens of Israel has increased since 1967 and is now their preferred descriptor. It was only under the influence of the *intifada,* however, that many Israeli Palestinians felt secure enough to begin to refer to themselves publicly in this way (as opposed to choosing the label *Palestinian* only in anonymous surveys on identity). With the signing of the Oslo Peace Accords, they are now legally able to claim a Palestinian identity and display its symbols. Israeli Palestinians have begun to question what the peace process will mean for them — they are focusing attention on Sami Michael's "most dangerous question" concerning their status.

The Israeli state's goal has been to make the Palestinians economically and politically dependent on the state while allowing them limited cultural and religious autonomy. The Jewish economy has absorbed Palestinian workers while Jewish political parties have vied for Palestinian votes directly or by creating affiliated Arab political slates. Palestinians are allowed a separate school system, ostensibly so that they can preserve their language and culture, but the Jewish establishment has supervised and controlled the appropriate cultural content of that system. Government ministries have established separate sections to deal with the problems or concerns of Palestinian residents. What this separation has meant in practice is very real inequality in the provision of government services and benefits to Israeli Palestinians. For example, research conducted under the direction of Henry Rosenfield in 1988 indicated that Jewish local authorities were receiving budgets three times greater than Palestinian local authorities of comparable size. His team also found evidence of inequalities in health care, education, social welfare services, and access to the legal system.[9] Finally, Palestinians are further segregated by religious affiliation because rights regarding personal status (marriage, divorce, inheritance) are vested in each religious community.

Ashkenazi refers to Jewish populations of European, American, Russian, or South African (i.e., "Western") origin. With 45 percent of the Jewish and 32 percent of the total population of Israel, they are the ruling economic, political, and social elite (Weingrod and Gurevitch 1977). Ashkenazi immigrants, many of them Holocaust survivors, were recast as Israelis: to be Israeli, one had to be (or become) modern and Western oriented. That many Ashkenazi immigrants did not meet these criteria was glossed over in the process of state and nation building. Ben-Gurion's Labor government did not perceive the new Ashkenazi immigrants as threats. European ethnicity, that is, continued identification with the immigrant's country of origin, was at its height during the first decade following his or her arrival in Israel (Weingrod 1979). Immigrant associations (*landsmanshaften*), ethnic synagogues, political organizations, and Yiddish- or Romanian-language newspapers enabled European immigrants to maintain their cultural ties to their fellow countrymen and women. Since the 1960s, however, these ethnic ties have gradually dissolved, to be replaced by a broader identity as Ashkenazim. A number of factors produced this dissolution, including the existence of few barriers to assimilation between veteran pre-1948 European immigrants and the newcomers, a willingness to adopt the new culture because of negative images of European diaspora culture, and the rapid economic and social mobility these new immigrants experienced (ibid., 57–58). The recent immigration from the former Soviet Union has served to bolster Ashkenazi domination. At the same time, however, the Russians are separating themselves culturally and politically (as in demands that Russian be recognized as an official language or the creation of Russian political parties) as they are also distanced by the prejudice and negative reactions they encounter on the part of veteran Israelis. It remains to be seen whether the Russians will dissolve into a larger Ashkenazi identity.

Mizrahi refers to Jewish populations of North African, Middle Eastern, or Asian origin (*ʿedot hamizrah*—literally, "Eastern communities"). They constitute 55 percent of the Jewish and 48 percent of the total population of Israel. While some writers advocate the use of the term *Sephardi* (literally, "from Spain") to describe these communities,[10] *Mizrahi* is the term members of these communities use in advocating group rights, while reserving *Sephardi* for more apolitical, religious contexts (Lavie 1992).[11] Veteran Jewish settlers and the new immigrants from Europe, North Africa, and the Middle East were all subsumed within the single category of Jewish nationality. Mizrahi Jews, however, were distanced from the center of power because the Israeli state was a Western, Ashkenazi state and Israeli national identity incorporated Western values and patterns of behavior. For the Mizrahim, political leaders wanted to make them completely dependent on the state so that they could be reeducated into the appropriate socialist Zionist identity. At the same time, some policymakers used Mizrahi dependence on the state as evidence of their cultural inferiority and lack of capacity to adapt to their new setting (Swirski 1989, 26–28). Government officials have encouraged the Mizrahim to lose their traditional identities and assimilate to a new Israeli identity.

In the first twenty years of statehood, Labor leaders used the Mizrahim to build their state. When the agricultural sector needed to be strengthened, government officials placed Mizrahi immigrants (who had no farming skills) on farms. When the state decided to develop the industrial sector, government officials sent Mizrahi immigrants to factory towns. They mobilized the national educational system to teach the children of Mizrahi immigrants how to be good Israelis. At the same time, however, the nation at large adopted elements of Mizrahi material culture (especially music and crafts) and the Sephardi dialect of Hebrew as "Israeli" folk culture. Institutional pluralism among Jews was allowed in only a single area, religion, with the recognition of separate Sephardi and Ashkenazi rabbinates (Ben-Rafael and Sharot 1987).[12]

Their absorption into Israeli society left Mizrahim second-class citizens. Government officials settled them at the margins of the new Israeli state, removed from the centers of power and growth in the central cities.

The official policy of equal treatment for all immigrants generated unequal outcomes because officials ignored differences in people's needs
and capabilities. Segregated in homogeneous communities, Mizraḥi immigrants were expected to assimilate to an abstract cultural norm, one
that they heard about but did not see modeled in their communities.
Separatist tendencies were severely frowned upon by the political establishment because the Jewish people had to be united. Ongoing military
conflicts with the surrounding Arab countries served to highlight this
need for unity among Israeli Jews. Government intolerance of Jewish
cultural pluralism began to dissipate in the early 1970s after the Black
Panthers, a Mizraḥi movement, rallied residents in underprivileged neighborhoods to protest against the state's discriminatory treatment. As their
movement gained in strength, government officials who at first dismissed
them as delinquents were forced to concede that there were social gaps in
Israel. The outbreak and aftermath of the Yom Kippur War in 1973
eclipsed the issues raised by the Panthers. It was not until 1977 that
Mizraḥi voters staged another protest. Their votes gave control of the
national government to the Likud Party, thus bringing to an end the
Labor Party's lengthy domination of national affairs. The change in government, however, did not mean a corresponding change in the identity
hierarchy. Mizraḥim have not experienced any real changes in terms of
their economic, political, or social position in Israeli society, regardless of
which political party rules.

These categories are part of a broader national ideology that links
state, nation, and religion in a particular configuration. The raison
d'être of the Israeli state is to defend and secure Jewish welfare. In
practice, this means that Israeli Jews receive preference for government
services and benefits. In addition, Israel is the state of the Jews, even
those not choosing to live within its territorial boundaries. Thus, the
interests of Israeli citizens are often neglected in favor of dealing with
the problems of Jewish communities in other parts of the world, as when
state funds are diverted to encourage further Jewish immigration. While
it is the state of the Jews, this does not mean that it is a religiously Jewish
state. Israel's founding fathers sought to develop a cultural Jewish identity based on the religious traditions yet at the same time divorced from
them. The status quo forged upon achieving statehood gave the religious
establishment control over personal status and certain other concessions, but the Labor Party established a democratic socialist state. Since
Israel is a democratic state, Israeli Palestinians continue to insist that the
Israeli national identity includes them as well and that national symbols
and celebrations must be changed to provide for their inclusion (see,
e.g., the debate between noted Israeli writers Anton Shammas, a Palestinian, and A. B. Yehoshua, a Jew, in Grossman 1993, 250–77).

Nationality and citizenship are separate in Israel. For Israeli Jews, their nationality is their Judaism, as inscribed on their identity cards. Thus, the burning issue is "who is a Jew?" since Jewishness provides privileged access to state resources.[13] For Palestinians, their identity cards list their nationality as Arab or Druze, not Israeli. Jewish nationalism, which separates Jews from non-Jews, is overlaid with a discourse of cultural racism wherein Israeli society is further divided and marked according to degrees of cultural inferiority and superiority. These ideologies mesh with a separate discourse, centered on notions of democratic citizenship, to create and highlight the boundaries that define who and what is an Israeli. In this formulation, the Mizraḥim must be included as Jews but the taint of their Arab heritage raises the question of how Jewish they truly are, while Palestinians are excluded as Arabs but partially included because they have rights as citizens. The Mizraḥim are Israeli because their hard work helped to redeem the country. The Palestinians of Israel are Israeli because, unlike Palestinians living elsewhere, they have shared in the common history and experiences that have shaped the Israeli state and society since 1948. In this way, Israeli Palestinians are more Israeli than new Jewish immigrants from Ethiopia or the former Soviet Union, who have yet to acquire an Israeli identity.

The various peoples who became Israeli citizens brought to the new state a variety of different cultures and identities. Rather than valuing these differences and adopting policies that fostered cultural pluralism, Israel's founding fathers felt compelled to sacrifice difference in order to create a homogenous, unified society. This society, however, was to be in their image. In striving for homogeneity, they actually spawned new categories of identity, as they ranked diverse groups of people according to how much they differed from the desired ideal. They developed distinct policy imperatives for each broad category of citizen according to whether or not they wished to facilitate their inclusion in Israeli society. These policy goals generated the present status hierarchy, with Ashkenazi Jews dominant, followed by Mizraḥi Jews and finally Israeli Palestinians. Government policies and societal categories combined to limit the upward mobility of large numbers of Israelis (Mizraḥim and Palestinians), thus producing the seeds of potential conflict and instability in Israeli society.

Studies of Israeli society generally recognize three broad cleavages that threaten Israel's stability: between Jew and Palestinian, between Ashkenazi and Mizraḥi Jews, and between secular and religious Jews. (That these broad cleavages represent the identity labels created by the Israeli state comes as no surprise. The close relationship between academic scholarship and government policy in Israel has been noted by several scholars [Bernstein 1980; Dominguez 1989].) Each of the paired terms represents a particular relationship of real or potential tension or conflict within Israeli society. Addressed at a macrolevel, it becomes possible to analyze each relationship of conflict as a separate entity. What happens, however, when Ashkenazi and Mizraḥi Jews and Israeli Palestinians live together in the same community? How do local residents manage the conflicts that are an inevitable part of life? Do they simply accept and reproduce the "common sense" of the national cleavages — Ashkenazi against Mizraḥi, Jew against Arab, secular against religious? Or are state categories subverted in these local struggles such that the outcomes of these conflicts are not necessarily predictable?

I look at how people in Acre adopt, reject, or change the state's messages and how they respond to the rewards and punishments that accompany those messages given that their daily lives lead them to develop ideas about and relationships with others that are not completely congruent with the national ideology. In the following sections, I develop my theoretical argument concerning the connections among identities, social relationships, and states. Then, in the chapters that follow, I explore how Acre's residents work through the contradictions in their lives in several key arenas. In chapter 2, I present a discussion of Acre's development as a community since 1948. This history, in which Arab and Jewish accounts are woven together to illuminate the city's development, provides a context for the events presented in the following three chapters. In chapter 3, I explore schools as sites for constructing identity. While the Arab and Jewish school systems in Acre are separate, local children are brought together in one of two ways — in programs intended to combat racism by teaching democratic values or in mixed Arab-Jewish kindergartens. Efforts by local officials and some parents to close down both of these forms of integrated schooling produced different outcomes. In chapter 4, I analyze the experiences of Arabs and Jews who live in the Wolfson neighborhood, which has been integrated since 1965. I look at how residents of this neighborhood construct their boundaries of identity. This process illustrates the interactions of local experience and nationalist prescriptions. Chapter 5 analyzes the 1989 municipal election campaign, which became a political battle over Acre's future: would it be an Arab or a Jewish city? In the summer of 1998, I returned to Israel and Acre after an eight-year absence. I wanted to assess what effect major external events such as the Persian Gulf conflict and the peace negotiations with the Palestine Liberation Organization (PLO) have had on how residents of Acre construct their identities and social relationships in their community as well as considering the effects of local events such as elections and immigrant absorption. Chapter 6 presents my findings from this visit. I continue to believe that processes at work in Acre may illuminate one possible future for Palestinian-Jewish coexistence in Israel and may prove relevant to similar situations in other pluralistic nation-states.

On Difference and Boundaries

To gain some insight into how analysts have approached the question of the boundaries of identity, consider the theoretical debate on ethnicity that raged during the 1960s and 1970s (and still orients some studies of ethnicity according to Bentley 1987). Primordialists such as Geertz (1963), De Vos (1975), Isaacs (1975), and Epstein (1978) view ethnicity as an innate form of group loyalty based on shared blood ties, race, language, religion, custom, and territory. The boundaries of ethnic identity are therefore given by nature. One is born into one's identity, and the boundaries persist because they protect their members from psychic stress during periods of radical social upheaval. "Primordial diversity" is here opposed to a modern (i.e., Western) civic identity and civic order, wherein ethnic identity gives way to a national identity that is grounded in the modern political community. Others are individuals who remain bound to primordial loyalties and have not yet begun the move toward civic society. Selves in this theoretical world, while they may retain some vague awareness of their ethnic heritage, have crossed the ethnic identity boundary into a new territory of civic identification with governing states.

Contrast this model of identity with the instrumentalist perspective on ethnicity, as represented in the works of Despres (1967), A. Cohen (1969), Smith (1981), and Young (1983). Instrumentalists view ethnicity as a means by which like-minded individuals can achieve particular economic or political goals in specific contexts. Ethnic groups are "in fact interest groupings whose members share some common economic and political interests and who, therefore stand together in the continuous competition for power with other groups" (A. Cohen 1969, 192). The boundaries of ethnic identity are therefore the outcomes of rational, goal-oriented human action. Instrumental explanations blend into other theories such as internal colonialism (Hechter 1975), the split-labor market (Bonacich 1972, 1979), competition (Olzak and Nagel 1986), and resource competition (See 1986) that link the development of ethnic stratification, by retaining (or creating) and reinforcing ethnic categories of identity, to the spread of capitalism and labor-market processes. Here the boundaries of identity are determined not by human action but by the impersonal forces of the market and capitalist development. Others are people who remain trapped in traditional forms by market processes or who choose, for the moment, to remain "trapped" as a strategy for securing access to scarce resources. Selves, as in the primordialist vision, have crossed into a nonethnic, homogeneous, capitalist cultural world.

The problem with both of these visions is that ethnicity is treated as a bounded, discrete thing — almost a possession — that one has or does not have. By extension, identity too becomes a thing since much about a person's existence is determined by the ethnic label. In one version, people have ethnic identities because they are born into them. In the other version, people have ethnic identities because they see advantages in adopting them. Identity is dichotomized: one is either a have or a have-not, modern or ethnic, a self or an other. Power inheres to the first term in the paired opposition.

We live, however, in a world of shifting possibilities and shared images, a mobile, never quite stable, global culture, many of whose members are bound together by fax machines, computers, television, and video machines. East and West, North and South meet and interact on a daily basis. The history of Acre is a chronicle of a series of encounters between West and East that occurred as merchants, soldiers, religious pilgrims, and residents mingled in the markets and streets of the town. In such a reality, it becomes important to focus on the ways in which people continue to establish and reinforce the boundaries of their identities, even as those boundaries are transgressed and compromised (as Barth suggested in 1969). Identities are "cultural phenomena embodied in customs, emblems, institutions, lexical categories, etc., and they imply relationships among people" (Canfield 1988, 185). Such a notion of identities implies a process of becoming, the unfolding of concrete life histories that are embedded in different relationships and shaped by different institutional forces, rather than a state of being, an essential sameness that never changes. It requires a vision of identity that focuses on the ways in which subjectivities are multiple and mobile rather than static and unified, what Bernstein (1992, 308) calls the "logic of tensed Both/And" and Benjamin (1988, 221) casts as the tension between a simultaneous need for recognition and independence.[14]

> Difference as uniqueness or special identity is both limiting and deceiving. If identity refers to the whole pattern of sameness within a human life, the style of a continuing me that permeates all the changes undergone, then difference remains within the boundary of that which distinguishes one identity from another. . . . Can identity, indeed, be viewed other than as a by-product of a "manhandling" of life, one that, in fact, refers no more to a consistent "pattern of sameness" than to an inconsequential process of otherness? (Trinh 1989, 95)

For these writers, difference does not imply conflict, it is not opposed to sameness, it does not have to result in segregation, and it is not separation. Difference means developing resilience in the face of contradictions and learning tolerance for ambiguity. As Anzaldua writes, "To survive the Borderlands you must live *sin fronteras* [without frontiers] be a crossroads" (1987, 195).

As Bernstein (1992, 296) notes, the question of how to conceptualize difference (i.e., self/other relations) in social life is at the heart of many debates within modern philosophical and social thought.[15] While conservative and liberal usages of the term retain an excluding notion of difference, an either/or vision of identity, the radical vision seeks to dissolve the dichotomy, to retain a tension in which self and other are both similar and different, both present in the same being. The self is continually constructed and reconstructed as it encounters variously defined others. Bentley (1987, 35) notes that an individual can possess several different situationally relevant identities that are also emotionally authentic, all of which may be symbolized in terms of shared descent. Sometimes other people provide the foils against which the self chooses to define itself, and sometimes the self incorporates aspects of those others. Identity is not a bounded, ordered whole but is only partially realized at any given moment in time. It is fractured, with its elements continually ordered and reordered according to the imperatives of the moment, in a historical shuffling of the parts. Different elements of identity will be privileged in different encounters to either forge connections with or highlight differences from variously defined others.[16] Afrikaners, for example, cling tenaciously to their historical memories of victimization at the hands of the English, thus inscribing an identity as victim in the sense of a collective self while at the same time refusing to acknowledge their own abusive practices toward the black population: "I don't think we have ever done the things to the Blacks that the English did to us" (quoted in Crapanzano 1985, 51). In this, identity is much like culture, which is also partial, fragmented, changing, and volatile.

Who Determines the Boundaries

While identity is only partially realized at any given moment in time, this is not to suggest that individuals are free to adopt any identity they choose. Indeed, claiming to be another can lead, under certain circumstances, to incarceration in prison or to confinement in a mental institution, as Trinh (1989, 95) notes in her discussion of identity and difference. Identities are constituted through the dual process of self-ascription and ascription by others. Cornel West (1992) notes that identity is about desires and death: desires for recognition, for affiliation, for protection and security. These desires can lead to death because some identities are constructed in such a way that their holders will either kill or be killed by or for them.[17] People construct their desires for recognition, affiliation, and security in social contexts not of their choosing that vary across time and space (West 1992, 20). Because identities are made concrete within the social arena of shared experiences, conceptualizing and concretizing identity occur in two contexts simultaneously — one cognitive and the other social, economic, and political (Dominguez 1986).

The primary vehicle by which people today try to realize their desires for recognition, affiliation, and security is the modern nation-state. How to deal with the state in such discussions, however, is a thorny issue. As Verdery (1983, 4) notes, what the state is has not remained constant over time; there have been shifts in forms of organization, the groups or social strata recruited into government, the relations between the state and other groups in society, the areas of social life that fall under state regulation, and so on. In addition, states do not act in and of themselves. They provide frameworks within which different types of human actors formulate policies and programs. That these actors usually consist of the dominant groups in a society is generally accepted, although the degree to which the state remains autonomous from such dominant groups is still hotly debated.

Who determines the boundaries of national identity is therefore an important question to consider. Nationalism is a slippery notion to analyze.[18] What is a nationalism? The often used political equation people = nation = state (or, put another way, that the people who constitute the nation have the right to be represented by a state) is extremely problematic, as Hobsbawm (1990) notes. Which people are included within the boundaries of the nation and which are excluded? Are the boundaries of nationhood determined by residence in a particular location, speaking a particular vernacular, and/or living a particular cultural lifestyle? Hitler, for example, persecuted and executed some people for being Jews who, were they alive today, would be excluded from claiming Jewish nationality by the modern state of Israel because they were born to Jewish fathers and non-Jewish mothers. Palestinians living as citizens in Israel may speak perfect Hebrew and live Israeli lifestyles, but this does not mean that they can claim Jewish nationality.

Anderson (1991, 6) provides a more useful definition of *nation* as an "imagined political community — and imagined as both inherently limited and sovereign," but the question remains, imagined by whom? Anderson's answer is a historical sequence of actors: first, marginalized, vernacular-based intelligentsia; followed by dynastic and aristocratic elites; and, finally, formerly colonized peoples. In answering the question "imagined by whom," it is evident that those who govern (which can include political and economic elites as well as the intelligentsia) and those who are governed are caught in an intricate web of identity that is woven from shared and opposed cultural understandings.

In "imagining the nation," the confrontation between elites and the populations they govern is of necessity a dialogue: each must speak to the other so that the requisite political and economic exchanges can occur (Sider 1987, 22). Despite the asymmetry of power evident in this exchange, state elites are limited in the extent to which they control the terms of the discourse. In particular, the confrontation itself is conditional; both governing and governed groups must incorporate into their interactions the recognition that their dialogue, and their respective positions within it, are tenuous and subject to rupture (Dwyer 1982, 274). For state elites, such a rupture would call into question their ability to control the social order, while for subordinant groups it would threaten their access to the social order. State elites simultaneously reject and create distinctive group identities, while subordinant (often ethnic) groups move toward assimilation as well as withstand state control. It is in this liminal area — of incorporating and distancing, colluding and resisting — that both identities and social orders are constructed.

State elites have motives for and methods by which to subsume other possible identities in their official identity. Through control over and manipulation of various state institutions (the educational system, media, courts, and/or state security forces), elites bolster and legitimate their dominance over economic resources and political power. National institutions are used to promote values that reinforce the elite position. Through bills of rights, legislation, and bureaucratic policies and programs, state elites permit or insist on certain identities infused with particular meanings while refusing others. In trying to achieve dominance, they consciously strive to establish their particular model of society as the *only* possible social order. In doing so, they produce a paradox: while attempting to homogenize difference in a single social order, they simultaneously impose distance between themselves and these groups by stressing the otherness of those they dominate (Sider 1987, 11).

If we begin with the notion that all people possess mobile subjectivities, then it becomes clear that what national elites are attempting to do is to suppress awareness of their own slippery identities by reframing them as a cohesive, unitary, and fixed identity that represents the true essence of the nation. Once the mobility of their own subjectivity has been closed and fixed, state elites use their new unitary identity to exclude others by expressly recognizing and stressing the partially realized, fluid character of other identities. Subordinate peoples are viewed as defective because they lack a cohesive, bounded identity. The very plurality of their identities provides state elites with an ideological justification for providing them with selective, usually discriminatory treatment. Because identity is multiple and changing, state elites will always be able to frame the national identity so that it includes certain groups of people and excludes others. Subordinate populations that attempt to advance within society by adopting the elite identity configuration are likely to find that the contours of the ideal identity constantly shift so that they remain excluded.

Israeli Jews not only struggle to control their own self-objectification; they also struggle to control the self-representation of other peoples with whom they come into contact. Dominguez (1989) shows how Ashkenazi groups dominate the processes of self-definition in Israel, despite attempts by Mizraḥi and Israeli Palestinian elites to participate in the process. Through research and academic writing, public debates on culture and heritage, and the manipulation of public rituals, the Ashkenazi elite controls the process of self-representation. A number of studies of identity in Israel (Ben-Rafael 1982; Ben-Rafael and Sharot 1991; Peres and Yuval-Davis 1969; Hofman and Rouhana 1976; Rouhana 1988, 1991; Smooha 1992) tap the saliency of national versus ethnic identifications by having respondents rank different possible identity labels in order of importance. Jewish respondents generally placed *Israeli* and *Jew* as the two highest labels in importance. Ben-Rafael and Sharot (1991) noted that European Israelis placed the *Israeli* label before the *Jewish* label, while Middle Eastern Israelis did the opposite. Not surprisingly, they interpret this to mean that European Israelis have accepted "the view of Zionism and the Israeli state as 'revolutions' against the Jewish tradition and way of life in the diaspora," while Middle Eastern Jews consider a separate religious identity (as Jews) to be more important than their civic identity (as Israelis) (129). Since none of the respondents was asked to explain how he or she did their ranking or what it meant to them, I find little justification for such an explanation except to note that it reinforces the images of Ashkenazim and Mizraḥim prevalent in Israeli society. An alternate explanation could just as easily be that the European Jews felt, as noted author A. B. Yehoshua does, that "For me, 'Israeli' is the authentic, complete, and consummate word for the concept 'Jewish'! Israeliness is the total, perfect, and original Judaism, one that should provide answers in all areas of life" (quoted in Grossman 1993, 253). My criticism is not that such research begins by assuming identity categories (my own work begins with assumptions that certain identity categories are more salient than others because of state policies) but rather that there is no acknowledgment that such assumptions are problematic. Claims to have ascertained exactly how a group of people frames its identity on the basis of how its members rank researcher-determined identity labels are weak at best.

The plural character of Arab identity is explicitly highlighted in most of these studies, but rather than recognizing this feature as an asset researchers present it as a liability. Arab respondents usually give the greatest weight to their Palestinian identity and the least to their Israeli identity. So Rouhana (1988) characterizes Israeli Palestinian identity as split and conflicted, with the Palestinian or Arab component experienced as sentimental and affective and the Israeli component as instrumental. For Rabinowitz (1990, 12–13), Israeli Jews possess an "overall coherent structure of ethnic affiliation, national consciousness, and sovereign statehood," while Israeli Palestinians are characterized as "engaged in a desperate juggling act, an urgent effort to keep three fire balls in the air," that is, continued possession of territory, Israeli citizenship, and Palestinian nationality. Grossman (1993) describes Israeli Palestinians as acrobats who have learned to stand still on a tightrope. In other words, Israeli Jews stride confidently in the vanguard of their national project, while Israeli Palestinians still stumble in the dark alleys of the old quarter, stymied by their contradictions. Even Lustick's (1980) control model and Zureik's (1979) internal colonialism analysis reinforce these notions of Palestinian dependence and submission. Jewish agency in these narratives is counterposed to Palestinian passivity. Smooha (1992) grants Jewish agency a primary role in defining Palestinian identity when he notes that it is Jewish desires and apprehensions that strain the Israeli and Palestinian components of Arab identity. Jewish unwillingness to accept Arabs as Israelis and to accept their Palestinian identity is responsible for the contradictions with which Israeli Palestinians must cope. One could as easily reverse this statement to say that Palestinian desires and apprehensions strain the Israeli and Jewish components of Jewish identity and are responsible for the contradictions with which Israeli Jews must cope. Implicit in all of the analyses just cited is a framing of Jewish identity as fixed and coherent while Palestinian identity is viewed as fragmentary and inchoate.

While there have been a number of studies of Arab-Jewish interactions (Smooha 1978, 1989, 1992; Romann and Weingrod 1991; Caplan 1980; Rabinowitz 1990, 1997; in the popular press, Shipler 1986; on Acre, Rubin 1974; E. Cohen 1969, 1971, 1973; Deutsch 1988; Deutsch et al. 1982), a number of these works accept the divisions by Arab and Jew as natural rather than asking if there are in fact cases in which these broad categories are not the most pertinent for understanding particular encounters.[19] Romann and Weingrod (1991) studied interactions in Jerusalem during the early 1980s. In his intensive analysis of border neighborhoods where Arabs and Jews live next to each other, Weingrod found that the ties between the two groups tended to be instrumental in nature. Arab and Jewish residents did not share varied interests, nor did they form the types of social relationships that involve close contact or long-term participation. There was a marked absence of shared cultural understandings, and individuals rarely crossed over to adopt other identities. Yet he also mentions a few cases in which Arabs and Jews have warm, personal, neighborly ties and real friendships. These Jews, it turns out, are from Middle Eastern families.

If we accept a vision of identity as a "tensed Both/And" (i.e., as mobile and only partially realized), then we must reject characterizations of intergroup interactions that reduce the identities of the actors involved to simple dichotomies. Both/And implies some level of interpenetration, most evident in the case of subordinate groups that have had to assimilate certain values and behaviors of the dominant society in order to survive — juggling cultures and switching codes. Israeli Palestinians share the same aspirations as many of their Jewish neighbors — to live quietly, educate and provide for their children, afford a few of life's luxuries, and live with dignity. Mizraḥi Israelis enjoy Arabic music, dance with the same rhythmic movements, and are comfortable with bargaining and fighting with a neighbor and then making peace through a *sulha*. Ashkenazi Israelis have taken cultural features from their Mizraḥi and Palestinian fellow citizens in order to create an "authentic" Israeli culture.

People throughout the Third World have been encouraged or forced to become bi- or tri-cultural, a legacy of the colonialism that once ruled their lives. Bentley (1987, 29–32) describes how one young Maranao woman exposed to the wider Filipino society now struggles with a sense of "ambivalent ethnicity" because she has internalized both the codes of conduct of her natal society and the behaviors, values, and norms of the "modern" world. The Mzeina of the South Sinai allegorize the ambiguities of their lives, once under Egyptian control, then Israeli, and again Egyptian (Lavie 1990): a new occupier, a new set of acceptable values and behaviors. We need modes of analysis that allow us to explore such ambiguities, to look more closely at the complexities of the identities of the people involved in these interactions, rather than simple causal models based on we/they frames of reference.

Imagining the community also produces different outcomes for citizens depending on whether those citizens are male or female members of the society. As a number of feminist analyses of citizenship and nationalism have clearly demonstrated, national identities are gendered identities.[20] As Cynthia Enloe notes, nationalist men may see women as "1) the community's — or the nation's — most valuable *possessions;* 2) the principal *vehicles* for transmitting the nation's values from one genera-

tion to the next; 3) *bearers* of the community's future generations —
crudely, nationalist wombs; 4) the members of the community most
vulnerable to defilement and exploitation by oppressive alien rulers; and
5) most susceptible to *assimilation* and cooption by insidious outsiders"
(1989, 54). She goes on to warn that when a nationalist movement
becomes militarized male privilege usually becomes more entrenched
(56). Thus, women in such communities may find that their most valuable role as a citizen is limited to that of a "mother" of the nation who is
restricted to her home in order to protect her from potential pollution
(sexual and/or cultural) by feared outside others.

While nationalism involves one form of imagining the community,
racism imagines that entity as rooted in the biology of blood and belonging, in the process often erasing the "nationness" (in terms of historical
destinies) of peoples in favor of visions of timeless contamination (Anderson 1991, 149).[21] Anderson claims that this process of erasure makes
racism antithetical to nationalism everywhere, but his claim is simply not
borne out. The "new racism" in Britain "link[s] discourses of patriotism,
nationalism, xenophobia, Englishness, Britishness, militarism and gender difference into a complex system which gives 'race' its contemporary
meaning" (Gilroy 1987, 43). Malcolm X's scribbled observation "Here
lies a YM (yellow man), killed by a BM (black man), fighting for the
WM (white man), who killed all the RM (red man)" (Haley and Malcolm X 1965, 389) captures the contradictions inherent in racist nationalism, wherein blacks could fight and die for "their" country, but that
same country denied them full status as "American" citizens upon their
return home.

If we see race as a social construction rooted in perceptions of some
combination of physical appearance, descent, historical or geographical
origin, dress, language, and cultural norms, then racism is one body of
ideas drawing on these perceptions and informing practices that create
and sustain racial categories (Reeves 1983, 7). Racial ideologies are
collective sets of beliefs that first account for events in the social world
through fashioning racial descriptions and explanations and assigning
major causal significance and persistence to these racial categories and
then using these racial evaluations and prescriptions to guide attitudes
and behavior.[22]

> Paradoxically, racism can be articulated in terms of race or of
> culture, mindsets, traditions and religions, i.e., in the vocabu-
> lary of "specificities" or of "collective identities." Racism does
> not just biologize the cultural, it acculturates the biological.
> Racist thought may be developed in terms of either of these
> registers or may even be presented as a syncretism of genetic
> reductionism and absolute cultural relativism. Its most radical

forms are not always the most visible, or the most easily re-
futed. (Taguieff 1990, 117)

Racism does not necessarily refer to any real difference rooted in genetics
or biology; any perceptible quality (origin, language, descent, culture)
that is seized upon and made "natural" can be the basis for racism and
racial practices. Race should not be viewed as essence; it should be
understood as "an unstable and 'decentered' complex of social meanings
constantly being transformed by political struggle" (Omi and Winant
1986, 68). Where nationalism provides subordinate populations with the
possibility that they can aspire one day to acquire the proper national
identity, racism puts this goal out of reach by converting this identity into
an essence that can be acquired only through birth. Lavie sees race in
Israel as "situated in the gap between identity as essence and identity as a
cultural construction" (1992, 30). It is situated in the gap because, while
Mizraḥim and Israeli Palestinians are aware that they are treated differently because of essence, they are also cognizant of the culturally constructed (and hence changeable) character of that difference.

One component of racism that is pertinent to my discussion has to
do with the way in which particular groups of people have been labeled
as violent. Once so labeled, violence can be legitimately used against
them. State oppression produces a paradox: violence is initiated by
those who oppress, who dehumanize others in order to retain their own
position of privilege, but it is these same oppressors who characterize
their oppressed fellow countrymen as violent, barbaric, or "not human"
when they react to the violence of their oppression (Freire 1970, 41).
Shapira (1992) traces the transformation of the Jewish people's self-
image from that of abhorring violence to the modern image of military
might. In this transformation, 'eyn brērāh (no choice) became the justification for every use of force by the new state. When Israeli state violence is disclosed, government officials or Israeli commentators present
it as an unfortunate but unavoidable consequence of Palestinian violence
against Israelis.

Violence, here, is perceived as essence. Often people speak of human conflict as inevitable, timeless, and unending; even the media at
times present this image of war and conflict. Consider how the Arab-
Israeli conflict is often depicted: a "war of brothers," with roots in the
struggles between Jacob (progenitor of the Israeli people) and Esau
(progenitor of the Arab people) or even Cain and Abel. The historical
conflict is described as outside the human ability to change because it is
part of man's nature and an order ordained by a divine being. This often
leads people to believe that it can only be solved through divine interven-
tion, some sort of deus ex machina. This vision of violence as natural
also precludes any critical examination of the identities that are in con-

flict. The division of people into groups and categories is also seen as natural and inevitable, thus obscuring the ongoing historical construction and reconstruction of such identities. State elites promote this process of "naturalizing" violence (and identities) because it provides an eternal evil other against which the society must struggle for its security (thus turning popular resentment outward and legitimating elite control) and it obscures elite involvement in the manipulation of such conflicts.

Generally speaking, Ashkenazi Israelis see intolerant attitudes and aggressive behavior as attributes of Mizraḥi Israelis, part of the essence of their identity.[23] The media and the Israeli political and social establishment explain this configuration of attitudes and behaviors by pointing to the backward character and cultures of the Mizraḥim. More recently, Mizraḥi intolerance has been linked in the popular discourse with intense hatred of Arabs; this is explained by reference to Jewish suffering at Arab hands. The Mizraḥi Jew, according to popular belief, knows from experience that Arabs only understand force. Recent surveys (1987 and 1990) continue to find an increase in intolerance and an erosion of democratic attitudes among the Jewish public in Israel (Peres 1990). These surveys note the following correlation: individuals who are lower income, religious, less educated, and of Mizraḥi origin are more inclined toward nondemocratic attitudes than their opposites. When reported in the national media, such surveys tend to reconfirm the already prevalent beliefs of Western Israeli Jews that Mizraḥim hate Arabs and lack democratic (i.e., Western) values.

Israel's Palestinian Arab citizens are also seen by Israeli Jewish society (both Mizraḥim and Ashkenazim) as violent in essence. Media coverage of the Arab sector, sparse at best, bolsters this image with reports of blood feuds between families in villages and honor killings in which a daughter or sister who has brought shame on the family name is killed by her father, brother, or other male family member. Since the beginning of the *intifada,* Israeli papers have reported an increase in the number of nationalist, antistate actions occurring in Arab villages. While most such actions are nonviolent (painting pro-Palestinian graffiti on walls, displaying the Palestinian flag, or singing Palestinian nationalist songs), there have been reports of more violent incidents in which Jewish citizens or soldiers reported being harassed or attacked. Even nonviolent activities are reported in such a way that they imply an underlying threat of potential, future violence.

Balandier puts the connection in a different way: "The manipulation of violence is one of the functions of power, which has its origin in violence and is maintained by managing it" (1986, 501). I use *power* in Foucault's (1980) sense of forces that are capable of producing things, inducing pleasure, creating knowledge, and producing discourses. To be useful, power must gain access to the bodies of individuals, to their acts, attitudes, beliefs, and everyday lives. Where power resides in the state, it is possible to examine how state elites maintain their positions by managing violence (see Zulaika 1988 on the Basque in Spain, Feldman 1991 on Northern Ireland, Taussig 1987 on Colombia, and Crapanzano 1985 on South Africa). Kapferer (1988) argues that every nationalist ideology is grounded in specific cultural logics or structures of reasoning that highlight certain existentially significant meanings over others. He claims that as nationalism begins to dominate alternative frames of meaning in a society these other frames of meaning take on nationalist messages. This ability of nationalism (and similarly racism) to entwine with and dominate the meanings and logic of daily life has important implications for understanding the violence that it often spawns. Such violence is not irrational but rather a product of a particular structure of reasoning; it is this logic of nationalism that gives it such tremendous power.

Dominant groups cannot totally constrain social life, nor do subordinate groups simply receive the dominant ideology passively. The latter are "active appropriators," who confront and partially penetrate that order (Willis 1977, 175). When political elites idealize a particular social order, they provide their dominated subjects with the means, the "symbolic tools," for use in a resistance that operates entirely within the hegemony (Scott 1985, 338). Social spaces exist in which the definitions and behaviors imposed by state elites can be critiqued and within which some form of resistance (ranging from symbolic to violent) can be framed. By fracturing certain groups of people from the cohesion of the national identity, state elites provide them with the social space within which to recognize their oppression. As they become aware of the artificially constructed character of the dominant identity and the arbitrariness of their categorization, these subordinate groups may begin to question the boundaries that state elites have imposed on their identities. Once they begin to question, these people may become aware that they share common experiences and fates with other categories of people (to whom they may have been opposed because of the national ideology). By reclaiming self-representation, groups excluded from the national identity may regain their agency. One interesting move in this direction in Israel is the growing recognition by Mizraḥi activists and intellectuals that they share a common oppression with Palestinians (see, e.g., Lavie 1991 and Shohat 1992). In July 1989, Mizraḥi Jews and Palestinians were brought together in Toledo, Spain, at a conference entitled "Jews of the Orient and Palestinians: A Dialogue for Arab-Israeli Peace." Groups such as the Black Panthers, East for Peace, and the Oriental Front in Israel and Perspetive Judeo-Arabes in Paris are active in promoting Mizraḥi self-representations that oppose the negative images prevalent in Israeli society. Whether these movements will eventually garner more widespread support among the Mizraḥim and Israeli Palestinians remains to be seen.

When state elites promote one particular version of a national identity, they dichotomize the social universe into those who belong to the nation and those who do not. They create a self/other discourse that is grounded in a specific cultural logic and that produces a particular form of lived experience, where some groups have better access than others to state resources and benefits. The nationalist ideology, however, by no means encompasses the full range of meanings and sets of relations present in a society. Citizens of the state continue to live in communities where they forge diverse economic and social relations with each other and experience others as complex beings and not the ciphers of the nationalist ideology. Violence results from this clash of the national and the local mode of practice, as people become aware of the contradictions in their lives. If individuals perceive threats to the racialized nation-state as threats to their self-constitution, they may resort to violence in an attempt to restore the social order. When individuals perceive their exclusion from the nation as a threat to their self-constitution, they may use violence in an attempt to restructure the boundaries of the nation. Understanding which response will be evoked when and with what result becomes a matter of empirical analysis of the specifics of particular situations.

Creating Boundaries in Israel

In order to understand the increased levels of violence and intolerance in Israeli society during 1988 and 1989, it is necessary to understand how Israeli nationalism constrains the identities of Israeli citizens. The culture of Israeli nationalism has as its central theme a national preoccupation with the issues of security and survival. Arian et al. (1988) see security as so firmly rooted in the Israeli Jewish belief system that they speak of the "religion of security." The key element in this belief system is the victimization of the Jewish people. The catalog of suffering begins with the Egyptian captivity and Babylonian exile; swells to include persecutions suffered in different lands at various times during their exile (diaspora); peaks during the horror of the Holocaust; and culminates in the losses suffered in five wars, in violent acts against Israel and its citizens, and, most recently, in the daily stone throwing and low-level violence of the *intifada* in the occupied territories. These historically specific experiences provide the legitimation for the national concern with security, in which the state of Israel, as the sole legitimate protector of the Jewish nation, stands alone against a hostile world.

Initiation into the security mentality starts at an early age in Jewish society. Beginning in nursery school and continuing through high school, Israeli Jewish children fantasize about, anticipate, and prepare for their period of army service. Army service, however, has very different outcomes for men and women. For men, becoming accepted as a full citizen in Israel is contingent on it. The model citizen of the Israeli state is the male citizen-soldier who serves three years of active duty and remains on reserve duty until he turns fifty-five.[24] For women, army service plays a different role in their lives. Most female soldiers spend their basic service as clerk-typists, working in base kitchens, or entertaining troops; or they may be loaned to various government ministries where they function as social workers, teachers, policewomen, and so on (Sharoni 1995, 45). Women's military service reinforces their subordinate role vis-à-vis the Israeli male soldier; women are expected to wait on and for their soldier husbands, brothers, fathers, and sons. As Geula Cohen aptly noted in an interview in the *New York Times,* for an Israeli woman her status as wife and mother is her military service (quoted in Sharoni 1995, 44).[25]

Many Israeli Jews have used the more than fifty years of Arab and Palestinian opposition to and aggression against the Israeli state as justification for the strengthening and hardening of their belief that they must defend themselves at any cost. Israeli Jews come to accept the preferential treatment they receive from the state as natural and right. Israel is the Jewish state and the ancestral Jewish homeland. Status as a "chosen people" provides the link to the second important element in constructing boundaries in Israel — a racism that sees Ashkenazi Israeli culture as superior and other cultures (Mizraḥi and Israeli Palestinian) as inferior.

For Israelis, both Palestinians and Jews, a different set of cultural images and experiences defines and structures their understanding of racism (*gaz 'anūt*). Racism is an ugly specter for many Israeli Jews (and Jews elsewhere) because of its intimate connections with the Holocaust of World War II. Debates about racism in Israel employ such alternate terms and frames as morality, mutual respect, rights, tolerance, and finally the Holocaust rather than explicitly addressing racism as a part of Israeli culture (Dominguez 1990, 10). The Holocaust is the master narrative that shapes Israeli understandings of and responses to racism.[26] This helps to explain why many Israeli Jews see their society as nonracist: a racist society is one that, like Nazi Germany, denies basic human rights to a segment of the population, concentrates them into camps and ghettos, and actively exterminates them through arbitrary shootings, gassings, and starvation. When many Israeli Jews look at their own society, they do not see a reflection of Hitler's Germany.

In the drive toward creating national unity and a true nation-state, survivors of the Holocaust saw their personal agonies and searing memories turned into national collective experiences.[27] Zuckermann asserts that "From the beginning Israel repressed the Holocaust and used a *Holocaust-image* as a quasi-concrete historical illustration for the right of the formation, existence and development of a Zionist state in all its phases—including the occupation after 1967" (1988–89, 45). Claimed by the whole society, public days of mourning replaced specific acts of remembrance, public memorials substituted for private graves, and the events of the Holocaust became codified in legends, myths, and rituals that obscured each individual's private past (Ezrahi 1985–86, 256).[28] *Shō'āh u'teqūmāh* (holocaust and rebirth) became the guiding metaphors for the task of state building, as the Jewish nation was constructed and rehabilitated in Eretz Israel (land of Israel). For Menachem Begin and his government, each Israeli act of aggression was justified because there was once a Holocaust and every act of aggression against Israeli Jews was simply a continuation of the Holocaust (Timerman 1982, 61). Under Begin's government, the image of a beleaguered Israel, alone and facing the world, was strengthened and developed. Israeli government spokespeople cited the 1975 United Nations Resolution 3379, that "zionism [*sic*] is a form of racism and racial discrimination" (which has since been rescinded), as evidence of a continued and pervasive anti-Semitic, anti-Israel bias within the world community.[29] The Holocaust serves as a powerful tool with which the Jewish leadership in Israel and abroad can police the Jewish community. Holocaust is past and future ('Evron 1981). Israeli Jews see threats of a repeat of the Holocaust when they consider the neighboring Arab countries and the PLO.[30] Every Palestinian thus becomes a nazi who seeks to eradicate the Jews from the land for all time.[31] Therefore, when Israeli commentators and political activists label the actions and remarks of certain public figures as racist, such labeling generally falls on deaf ears among the general public because to be racist is to be a nazi, something logically impossible for an Israeli Jew. As Liebman and Cohen state, Israeli youth has received at home, at school, and in the army, with growing intensity, the message that "racism is a crime against Jews; not a crime Jews are capable of inflicting upon others" (1990, 92).

While Israeli Jews deny any similarity between Nazi Germany and the actions of the Israeli state, Israeli Palestinians see a number of parallels between how the Jews were treated in Germany and how Arabs are treated in Israel. The most obvious parallel is that between the anti-Jewish regulations adopted in Germany in 1939 and the anti-Arab regulations that Meir Kahane repeatedly proposed during his term in the Knesset (1984–88).[32] Israeli Palestinians also draw comparisons between Nazi actions against Jews and Israeli military actions in the West Bank and Gaza Strip such as deportation, the destruction of homes, expropriation of property, curfews, searches, and collective punishment. In 1989, when the town of Ariel required that Palestinians working there wear a badge with the words *foreign worker,* comparisons were drawn with the yellow stars that Jews were once required to wear. The Kufr Qasim massacre of 1956, in which forty-nine Israeli Palestinians — men, women, and children — were killed for breaking a curfew imposed while they were absent from the village, has not been forgotten. Israeli Palestinians remember that the senior officer responsible for the murders was fined a token one and a half Israeli piastres (about two cents). They also know that the municipality of Ramleh hired one of the officers who participated in the killings as their adviser on Arab affairs when he was released from jail (Davis 1977, 147–48). Finally, they question how it is that Israeli Jews can behave this way toward the Palestinians given what they suffered during the Holocaust. As one professor describes his students' reactions, "The Holocaust was a very bad thing for us Palestinians, because the final development of the Holocaust was the creation of Israel in this part of the world against the Palestinians, which means we were the main losers of the Holocaust" (quoted in Shipler 1986, 342).

Israeli Jews who do not make the racist-equals-nazi connection believe that theirs is a nonracist society because they have no history of biological racism.[33] The argument here revolves around the lack of a biological basis for discrimination since both Jews and Arabs are Semitic peoples. In fact, however, physical appearance is commonly used to mark significant others. The *sabra* (a term used to describe an Israeli-born Jew) has often been portrayed in Hebrew literature as blond and blue-eyed, with European features (Shohat 1989, 41). Mizraḥim, with their darker coloring, are often mistaken for Arabs; for Eli Ben-Simon, this meant a severe beating by two Jewish men — "They hit and hit, only because they thought I'm an Arab."[34] Conversely, some Israeli Palestinians are able to pass as Ashkenazim due to their fair coloring. Distinguishing Arabs from Jews and Ashkenazim from Mizraḥim becomes a matter of amateur biology and common sense. Arabs, one is told, cannot pronounce the letter *b;* Mizraḥim affect a particular style of dress and ornamentation. In a 1987 national study of 605 Israeli Jewish adults, Moughrabi and Zureik reported that 77 percent of the respondents felt they could determine at first sight whether a person was a Jew, with 81 percent believing they could tell whether someone was an Arab (1988, 7). These forms of differentiation are reinforced through media images that serve to engender, coalesce, and nationalize images of Palestinians, Mizraḥim, and Ashkenazim.[35] The recent immigration to Israel of Jews from Ethiopia, who are biologically distinct, has produced a marked sensitivity to biological racism in the general society (see Dominguez 1989, 70–95). Ironically, at a time when biological racism is being downplayed geneticists at Tel Aviv University have been analyzing the genetic distinctiveness of Israeli Jews, with one researcher stating that her studies show that non-Jewish populations have contributed little to the Jewish gene pool (Bonné-Tamir 1980). Tekiner (1991) questions this new Israeli trend toward reclaiming separate "racial" status for Jews, especially given the contributions of many Jewish scientists to debunking racial distinctions in the post–World War II world.

Intolerance has been present but largely unremarked in Israeli society since the beginnings of Jewish settlement in Palestine in the late 1800s. Zionist "pioneers" brought with them as a legacy the unremitting racism of European orientalism. Aḥad Haʿam, writing in 1891, sounded a warning note in protesting the view that "Arabs are wild men of the desert, an ignorant people who did not see and do not understand what is going on around them. . . . [I]n time, when our people in Palestine . . . will begin more or less to push aside the natives, the latter will not easily give way" (quoted in Elon 1971, 172). As Edward Said (1990, 227) has noted, Zionism adopted the European typology of a fearsome Orient menacing and confronting the Occident, except that Zionism as a redemptive occidental movement confronted the Orient in the Orient.

More than fifty years of coexistence have not fundamentally altered the Israeli Jewish vision of their Palestinian cocitizens. Stereotypes of Arabs as irrational, emotional, able to understand only force, violent, childish, and primitive infiltrate many levels of discourse. While serving as chief of staff of the Israel Defense Forces (IDF), Rafūl Eitan (a Knesset member from 1984–99), in testimony before a legislative committee in April 1983, declared that "When we have settled the land [referring to the West Bank and Gaza Strip], all the Arabs will be able to do about it will be to scurry around like drugged roaches in a bottle" (quoted in Shipler 1986, 234–35). Friends of ʿAmi Popper, the young Israeli Jew who gunned down seven Palestinian men from the occupied territories who were waiting for work in 1990, had the following remarks to make about Arabs:

> They come to the junction of the slave market, but they don't come to look for work. They come to steal. When a car comes along with someone looking for a worker, they fall on him, fifty at a time, and strip him of everything. They fuck donkeys in the orchards and rape girls in the park, they steal prams and shoes, they steal clothes off the clothesline and hubcaps from cars. . . .
> The Arabs slaughter us night and day, so the time has come for someone to do it to them. Everybody here was dreaming about doing it.[36]

These popular understandings of Palestinians have their corollaries in economic and political structures and public policies that the Israeli government has developed over the last fifty years to deal with this segment of the population. Viewed as a potential enemy fifth column by both the Israeli state and its Israeli Jewish citizens, Israeli Palestinians were long subjected to a pervasive system of state domination and control centered on a separate military government that controlled the Arab areas and citizens of Israel from 1948 to 1966. The Israeli state systematically segmented, co-opted, and made Israeli Palestinians dependent on it and Israeli Jewish society.[37] Israeli Palestinians faced land expropriation, travel restrictions, quotas on agricultural production and water use, black lists, delays in approving village master plans, delays in provision of basic infrastructural services, and separate wage and welfare payment scales. Noting that the primitive customs and traditions of Arab society mitigated against modernization, many Israeli public officials actually congratulated themselves on helping to bring political, social, and economic progress to Israeli Palestinians. In reality, although they continued to live in a familiar and known landscape, Israeli Palestinians were now marginalized and made strangers in and to their own land — dependent on the good graces of the larger, alien society.[38]

While the Israeli government officially pursued a policy of *kibbutz ha'galuyōt* (ingathering of the exiles), certain population segments were more welcome than others. From 1948 onward, as they publicly proclaimed the homogeneity and unity of the Jewish population, Ashkenazi politicians and public officials stigmatized Mizraḥi Jews as the "generation of the desert" (Segev 1986; Smooha 1978). The following excerpt from an article by Arye Gelblum, correspondent for the daily *Ha'aretz* (Israel's leading intellectual newspaper), that appeared on 22 April 1949 illustrates vividly Ashkenazi views of their Mizraḥi brethren:

> This is a race [North African Jews] unlike any we have seen before. . . . The primitiveness of these people is unsurpassable. They have almost no education at all, and what is worse is their inability to comprehend anything intellectual. As a rule, they are only slightly more advanced than the Arabs, Negroes, and Berbers in their countries. It is certainly an even lower level than that of the former Palestinian Arabs. . . . [T]hey are entirely dominated by savage and primitive instincts. . . . What will happen to the State of Israel and its standards with this type of population? . . . The peculiar tragedy with these immigrants, in contrast to the bad human material [i.e., the survivors of the Holocaust] from Europe, is that there is nothing to hope for from their children, either. To raise their general standards from their communal depths would take generations! (quoted in Segev 1986, 159–61)

This intolerance manifested itself in public policies that sought to deculturize and resocialize immigrants from African and Asian countries. These immigrants "were airlifted or shipped, housed, educated and medicated by government representatives of the veteran European Jews who planned and managed their lives" (Smooha, quoted in Elazar 1989, 48). Smooha (1978) notes that government officials forced the Mizrahim into a pattern of absorption that had high utility as far as the absorbing society was concerned but failed to take into account the needs of the immigrants themselves. A typical Ashkenazi family of four received the same two-bedroom apartment as a typical Mizrahi family of eight. Mizrahi immigrants were forced to live in transit camps and other temporary housing for longer periods than Ashkenazi immigrants. In some cases, Mizrahi parents sent their children away to live with strangers on kibbutzim in order to spare them the conditions in the transit camps.[39] When immigration from Eastern Europe increased in the late 1950s, these new immigrants received special treatment such as tax exemptions and job reservations. At a time when 127,000 immigrants (mainly Mizrahim) were still living in transit camps, the Eastern European arrivals were directed to the highly desired coastal strip and housed in apartments purchased from private contractors. Government funds were redirected from the low-standard construction budget into the building of high-standard apartments for the newcomers (Smooha 1978, 91).

That these policies also supported the continued domination of national affairs by an Ashkenazi elite was either ignored or explained as temporary by Israeli social commentators. Lewis calls this the "culturally disadvantaged model" and indicates that it is the preferred explanation of Ashkenazi Israelis for the social inequalities in Israeli society (1979, 75–78, 188). As the "inferior" culture of the Mizrahim disappeared and they were absorbed by the new society, these immigrants would also gain their rightful share of and place within the new nation.[40] In interviews with people of Mizrahi background, Swirski (1989) found that many of them had internalized these notions of cultural inferiority. They had come to believe that the Ashkenazim are more intelligent and therefore entitled to better economic, social, and political positions.

Even after the Levantine culture that previously threatened to pollute and destroy the pure fabric of Israeli life suddenly became a treasured part of the national heritage, the domains of political and economic power remained in the hands of the Ashkenazi elite. Mizrahi Israelis were co-opted with marked versions of cultural forms (ethnic art vs. art), while the hierarchical ordering that favored one form of culture and one sector of the population remained essentially untouched (Dominguez 1989, 123). Resocialization policies were replaced with new social welfare programs such as education "for children in need of special care" and Project Renewal.[41] These new programs, while targeting the same populations as earlier ones, no longer have as their stated goal cultural effacement, but the paternalism of earlier projects remains essentially untouched. Mizraḥim usually improve their class position within society by one of two routes: marriage to an Ashkenazi partner or higher education. Both imply loss of a distinctive Mizraḥi culture and assimilation into a more universal, Western culture. Underlying the celebration by Israeli politicians and social scientists of intermarriage as heralding the end of the ethnic problem is an unspoken belief that such marriages "uplift" the Mizraḥi partner either through the transfer of Ashkenazi genes to the children or through the "cultured environment" that the Ashkenazi partner brings to the home (Swirski 1989, 23).

Fifty years after many Mizraḥi Jews immigrated to Israel, they remain confined to the lower echelons of society (although they rank above Israeli Palestinians). In 1988, research on income and educational advancement indicated that gaps had widened between second-generation Mizraḥi and Ashkenazi Israelis.[42] Mizraḥim are the settlers sent in the early years to occupy lands expropriated from Israeli Palestinians; they are the low-level functionaries of the Secret Service, the military government, and various "Arab affairs" departments in the ministries; and they are the workers whose livelihoods are threatened by the availability of cheaper Palestinian labor. As the agents of policies and programs devised by the ruling Ashkenazi elite, Mizraḥim have been forced into direct confrontation with Palestinians (Swirski 1989, 54–55). These confrontations are then cited by Ashkenazi commentators to prove that Mizraḥim "hate" Palestinians. Ella Shohat delineates the "divide and conquer" strategy of the Ashkenazi establishment: Mizraḥim learn to see Palestinians as terrorists, while Palestinians learn to see Mizraḥim as Kahanist fanatics (1988, 26). As she puts it, "A spectre haunts European Zionism, the spectre that all of its victims — Palestinians, Sephardim (as well as critical Ashkenazim, in and outside Israel, stigmatized as 'self-hating' malcontents) — will perceive the linked analogies between their oppressions" (32).

The Israeli state was created in order to secure the life and liberty of its Jewish population, and its main responsibility continues to be security. The emphasis on security has always been tempered, however, by an alternative ideology drawn from Jewish ethics and morality. Even defense activities are contained within moral limits. Israelis are proud of their *tōhar ha'nesheq* (purity of arms), an ethical system of values taught to every Israeli soldier that limits the use of arms to situations in which the soldier's life is threatened.[43] Israelis are quick to point out that no other army in the world holds to such high moral standards.[44] The concept of *tōhar ha'nesheq* itself represents an attempt to merge security imperatives with Jewish morality. The *intifada,* however, with its continuing low-level violence, has presented the Israeli state with a powerful challenge. The Israeli state has been unable to provide complete security for its Jewish citizens in the current situation of civil unrest. Most importantly, it has not been able to contain the conflict or prevent violent acts from occurring within its borders.

For the majority of Israeli Jews, the ongoing conflict calls into question the ability of the government to provide security (thus also questioning its legitimacy to a certain degree). Some Israelis have called for the formation of vigilante squads to restore order, while others have urged the government to negotiate with the PLO. Within this context of constant, potential aggression and threats to their existence, security nationalism has become the dominant vehicle by means of which many Israelis apprehend reality and assign meaning to their daily experiences. Thus, the business of defense becomes individualized and is brought to the level of daily life. Ordinary citizens may be motivated to take this responsibility upon themselves in order to restore the requisite relation between state and nation in a context in which they feel their existence or control over society is being threatened. The assassination of Prime Minister Yitzhak Rabin in 1995 can thus be read as a logical consequence of the deep embedding of security nationalism within Israeli life rather than the act of a lone madman, the result of religiously inspired fundamentalism, or a politically motivated action (the antipeace process).

Since Israeli society is not a homogenous cultural and social entity, the ways in which individuals respond to security nationalism are conditioned by their class position, ethnicity, religiosity, age, gender, and personal history. Security nationalism, by meshing with other discourses present in Israeli society (on class, culture, ethnicity, and religion), draws upon the elements of these cultural constructions, which strengthen its own logic, in creating a hybrid in which nationalistic meanings dominate. One result of this process in Israel has been an increase in acts of intolerance and violence and the legitimation of formerly marginal and racist political ideologies (advocating concepts such as "transfer," the idea of expelling Arabs from Israel, the West Bank, and the Gaza Strip) in Israeli political discourse.

Security nationalism does not go unchallenged. Some Israelis (Jews and Palestinians) choose alternative frameworks of meaning to structure their lived experiences. One such framework is based on the ideals of Jewish ethics and morality. This system of values is a product of two thousand years of Jewish life as minorities in a number of host societies that were often intolerant of, or even hostile to, their presence. Against the often capricious brutality of the larger society, Jews attempted to shield themselves within a moral community based on family, religious, and communal institutions and sustained by a humanistic tradition. The founding fathers of Israel employed this ethic in seeking to establish a state that would serve as a model society for the rest of the world in response to the horrors and destruction of Nazi oppression. By its condoning of force and oppression to guarantee Jewish security, however, some Israeli Jews see Israeli nationalism as threatening what for them is the essence of Jewish identity — concern for basic human rights and abhorrence of injustice. For these people, to continue on an intolerant nationalist path will destroy this essence, and thus Judaism, and without Judaism they see no need for a Jewish state.[45]

A more oppositional alternative is based on Palestinian Arab nationalist aspirations. Palestinian nationalism is historically and culturally grounded in a particular experience of oppression — the loss of Palestine in 1948. Palestinian nationalists claim intimate connections to the land, deep historical roots in the region, and a cultural authenticity lacking in Jewish settlers, who will always remain alien to the land and region. While all Palestinians share the same aspiration — a Palestinian state — they vary in their willingness to compromise on the eventual boundaries of it. For some, a state comprised of the West Bank and Gaza Strip will suffice; for others, nothing but the United Nations partition boundaries of 1947 will do; and still others desire the entirety of Mandate-period Palestine. Different lived experiences — within Israel, in the West Bank, in a refugee camp in Lebanon, in the cities of the Middle East, or in the West — have produced differences in what Palestinians desire and seek for their futures. Said (1985) sees two images encapsulating Palestinian existence: the identity card (passport, travel document, or laissez-passer), which is always something else and never Palestinian; and Emil Habiby's fictional creation the Pessoptimist, half there and half not, like his compound name. For Palestinians who became refugees in 1948, the home in Palestine now exists only in memory because many villages were destroyed or altered by subsequent Jewish settlement. Those who live in the camps of Lebanon, Jordan, or Syria may never see their village homes again; those who remained in Israel have had to cope with seeing their homes in ruins or occupied by Jewish families. Israeli Palestinian society and identity are structured around the family, the village, and their relationship with the larger Palestinian community and the Arab world. As citizens of Israel, they demand an Israeli nationalism that does not relegate them to outsider status. As Palestinians, they support the establishment of an independent Palestinian state in the West Bank and Gaza Strip. In comparing their plight to that of Jewish populations prior to 1948, they poignantly ask how the Israeli state can victimize another people.

Even within these alternative frameworks, security remains at base the central issue, and it serves to limit the parameters of these discourses. Israeli Palestinians can forward humanitarian aid to their relatives, but until very recently they were forbidden to display any emblem of their Palestinian nationality. The Israeli peace movement demands territorial compromise but frames it as necessary for the security and well-being of the Israeli state and people (implicitly, the Jewish state and people). These structures of meaning act to both dampen and amplify the potential for violent outbursts as ordinary Israelis seek to cope with the unpredictable reality of their lives.

CHAPTER 2

Acre: Defining
Communal Boundaries

> In the days of the generation of punishment, when humans
> began to sin against God and to make themselves idols, God
> called to the sea to flood the world, and when the sea arrived
> at Acre, God told it "To here you can come and no farther,"
> and from this the name "ʿAkko" — ʿād kōh [Hebrew: "unto
> here"]. (Yashar 1953, 59; in Hebrew)

ʿAkka, Accho, ʿAkku, Ake, Ptolemais, Colonia Claudia Felix Ptolemais, ʿAkko, St. Jean d'Acre, Acre, Acri — these names reflect the differ-
ent powers that at various points in time have controlled the city
(Makhouly and Johns 1946). Conquest has followed conquest for five
thousand years of the city's history — Egyptians, Assyrians, Greeks,
Seleucids, Romans, Byzantines, Arabs, Crusaders, Mamluks, Turks, the
British, and finally the Israelis.[1] Modern Acre still bears the marks of
some of these conquests. Under the streets of the Ottoman-period Old
City, archaeologists have discovered the vaulted halls and corridors of
Crusader-period Acre. When the Bedouin Shaikh Ẓāhir al-ʿUmar began
to rebuild the city in the mid–eighteenth century, he filled the remains of
the Crusader buildings with sand and rubble and built on top of them.
The walls built by Ahmad Pasha al-Jazzâr (A.D. 1775–1804) bear the
marks of his battle with Napoleon Bonaparte (A.D. 1799) and of the
battle waged in 1840 by the British and Turks to recapture the city from
Ibrahīm Pasha, the Egyptian leader who conquered it in 1831. During
that battle, British naval gunners scored a direct hit on the town's pow-
der magazine. The resulting explosion caused great loss of life within
the walls and forced the Egyptian forces to withdraw. The building's
rubble was finally cleared away in the 1960s; local residents still remember the area (now a parking lot) as the site of the explosion. Along the
coast to the south, the palm trees that grow in clusters are said by local
residents to be evidence of Crusader settlement in those areas during the
tenth and eleventh centuries. To the east of modern Acre, Tel Napoleon
has provided archaeologists with evidence of settlement dating back to
the middle Canaanite period (ca. B.C.E. 2000–1800).

The city of Acre was never part of the biblical Israelite state. Although located in territory allotted to the tribe of Asher, the city itself was never conquered (Judg. 1:31–32). Acre remained outside the boundaries of Eretz Israel (the Land of Israel, or sacred territory). Rabinovich (n.d., 3) reports that rabbinical authorities did not regard the city of Acre as part of Eretz Israel, and so the Jews of Acre buried their dead fifteen miles south, at the foot of Mount Carmel. H. Dromi, writing in 1945 on the history of Jewish settlement in Acre, notes that "in almost every historical period, Acre was inhabited by foreigners, while her agricultural surroundings were inhabited by Jews. In the city itself, the rule was always foreign."[2] Efrat, in his work on urbanization in Israel, describes Acre as the most extraordinary town in Israel because after so much historical change it is still inhabited by both Jews and Arabs (1984, 101). He also states, however, that it was the least Jewish of all the towns and that, although Jews lived there in many different eras, they left no significant mark on it. He echoes Dromi in saying that Acre was always under outside influence, either European or Muslim.

Zionist leaders asserted the legitimacy of establishing a Jewish state in Palestine by linking their movement to the biblical covenant between Yahweh and the Jewish people. They were not colonialists taking over another people's land but the rightful tenants who had been wrongfully evicted and were returning after two thousand years of exile to reclaim their rights of occupancy.[3] Yet, if biblical boundaries are the basis for the modern state's control over territory, how did Acre, which lay outside those boundaries, come to be incorporated into Israel? In this chapter, I explore how municipal and national government officials pursued policies to Judaize the city and establish Israeli control over it. Creating a community in Israel during the first twenty years of the state involved such things as "making the desert bloom" and absorbing Jewish immigrants from more than one hundred countries and turning them into a reborn people. Land and nation were to blossom simultaneously. These beginnings of the state and society have assumed almost mythic proportions for many Israelis as well as many outsiders. It is the Horatio Alger story par excellence. Starting from nothing, a thriving, energetic, Westernized, democratic state came into existence in the space of only twenty years. It is only recently that some Israeli historians have begun to probe this myth (e.g., Segev 1986; Morris 1987; Flapan 1987).

What exactly happened in Acre during those mythical years of the early state's development? How did the events of the early years of state making affect later economic, political, and social developments in the city? This chapter explores the city's development from 1947 to the late 1980s. It provides a context for events presented in the following chapters. It also represents an attempt to juxtapose Arab and Jewish accounts of history into one united narrative about Acre's development.

I examine how municipal officials and local residents defined Acre as a community in contrast to perceptions of it on the part of national government officials. I also explore the different forces that affected how Acre's Palestinian, Mizraḥi, and Ashkenazi citizens established their communal boundaries in the city. The processes and practices developed during those early years continue to inform the current state of affairs in the city. Acre has not been successfully Judaized. More than any other city in Israel, it has retained a mixed aura—as Efrat notes—neither unambiguously Jewish nor Palestinian. This chapter also provides insight into what happened to Israeli Palestinians during these same years. The Palestinian residents of Acre have actively worked to promote their interests in the city during the past fifty years. Their agency contrasts markedly with the passivity imputed by some researchers to the Palestinian population during this time period (especially the years of the military government from 1948 to 1966) when they present them as silent and controlled by the Israeli state.

Geographical Boundaries

Acre is located at the northern end of Haifa Bay, about twelve miles north of the city of Haifa and twenty miles south of the Lebanese border (fig. 1). As people travel north on the coastal highway, the first glimpse they get of Acre across the beach is a magnificent view of the port of the Old City—the clock tower of the Khan Al Umdan and the Mosque of Sinan Basha. From this point the road swings eastward, past the light industrial zone, to skirt the central bus station and the Wolfson neighborhood, before once again heading north toward Nahariyya and the Lebanese border.

Acre is the capital of the Acre Subdistrict, which covers an area of 936 square kilometers.[4] Until 1946, the city covered only 1,577 dunams of land (one dunam equals about a quarter acre). In 1946, the British Mandate government proposed widening the boundaries to cover 4,917 dunams. The first Israeli mayor, Baruch Noy, requested that the city's boundaries be widened to include 16,173 dunams of land and that borders be fixed (Bernblum n.d., 11). In 1950, the Israeli government authorized enlarging the municipal boundaries to 11,617 dunams (Rubin 1974, 21), but in 1971 1,187 dunams were transferred to the nearby Ga'aton Regional Council without compensation. In 1988–89, the city's jurisdiction covered an area of 10,600 dunams.

To the east of the city lies the Plain of Acre, an area of rich agricultural land that is now divided among various agricultural settlements. To the north, the city is bounded by the agricultural lands of Bustan

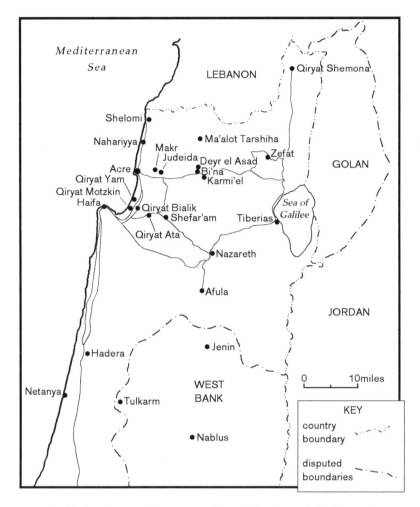

FIG. 1.   Acre and its surroundings. (Map by Ardeth Abrams.)

Ha'Galil, a kibbutz (communal settlement). Efrat notes that the town's location between geographical regions (the sea on one side, valleys to the east [Acre] and south [Zevulun], the coastal plain to the north) and outside of the swamp that once existed in the area means that a number of transportation routes ran through the city — making it "the capital of the northern Land of Israel" (1984, 101–2). Throughout a major part of its five thousand years of existence, Acre served as an important port city. During the period 1856–82, it was the main port for grain exported

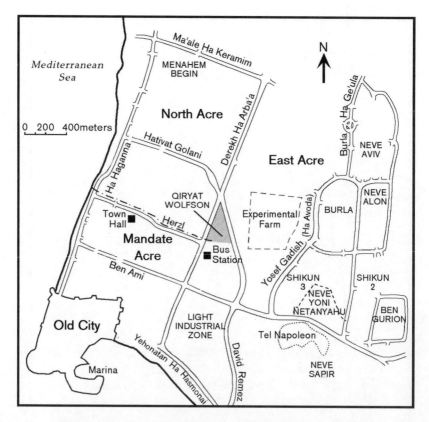

FIG. 2.   Acre's residential areas. (Map by Ardeth Abrams.)

from the Hauran region of Syria (Schölch 1981, 37). Acre's harbor was
shallow, however, and could not handle large steam vessels. As the
harbor at Haifa developed in the early twentieth century, Acre declined
in importance as a port city. By 1988–89, its harbor served only as a base
for local fishermen and a marina for yachts.

The city itself is divided into two parts with four distinct residential
areas: the Old City and the New City, which includes Mandate Acre,
East Acre, and North Acre (fig. 2). The municipal boundaries stretch far
to the south to incorporate a heavy industrial zone that includes Acre
Steel City, Tambour Paints, and the Frutarom chemical plant. Just south
of Mandate Acre is the light industrial zone that contains various ga-
rages, food-processing facilities, and a leather goods factory. The main
north-south highway and the railway line used to divide East Acre from
the rest of the city. With the completion of a bypass road in 1993–94, the

two halves of the city are more united. The east-west, Acre-Safed highway further divides the city. To the south of this highway, about a kilometer from the city center, is Tel Napoleon, an archeological site that is believed to be the original location of the city. A government experimental farm that dates from the British Mandate period covers 1,187 dunams of land situated between the railway line and East Acre, further isolating that neighborhood from the main part of the city. It was this land that was transferred to the control of the Ga'aton Regional Council in 1971.

The Old City is located on a small peninsula that juts out to form a shallow harbor at one end. It is a traditional Middle Eastern city, with narrow streets and alleyways, a covered market (*suq/souk* in Arabic, *shūq* in Hebrew), houses that face inward to courtyards, and several caravanserais in an area of four hundred dunams (fig. 3). Within its walls are found the mosques and churches that serve local Arab residents. Shops selling spices, household goods, school supplies, jewelry, and crafts line the narrow streets. Near the harbor, one finds cafés and coffee shops that cater to both local residents and tourists. Schools, day-care centers, banks, a health clinic, and youth clubs are located within the walls. The massive walls that enclose the Old City have been breached in two locations to provide some access by car to points in the old quarter. Most of the buildings date to the eighteenth and nineteenth centuries. Most streets are cobbled, with gutters running down the middle to carry away rainwater. Under these buildings are the subterranean remains of Crusader Acre — vaulted halls and narrow winding passageways, some of which have been cleared and restored as tourist attractions. A municipal garden near the entrance to the Crusader ruins is home to the Acre Theater Center, a resident company of actors. Every year during the Succot holiday, the Old City comes alive with street theater, puppet shows, and music during the Israeli Alternative Theater Festival. For a number of years during the spring, at Pesach, the Old City's walls reverberated to the sounds of the Vocalisa, an international music festival.

Mandate Acre takes its name from the period of British rule over the city (1918–48). Single-family, Arab-style houses were built to the north and northeast of the Old City using the gridiron scheme developed by Gottlieb Schumacher, a town planner, in 1909 at the request of Turkish authorities (Waterman 1969, 19–21). After 1948, some of these houses were taken over to serve as government offices or school buildings. Others were converted into apartments. Additional buildings were added after 1948, but the name *Mandate City* remains to this day. It is the commercial heart of the city, with banks, shops, restaurants, and coffee shops that draw residents in the evening hours and on Saturdays at the end of the Jewish Sabbath (fig. 4).

East Acre was built in the early 1950s on the remains of the Arab

FIG. 3.   An aerial view of the Old City (1953). (Photo by Teddy Brauner. Courtesy of the state of Israel, the Office of the Prime Minister, Government Press Office, Photography Department.)

FIG. 4. An older Arab house in the Mandate City in front of newer high-rise construction (1988). (Photo by author.)

village of Al Manshiyya. It is connected to the main part of the city by a single footbridge located at the northern end of the neighborhood. In 1987–89, two bus lines and a taxi service ran between East Acre and the city center. Its southern limit is the Acre-Safed highway, its northern limit the Baha'i gardens, its western limit the railroad, and its eastern limit the fields of nearby agricultural settlements. A permanent neighborhood that has grown up at the foot of Tel Napoleon, south of the highway, is also included in this residential section. The first buildings here were one-story, wooden huts quickly constructed to handle the flood of new immigrants entering the country. In many cases, residents enlarged these dwellings over the years by adding a room here and a room there, the result of which is a hodgepodge of architectural styles. Later construction favored four- or eight-story, concrete block apartment buildings. This area does include one section designated as "Build Your Own Home" where a number of large, single-family homes are under construction. The Neve Alon section contains large, single-family villas, while another new development, the British Cottages, is a series of red-brick, two-story houses with sloping roofs. In 1987–89, East Acre included twenty-two synagogues, a *mikvah* (ritual bath), a bank, a Kupat Holim (one of the national health funds) clinic, seven schools (including the middle school for the city), and a number of small grocery stores, vegetable stalls, and shops that sell school supplies and household goods (fig. 5).

North Acre was constructed in the 1960s and 1970s, and the city has continued to expand to the north. While this area also contains multistory, concrete block apartment complexes, the apartments themselves are larger and more spacious than those of earlier periods. Planners, learning from previous mistakes, included enclosed spaces for children's playgrounds and spaces for shops, a bank branch, and a supermarket so that residents would not be forced to travel to the city center to take care of shopping and other business. This section also includes an area of single-family dwellings, surrounded by a wall, which house many young professionals who work in Haifa. The high school and the only MATNAS (cultural center) operating in the New City in 1987–89 are also located in this section of town.

Stanley Waterman (1980) investigated spatial images of the town and found that Arab and Jewish urban images were markedly different. As part of his study, he initially asked respondents to draw a map of the city. Jewish respondents generally tried to draw a map that included both the Old and New Cities. Waterman calls their maps modern because they depicted networks of streets with occasional buildings marked as landmarks. They oriented themselves around the main commercial streets of the New City, and their maps lacked definite peripheries. Arab respondents restricted their maps to the Old City. Theirs resembled "mediaeval city maps, replete with ornamentation," with quite clear peripheries at the seacoast and city walls (Waterman 1980, 280). Specific points, such as mosques, khans, coffeehouses, and the harbor, were

FIG. 5. A view of East Acre, looking west from the Ben-Gurion neighborhood (1988). (Photo by author.)

used to provide detail on the maps. The only locations marked for the New City were City Hall and the police station. While each group (Arab and Jew) had a much clearer image of their part of town, Arab images of the New City, though vague, were much closer to reality than were Jewish images of the Old City. Waterman attributes this to the nature of the relationship between the two communities. Arab residents had to go to the New City to handle certain types of business, while Jewish residents had little need for the services of the Old City and had switched their shopping to newer shops and markets located in the New City. In a similar study of Jewish and Arab high school students in Jerusalem, Romann and Weingrod (1991) also found that Arab students were generally better acquainted with the Jewish sections of the city than Jewish students were with Arab parts. They, too, attribute this to the nature of the relationship between the two communities. Jerusalem Arabs are dependent on Jewish employment or public service centers, while Jerusalem Jews can freely choose whether to visit the Arab parts of the city.

Defining Boundaries: 1948–49

Prior to 1948, Acre was clearly an Arab city. Farah and Khoury (1936) reported that in the 1928 census Acre's population of 7,897 residents included 6,076 Muslims, 1,523 Christians, 237 Jews, 10 Druze, 35 Bahais, and 12 foreigners. By the 1931 census, the city's population had grown considerably — to 9,155 residents — and it continued to grow, to 13,244 in the 1942 registration for food control and an estimate of 15,900 to 16,000 by the deputy district commissioner in 1943, according to the Winter Report (Winter 1944, 45). In early 1948, Acre's population was all Arab and numbered approximately 15,500 individuals. During the Mandate, the British had turned the former Turkish citadel in the city into a maximum-security central prison. They constructed a police barracks along the seacoast in the New City and quartered additional troops on the northern boundaries of the city (Sir Sidney Smith Barracks). The prison at Acre was sufficiently isolated from both Palestinian and Jewish strongholds so that the British could carry out sentences with little fear of demonstrations or rioting. In 1947, there was a massive escape from the fortress by Jewish underground members (and several hundred Arab prisoners as well), which was immortalized in the book and film *Exodus*.

During the nineteenth and early twentieth centuries, a small Jewish community was resident at Acre. Rabbi Baruch Yashar claims there were eight hundred Jews in 1821, thirty-five families in 1935 (twenty Sephardi and fifteen Ashkenazi), and 350 residents in 1936 (1953, 83). The 1928 census recorded 237 Jews,[5] while that of 1931 registered 231.[6]

The Jewish residents, however, left the city during the 1936–39 Arab Rebellion and did not return.

When the United Nations voted on 29 November 1947 to partition Palestine into an Arab and a Jewish state, Acre fell within the borders of the proposed Arab state. The battle over Palestine began shortly after the UN decision. The presence of the British from December 1947 to March 1948 prevented the Israelis from launching full-scale attacks because they believed that the British would not permit any major change in the Jewish-Arab military balance before their withdrawal from Palestine (Morris 1987, 36). Reprisals by the Haganah (later the Israel Defense Force) during this period, however, had the effect of widening the circle of violence. From December 1947, Acre was ruled by a Palestinian National Committee, which organized a national guard comprised of youths from the city and fighters from nearby villages (Yehieli n.d., 111). To Israeli military commanders, Acre and the Arab villages around it posed grave threats because they cut off Nahariyya and the kibbutzim of the Western Galilee from Jewish Haifa (Morris 1987, 61). In early March, Haganah leaders produced a blueprint for securing the Jewish state and Jewish settlements outside the state's borders from the expected Arab invasion after the British withdrawal on 15 May (62). This was Tōkhnīt Dalet (Plan D), which the Haganah began to implement in April and May. Plan Dalet provided guidelines for dealing with Arab villages. They should be surrounded and searched for weapons and fighters. If the village was hostile, its armed forces would be destroyed and its inhabitants expelled from the state. If the village did not resist, it would be disarmed and occupied but its inhabitants would be allowed to remain in their homes (63). Using Plan Dalet, the Haganah went on the offensive and carried the fighting outside the boundaries of the proposed Jewish state.

When Arab Haifa surrendered to Israeli forces on 22 April 1948, thousands of refugees crossed the bay to Acre. By 5 May, according to the British, Acre's population had swelled to forty thousand.[7] The Haganah turned its attention to Acre and increased its harassment of the city. In the last week of April, the Haganah launched mortar attacks on the city, cut the aqueduct that supplied Acre's water, and cut the town's electrical lines, which increased the panic in the city (Morris 1987, 107; Palumbo 1987, 119). The overcrowding in the city led to an outbreak of typhoid in early May, which affected even the British soldiers stationed nearby and precipitated a further exodus from the city (Morris 1987, 108).

Acre was captured by the Carmeli Brigade in Operation Ben-Ami, which began on 13 May and ended on 18 May with the conquest of the city. The Haganah moved to capture all positions around the city, thus isolating it, before attacking it directly on 17 May. The political and military leadership had departed prior to the attack, but those residents who remained fought valiantly. When the Haganah captured the police station on the northern edge of town, the residents' resistance collapsed. During the night, a priest emerged from the city to request surrender terms, and he later returned to accept them. The Haganah moved into the city on the morning of 19 May, collecting weapons and detaining foreign fighters. The brigade immediately moved to set up a military administration in the town, headed by Major Rehav'am 'Amir. According to Morris, looting and abuse of local residents were held to a minimum. They were not pressured to leave, and no expulsion orders were issued (Morris 1987, 109). Acre was now part of the new Jewish state.[8]

Palestinians who lived in the New City, outside the walls, had moved into the Old City for protection from Israeli attacks in the months prior to the fall of Acre. In some cases, men moved their families to nearby villages or from the villages to Acre to protect them from attack.[9] With the surrender of the city, all Palestinians were collected within the walls of the Old City, which was declared closed and under military administration.[10] Barriers were placed across the two roads that breached the walls to keep the Palestinians within.[11] By the time the town surrendered to the invading Israeli forces on 18 May 1948, only five to six thousand inhabitants remained, many of whom were the original inhabitants of the city.[12] Morris reports that people continued to flee the city after its conquest. By 8 November, when the first official Israeli census was taken, the Arab population had shrunk to 3,100.[13]

The Haganah had begun to implement a policy of destroying conquered Arab villages during the April–May 1948 fighting, ostensibly to prevent hostile forces from returning and initiating new attacks on Israeli forces (Morris 1987, 156–58). The policy was quickly turned to a more political end, however, as Yosef Weitz (head of the Jewish National Fund) used destruction to implement a permanent transfer of Arab inhabitants from Israeli-held territory.[14] Weitz, Zalman Lifshitz, a surveyor and cartographer, and Ezra Danin, an Arabist, formed an unofficial Transfer Committee that brought recommendations to David Ben-Gurion, leader of the new Israeli state, concerning what to do about Palestinian refugees (see Morris 1986 for a detailed discussion of the committee's activities). On 7 June, Weitz asked Danin what was to be done with Acre (along with Beit Shean, Jaffa, and Qaqun).[15] On 16 June, Ben-Gurion recorded in his diary a partial list of destroyed villages that included Al Manshiyya near Acre (1982, 523–24). As word of the Transfer Committee's activities began to spread, opposition to its policies crystallized in Mapam (the Socialist Labor Party) and among Cabinet members such as Agriculture Minister Zisling and Minority

Affairs Minister Shitrit. The policy made no economic sense to them because valuable property and buildings that could benefit the new state were being destroyed. Cumulative pressure resulted in the 6 July IDF General Staff's general order, stating, "Outside of the actual time of combat, it is forbidden to destroy, burn and demolish Arab towns and villages [and] to expel Arab inhabitants from the villages . . . without special permission or an explicit instruction from the minister of defense in each case."[16]

The IDF Northern Front did seek to evict the Palestinian inhabitants of Acre (see Morris 1987, 109–10). It proposed either moving them to Jaffa or expelling them across the border. Ya'acov Shimoni, the acting director of the foreign ministry's Middle East Affairs Department, was approached for the ministry's opinion on the matter. He asked the minister, Moshe Shertok (later Sharett), who expressed no objections to a transfer but did foresee problems with maintaining the Acre residents in Jaffa. Shimoni then approached Minority Affairs Minister Bechor Shitrit for his opinion. Shitrit had heard nothing about this proposal and was upset since his ministry was supposedly dealing with such matters. On 19 July 1948, he informed Shimoni that according to the standing order of 6 July a written order from the defense minister (Ben-Gurion) was required to move any inhabitants. The inhabitants of Acre could not be evacuated. Jaffa could not serve as an Arab absorption center, nor would the ministry fund any maintenance costs. The empty housing in Jaffa was required for Jewish settlers.[17] Shitrit told Finance Minister Eliezer Kaplan that the military commander of Acre was a "moderate and easy-going young man" and that the Arab representatives in the town were satisfied with him. "Acre is today a very miserable town; no sources of income exist for those who remained."[18]

Lieutenant Petit, a UN observer from France, was sent to Acre on 27 August 1948 to investigate charges made by Azzam Pasha (secretary general of the Arab League) that the Palestinians who remained there were being mistreated.[19] In his report to his superiors, he includes the testimony of an unnamed witness (who had requested anonymity because he was afraid of reprisals) that the Jews had killed at least eighty Arab civilians, most for no reason. Some of the deaths occurred as people were fleeing; others were due to "curfew" violations. This witness also reported that he knew of six incidents of rape. Petit provides the testimony of one man, Mohammed Fayez Soufi, who received permission to return to his house in the New City to get food. Soufi reported he was coming back with four other Arabs when they were stopped near the police station by a group of fifteen Jews. At gunpoint, the Arab men were forced to drink poison (an acid of potassium). Soufi did not swallow the potion. He fell down like the others, and rolled around until the Jews left. Three of the men died, and their bodies were thrown into the sea. Soufi went to a doctor for treatment. Four or five days later, the bodies of the three men washed up on the beach. Petit noted his suspicion that the soldiers were acting on their own initiative and without orders from their superiors.[20] He also discussed reports that children were being kidnapped and killed:

> The question of the kidnapping of the children during the last 10
> days is still pending—no complaint of one or other party had
> been introduced to me. It has only been reported as a mystery.
> The mothers are terrorised and do not dare leave the children
> alone in the houses or in the streets. It is possible the kidnapping
> is the fact of some hidden Arabs trying to excite the population
> against the Jews. It's also possible that it's the fact of some
> isolated Jewish soldiers. Indeed I met several of the same cases
> during the first truce.

He also reported that the Israeli army was systematically looting uninhabited homes and that he had seen similar evidence of looting when he had visited the town on 3 August. Soldiers were carrying off furniture, clothing, and any other household goods that could be used by the new Jewish immigrants.

Among the first Jewish settlers to arrive in Acre after its capture were soldiers of the brigades that had taken the city and their families. The brigade commander encouraged his soldiers to consider relocating in Acre. A Military Settlement Committee, composed of members of the two brigades that had conquered the city, divided the empty apartments between soldiers and the first immigrants, who arrived from Romania, Bulgaria, Morocco, and Poland. The committee also worried about repairing the houses and the water and electrical systems. The military commander of the city had formed a local committee that was responsible for dealing with things like sanitary problems and providing for needy residents (Bernblum n.d., 4). One soldier, Mordehai Yehieli (who later became the manager of the Acre Municipal Museum), told of having to work frantically throughout the night to repair his apartment because his unit was ordered to move shortly after he brought his family to their new home. He was able to connect pipes to the water system, install a kitchen sink, connect two rooms to the electrical system, and cover some windows.[21] Another local resident had immigrated to Israel with his wife and daughter from Oujda in Morocco in 1948. They were sent to a transit camp in Binyamina and moved to Acre in August, where they were settled in an empty house in the New City. Thirty days later he was called for army service, and he was not discharged until two and a half years later.[22]

It was common for men to settle their families into new homes in

Acre and then to leave to join their army units. Former mayor Israel Doron and his wife came to Israel in 1948 with their three-year-old daughter from a UN camp in Milan, Italy. They spent two months in a transit camp in Hadera, where they lived in tents. Their daughter was taken to live in a children's tent, where she became ill with dysentery. Doron went to Haifa to get medicine for her, and when he returned he found that both his wife and daughter were gone from the camp. They had been transferred to the hospital at Afula, where he found them after a frantic search. They remained in the camp only a short time. He brought his family to a house in the Mandate City that they shared with two other families. He described it as an Arab home that had probably belonged to a man with several wives. There were three rooms (one for each family) around a central courtyard with a common kitchen. He was conscripted into the army and had to leave his wife there. She was left to survive on his monthly army pay of fourteen līrōt (about fifty-six dollars) and whatever he could earn while at home on leave. He was not discharged until 1950.[23]

The Absentee Property Regulations of 1948 defined as an absentee any person who left his or her town, village, or "ordinary place of residence in Palestine" after 29 November 1947. Any Palestinian who held property in the New City but had moved to the Old City was therefore classified as an absentee and the property passed to the control of the Custodian for Absentee Property (Peretz 1958, 152). Once the Custodian took charge of the property, it was used to settle Jewish families. The military commander of Acre initially blocked settling Jewish immigrants in the town because he was worried about local Arab-Jewish relations. Minority Affairs Minister Shitrit supported this decision because he did not want a repeat of the problems that had occurred in Jaffa, where anarchy had reigned and some Arab families had been evicted from their homes by Jewish squatters.[24] By 18 September 1948, the problem had apparently been solved because Shitrit, Ben-Gurion, General Elimelech Avner (commanding officer of the Military Government-Conquered Territories), and the Custodian for Absentee Property decided to begin the settlement of Acre. By 22 November, two thousand Jewish settlers were resident.[25]

The municipality of Acre was established on 5 May 1949 when Moshe Shapira, minister of the interior, appointed a municipal council of ten members. Baruch Noy, who served as the representative of the military government in Acre until 25 January 1950, was chairman of the council. It also included representatives of the Jewish Agency, the Minorities Department of the Ministry of the Interior, the Ministry of Health, Mapai (later the Labor Party) and Mapam (the Socialist Labor Party), and three members of the local Arab community (Yashar 1953,

85). They faced a formidable task. They had to reestablish basic services like water, sewage, trash disposal, and electricity. They needed to settle the new immigrants and veteran Israelis who were arriving to inhabit the empty houses and provide employment opportunities for them. They had to provide for the Palestinians who remained in the Old City and were under travel restrictions, and they had to establish order in the town. At municipal meetings throughout 1949, numerous decisions were made. A budget in the amount of 34,290 līrōt (Israeli pounds, equivalent to $137,160) was adopted for the period 1 June 1949 to 30 November 1949. They took out two loans from the Israeli Treasury — one for 8,000 līrōt ($32,000) to build a center of light industry and another for 15,000 līrōt ($42,000 due to devaluation of the līrāh) to expand the light industrial center, build a vegetable market, and clear ground for a Jewish cemetery (Bernblum n.d., 22–23).

At the time of Acre's conquest, all of the municipal records were destroyed, apparently burned by the Israeli army during the fighting. The new municipal council had to begin all over again. It was aided in its endeavors to establish which properties had belonged to the municipality by an Arab resident who had been a municipal clerk under the British and had taken his files with him when he fled to Lebanon. He returned to Acre under the Family Reunification Program and brought the file to Yosef Katran, the town clerk.[26] The file contained a listing of municipal property — land, houses, stores, desks, and other furnishings and equipment. Katran used British land records in the Settlement Office in Haifa to establish exactly which properties had belonged to people who had remained and which to those who had fled. In this way, the municipality knew which properties they had to purchase from resident owners and when they had to turn to the Custodian to gain control over a piece of land.

By 2 August 1949, 4,200 immigrants had been settled in Acre by the Jewish Agency's Absorption Department.[27] They had been settled in the uninhabited homes of the New City.[28] Noy reported to Kalman Levin, head of the Absorption Department of the agency in Haifa, that most of the immigrants were paying taxes and were beginning to build new lives. He informed Levin that he had 640 apartments to fill and requested immigrants who were already employed in factories in Haifa, were experienced craftsmen whose skills were needed in the city (bakers, builders, plasterers, tilers, carpenters, locksmiths, or fishermen), or had brought with them tools or machines. The municipal council had no control over which immigrants were settled in Acre. The Jewish Agency would put together lists of those who were eligible for settlement and forward them to the municipality. These immigrants would be given permits that they could present to the local office of the Custodian in order to receive an apartment. On 29 August, Noy received a response to his request from D. Goldstein, Absorption Department, Jewish Agency, Tel Aviv, in which Goldstein told him that they had concluded at their last meeting that they would send to Acre only immigrants who were employed, with small families (no more than three people), and under the age of forty.[29]

On 19 August 1949, Noy wrote to Yehoshua Palmon in the Prime Minister's Office to request permission to settle 100 to 150 Jewish families in the Old City.[30] He noted that the municipal council had decided this was advisable from the standpoint of the future development of the place and particularly for purposes of security. He mentioned that problems had arisen between the Christian and Muslim communities.[31] On 23 August, Palmon wrote to the headquarters of the military governor indicating that Noy's request had been approved and he should now request the approval and assistance of the Jewish Agency in carrying out the plan.[32] On 26 August, Noy wrote to Kalman Levin and M. Sirutah at the Jewish Agency in Haifa to inform them of the proposed plan. In the memo, he also noted that the military governor, Rehav'am 'Amir, wanted to settle a considerable number of families of discharged soldiers in the Old City. He requested that their Technical Department contact him about repairing the apartments. He also asked that the immigrant families chosen for the housing be select, since they would be part of a mixed population.[33] It took several additional months to clear up various problems that arose among the different offices.[34] A list from 25 December provides details on 17 immigrant families who were chosen for Old City housing.[35] The men varied in age from twenty-five to fifty-seven, with most in their twenties or thirties. The immigrants were mostly from Europe — Hungary, Czechoslovakia, Romania, Germany, and France — although one family came from Egypt and another from Argentina. The typical family size was two individuals.

The Jewish Agency built a new neighborhood east of the city, across from Tel Napoleon where the village of Al Manshiyya had once stood. A memo of 8 August 1949 from the Absorption Department, Northern District, to the department in Tel Aviv spelled out the services that would need to be provided in the new neighborhood. These included a kindergarten, a clinic, a *tipāt ḥālāv* (postnatal care clinic), offices for two doctors, office space for the Welfare Office and the labor exchange, stores and workshops, and a club for youth.[36] On 5 September, Baruch Noy complained to the local police that trucks were coming to the new housing project and taking dirt from the area. Arab workers from the villages, who did not have permission to be there, were loading the trucks. He requested that the police stop those responsible.[37] The first families arrived at the new neighborhood by 1 November. Noy wrote again to the local police, this time to request that they either establish a small force there or arm the new residents and form a neighborhood guard. He noted that security was difficult in the neighborhood because it is located at a crossroads where the Arabs pass day and night. He mentioned rumors that armed gangs (presumably composed of Arabs from nearby villages) had been seen near the Baha'i gardens, just north of the new housing quarter.[38]

Mordehai Sarid was the national government official in charge of resettling Acre in 1949. Using a map, he would consult with engineers to determine what repairs each unit required — paint, flooring and sewage, sinks installed. The Jewish Agency paid the costs of the repairs and improvements. He told of once inquiring about some immigrants only to be told they were "getting organized." An aide explained to him that the phrase meant they were stealing furnishings for their apartments from the uninhabited Arab homes. Sarid summoned the most influential people among the immigrants and demanded that the stolen property be returned. He reported that almost everything was returned (Segev 1986, 76–77).

The office of the Custodian of Absentee Property in Acre was organized by 1949 and its workers began to remove all the furnishings from the empty houses in the Old City in order to store them in warehouses in the New City. Ramzi Ḥouri, a local resident who was active in the Communist Party, described what transpired next.[39] The workers from the Custodian's office were assisted in their labors by a local Arab man. After all the empty houses were cleared out, they moved to houses that were occupied. Many Palestinian men were still being held in prisoner-of-war camps at this time, so many women and children were living alone and unprotected in Acre. The Arab worker would enter a home and determine what belonged to the family and what did not. If the furnishings in the house were any good, the Israelis would claim that they were the property of absentees and take them away. Ḥouri organized the Arab residents to demonstrate in protest over the seizures. This, the first demonstration in Acre, was a demonstration of women — he was the only male who participated. They passed the covered *suq* and went to the governor's building. On the way, people stopped the Arab man who had been helping. The women began to trample him, and a man who had been watching shouted at them to clear the way so he could kill him. Ḥouri had to rescue him from the crowd. The women were successful in their demonstration, however, and the illegal seizures were stopped.

On 22 September 1949, Noy wrote to Kalman Levin again, this time to request assistance with providing the proper equipment for four policemen whom the municipality had hired. The policemen were given the task of evicting Jewish squatters so that the municipality could give the homes to families who were supposed to receive them. Noy said that the men had been working without proper clothing or weapons and were receiving blows from the Jewish intruders.[40]

As the representative of the military governor in Acre, Baruch Noy was inundated with requests from the Arab residents of the city, who were under his direct administration. A number of individuals, men and women, requested compensation for olive crops that had been harvested and processed by the Custodian. One woman, for example, sought restitution for the fruit of 130 trees that were located in Bassa Village at six different sites. She estimated that the trees produced 320 gallons of olive oil.[41] Noy also had to establish which residents of Acre were "present absentees." Any resident of the Mandate City who had moved to the Old City after 29 November 1947 was declared a "present absentee" and their property was forfeited.[42] Individuals classified as nonabsentees could reclaim their property. Noy received a number of letters from residents of the Old City requesting identity cards as nonabsentees. To prove that a resident had not left, a respected member of the Arab community often served as a witness.[43]

The Israeli authorities began to release local men who had been held since the summer of 1948 in prisoner-of-war camps. There were two types of POWs — foreign soldiers and Arab irregulars (such as members of the Arab Liberation Army), and Palestinian Arabs who had been captured in the fighting over their villages or towns. Being of military age was often a sufficient reason to be sent to a prison camp, even if one had not participated in any fighting (Kamen 1987, 475–76). By January 1949, at least five thousand men were being held in such camps.[44] As the men were released, they were transported to their places of residence, where they were issued identity cards. The voucher for one Arab resident of Acre indicates that he was held at POW Camp 793 from 23 June 1948 until 12 August 1949, when he was allowed to return to his home.[45]

As the magnitude of the Palestinian exodus became apparent to national government authorities in 1949, they crystallized a policy of not allowing internal refugees to return to villages that had been declared abandoned. Individuals who were refugees from localities that continued to exist were allowed to return if they could prove that they had homes there.[46] On 4 March, the Inter-Ministerial Committee for Nazareth decided that it needed to reduce the population for security reasons. It recommended that internal refugees whose permanent place of residence before the war had been Haifa, Acre, or Jaffa be allowed to return to those locations if they could find housing.[47] On 2 November, Noy wrote to Lieutenant Colonel ʿAmnoel Markovsky at the military government headquarters in the occupied territories, regarding the return of Arabs to Acre. He had received information that the military governor in Nazareth was allowing refugees who had fled to Nazareth to return to Acre. He informed Markovsky that the Jewish Agency was settling Jewish immigrants in the Old City at that time. He also reported that the security situation was unstable and asked Markovsky to direct that no Arabs should be returned without consulting local authorities.[48] On 25 November, Noy received a response from Rehavʿam ʿAmir, military governor of Western Galilee, in which ʿAmir assured him that Nazareth was giving permission for single visits only to individuals who wanted to request permission for a fixed residence in Acre from Military Governor Noy there. Noy was assured that he would be consulted before such permission was given.[49]

Some Arab residents of Acre adapted quickly to the change in their national status. They made demands on the local military governor in the hope that he would respond favorably. The letters in the military governor's file provide some insight into the transition that Acre's Arab residents experienced during 1948 and 1949. The first priority was to be registered as a nonabsentee and receive an identity card.[50] When hostilities ceased in early November 1948, the IDF moved over the next nine months to secure Israel's borders. Individuals who lacked identity cards were arrested as "illegals" and expelled across the border. The army repeatedly raided villages and mixed cities to locate illegal residents and deport them.[51] On 24 September 1949, an Arab resident of Acre turned to Baruch Noy for help in locating his fourteen-year-old son, who had been deported two weeks previously. The father, who was registered as an Israeli national, explained that his son could not produce an identity card because he was registered on his father's card (since he was under the age of fifteen). The family had received no news of its son since the deportation.[52] The Israeli government allowed a few thousand Arab refugees to return to Israel under a family reunification plan.[53] The municipal archives contain two lists of the names of people allowed to return.[54] They returned via Rosh Ha'Niqra on 13 December and 30 December 1949. From the names and ages provided, it is clear that most of the returnees were women and children whose husbands had remained in Acre.

Once their status as nonabsentee and legal residents had been established, residents began to press claims to regain access to their property. One man requested help in recovering his Chevrolet automobile, which had been seized when the city was captured. The requests for compensation for olive harvests have been mentioned. Businessmen requested permission to reopen their shops and warehouses. The military governor was also approached for help in maintaining order in the Old City. In an interesting series of letters over the period 17 June to 28 June 1949, a Muslim religious official requested that the town commander order a woman engaging in prostitution to move from the house she had rented from the Muslim *waqf* (religious foundation). Noy turned the matter over to the local police, who reported that the woman had previously been a prostitute but she was now fifty-five and no longer causing problems. They found no evidence that her house was serving as a brothel. They indicated, however, that if she were expelled it would probably be a good thing. The final letter is a request from Noy to the military governor, the Western Galilee, to expel the woman because of serious complaints against her by the citizens of Acre.[55] The archives are silent on the woman's fate.

Throughout 1948 and 1949, Arab-Jewish communal boundaries were clearly defined. In the interests of military security, local Israeli officials confined the Palestinian residents of Acre within the walls of the Old City. These same officials enforced new laws such as the Absentee Property Regulations of 1948 to take over the empty houses of the New City for Jewish settlers. There was little interaction between the two communities except for those Jewish immigrants who were settled in the Old City. Both communities had experienced a complete disruption of their lives. Palestinian residents lost homes, belongings, and family members — their way of life changed completely almost overnight. Jewish residents, many of them immigrants who had entered the country only months before coming to Acre, arrived with little but the clothes on their backs. It is no wonder that the empty houses were looted. As the Custodian noted in a secret report, "Passions of revenge and temptation overcame great numbers of people. Under those conditions only an extremely firm action by the military, administrative, civil and judiciary authorities might have saved, not only the property, but also many people, from moral bankruptcy. Such firm action did not take place, and perhaps could not, given the circumstances, and so things continued to go downhill without restraint."[56] Both communities had to deal with the new civilian and military authorities of the town — Palestinians mainly with the military government, Jewish residents with the offices of the Jewish Agency, the Custodian, the labor exchange, and municipal officials. The presence of the remaining Palestinian community and its active resistance placed constraints on looting and seizures by the new Jewish residents and the Jewish state (through the Custodian). The presence of the Jewish residents meant that members of the Palestinian community benefited from a quicker restoration of basic services such as water, electricity, and trash disposal than would have been the case if Acre had remained an all-Arab locality. The municipal council, from its inception, was integrated, with both communities represented. Town clerk Yosef Katran, who himself was born in Damascus, served as a translator at the early council meetings because

the three Arab representatives did not speak Hebrew. He would prepare the protocols of the meetings in Hebrew and then translate them
into Arabic. As Katran noted, there was no separate entity in Acre to
take care of the problems of the Arab residents; the municipal council
dealt with the needs and problems of both its communities. Decisions
made informally during the first two years of Acre's existence as part of
the state of Israel thus lay the foundations for the later development of
relations between the two communities.

Consolidating Community: The 1950s

The decade of the 1950s brought further changes to the face of Acre.
One of the most significant changes was the termination of military rule
over the city in 1951. In a memo to the interior ministry dated 5 February 1951, Noy initially indicated his opposition to the termination of
military rule in Acre if it meant that control over administrative and
financial matters in the surrounding villages would be transferred to
Nazareth. He noted that Acre had been the natural central point for the
villages of the Western Galilee for many years. He pointed out that
many businesses and large factories connected to the surrounding villages had their headquarters in Acre. By this means, the city was able to
provide employment for Jewish immigrants who settled there. Cutting
the surrounding villages off from Acre would severely hamper the local
council's efforts to further the city's economic and social development.[57]
There is no evidence in the files that the interior ministry responded to
Noy's concerns. The government transferred administration of the city
to the local municipal council and civilian rule. With this, the barriers
were removed from the Old City and Arab residents were able to move
freely around the city, although they still had to get permits to travel
outside it (and Arab residents of villages in the surrounding area needed
permits to enter Acre).

During the early years of the new Israeli state, the fledgling government struggled to cope with the massive influx of Jewish immigrants and
to build a functioning economy. The government controlled the production, distribution, and prices of necessities such as food, housing, and
clothing. Rationing was instituted, and residents remember needing cou-
pons for everything. During this period, unemployment was high in
Acre (as elsewhere in the country). Some residents started vegetable
gardens and began to raise their own chickens in order to have adequate
food supplies. To deal with unemployment, the city's mayors pressured
the government to provide public works projects for Acre's residents,
both Arab and Jewish. One man recalled that he would go to the local

Labor Branch to obtain work. At most, he received three days of employment at a time. He worked building roads and was then sent to the experimental farm to serve as a shepherd. At the beginning of 1953, women, men, and children who lived in Shikūn Amidar (*shikūn* means "neighborhood") in the eastern part of the city held a demonstration to protest living conditions there. They carried signs reading, "Bread, Work," and marched to the city hall. They were met there by Yosef Gadish, who had taken office as mayor only one day previously. Gadish asked them to give him several days to do something about the situation. He traveled to Jerusalem to talk to officials at the Ministry of Labor, begged for assistance, and brought back four hundred days' worth of work for Acre's residents.[58]

The first municipal council elections were held on 6 September 1951.[59] To be eligible to vote, persons had to be at least eighteen years of age and have been resident in the city for at least six months. They city was divided into ten voting areas, seven in the New City and three in the Old, with voting stations designated for each area.[60] Candidates were nominated by Mapai, Mizraḥi (later the National Religious Party), the General Zionists, Herut (later part of Likud), Mapam, the Communists (later Rakah), and a Labor-affiliated Arab independent list. Baruch Noy, who was now the mayor, made a series of special requests to different army units to allow soldiers and reservists who were Acre residents to return home that day to vote in the elections.[61] Thirteen municipal council members were elected, with Mapai and Mizraḥi forming the governing coalition. Noy continued as mayor. The Arab independent list joined the governing coalition, and an Arab deputy mayor was appointed to handle the affairs of the Arab community, a pattern that has continued throughout five decades.

Noy argued forcefully and persuasively with national government representatives to advance the development of the city. By 1952, the local municipality had constructed roads, developed a new water-supply plan, begun a main drainage scheme, built factories and schools, and attracted a number of industrial enterprises of various sizes to the city.[62] Noy fell victim to a local power struggle, however. Members of opposition factions circulated rumors that he was personally profiting from his position as mayor and that the local administration was not following proper financial procedures.[63] He was eventually investigated by an internal affairs committee of the Knesset. Although he was cleared of all charges, he resigned his office on 29 October 1952 and the Ministry of the Interior took control of local government in Acre. On 30 December, Yosef Gadish (of Mapai) was elected mayor.

By 1950, Acre's Jewish population had increased sevenfold to over eight thousand. On 8 October, a temporary tent camp for 150 families was opened in Acre to help deal with the flood of immigrants that was arriving at the port in Haifa.[64] When housing became available in the new eastern neighborhood, residents were moved out of the tent camp and it was destroyed. During the first winter, the tent encampment had been a disaster, as all the bedding had been damaged by rain and humidity. Other immigrant transit camps (singular *ma ʿabārāh,* plural *maʿabārōt*) were built in Acre.[65] Tin huts (later replaced by wood or asbestos huts) were put up in the northeast corner of the city (Shikūn Rassco) and in the northwest corner of the city (Mazra), next to the army camp. A third camp, Maʿabārāh Napoleon, was built at the foot of Tel Napoleon (Yehieli n.d., 114). The camp at Mishmar Ha'Yam, south of the Old City, was meant to house 200 to 250 families on a temporary basis.

One man, who arrived from Romania with his wife and five-year-old son at the beginning of 1950, described how he found a home.[66] He worked for a week or two in the transit camp to earn money and then brought his family to Acre, where his brother was living. He went out and looked for a place to live. He claimed that there was no one in Acre who could assist him in locating housing. The Old City was empty, with houses standing empty. The Arabs still living there stayed inside their houses. He moved into a building in the Old City with another nine families; each family had a room and a half. They occupied the building without permission from either the Jewish Agency or the Custodian. The Jewish Agency wanted to evict them all, but one family created a real scandal, so all the families were allowed to remain.

The character of the Jewish immigration to Acre continued to be of concern to local municipal authorities throughout the 1950s. In 1950, Mayor Noy complained in a memo to Kalman Levin of the Absorption Department in Haifa that Acre had just received another twenty families whose members were in such poor health that they could not perform physical labor. He added that 40 percent of the families in the new neighborhood were in such a condition. He requested, once again, that Acre be sent people who could handle hard work and who belonged more or less to the same ethnic group so that they could develop a "common language" in the future.[67] In 1956, Mayor Gadish asked the Jewish Agency in Haifa to send immigrants with professions that the city could use, such as electricians, metalworkers, welders, and engravers. He added that Acre had no need for tailors, carpenters, shoemakers, or barbers.[68]

The Arab residents of the city faced a new crisis during 1951 regarding the actions of the Custodian. Once again, Arab homes were being searched for furnishings that belonged to people who had been declared absentees.[69] The social worker for the Arab sector delivered a report on the matter to her supervisor in the Welfare Office in Haifa. This woman, who was in charge of minority care, forwarded the complaint to Baruch Noy and the military governor of the Galilee on 26 January. The complaint centered around the removal of essential furnishings, such as mattresses and blankets, from the homes of needy Arab residents in the Old City.

Mayor Noy pursued the matter by contacting the supervisor of absentee property in Haifa and requesting an investigation. He received a response to his inquiry on 7 February from the representative of the Custodian in Acre, who denied that there had been seizures from the homes of the needy and stressed that his office was carrying out instructions it had received from the office in Haifa. Mayor Noy responded on 13 February, noting that since the confiscation activities had begun many Arab residents had turned to the local Welfare Branch with requests for furnishings and mattresses. He was well aware that many of the needy were refugees who "with the rulers' permission, kept for themselves the necessary furnishings, most of which belonged to the absentees." Although Noy received a memo on 19 February stating that the Acre office had been instructed to stop confiscating abandoned property held by poor people, he did not let the matter rest there. In the meantime, the Arab social worker whose report had begun the whole affair was subjected to investigation and action by the Custodian's office in Acre. Noy was incensed at this and wrote directly to the Custodian in Jaffa to again request a commission of inquiry. He received a response on 15 April from M. Porat, the Custodian. Porat had ordered that new measures be put into place so that all future searches and seizures would be legal and properly conducted. He acknowledged that there had been problems. He ordered the connection broken between the office in Acre and the Arab man who had assisted in the searches. He had decided to discontinue the practice of general searches but indicated that when his offices had definite information that an individual was holding abandoned property they would take appropriate legal action. The residents of the Old City wrote a letter of thanks to Mayor Noy for his assistance in stopping the searches and seizures.[70]

Mayor Yosef Gadish was known as the Napoleon of Acre because he was able to advance a number of major schemes to develop the city (Rubin 1974, 25). He took charge of the city as the period of austerity began to ease in 1952–53. During his term as mayor (1952–61), the tourist potential of Acre was first developed. Gadish negotiated with the Prime Minister's Office and the Ministry of Tourism for funds to restore the seawall, the Hospitaler Crypt of St. John, the El-Jazzâr Mosque, and the Hammam (bathhouse) (25–26). Cafés and promenades were developed to promote Acre as a modern beach resort. Gadish made a point of learning Arabic and studying Arab customs and traditions in order to better communicate with local residents — Muslims and Christians as well as Mizraḥi Jews. An Arab folklore museum was established on the premises of the Hammam. Its "Exhibit of the Folklore of the Minorities" was lauded as one of the best in the country. In the words of the mayor, "The exhibit symbolizes our desires for peace and demonstrates the peaceful life that survives in our mixed city, Acre."[71]

By 1954, the country was experiencing rapid economic growth, with annual increases in the gross national product of 10 percent and a concomitant rise in living standards (Ben-Sasson 1976, 1094). Reparations payments to Holocaust survivors from the West German government ($720 million paid over twelve to fourteen years, beginning in 1952) allowed those Israeli Jews who received them to rapidly improve their economic situation. By the mid-1950s, these payments were reaching Jewish residents of Acre, many of whom used them to set themselves up in business. During this period, Jewish residents purchased a number of shops in the Old City from their Arab owners. In fiscal year 1951–52, the Old City's *suq* was home to 131 Arab and only 37 Jewish shopowners. By fiscal year 1957–58, there were 98 Jewish and only 78 Arab shops (Cohen 1973, 8).

The period of the austerity lasted much longer for Acre's Arab residents. In 1953 and 1954, the municipality was still requesting financial support in workdays for the Arab "refugees" from the Minorities Department of the Ministry of Labor.[72] In 1953, at least 180 Arab men were registering daily at the Labor Exchange and the municipality had nothing for them. Majid Al-Haj provides data from private diaries about the economic situation in Shefar ʿAm (a large Palestinian town near Haifa) during the 1950s, which is strikingly similar to conditions among the Arab residents of Acre. The Shefar ʿAm residents reported steep rises in prices, an increase in black-market activities, and high rates of unemployment. By January 1957, the employment situation was beginning to ease, although internal refugees were still having difficulty finding work in 1958 (Al-Haj 1987, 41–42). A number of Arab residents gave up in their search for work and applied to leave the country. The municipality was contacted when Israeli citizens applied to leave the country, so that debts to the municipality could be cleared before permission was given. During 1954, 29 Jewish and 63 Arab residents applied for permission to leave the country permanently. Arabs who applied to leave generally listed one of three destinations: Lebanon, Jordan, or ʿEver Jordan (across the Jordan, i.e., the West Bank).[73] In 1955, only 3 Jewish residents petitioned to leave permanently, but the number of Arab residents asking to leave rose to 79. In 1956, 38 Arab residents left. In 1957, the number leaving dropped to 20. Many of those who left between 1954 and 1956 were women who were probably rejoining husbands who had either been expelled or never allowed to return to Acre after 1948. A number of men, however, indicated that they were leaving because they lacked employment. Sometimes they left alone; at other times they took their entire families with them.

Gadish tried to solve the housing problem for Old City residents. On 21 May 1953, he wrote to Mr. Houbeishe, the manager of the Minorities Department of the Ministry of Labor office in Haifa, with a copy of a letter directed to Yehoshua Palmon, the Prime Minister's Adviser for Arab Affairs.[74] In the letter, Gadish described the living conditions of eight hundred Arab refugee families living in the Old City. Families with seven to ten children were living in one room without a kitchen or a toilet. Some of the buildings were dangerous and ready to collapse; others were historic buildings that the municipality wanted to renovate in order to promote tourism. Gadish proposed building two hundred apartments on sixteen dunams of land that, while outside the walls, were close enough so that residents would remain connected to services available to them in the Old City. The land belonged to the Muslim *waqf*, which had agreed to make it available for housing construction. Gadish pointed out that the refugees themselves could be employed to construct the units and that quantities of building stone were available from ruined houses in the Old City itself. This would greatly decrease building costs. There is no record of any response to this request, but the proposed housing quarter was not built.

This was the first of many attempts by municipal officials to provide better housing for the Arab residents of Acre. It highlights the dependent relationship between local municipalities and national government ministries. Gadish's plan was a pragmatic solution to two very real problems for Acre's Arab residents — housing and employment — that clearly had the support of the local Arab community. It would have done much to improve the lives of the most disadvantaged of the Arab families in the Old City. The plan, however, needed the approval and financial support of national government ministries in order to be realized. In 1953, Arab housing projects were not a national priority. The local municipality was therefore powerless to bring its proposed plan to fruition.

Acre remained an important center for Israeli Palestinians. The Communist Party was very active, scheduling meetings and public lectures in its clubhouse in the Old City. On 6 July 1958, Yanni Yanni, chairman of the Kfar Yasif local council, and Taher Fahum of Nazareth issued an invitation to a public meeting in Acre, with a similar meeting scheduled in Nazareth the same day. The meetings were attended by about 120 people, while the military governor placed 40 others under house arrest to prevent them from attending. These meetings led to the formation of the Arab Front, which became the Popular Front when the district commissioner refused to recognize or register it because the name sounded "national-ist." By the end of 1958, the Popular Front had branches in Nazareth, Acre, Haifa, Taibe, Kfar Yasif, and Yafa al Nasra (Jiryis 1976, 186).

For both Arab and Jewish residents, the decade of the 1950s was a time to rebuild and consolidate their lives and families. All residents had to endure the hardships of austerity. Although local government officials worked to improve living conditions for both Arab and Jewish residents, clearly Jews were favored in both housing and employment. Unemploy-ment continued to be a problem in the Arab sector long after the Jewish sector had begun to see improvements. Housing construction and the provision of services, funded as they often were by the Jewish Agency, were targeted for Jewish residents. The Arab residents of Acre did see a few benefits during this period. They passed from military to civilian control and regained the right to move about the city freely. They elected representatives for the municipal council and had a deputy mayor to look after their affairs. Both Noy and Gadish had a certain degree of respect for their Arab constituents and so paid some attention to their welfare rather than completely neglecting them.

The decade of the 1950s solidified a particular dependent pattern of relationships between the two communities. The Arab Old City, with its exotic aura, shops, market, and housing, was valuable to the Jewish sector for its tourist potential and because it provided new immigrants with housing and often livelihoods (as they purchased or opened their own shops and kiosks). The Arab sector benefited from the improve-ments and basic services that Acre received for its Jewish residents and from having Jewish officials looking after their social welfare and mediat-ing with national government ministries on their behalf. This pattern would be developed and amplified in the ensuing years.

Coexistence from the 1960s to the 1980s

Each of the next three decades saw Acre go through a period of renewed immigrant absorption, new housing construction, and recession and un-employment. In the 1960s, new housing was constructed north of the Mandate City to provide dwellings for those residents who still lived in the Old City or in one of three transit camps. The bulk of the immigrants coming to Acre in the 1960s were Mizraḥim, mainly from Morocco. The local municipal council continued in its efforts to provide a stable eco-nomic base for the community. Besides trying to convince a variety of industries to locate in the city, efforts were made to develop the tourist potential of the Old City. In 1963, the municipal council received a grant from the interior ministry for the purpose of renovating the Old City.[75] By

1965, almost half a million Israeli pounds had been invested in restoring the Old City and developing facilities for tourism.[76] That same year, the Acre Development Corporation was established with representatives from the municipal council, a number of government ministries, the National Parks Authority, Amidar (the national housing authority), the Custodian of Absentee Property, the Government Tourist Corporation, and the Department for Preservation of Historic Sites.

Mapai continued to dominate the municipal council by forming governing coalitions with its affiliated Arab list and the National Religious Party. Gadish resigned as mayor in December 1961 to take a position in the Ministry of Education (as an expert on Arab education). He was followed as mayor by first Shmuel Efrat (1962–65) and then Yosef Katran (1965–69). Katran's election was seen as particularly appropriate by the Arab residents of the city, many of whom remembered his great-uncle, Yosef Farhi, who was the governor of the city from 1903 to 1910. Katran was mayor at the time of the national recession of 1966–67. He noted that Acre was not as severely affected as other cities because its industrial base was diversified, with both light and heavy industry. No single factory employed all the workers of the city (as was the case in towns like Dimona or Beit Shean). Acre survived the recession, and its industrial base was even stronger than before.

Acre in the 1960s was an immigrant, workingman's town. The municipality began to publish a monthly newsletter to inform residents about deadlines for school registration and the payment of tax and water bills as well as news of local cultural and educational events. During 1966, besides local news and information, the *Yedīʿon ʿĪriyāt ʿAkko* (Bulletin of Acre's municipality) featured a series of cartoons in every issue that warned local residents about properly disposing of garbage, preventing fires, proper storage of food at home, purchasing from shops that kept food covered and properly stored, and personal sanitary practices. Rubin notes that local officials wanted to modernize the city to make it more attractive to young couples and the middle class (1974, 22). They cleaned up the city's main street by removing several small Arab houses and a match factory and extended the areas of public gardens into the Old City.

During the decade of the 1960s, Arab and Jewish residents of Acre went through periods when they interacted cooperatively and amicably and periods when relations were tense and stormy. The first period of tension occurred in September 1961 after five Arab youths were killed by an Israeli border patrol as they attempted to cross into Gaza. Rumors spread throughout Arab villages and towns that the boys' bodies had been mutilated. The killings set off a series of demonstrations in Haifa, Nazareth, Acre, Shefar ʿAm, and Kafr Yasif. In Acre, students at the

Terra Sancta school, led by the wife of the leader of the local Rakah
faction, held an antigovernment demonstration and marched to City
Hall. Matters turned violent when the students were attacked by young
Jewish residents. Five Arab students were injured, two seriously.[77] A
police barricade was erected to keep Arab and Jewish residents in their
respective quarters of the city, and special police details were brought in
to patrol. The police arrested twenty-five people, including eleven Jewish residents who had tried to interfere in the march. Mayor Gadish held
meetings with local leaders (Jewish, Muslim, and Christian) to encourage moderation.[78]

Nationalist sentiments continued to create breaks in local communal relations throughout the 1960s. During 1958–65, Arab nationalists
tried to create an Arab political movement — al-Ard (The Land). Al-
Ard had its roots in the Popular Front. Its members fought against the
military administration and land expropriation and worked for a united
Palestine. The movement was finally outlawed by the government in
1965, and four of its leaders were banished (Zureik 1979, 172–75).[79] In
August 1964, ten students from the Arab high school were arrested after
Egyptian flags and anti-Israeli posters appeared in the Old City. The
posters declared, "We are *feda'yeen* in the cause of freedom," and were
signed, "Palestine Liberation Front."[80] In the summer of 1965, a memorial assembly was held in Acre for Eli Cohen, an Egyptian Jew who,
when caught spying for Israel, was hung by the Syrians. Jewish military
youth groups organized a relay race from the Syrian border to the Cohen
home south of Tel Aviv, and the runners halted at dusk in Acre. At the
memorial, the mayor and an IDF officer extolled the heroism of Cohen
and noted his Egyptian origins as a source of pride for Mizrahi immigrants (Rubin 1974, 74). That night several Arab youths who were ru-
mored to have spoken approvingly of the Syrian action were beaten on
the main street of the New City.

During this same period, Arab members of the municipal council
cooperated closely with Jewish councilors in order to realize some benefits for the Arab residents of the city. Some Arab families had begun to
purchase or rent apartments in the Mandate City as they became available. During this decade, Arab residents received a municipal clinic, a
home for the elderly, apartments in a new housing project (Shkhūnāt
Wolfson, discussed in chapter 4), and a new kindergarten and schools.
The Arab deputy mayor, Mohammed Houbeishe, in return gave his
support to the municipality's plans to restore and develop parts of the
Old City, including the Khan Al Umdan and other Crusader buildings.[81]
Houbeishe functioned much like a *mukhtar* (village headman under
Ottoman rule); Arab residents brought their problems to him at his
home to be discussed over coffee. Houbeishe served as the intermediary

between the Arab residents of Acre and municipal and national government officials and offices. Municipal officials blamed tensions and problems between Arabs and Jews that did arise on the interference of local
Communist Party leaders, who opposed the Labor coalition (Rubin
1974, 26).

Military jurisdiction over all Israeli Palestinians was finally removed
in 1966. The Six Day War of 1967 signaled a major turning point in
relations between Israeli Palestinians and Jews. For Israeli Jews, the war
was a miracle. The rapid destruction of the combined armies of Egypt,
Jordan, and Syria and the capture of Jerusalem, the West Bank, the
Gaza Strip, the Golan Heights, and the Sinai were events they never
dreamed would occur. Israel came out of the war holding territories
three times its size, and Israeli Jews became convinced that their army
and society were invincible. Imperialist visions of a Greater Israel were
now reality. For Israeli Palestinians, the war represented an additional
humiliation and defeat. The capture of the new territories, however,
brought Israeli Palestinians and Palestinians from the West Bank and
Gaza Strip into direct contact. Israeli Palestinians emerged from this
contact more politicized.

In Acre, tensions were high in the months prior to the outbreak of
the war. Some Arab families who had moved outside the Old City's
walls returned to their protection during the conflict, while others went
to relatives in the villages. In the mixed Wolfson neighborhood, Arab
and Jewish neighbors shared bomb shelters and Arab neighbors helped
Jewish women get into the shelters with their families. Arab residents
remembered this period as one of tension. Eggs were thrown at them,
Jewish neighbors hurled insults, and they felt humiliated. Jewish residents of Acre danced and sang to celebrate the capture of East Jerusalem and the Old City; this angered Arab residents.

In the war's aftermath, a national debate ensued about what Israel
should do with the conquered territories, a debate that reverberated in
Acre as well. Journalist Dov Goldstein interviewed Mohammed Houbeishe, then deputy mayor, and Hassan Sirwan, assistant town clerk, for
an article in a series called "Arabs in Israeli Cities" that appeared in *Ma-
'ariv* on 15 November 1968. Houbeishe and Sirwan discussed what life
was like for Acre's Arab population and their ideas concerning what
Israel should do with the conquered territories. Sirwan told Goldstein,
"When I saw the Jewish and Arab children running around on the grass
of my yard, I knew — It's all a matter of time. Not only that we can live
together in peace but that we're capable of producing mutual pleasure
from life. And I asked myself with great excitement: Maybe this is what
peace looks like? Maybe this is its hoped for shape."[82] He supported the
idea of a binational state and said that anyone who thought it would not

work should visit Acre and see how Jews and Arabs live together and have found a common language. Houbeishe saw two possibilities — that a binational state would arise (his greatest ambition) or that a Palestinian state would be established, in which case Acre would need to be a part of it as an Arab city. Sirwan also echoed this feeling that Acre, as an Arab city, should be part of the Palestinian state if one were founded. He insisted that any Arab who thought otherwise was a traitor to his people. Both men, however, were very clear that their hoped-for solution was the establishment of a binational, Jewish-Palestinian state, similar in structure to the Lebanese state.

Shortly after this article appeared, *Ma'ariv* published a second piece under the headline "Suspected Link between Fatah and the Deputy Mayor of Acre under Investigation." The article alleged that Houbeishe had received money from two Nablus men for "distribution among Acre's poor." Because of the identity of the two men, the article continued, Israeli security authorities suspected that the deputy mayor's earlier published statement about returning to the 1947 partition plan borders was coordinated with Fatah agents.[83] The two pieces created an uproar both within Acre and nationally. "Most of Acre's Arabs See It as an Arab City — Like the Partition Plan," announced headlines in *Ha'Aretz* on 3 December 1968. The incident received coverage in *Davar, Ha'Aretz, Al Ha'Mishmar,* and *Ha'Tzofah.*[84] Top officials of the Arab Affairs Committee of the Labor Party (with whom Houbeishe's independent list was affiliated) met in Tel Aviv and decided to seek his resignation as deputy mayor.[85] Houbeishe's earlier political moderation did not protect him now. He resigned his post on 5 December, although he refused to resign his council seat. Jewish municipal officials in Acre also sought to have Sirwan fired because of his statement that "any Arab who does not regard Acre as an Arab town is a traitor to his people." Sirwan, who had worked for the municipality for eighteen years, received a reprimand from an internal committee.[86] A very clear message was sent to the Palestinian residents of Acre and Israel as a whole. Acre was a Jewish city, and claims to the contrary were not allowable.

No sooner had this scandal faded away than residents of Acre received a new blow. In late November 1969, the Police and Security Services arrested six Arab men from Acre on suspicion of terrorist activities. The six, all Muslims in their twenties and thirties, held good jobs and were financially secure. Two were taxi drivers for Jewish cab owners, two were fishermen, one was a housepainter, and the sixth was a carpenter. All but one were married and had children; they had never been politically active. The men were accused of nine acts of sabotage between 6 June and 23 October, which included blasting oil pipes and power transformers, damaging water pumps, and exploding five houses in Haifa in which two people were killed and seventeen injured. At the carpenter's shop, police found a cache of weapons and explosives that included Russian hand and antitank grenades and electrical detonators.[87]

Jewish residents of the city responded to the news of the arrests with horror and anger. Five hundred Jewish residents, mostly young people, marched on the Old City on 22 November but were turned back by police. They carried signs that said, "We want military government back to restrain the Arab citizens," and, "Our thanks to the security forces. But we have to live in Acre even without the security forces."[88] The police patrolled the city throughout the night. The terrorist attacks were condemned by the Nazareth Municipal Council, principals of Arab schools, and the Acre Muslim *Waqf* Committee, whose message stated: "We are confident the acts of a few individuals will not stain the name of our community and that of the Arab residents of Israel generally."[89]

The tension in Acre was further exacerbated when an automobile driven by two Arabs from Majd el Kurum blew up after it stopped sharply at a traffic light at one of Acre's main intersections on the Saturday night after the first arrests. The police speculated that the driver had sped up because of a patrol car behind him but then had to brake for the red light. The sudden stop jarred the explosive charge being carried in the car and caused it to explode prematurely. The bomb demolished the car, and both occupants were thrown into the street. One of the men was killed outright, while the other died en route to the hospital.[90]

Once again, rioting broke out and the police prevented a Jewish mob from entering the Old City. Jewish youths responded by stoning the police. Four rioters and three policemen were injured in the incident. A *Jerusalem Post* reporter claimed that Arab residents of the Old City believed that a number of Jews had been killed in the explosion and "groups began marching in the streets singing."[91] Once again, a newly elected mayor, barely in office one day, had to act to restore order. Israel Doron went from factory to factory to try to calm Jewish workers. He issued a proclamation calling for peace and quiet in the city. In the evening, military police and border police units were brought to the town to help local police maintain order.

Over the next few weeks, an additional five men and two women (one of them Jewish) were arrested on suspicion of cooperating or shielding members of the terrorist cell. The women were the wives of two of the original six suspects. The men included relatives of the first six men, a locksmith, a tinsmith, a café owner, and an officer of the Acre Fire Brigade. The fireman, who had served with distinction for eleven years, had frequently visited the occupied territories since the Six Day War to see friends and relatives. Local Arab leaders and businessmen condemned the group's actions and sought to distance the local Arab community from the suspected terrorists. For many Jewish residents, these events seemed to justify their fears that Israeli Palestinians were indeed a fifth column. It was necessary to act forcefully. As one Jewish youth who had participated in the riots put it:

> You have to beat them in order to teach them where they belong, so that they know their place. If we continue to be lenient toward them, we will wake up one day to discover that the city has been taken over by al-Fateh. . . . We have reached the conclusion that it is impossible to continue to tolerate the situation. They have to fear us, otherwise out [of the country] they will go.[92]

Coexistence was no easier during the decade of the 1970s. In July of 1970, Mayor Doron sent a confidential report to the prime minister and several Cabinet ministers. Doron characterized Acre as "a city of refuge, riddled with social problems" and detailed its problems — prostitution and drugs, housing unfit for human habitation, and a potential Arab-Jewish demographic imbalance in the future.[93] His report prompted national officials to establish a commission of inquiry to examine the city's situation. The commission reached the conclusion that without assistance Acre could turn into a city with a large Arab population and a weak and poor Jewish one. It recommended immediate action to prevent this possibility: preferential development status, increased private construction, special grants to young couples for housing, and construction of better-quality housing. The commission also recommended the construction of more modern housing for the Arab population.

Doron's report had been preceded in May by a letter to the same government officials from Arab municipal councilors Houbeishe and Houri, who demanded that something be done to improve living conditions in the Old City.[94] There were houses whose roofs were likely to collapse at any moment and people living in rooms half open to the elements. They demanded that a solution be found. They also demanded better health and sanitary services, cleaner streets with lighting, play areas and parks for children, and new school buildings. They asked that the municipality hire Arab workers in proportion to the number of Arab residents in Acre and that municipal correspondence to Arab residents be in Arabic and not Hebrew. They also asked that a deputy mayor be appointed from among the Arab councilors. The letter was signed by leaders of all the religious communities and other leading Arab citizens.

The battle over the Old City began during this period. For Jewish municipal leaders and residents, the Old City took on a more sinister aura. Journalists described it as a "hatchery and hothouse for anti-Israeli elements, which find among the walls of the Old Town ample and easy ground for their hostile activity."[95] By this time, almost all Jewish residents had moved from the Old City to housing elsewhere in Acre. The only Jewish presence in the quarter was the shopowners in the *suq* — 102 Jewish shops compared to 75 Arab (Cohen 1973, 8). For the Arab residents, the Old City was an important center of autonomy and a symbol of national identity. At the same time, the physical deterioration, congestion, and unsanitary living conditions were oppressive. The quarter came to be known as the ghetto of Acre. Jewish municipal officials wanted to convert the Old City into a living museum as part of their strategy for the city's development. Such a strategy required reducing the Arab population within the walls.

The municipality was in the process of developing a new master plan at this time. One of the national committees that studied Acre's problems had recommended solving the Arab housing situation by constructing a new neighborhood *outside* the municipal boundaries of Acre (Cohen 1973, 15). Local leaders enthusiastically adopted this suggestion, and planners were told to include this provision in the new master plan. Reducing the size of the Arab population in the city would serve a dual purpose. It would ensure Jewish demographic control and strengthen Jewish political control of the city. Arab residents in Acre generally elected four of the fifteen municipal council members. With fewer Arab residents, there would be proportionately fewer Arab elected officials.

Acre received another wave of Jewish immigrants during the early 1970s. In 1972 and 1973 alone, more than 66,000 Soviet Jews entered Israel. The new immigrants were enthusiastically embraced by Israeli officials and provided with modern housing and employment. The Arab-Jewish demographic balance had been of great concern to policymakers. For Acre, this wave of immigration resulted in an infusion of Jews from the Soviet Republics of Georgia and Azerbaijan. In 1972, Acre's Jewish population reached 25,500, while its Arab population was 8,200.

The 1973 Yom Kippur War reinforced Jewish fears and suspicions regarding their Arab fellow citizens. This war destroyed the sense of invulnerability that Israeli Jews had held since 1967 and brought a return of the siege mentality. The failure of the national government to foresee the attack, the evidence of corruption and incompetence that came to light in the Agranat Commission's report, and the massive loss of life in the war left many Jewish citizens feeling vulnerable and disillusioned.

For Acre, 1974 brought a number of changes. Early in the year, the government announced that it was taking over 560 dunams of land in Acre for housing and development projects.[96] The government decided to close down the *ma'abārāh* at Tel Napoleon and house its families elsewhere. The municipality's proposal to build an Arab neighborhood outside the municipal boundary was accepted by national government ministries. In September, Housing Minister Avraham Ofer announced that an Arab development town for five thousand families would be built four kilometers east of Acre on a site adjoining Makr. That same month, a new bus terminal, located next to the Wolfson neighborhood, opened for business.

Intercommunal tensions brought on by the Yom Kippur War were heightened by several Palestinian attacks during the year. On 11 April, eighteen Israelis were killed and sixteen wounded in a Popular Front for the Liberation of Palestine (PFLP) attack on Qiryat Shemona. On 15 May (Israel's Independence Day), members of the Democratic Front for the Liberation of Palestine (DFLP) seized a school building in Maʿalot and held more than one hundred students and teachers hostage. During a flawed rescue operation, twenty-seven children were killed. This was followed on 24 June by an attack on Nahariyya (just north of Acre) by members of Al-Fatah in which a woman and two children were killed.

Some government officials perceived the strong Arab presence in the Galilee as a threat, especially since efforts to establish a Jewish presence there had not been especially successful. In 1976, Yisrael Koenig, the interior ministry's representative for the Northern District, wrote a private memo in which he proposed a series of measures that should be taken to restrict Arab population growth in the Galilee. He urged cutting government subsidies to Arab families, encouraging Arab youth to study overseas and remain there, restricting the number of Arab workers employed in Jewish-owned businesses, cracking down on Arab tax evaders, and increasing surveillance on Arab political activities. His report caused a storm of protest when it was leaked to the media, but Koenig retained his post. The Jewish Agency and government ministries intensified the Yahud Ha'Galil (Judaize the Galilee) initiative by constructing a number of new Jewish settlements throughout the region. Resettlement of Arab families from Acre's Old City to new housing in the village of Makr began in 1976 (Lustick 1980, 132). In December, it was announced that one-third of the government's development budget would be spent in the Galilee.[97] Acre would be included in these developments, and a new master plan would be ready by the following summer.

The Arab residents of Acre were not the only ones with complaints. Municipal officials found themselves in a battle with the Black Panthers, a national Mizraḥi protest group, during 1973 and 1974. The municipality closed down the chicken slaughterhouse of a local Mizraḥi man, claiming that it was a health hazard. The slaughterhouse's owner, who had made an unsuccessful bid for mayor of Acre as a Black Panther candidate, fought back. Mayor Doron resigned his office twice in protest over how matters were being handled. The issue came to a head when the Mizraḥi man threatened to commit suicide and proceeded to douse himself with gasoline. When the mayor capitulated to his demands, municipal employees went on strike to protest giving in to a suicide threat. The slaughterhouse's owner was backed by the national Black Panther leadership. Naim Giladi, their spokesperson, said that branches throughout the country had been ready to converge on Acre with trucks and oil if the Acre man had committed suicide. "There would not have been one government or municipal office left whole in Acre," he said.[98]

The other protest was by residents of the Tel Napoleon *maʿabārāh*, who in 1975 were still waiting for the government to fulfill a promise to relocate them made two years previously. The *maʿabārāh* of asbestos huts was a haunt for thieves, prostitutes, and drug addicts. Trash was collected only once a week. Rats, snakes, scorpions, and mosquitoes flourished in the debris of demolished huts. There was no place for children to play, the kindergarten was closed, and the nursery school was scheduled to close the following year. Many of the residents of the area were young couples who had grown up and married there. The residents sent petitions and delegations to the Ministry of Housing, demonstrated, and even squatted in homes built for new immigrants that had been sitting empty for five months. As one resident asked, "Why are hundreds of homes waiting empty for newcomers, while we must live in this kind of environment with small children for another two years? One should have thought that after fourteen years at such a place we too would have some right to rent decent homes, like newcomers."[99]

By December 1976, a new housing quarter in the north of the city had been finished and five hundred apartments were waiting for new residents. Special mortgages were made available to young couples to encourage them to remain in the city. Throughout the rest of the 1970s, municipal officials worried about continued Jewish out-migration from the city, because the families who were leaving were the more established and educated middle class. In 1977 and 1978, layoffs and plant closures increased the rate of unemployment in the city, further raising concerns about its future. Municipal officials continued to clamor for land for higher-quality housing so that the more established residents would remain and a more sophisticated working population could be attracted to the city.[100] In the municipal elections of 1978, the Labor Alignment won six seats and the religious front two seats, while the United Arab list won four seats and Rakah one.

The decade of the 1980s repeated patterns seen in previous eras. The Israeli invasion of Lebanon, Operation Peace for Galilee, in 1982, once again increased tensions between Arab and Jewish residents. One Arab woman summed up the effects of the Lebanon War:

> The Lebanon War—it was the beginning of racism on both sides. It was a period of taking away the blindfold and revealing what was hidden in hearts. When the Lebanon War started, volcanoes of blind hatred and racism erupted from people's hearts. The Arabs want to defend the land because it's theirs—and the Jews want to conquer it with all their strength.[101]

In September 1982, eight Arab youths (aged sixteen to nineteen) were arrested on suspicion of rioting in the Old City. The police claimed their actions were a protest against the war in Lebanon; the youths said that they were celebrating a traditional feast. The following week, Ramzi Houri, the Rakah municipal council member, called for a parliamentary inquiry into police brutality in Acre. He claimed that ten youths had been arrested and that other young people had been beaten by police. The bonfire was part of an annual Catholic celebration and was always held in the same spot.[102]

In 1983, Acre elected a new mayor—Eliahu de Castro. In municipal elections that year, his Labor Party had won five seats, Herut got three, and local lists took the remaining seats.[103] De Castro immediately set up a Tourism Department to renovate historical buildings and work on finding investors who would be willing to construct hotels in the city. The municipality embarked on a number of high-profile construction projects—a war memorial to Israeli Jewish war dead (for 640,000 Israel; Shekels [IS]), a four-hundred-seat auditorium for East Acre (at a cost of $1 million for the first stage), and a new municipal library (for $500,000). The municipal government at the same time was running a deficit. In 1984, the combined deficits of Nahariyya, Acre, Shelomi, and the Mateh Asher Regional Council amounted to over IS 1 billion.[104]

Municipal officials commissioned another report on the city's urgent needs in 1984 to help with the preparation of a new master plan.[105] This report included a number of recommendations that were similar to those of earlier years: expand Acre's municipal boundaries, provide land for high-quality housing, introduce housing and industrial opportunities that would attract a better class of resident to the city and would hold those members of the middle class already there. It again raised the need to find a solution to the problem of Arab housing in the Old City. The report's author, Karlos Lomovsky, also stated that the municipality needed to devote resources to strengthening mutual awareness between Arab and Jewish residents of the city. He recommended that the various educational networks in the city be directed to finding ways to address this issue in their activities. In a 1985 municipal report that went to government ministries, the problems within the Arab sector were again enumerated—dangerous housing, overcrowding, dilapidated school buildings, infrastructure deficiencies, and poor or inadequate services.

The report noted that the municipality was concentrating its efforts on moving families with many children to Makr and giving preferential assistance to young couples who moved there. The housing ministry had agreed to come up with a suitable building project for Arab residents — in Makr, where an additional two hundred housing units were planned.

Relations between Arabs and Jews continued on a rocky course throughout the 1980s. In October 1985, swastikas and slogans — "We're all PLO, all Palestinians, Jews out" — were painted on the doors of Jewish-owned shops in the Old City. Two weeks previously there had been a bombing, and Israeli flags were defaced during the Alternative Theater Festival.[106] In May 1986, Mayor de Castro decided that he wanted a special adviser on planning and tourism development and announced that he would give the position to Yisrael Koenig, who had just resigned from his post in the interior ministry. The announcement produced an outpouring of anger on the part of Acre's Arab residents, many of whom had not forgotten (or forgiven) Koenig's 1976 memo on curbing the Arab presence in the Galilee. Hadash (the united list of Rakah and the Black Panthers) spearheaded a campaign to protest de Castro's decision. Finally, in February 1987, de Castro announced that he was dropping Koenig as a candidate for the position. In September 1986, a crowd of fifty Arab youths turned on police in the Old City and successfully freed three youths who had been arrested. The riot was described as one of the most serious attacks on police in many years.[107] In October 1986, a fire was started at the Amal elementary school. Racist slogans such as "Arabs out of Israel," "Kahane for leader," and "Death to Terrorists and Arabs" were found chalked on the blackboard in the room where the fire was started.[108] Kahane activists struck again the following year in April when a fire was laid in a Protestant church in the city center. Again, slogans called for the expulsion of Christians and other Arabs from Israel.[109] Ironically, in 1986, Acre received a national prize for tolerance as an "example of how Jews and Arabs can live together in peace and harmony."[110]

The history of Israeli Acre's first forty years is a history of struggle and unfulfilled promises, of local efforts to develop and improve the community being subverted by national imperatives, and of national conflicts impinging on and affecting local communal relations. Acre's political leaders have had to fight for adequate housing, services, and employment for their consituents, but they have fought harder and been more successful in acquiring benefits and services for their Jewish than for their Arab citizens. Acre's Arab citizens have good reason to feel like second-class citizens. For forty years, they have looked to the local and national governments for solutions to their housing, education, and employment problems. For forty years, they have been given halfhearted solutions and promises. The neglect has led some Arab residents to pursue more radical, nationalist solutions to their difficulties. Others continue to believe that compromise and coexistence will eventually bring the rewards of a better life. Had Acre's residents been able to adjust to life in a mixed city during forty years of peace, a stronger fabric of intercommunal connections and trust might now exist. Instead, each decade has brought its conflicts — both local and national — so that trust and understanding have constantly been strained and broken. With the outbreak of the *intifada* in the West Bank and Gaza Strip in December 1987, the residents of Acre entered a new cycle of tension and communal strife.

Acre in the 1980s: Demographics

In 1989, the city of Acre included 37,400 inhabitants, of whom 28,700 were Jews (76.7 percent) and 8,700 were Arabs (23.3 percent) according to the Israeli Central Bureau of Statistics. According to the 1983 census, its population was divided among the four different residential quarters as follows: East Acre, 2,521 households, 9,061 individuals; Old Acre, 950 households, 4,698 individuals; Mandate Acre, 1,529 households, 5,686 individuals; and North Acre, 4,817 households, 16,951 individuals (table 1).[111] Locally there has been recurring debate about the size of the Arab population of the Old City, which some people claim approaches 11,000 residents, not the 5,000 of the official statistics. This would give Acre a population closer to 43,000, about one-third Arab and two-thirds Jewish. It is the most heterogeneous of the seven mixed Arab-Jewish cities in Israel, with the exception of Jerusalem.[112] The proportion of Jewish to Arab residents (three to one) has remained fairly stable from 1955 to 1989 (table 2). Unlike all the other mixed localities, which are characterized by high degrees of residential segregation, Acre exhibits a degree of residential integration that makes it unique in Israel.[113] Al-

TABLE 1. Population in Acre by Residential Quarter, 1983

Residential Quarter	Number of Households	(%)	Number of Individuals	(%)
East Acre	2,521	25.6	9,061	24.8
Old Acre	950	9.6	4,698	12.9
Mandate Acre	1,529	15.5	5,686	15.6
North Acre	4,817	49.0	16,951	46.5
Total	9,817		36,396	

Source: 1983 Census of Population and Housing, Geographic Version, Israel Social Sciences Data Archive, Hebrew University.

though the population of Old Acre is exclusively Arab, Arab families can be found living in all the other neighborhoods in the city. In Shkhūnāt Wolfson, they comprise more than half of the residents of the neighborhood. Shkhūnāt Ben-Gurion, in East Acre, also has drawn a larger number of Arab residents.

Acre's Jewish population is divided among immigrants from Europe, the Americas, Africa, and Asia, and their Israeli-born children, and among veterans (those who immigrated before 1948) and newcomers (those who arrived after 1948). From 1948 to 1964, Acre absorbed immigrants who were arriving in Israel from North Africa (5,734 people), Asia (942), and Europe (3,094). The Ashkenazim and their Israeli-born children account for 38 percent of the Jewish population, while the Mizraḥim and their Israeli-born children comprise the remaining 62 percent. Less than 1 in 10 Jewish heads of households are classified as veterans; all veterans in Acre are Ashkenazim (262 individuals). Among the Ashkenazim, the largest groups are the Romanians (33 percent), the Poles (17 percent), and the Soviets (40 percent), with much smaller contingents from Hungary, Czechoslovakia, Germany, Austria, Latin America, and North America. Among the Mizraḥim, immigrants from Morocco make up 60 percent of those who have settled in Acre, while the next largest contingent is from Algeria and Tunisia (15 percent). The Mizraḥi community also includes people who immigrated from Turkey, Libya, Bulgaria, Greece, Egypt, Sudan, India, Pakistan, Iran, Yemen, Iraq, Syria, and Lebanon (table 3).

Of the five thousand residents included in a geographic subset of the 1983 census,[114] 66 percent of the Arab population lived in housing that was constructed prior to 1948. An additional 23 percent lived in housing constructed between 1948 and 1965. Only 10 percent lived in

TABLE 2.   Population in Acre, 1948–89

	1948	1950	1955	1961	1972	1980	1983	1985	1988	1989
					A. In thousands					
Jews	.9	8.2	14.2	19.0	25.5	29.6	28.6	29.3	28.7	28.7
Arabs	3.1	4.0	5.0	6.2	8.2	9.1	7.8	8.1	8.5	8.7
Total	4.0	12.2	19.2	25.2	33.7	38.7	36.4	37.4	37.2	37.4
					B. In percentages					
Jews	22.5	67.2	74.0	75.4	75.6	76.4	78.5	78.3	77.1	76.7
Arabs	77.5	32.8	26.0	24.6	24.4	23.6	21.5	21.7	22.9	23.3
Total	100	100	100	100	100	100	100	100	100	100

Source: Israel, Central Bureau of Statistics 1990.

newer housing, with 4 percent resident in housing built after 1975. The bulk of the Jewish population lived in housing constructed between 1955 and 1980 (73 percent), with 30 percent living in housing built in 1975–80. Only 20 percent lived in housing constructed prior to 1954, while 8 percent lived in housing built in 1981–83. A municipal report from 1985 provides data on the details of Amidar's housing stock in Acre prior to 31 December 1984. Out of a total available stock of 6,935 units, 99 (1 percent) were vacant, 3,995 (58 percent) were privately owned, and 2,841 (41 percent) were rented. Housing was divided among the neighborhoods as follows: East Acre, 32.7 percent; North Acre, 62.5 percent; and Mandate Acre, 4.7 percent. Amidar administers more than 90 percent of the housing stock in Old Acre, which it received from the Custodian.[115] Thus, most of the Arabs who are residents of the Old City are tenants of Amidar. Amidar's rental units are notorious for being poorly maintained. Residents of Shkhūnāt Wolfson, for example, told of being given apartments that lacked glass in the windows and blinds to keep out bugs and intruders. The housing stock in the Old City, much of which dates to the eighteenth century or earlier, is beyond the capacity of Amidar to maintain. Heavy rains and strong winds break off chunks of masonry. Ceilings, balconies, and walls often collapse with no warning.

TABLE 3.　Jewish Immigration to Acre by Country of Origin, 1948–88

Country of Origin	Statistical Area										
	1	2	3	4	5	6	7	8	9	10	11
Latin America	3	21	9	4	14	62	59	11	1	1	17
North America	1	2	3	1	1	5	4	2	–	1	8
Hungary	6	14	26	18	13	19	34	23	5	7	46
Czechoslovakia	5	13	10	23	4	14	11	12	15	7	61
Germany/Austria	10	19	21	17	8	21	38	28	25	14	41
Bulgaria/Greece	5	10	30	41	8	12	41	37	32	12	126
Romania	82	120	185	479	141	238	323	403	144	113	582
Poland	66	79	76	132	30	86	135	220	107	55	454
USSR	19	665	299	72	55	1,220	780	92	28	52	145
Egypt/Sudan	88	131	216	97	64	109	140	135	62	30	119
Libya	22	26	37	18	2	16	29	14	6	9	24
Algeria/Tunisia	212	263	393	247	296	300	228	210	132	69	248
Morocco	546	794	1,243	1,176	1,326	1,439	1,269	955	523	264	689
India/Pakistan	6	11	24	9	6	15	27	14	13	6	9
Iran	99	25	35	15	12	28	16	12	13	10	33
Yemen	102	73	109	9	8	13	28	7	3	5	15
Iraq	21	36	76	23	18	42	94	54	65	25	121
Syria/Lebanon	4	8	12	10	4	20	33	12	11	9	15
Turkey	56	107	129	87	137	123	139	90	55	51	102

Source: Israel, Central Bureau of Statistics 1988.

At least 250 homes there have been declared unfit for human habitation, with 70 ordered demolished, although nothing has been done to carry out the demolition orders.[116]

Purchasing a home is a major expenditure for most Israelis as well as their primary form of investment. In central cities such as Tel Aviv and Jerusalem, the housing market is inelastic; it is not uncommon to find a two-bedroom apartment selling for a hundred thousand dollars or more.[117] One of the attractions of development towns such as Acre, where the housing market is more elastic, is that individuals can purchase more housing for their dollars than in the larger cities of Haifa, Tel Aviv, and Jerusalem. Among Jewish residents in the 1983 census subset, 69 percent owned their homes, while 29 percent rented. Of those families renting, 91 percent were the tenants of Amidar or Rassco, while 9 percent rented from private owners or another source. For Arab residents, 31 percent owned their homes and 66 percent rented. Of those families renting, 72 percent rented from Amidar or Rassco, while 28 percent rented from a private owner or another source. Most of the Arab families who rented were residents of the Old City.

The working-class character of the city's Jewish residents can be seen by comparing Acre to the neighboring cities of Nahariyya and Karmi'el (which have larger proportions of Ashkenazi residents) and to national Jewish averages on several key population indicators (table 4). Living standards and conditions in Nahariyya and Karmi'el are used by local residents to determine their own status in the region. More than 33 percent of Acre's Jewish residents are employed in industry, compared to a national average of 22.7 percent and averages of 28 percent for Nahariyya and 36 percent for Karmi'el (which is an industrial center). Only 18 percent of Acre's Jewish residents hold professional or managerial positions, compared to a national average of 32.6 percent and averages of 27 percent for Nahariyya and 26 percent for Karmi'el. Income

TABLE 4.   Socioeconomic Characteristics of Acre Compared to National Averages and the Neighboring Cities of Nahariyya and Karmi'el, 1990

Characteristic	Acre		Israel			
	Jews	Arabs	Jews	Arabs	Nahariyya	Karmi'el
0–4 years of education (%)	14.3	29.0	9.0	21.1	11.7	5.9
Academic degree (%)	1.9	1.4	8.9	3.0	5.6	8.0
Industrial occupation (%)	33.4	39.5	23.7	52.0	27.9	36.0
Professional/managerial occupation (%)	18.3	10.7	30.1	12.0	26.8	25.8
Income per person (NIS 1,000)	11.8	6.7	14.1	12.3	13.3	13.0
Car ownership (%)	30.4	17.5	46.4	—	40.6	47.8

Source: Haifa and Galilee Research Institute 1989; Israel, Central Bureau of Statistics 1990.

levels are correspondingly lower for Acre's Jewish residents. The average annual income per person is 11,800 new Israeli shekels (NIS), while nationally the level is NIS 14,100. In Karmi'el, incomes average NIS 13,000, while in Nahariyya the rates are NIS 13,300. Educational levels, not surprisingly, also reflect the city's working-class character. Few of Acre's Jewish residents hold academic degrees (2 percent), while more residents of Acre (14 percent) than of Nahariyya (12 percent) or Karmi'el (6 percent) have completed less than five years of schooling. Since Nahariyya is known as a popular retirement location, its low level of education may be explained by the higher proportion of elderly residents whose educations were interrupted by events in Europe or Israel. In Israel, car ownership is a status marker, because of the costs involved in purchasing (ten thousand dollars or more), operating, and maintaining an automobile. About 30 percent of Acre's Jewish residents own cars, while 41 percent of Nahariyya's and 48 percent of Karmi'el's residents do.

Acre's Arab residents present a somewhat different picture. About 39 percent of Arab residents are employed in industrial occupations, compared to a national average for Israeli Palestinians of 52 percent. Professional and managerial occupations employ 11 percent of Acre's Arab residents, which compares favorably to the national average of 12 percent. In terms of income levels, education, and car ownership, however, Acre's Arab residents are far behind its Jewish residents. Twenty-nine percent of Arab residents have less than five years of schooling, compared to a national average for Arabs of 21.1 percent. Income levels show a considerable discrepancy: the average annual income of Acre's Palestinian residents is NIS 6,700 (compared to 11,800 for Acre's Jewish residents and 12,703 for Arabs nationally). Given such low income levels, it is not surprising that only 17 percent of Acre's Arab residents own cars.

When Jewish residents of Acre improve their status, either through education or employment, they often leave the city and purchase homes in higher-status communities such as Nahariyya, Karmi'el, or the Qrayot suburbs of Haifa. There has been slow but constant out-migration of middle- and upper-class Jewish residents from the city. These individuals are often replaced by Jewish working-class residents, who find Acre an affordable place to live, or people who are dependent on state welfare services, who are given no choice as to where they will live. For the Arab residents, a different settlement pattern is at work. While some established Arab families choose to leave the city and settle elsewhere, a number of middle-class Arab families remain in the city because they prefer the amenities it offers. The high proportion of rental housing available in the Old City provides an entrée for poorer Arab families from surrounding areas, who thus replace the Arab families that have moved to better housing elsewhere in the city. Local and national policymakers often characterize Acre's residents as "weak" and blame the city's inability to develop and progress on their low socioeconomic status.

Acre retains the aura of an Arab city. It has served as a development town but does not receive the special status and benefits accorded to all-Jewish settlements. For its Jewish residents, it represents a way station on their journey toward Ashkenaziness and a settled middle-class existence. For its Arab residents, it represents the homeland, a monument to a continuous Palestinian presence that will not be erased from the land. Acre remains on the margins of Israel in many senses, a border zone between Arabs and Jews. As a border zone, it provides a possible model for Arab-Jewish relations in the Israeli state. Yet whenever the state has intruded into life in Acre, good relations have suffered. It is only when Acre is on the margin, a liminal area, that peace is maintained between the two communities.

CHAPTER 3

"Educating for Democracy": Schooling and the Politics of Identity

> . . . and I thought about Eve the kindergarten teacher behind
> the cardboard ship with the two funnels, who taught us to
> hate in an orderly way, the Greeks at Hanukkah, the Persians
> at Purim, the Egyptians at Pessach, and who wasn't there now
> to help me orchestrate the row of corpses which belonged to
> her, which came from her, into a choral recitation of some
> heroic poem; no, she wasn't there to organize and supervise
> and I thought with the bitterness of the boy I had been up to
> then, why aren't you here with your hard eyes and lined face,
> you who may perhaps have suffered real suffering that you
> didn't know how to teach us instead of Hannah sacrificing her
> seven sons and Haman's children hung on a tree, in three
> voices . . . (Kaniuk 1988, 36)

The educational system was a key component in the Zionist plan to build a new Israeli society. Its purpose was not to reproduce values, skills, beliefs, and behaviors already in place but to produce a new generation of citizens who were consciously separated from the cultures of their parents. Rather than creating cultural continuity, the pre-state Zionist educational enterprise deliberately fostered cultural discontinuity. These early Israelis tried to turn away from the upbringing they had received from their parents and communities. The new state required a new Jew, the mythological "Elik born from the sea," foundling children who were nurtured by the land into which they were born (Shohat 1988; Lavie 1992). The sabra (native-born Israeli Jew) was to be the physical, psychological, and emotional antithesis of the diaspora Jew. Brawny and tanned, these new children were to be confident, brave, and tough, men and women of action, prickly outside but tender inside like the cactus after which they were called. The pioneering generation, however, only partially succeeded in the endeavor to create a new culture because its children continued to be socialized by adults who were themselves products of different cultural systems. In trying to bring about planned cultural change, the Zionist founders unconsciously reproduced in the new generation certain beliefs, values, and behaviors that were at odds with their stated vision of an egalitarian socialist society.

After 1948, the educational system was eventually brought under the control of the national government. Israeli educators were faced with new challenges. Out of the educational pluralism that existed under British rule, they had to develop a unified national curriculum that would foster loyalty to the state in the younger generation. This system had to serve multiple purposes: to reproduce Zionist values, beliefs, and behaviors in the children born to the new generation of Israelis; to produce this culture in the children of new Jewish immigrants (and through them in their parents); to prevent the reproduction of the existing Palestinian culture, given its nationalist aspirations; and to produce a new "Israeli Arab" whose values, skills, and behaviors would be congruent with his or her status as an Israeli citizen. Israel's national leaders saw themselves as consciously leaving behind their old cultures. They never stopped to question whether, in fact, they had left everything behind. Nor did they stop to question whether the new Jewish immigrants entering the country or the Palestinians who remained felt the same urgent need to rework their cultures and identities. Their lack of introspection has had major consequences over the years. In Israel, truly, "[E]ducation is at once the result of contradictions and the source of new contradictions" (Carnoy 1989, 9). In this chapter, I explore how schools have served as sites for constructing identity. That schools in Israel have an important role to play in transmitting national values is accepted by most Israeli Jews. Yet schools are also sites for the transmission of the particularistic values of the dominant sector of society as well as places where students and teachers can contest and resist those values. After examining how the state has approached educating Israelis (both Jews and Palestinians), I analyze two ways that schools bring together Arab and Jewish children in Acre, the contradictions embodied in each of these processes, and their outcomes.

Educating Israelis

During the last quarter of the nineteenth century, the Ottoman *wali* (governor), located in Acre, established four-year elementary schools (the *rushdi*) in Palestine that provided a basic Islamic education in Turkish, with Arabic taught as a second language.[1] During the early 1870s, the Association of Good Will was established in Greater Syria as a Muslim organization, one of whose goals was to provide schools for boys and girls. They began by opening private Arab-Muslim schools in Acre and Jerusalem.[2] During the time of the Mandate (1922–47), a

number of schools existed in Acre.[3] The British established a government school that was also attended by members of Acre's Orthodox
Christian community. For the Catholic community, there were two
schools, one for girls and one for boys.[4] The Muslim community was
also represented by the religious seminary of the Al-Jazzâr Mosque, an
important center for training Muslim clergy, and by a private school.
Arab educators battled with British officials for control over the content
of the curriculum in their schools. The British denationalized the formal
curriculum, so Arab educators were forced to use hidden or implied
lessons to impart their nationalist values or to model such values
through their own political activism (Marʿi 1978, 18).

The Jewish educational system during the Mandate consisted of
three ideological trends (General, Mizraḥi,[5] and Labor) as well as more
traditional religious schools such as the *ḥeder* and yeshiva.[6] Each of the
trends offered the same basic curriculum but supplemented that material
differently. Mizraḥi schools devoted considerable time to religious education, while the General schools combined Zionism and modern education with a positive religious component. The Labor schools emphasized
progressive education, the value of work, and a literary or historical
reading of the Bible (Cohen 1992, 237–38). The Jewish community in
Acre prior to the 1936 riots had a school of thirty-two students and one
teacher. The British also established an experimental school for delinquents in Acre, the site of the central prison.

The educational system was disrupted by the fighting in 1948 and
1949. Opening schools in Israeli Acre was not a structured process.
Pninah Gofer founded the first Jewish school in 1948.[7] Her husband
served with the brigade that had captured Acre, so his commander gave
them the opportunity to settle in one of the many vacant houses of the
Mandate and Old City quarters. Captivated by the view of Acre from
the south, they decided they would move there. Two days later, Gofer
sallied forth to begin her school. In her words:

> I entered houses, but the languages I spoke didn't count — no
> Romanian and no Maro'cait [a Jewish-Arabic dialect spoken in
> Morocco]. When I tried to explain with hand signals that I was
> looking for children, they thought I was a nurse or doctor and
> brought a child whose stomach hurt. I returned home, took a
> satchel and paper. . . . I collected a group of children that I
> could separate into five classes according to age and knowledge
> of arithmetic. Two or three children in every class and I would
> travel among all the rooms that were the school, which was in an
> old Arab building that today houses Ha'Tomer School. I didn't
> want to mix two classes in one room so that parents would know
> that this was to be a school and not a *ḥeder*.

Gofer was soon joined by two additional teachers, who were put to work enlisting students, teaching half the day, and making home visits. One of the major problems was that none of the students knew Hebrew and the teachers couldn't help in another language. The children spoke different languages, so there was no choice but to teach in Hebrew. Soon three more teachers arrived, and the school began to function like "every regular school."

In September 1949, the first Knesset passed the Compulsory Education Law, which provided free and compulsory education, to be implemented by the 1951–52 school year, for all children aged five to thirteen years. The course of studies was organized as one year of kindergarten and eight years of primary school. In addition, children aged fourteen to seventeen who had not completed primary school were required to attend schools for "working youth" that offered afternoon or evening classes.[8] The law left intact the preexisting division of the educational system by trends — General, Mizraḥi, and Labor — which were guaranteed their autonomy but placed under the Ministry of Education and Culture. In addition, the law provided for "non-official but recognized schools," which included those of Agudat Israel, a non-Zionist, ultra-Orthodox group, as well as various Christian and Muslim schools.

The General trend schools were coeducational and secular. While they stressed national education and the special role of the *ḥālūts* (pioneers), no specific social theory informed the curriculum. Students studied Hebrew language and literature, Zionism, and knowledge of Palestine, as well as Jewish subjects for nine to eleven hours a week. In the Mizraḥi trend schools, boys and girls were separated. The curriculum stressed the Bible and prayer, with students spending more than half of their time on Jewish and Hebraic subjects. Teachers were religiously Orthodox and largely ignored modern educational theories and techniques. The Labor trend was the most innovative in terms of educational practice. In keeping with their socialist ideology, teachers exposed their students to the value of physical labor along with training in social studies, history, and the natural sciences. In teaching the Bible, teachers used a critical, literary, or historical perspective to stress the attachments of the Jewish people to the land of Israel. They developed noncoercive environments in their classrooms and functioned more like counselors than traditional authority figures. The schools provided opportunities for student democracy and communal organization. Unlike the other trends, they also provided vocational training and shop, handicraft, and gardening classes.

The events of 1948–49 devastated the Palestinian educational framework that had existed prior to Israel's creation. Many educated Palestinians left the country during the social and political upheaval of the military campaigns, which meant that when schools were ordered to reopen after the declaration of Israel's statehood there was a shortage of teachers (Marʿi 1978, 18). During the early 1950s, a full 70 percent of Arab teachers lacked valid certificates from the Ministry of Education (ibid.). High school graduates were often hired to teach, thus lowering the quality of instruction in Arab schools.[9] Because the military administration appointed teachers and paid their salaries, many residents of Arab villages and towns suspected teachers of being government informers. In Acre, Arab schools sometimes hired Mizraḥi Jewish teachers (although they constituted a decided minority in the Jewish system, which was staffed mainly with Ashkenazim). Ministry officials canceled the curriculum of the Mandate period because of its nationalist content but did not provide a substitute. They banned textbooks that included anti-Zionist material, but no substitute textbooks were available in Arabic. Arab teachers had to either use obsolete materials in their classes or rely on extensive lecturing and note taking, to the detriment of the educational process.

The linking of schooling to ideological movements was a disaster, as each of the political parties competed to open schools in every immigrant settlement camp. "The infection spread to the old-established settlements as well. . . . Scarcely a month passed without some newspaper sensation about stormy clashes, even leading up to violence, in this or that village or settlement" (Bentwich 1965, 40). From its beginnings, the public educational system in Israel had political implications. Leaders of the political parties saw the schools as arenas for capturing students' minds and therefore gaining their parents' political allegiance.[10] The different parties cared mainly about securing votes, not about providing an adequate education to the new immigrants. The trends conflict finally led to a coalition crisis in February 1951. The government resigned, the Knesset dissolved, and new elections were held in July (Kleinberger 1969, 119).

In 1953, a new law was passed to correct the deficiencies of the trends system. The State Education Law provided for an educational system that was not linked to a political party. The state would provide education through a curriculum prescribed and supervised by the minister of education and culture, with no attachment to any outside "party or communal body or any other organization outside the Government" (Kleinberger 1969, 123). While parents could supplement up to 25 percent of the curriculum of a specific school according to their ideological orientation, teachers and other school employees were forbidden to conduct political organizing in the schools. The former General and Labor trends were merged into a state (*mamlakhtī*) track while the Mizraḥi trend became a state religious (*mamlakhtī-dātī*) track. The law retained options for "nonofficial recognized" schools (mostly those run by Agudat Israel, the anti-Zionist political party representing ultra-Orthodox Jews) and "exempt, unofficial and unrecognized" schools (such as different types of Orthodox Jewish religious and foreign and missionary schools) (Franks 1987, 10). Arab education was handled with an entirely separate state system. In merging the General and Labor tracks, socialist education disappeared to be replaced with a system that promoted the transmission of statist symbols and values (Liebman and Don-Yehiya 1983, 84). Ben-Gurion sacrificed a socialist, labor orientation in order to achieve his goal of *mamlakhtī* — or statist education — which would instill a national (rather than class) consciousness in future Israeli citizens (Cohen 1992, 242–49).

The Educational Reform Act, passed by the Knesset in 1968, introduced the notion of integration into the Hebrew school system. Integration in Israel refers to the process of eradicating ethnically segregated Jewish schools. It has never had as a goal ending the separation between the Hebrew and Arabic school systems. The new legislation established a six-three-three (elementary school, middle school, high school) plan. More importantly, the Knesset approved a reexamination of all the elementary school districts in the country so that Jewish children of different social and ethnic backgrounds would mix in school at as early an age as possible (Blass and Amir 1984, 70). Educational officials carried out these integrative reforms mainly at the middle-school level, through the establishment of regional or districtwide schools that drew a more diverse student population. The neighborhood character of elementary schools has hampered such integrative efforts. Also, many development towns and rural settlements (*moshavim*) are ethnically homogeneous; for these areas, integration could only be accomplished through a comprehensive busing program, difficult to accomplish in Israel (Minkowich et al. 1982, 423). In addition to integrating the schools, the reform act provided for revisions in the curriculum not only to update knowledge acquisition but "to provide adaptations and considerations for the lower socioeconomic elements of the Jewish population" (Franks 1987, 19). These efforts at the middle-school level were completed by 1978; between 1978 and 1980, similar reforms were implemented at the elementary level (ibid.). The ministry encouraged the establishment of a broad network of vocational high schools for students for whom an academic high school was not appropriate (Swirski 1989, 26).

Since 1968, the Israeli school system has consisted of a primary level of six years, an intermediate level of three years, and a secondary level of three years.[11] Amendments to the Compulsory Education Law in 1978 and 1979 raised the age for mandatory schooling to grade ten, and a further revision in 1978 extended free (but not compulsory)

education through grade twelve (Franks 1987, 9). This is the system
that remains in place today. State schools provide 95 percent of formal
education (*mamlakhtī*, 75 percent; *mamlakhtī-dātī*, 20 percent), with
Agudat Israel schools accounting for most of the remaining 5 percent.
State schools are divided into separate Hebrew and Arab systems, each
with its own curricular requirements.[12] Secondary schools offer a general, technical, or agricultural focus, although some (the *māqīf*, or
comprehensive, schools) provide more than one track from which their
students may choose. For each track, the Ministry of Education and
Culture determines the minimum compulsory units required for a matriculation certificate. Within the general track (similar to the American college preparatory system), secondary students select their programs of study, choosing subjects and areas for which they have ability
and interest. At the completion of their secondary studies, students sit
for either final or matriculation exams. A student who successfully
completes his or her program and passes the final exams will be issued
a final diploma (*te ʿudāt gemer tikhonīt*), which certifies only that he or
she has completed grade twelve. Students who wish to enroll in the
universities must sit for and pass matriculation exams (*bagrūt*).

Educating Mizraḥi Students

The 1953 State Education Law outlines the aim of education in Israel as
"to base education on the values of Jewish culture and the achievements
of science, on love of the homeland and loyalty to the state and the
Jewish people, on practice in agricultural work and handicraft, on pio-
neer training and on striving for a society built on freedom, equality,
tolerance, mutual assistance and love of mankind" (Kleinberger 1969,
123). Given a state policy of encouraging Jewish immigration from many
countries, the schools have had an important role in the process of
absorbing and creating "Israelis" from the masses of immigrants. In the
words of one commentator, "[T]he majority of children in the elementary schools come of immigrant parents, with all kinds of different habits
and mother-tongues, and many of them primitive, even illiterate. To
weld all these together, to create one people, with a common language
and common values, strong enough to withstand outside influences, the
school is required to initiate, even to re-educate" (Bentwich 1965, 63).
In meeting this objective, the Ministry of Education and Culture moved
through three distinct phases of policy development, each of which had
implications for the students.

     From 1948 to 1958, a policy of formal equality held sway. How-
ever, the curricula and methods were based on Western culture and

values, as carried over from the Hebrew school system established prior to the formation of the state. The first Hebrew secondary school, the Herzlia Gymnasia, which opened in 1905 in Jaffa, attracted many of its students from Eastern Europe. Fervent supporters of the Zionist movement abroad willingly sent their children to Israel to be educated. Teachers trained in European universities translated textbooks from German and Russian into Hebrew; the syllabus was a translation of that of a continental school, with a few Jewish studies added (Bentwich 1965, 11–12). Given that the new state's goal was to create a unified Israeli-Jewish-Western culture, government officials believed that any recognition of cultural differences in the schools would hinder the melting-pot process. By exposing Mizrahi students to the same curricula and methods used with European students, educators assumed that they would also assimilate a Western-oriented culture. Through the educational system, Mizrahi Jews, that "generation of the desert," were to be trained and remolded to replace Jews lost in the Holocaust, those who had been "the leading candidates for citizenship in the state of Israel" (Va'ad Hapo'el Hatzioni 1949, 118).

Ben-Zion Dinur, education minister from 1951 to 1955, believed strongly that equality in educational input would automatically produce equal outcomes (Cohen 1992, 245). As he put it, "There must obviously be a single curriculum for all students. . . . All Jewish children throughout the country share this curriculum. And this must be our ambition: the achievement of intellectual and cultural equality for all Jewish children" (ibid.). He based his belief on the positive results achieved with European Jewish immigrants in the pre-state period. As early as 1938, however, educators had noted that Mizrahi children were failing in schools where the course of study had been established by Ashkenazi teachers (Shumsky 1955, 112). This evidence was overlooked in planning for the new national curriculum. Even when faced with evidence in 1953 that Mizrahi students were failing at an alarming rate, Dinur refused to adjust the curriculum to suit their capabilities and needs; to do so, in his view, would consign them forever to positions as "hewers of wood and drawers of water" (quoted in Kleinberger 1969, 295).

When Zalman Aran became education minister in 1955, he championed programs of preferential treatment for Mizrahi children so that "real" equality could be achieved rather than the "formal" equality that had been the norm. New research reports in 1957 provided further evidence that Mizrahi students were performing substantially below minimum standards. Aran pressed for the development of compensatory programs and for changes in Israeli textbooks and curricula that tended to focus only on the Ashkenazi Jewish heritage. However, Aran lacked the political strength in his own party to initiate the reforms he felt were necessary, and he resigned his post in 1960, partly due to his frustration at the lack of attention given to education at the top levels of the government.

During this ten-year period, significant differences became apparent in the performance of children from Ashkenazi and Mizraḥi backgrounds. In explaining these differences, government officials and popular opinion blamed the impoverished cultural backgrounds of the Mizraḥi students. While it was true that some Mizraḥi Jewish communities (such as the Yemenites) had never been exposed to modern forms of education, this was not true of all Mizraḥim. Upper-class, educated, Jewish communities could be found throughout the Middle East and North Africa in Iraq, Egypt, Morocco, Algeria, and Tunisia. In Israel, government officials and veteran Israelis (as well as new European immigrants) characterized these peoples as primitive, uncultured, and backward.

Rather than blaming the students for their failures, an alternative explanation is obvious. Did the Israeli government really provide equal inputs, that is, were Mizraḥi students really receiving the same education as Ashkenazi students? Shama and Iris (1977), in their study of immigrant absorption, provide a partial answer to this question. From 1948 to 1952, Israel's population more than doubled. From May 1948 until mid-1950, the new immigrants were settled in the empty houses of Palestinian refugees throughout the country, many of which were in major cities such as Lod, Ramleh, Jaffa, Haifa, and Acre. The beneficiaries of this policy were mainly Ashkenazim because they formed the bulk of immediate postindependence immigrants. There were functioning school systems in most of these urban areas, into which the immigrant children were absorbed with only minor difficulties. By mid-1950, the composition of immigration was shifting to a greater preponderance of Mizraḥim. As available housing stocks had been exhausted, these immigrants were directed to the *ma'abārōt*. The political movements established schools in the camps, but they were plagued with problems. Well-qualified teachers were not interested in leaving good urban schools to teach under the harsh conditions in the camps. Novice or no teachers, language problems (a variety of languages were spoken and few children spoke Hebrew), inadequate physical facilities (classrooms frequently had no blackboards and students sat on the floor), and the chaotic living conditions of the camps all combined to impede the educational process.

In 1953, when the trends system was eliminated, the national government could have acted to remedy the inequities in the camps. All schools came under the administrative authority of the Ministry of Education and Culture. The minister could have required experienced teachers to leave established schools and work in the immigrant camps to improve the quality of education there. Such a strategy would have been consistent with the pre-state emphasis on pioneering and with national goals for absorbing the new immigrants. I can only speculate that such options were not explored because government officials saw the problem not as one of inequality in the provision of services but in terms of the cultural inferiority of the students. Klein and Eshel (1980, 11) suggest that the veteran settlers were beginning to close in on themselves as Israeli society became increasingly bureaucratized. They also note the development of stereotypical images of the Mizraḥim as lower class and of pervasive, though often unspoken, fears of contagion. The established Ashkenazi population worried that somehow the Mizraḥim would lower the standards and reduce levels of aspiration and achievement for the whole society.

In 1959, riots broke out in the Wadi Salib neighborhood of Haifa after a Moroccan Jewish resident was shot and killed by the police. The Wadi Salib riots became the focal point around which Mizraḥim throughout the country rallied to protest discriminatory treatment on the part of the government.[13] Due to public pressure, the government appointed a commission of inquiry that found ample evidence of problems with ethnic integration but that denied the charges of ethnic discrimination. The commission recommended that the government take action to deal with housing problems, improve education, and make better efforts to facilitate absorption of the immigrants. It issued its report during an election campaign; after the election, the report was shelved, and no action was taken because public pressure had dissipated. Widening gaps in school performance between Mizraḥi and Ashkenazi children, however, prompted the Ministry of Education and Culture to institute a new series of educational policies, initiating the phase of compensatory education (1959–68).

The ministry added hours of Hebrew and math instruction to the curriculum for Mizraḥi pupils (Marʿi 1978, 91; Kleinberger 1969, 297). It replaced the practice of grade repeating with "social promotions based on attendance and deportment" (Stein 1985, 209) but failed to take special remedial measures to help slow learners advance (Kleinberger 1969, 296). Ministry officials established a lower passing standard, "norm B," for the *seker* (a survey test given in grade eight that determined a student's placement in secondary school and eligibility for scholarship support) (ibid.). Toward the end of this period, it implemented new measures: an extended school day and academic tracking, new textbooks for disadvantaged students, and an expanded boarding-school program for gifted students (Blass and Amir 1984, 67).[14] In 1962, a new Centre for Educational Institutions in Need of Special Care (*te ʿūnei tipūaḥ*, what Kleinberger [1969, 298] calls the Israeli euphemism for schools in development towns or urban slums with a preponderance of pupils of Mizraḥi origin) began operating with 228 primary schools and about 91,500 students. All of these reforms reinforced prevalent societal notions of Mizrahim as culturally deficient and deprived and as less intelligent, slow learners.[15]

Lewis (1979) notes that the school in one community was effectively divided into two classes. In one class, the children of veteran Israelis and new Ashkenazi immigrants progressed along a track that prepared them for an academic high school. School officials placed the children of Mizrahi immigrants in separate classes that stressed reading, writing, and basic skills. Their education prepared them only to enter a trade because it did not meet the standards for admission to the academic high schools. This pattern of separation persisted until 1966, even though by 1960 more than 70 percent of the students at the school were Mizrahim. Shama and Iris (1977) note that students living in public housing projects near the immigrant transit camps faced serious educational problems. Children had no quiet space where they could do their homework because apartments generally were overcrowded, with considerable noise and distraction. These students were segregated in schools that catered to the projects and "grew to accept norms of poor, apathetic performance and cursory preparation of class assignments" (Shama and Iris 1977, 90). Once again, teachers assigned to these schools usually were poorly qualified to deal with the problems of their students.

Government officials tried to solve the problems in the system by providing quantitative solutions—more class hours, longer school days, lower passing exam scores. They continued throughout this period to view the problem as one of cultural disadvantage on the part of the Mizrahim. These officials could not afford any hint that their policies and programs were harming rather than helping Mizrahi immigrants. Such recognition would have damaged the image of the Israeli state as the guardian of the Jewish people and fractured the professed unity of the Jewish people. In addition, during this period there was a consensus that national security took precedence over domestic problems.

The third phase of educational reform, school integration, came about as a result of organized protest by Mizrahi parents. In 1966, a group of parents in a Mizrahi neighborhood in Jerusalem organized a protest against segregation in neighborhood schools (Klein and Eshel 1980). These parents, upwardly mobile and better educated than many of their neighbors, had initially tried to have their children transferred to more prestigious schools. When their applications for transfer were rejected, they began to organize public meetings around the idea of integration. Because their protest coincided with an election year, school integration became a serious political issue, which forced the Ministry of Education and Culture to investigate the situation and issue recommendations. The results of the 1966 Equality of Educational Opportunities

Study in the United States, with its finding of a correlation between classroom composition and minority achievement, were widely discussed in Israel. This initial protest led to the Educational Reform Act, which was passed by the Knesset in 1968.

The reform act, as noted, established a new six-three-three structure for the schools and redrew boundaries at the middle-school level to promote integration. When the Ministry of Education and Culture proposed to preview the proposed reforms in six communities (Or Yehuda, Migdal Ha'Emek, Nazareth, Qiryat Gat, Shafit, and Acre) by moving grades seven and eight to the high school, the Teachers' Union threatened noncooperation unless the ministry promised to protect the positions of the principals and teachers displaced by the transition.[16] The union strongly opposed the proposed reforms and threatened noncooperation and a general strike when the Knesset Education Committee approved them in May 1968. When the proposal passed the Knesset almost unanimously, with massive public support, the union did a quick about-face and declared itself willing to cooperate in implementing the reforms (Kleinberger 1969, 149–50). This reversal, however, did not signal their acceptance; as Kleinberger (150) notes, there were "plenty of ways to sabotage the reform surreptitiously."

To publicly oppose school integration in Israel was extremely difficult. Integration, as Klein and Eshel (1980, 145) note, was "a way of reiterating the official goals of absorption, assimilation, and 'intermingling,' but now fleshing out the bare framework of these goals with more specific concerns for improved educational and social impact." Mizrahi parents were not revolting against the state; rather, they were demanding more effective programs to promote their assimilation within it. Halper, Shokeid, and Weingrod (1984) explored the local process of school integration in three communities: in one residents were apathetic, but in the other two Ashkenazi and Mizrahi parents clashed over class composition and enrollment policies. While most Israelis supported the goal of school integration in theory, some were reluctant to see their particular schools used as a means to achieve this goal. The Ministry of Education and Culture diffused the concern of many Ashkenazi parents by assuring them that their school's curriculum and standards would not change. "They [the schools] would continue to serve as 'cultural models' for the Middle Easterners, who would be expected to adopt their attitudes and behavior patterns" (Halper, Shokeid, and Weingrod 1984, 49).

Elements of separation and differentiation continued in the new comprehensive schools, as students were tracked into different class levels. In 1974, the Ministry of Education and Culture developed a new, "socially based" index to determine which schools should be targeted for special treatment. The index was based on father's education, family size, and ethnic origin (although in the 1950s ethnic origin had been rejected as the basis for a definition because it contradicted the national ethos of solidarity and uniformity; see Adler 1984, 32). According to this index, in 1971–72, 44 percent of Israeli and 95 percent of Mizraḥi students were disadvantaged (ibid., 33). Mizraḥi students continued to be categorized as *te 'ūnei tipūaḥ,* in need of fostering, a process that sometimes resulted in entire Mizraḥi student populations being placed in special education classes or categorized as slow learners or educable mentally retarded (Stein 1985, 211, 213).

There is considerable evidence that teachers in Israel continued to hold negative stereotypes about Mizraḥi students, even after school reform was instituted. This is an important finding because it is through the teachers that government policies are implemented in the schools. The Ministry of Education and Culture might explain student failure through the use of notions of cultural disadvantage, but such explanations would have little effect in the classroom if teachers refused to accept its premises. In one experiment intended to test the effects of stereotypes in education, teachers were given an examination to grade. Half were told it was written by a Mizraḥi student, while the other half were told an Ashkenazi student had composed it. Teachers grading the Mizraḥi examination gave it much lower scores than those grading the same exam as the work of an Ashkenazi student (Shtal, Agmon, and Mar-Haim 1976). In his study of the process of education in a small Mizraḥi rural settlement, Lewis (1979) finds direct evidence that teachers' attitudes toward students affected their academic achievement. The only class in the school to achieve the national level for its age-group in reading, arithmetic, and other basic skills was taught by a woman who rejected the notion that her students were culturally disadvantaged and believed that if a child had trouble learning it was the fault of the teacher. In all other classes, teachers had low expectations of their students' abilities.

More importantly, Lewis found that students demonstrated four types of behavior in the classroom: obedience, active resistance, passive resistance, and disruption.[17] Obedient students adjusted to the classroom routine and answered most of the questions. Passive resisters did not complete homework, brought no books to school, and would spend the class period sitting quietly looking out the window or playing games. Active resisters, the majority of the students in the class, had a sophisticated repertoire of responses to simulate involvement while actually withdrawing from the lesson. They prepared homework but in a slipshod fashion, or they would raise their hands to answer questions a fraction of a second after someone else was called on. They played a variety of table games, involving books, paper, and pencils, but quietly so as not to draw the teacher's attention. Disrupters would actively battle the teacher by shouting across the room, fighting, and calling other students names. As early as grade two, these Mizraḥi students had developed an image of school as boring and unimportant and had learned behaviors that, while allowing them to control their boredom, did nothing to promote the learning process. Lewis speculated that by the time these students graduated they would have refined their active tactics into forms of aggressive resistance and would no longer make even a pretense of trying to learn. None, he predicted, would move on to an academic high school.

More recent studies of income and educational levels of Ashkenazim and Mizraḥim indicate that the gap between the two groups grew throughout the 1970s.[18] Mizraḥim lagged behind in both educational achievement and the proportion of students who successfully complete the matriculation exams and continue on to university studies. In 1981, only 11.6 percent of Israeli-born Mizraḥim had more than thirteen years of formal schooling, compared to 41.8 percent of Israeli-born Ashkenazim (Swirski 1989, 26). Mizraḥi students were disproportionately represented in the technical-vocational track of secondary schooling. In the early 1980s, fully two-thirds of students in development towns were following vocational tracks, compared to 47 percent of students in large cities (many of whom were also Mizraḥim) (Israel, Ministry of Education and Culture 1981, 34–36).

In the early 1980s, the Ministry of Education and Culture began to make available to schools history and reference works about Mizraḥi Jewish communities prior to immigration in a new effort to improve the performance of Mizraḥi students.[19] This was partly in response to increased demands by Mizraḥim for societal recognition of their cultural heritage. However, as Mizraḥi high school teachers note, these materials do not form an integral part of the regular program of studies (Swirski 1989, 115). Teachers in the academic high schools prepare students for the *bagrūt*. While teachers are not required to use particular books in their classes, they are required to cover specific material. Since passing the *bagrūt* permits a student to study at the university, there is tremendous pressure to teach only that material which appears on the matriculation exams. The exams don't focus on the Mizraḥi heritage, so students prepare for them accordingly.

Educating Palestinian Students

For Israeli Palestinian students, many of the reforms implemented in the Jewish sector were irrelevant. Changes in the Hebrew schools usually take effect in Arab schools about ten years later (Franks 1987, 19). For the first three decades of Israel's existence, the Arab schools functioned without a defined goal. For example, Khawla Abu-Baker analyzed the instructions issued each year by the Ministry of Education regarding "political education" and how the schools should approach this topic. Each week there were numerous directives for the Jewish school system, but not until some time in the 1970s did these instructions also refer to the Palestinian schools.[20] The minister of education was empowered to adapt the goals for Jewish education, as defined by law, to the Israeli Palestinian educational system but at the elementary level only.

Mar'i (1978, 51–52) notes that Israeli educators debated at least four possible goals for Israeli Palestinian education during this time. The first strategy sought to blur Palestinian national identity and develop an identity as Israelis. The second strategy sought to preserve a unique Arab cultural and national identity but had little to offer in dealing with the contradictions inherent in their status as Israeli citizens. The third strategy advocated a balance between Arabness and Israeliness — a hyphenated identity as Israeli-Arabs, with loyalty to both nation and state. The final strategy was that nothing should be done either way and the problem would work itself out over time; this was the strategy that was primarily implemented.

An initial attempt to develop goals for the Israeli Palestinian system in 1972 resulted in the Yadlin Document.[21] Just as the Mizraḥi population was to be reeducated and remolded, so, too, were Israeli Palestinians. The committee established as its target the formation of a plan that would make it easier to socially and economically absorb them, with goals such as educating Palestinian females to foster autonomy and improved status and inculcating the values (democracy and social ethics) and culture of interpersonal relationships accepted by Israeli Jewish society.

In 1973, a new committee, composed of seven Arabs and seven Jews, was formed "to define the national and cultural framework for the education of minorities" and to propose plans and policies for Arab education during the 1980s. This committee saw the earlier Yadlin Document as an attempt both to blur Palestinian national identity and to cancel out Palestinian culture by imposing the values and morals of Israeli Jewish society through a national educational system (Mar'i 1978, 52–53). Instead, the Committee on Arab Education for the Eighties recommended that education in the Arab sector be based

> on the foundations of Arab culture; on the achievement of
> science, on the aspiration for peace between Israel and its
> neighbors, on love of the shared country by all citizens, and
> loyalty to the State of Israel — through emphasizing their com-

mon interests and through encouraging the uniqueness of Israeli Arabs, on the knowledge of the Jewish culture, on respect
for creative work and on the aspiration for a society built on
freedom, equality, mutual help and love of mankind. (Israel,
Ministry of Education and Culture 1975, 14)

Marʿi stresses that one of the main problems with all of these efforts was
that they treated the Palestinian minority as an object, a periphery.
"These committees on Arab education have either been all Jewish or
Jewish dominated, and the basic question behind all these efforts has
been, in effect, how to manipulate the peripheral Arab minority through
education in such a way that the central Jewish majority can maintain its
interests" (1978, 54). One teacher I interviewed provided an example of
how the committees were manipulated. The Ministry of Education and
Culture finally added a few Arabs to the curriculum committee that
determines what is taught in Arab schools. These members suggested
adding additional materials to the Arabic literature portion — poetry and
prose by contemporary Arab authors. Every piece they proposed was
rejected; what was finally accepted was a poem by a famous Palestinian
poet that he had written in his youth on the topic of nature. These
committee members were then severely criticized by their fellow Arab
teachers, who thought that this was their idea of something worth adding
to the curriculum.

Mahmood Meʿari's content analysis of the curricula for Arab
schools in the mid-1970s further highlights the identity-blurring aspects
of the Israeli-established educational system. He found a tremendous
emphasis on Jewish nationalism: "In 7th grade the Arab students learn
about the relation of the Jewish Diaspora to the land of Israel and in the
8th grade they learn about the Zionist movement and its development,
the thrust of Jews to come back to the land of Israel, Jewish immigration,
the revival of the Hebrew language and pioneering" (1975, 34). The
curricula ignored modern Arab history and the Arab (and Palestinian)
national movements. Students learned about the Ottoman Empire and
the Middle East in the nineteenth century only through scattered comments incorporated in various chapters (Meʿari 1975). In Acre in 1988–
89, all high school students were required to complete one unit of history, which consisted of two main topics: (1) the Islamic state (elements
of rule and society from the time of Muhammad to the Abbasid caliph-
ate) and (2) the history of the Middle East in the New Age (which covers
the Ottoman Empire to the twentieth century with a regional focus).
Students learned about the history of Palestine only indirectly, through
lessons on the history of the Israeli people or through learning about
nationalist movements in Egypt and Syria (but never Palestine).

As Shipler (1986, 454) notes, Arabs themselves describe the

educational program in their schools as "Bialik and the Bible" given its emphasis on Jewish culture and religion.[22] Fouzi El-Asmar, in his book *To Be an Arab in Israel,* comments: "Daily we experienced the close connection between the Hebrew literary works we were learning and the Arab-Israeli conflict: while the Jewish works gave expression to a live and conscious people united in its feelings and actions, the Arab works that we were taught did not concern themselves at all with any nationalist ideals but were mostly works describing nature and lyrical moods" (1978, 46). One teacher noted that Arab students now learn Bialik and relate his poetry to their own situation; in a subversion of the intended curricular message, they use Bialik's verses to speak about their own feelings about Palestine. While much of their formal education is culturally or nationally irrelevant to Arab students, nonformal education has played an important role in providing nationality-related material for Israeli Palestinian youth (Marʿi 1978, 88). Through radio and television programs from Egypt, Lebanon, Syria, and Jordan, Arab youth have alternatives to the identity blurring found in the formal school curriculum. Marʿi sees these resources as important means by which Israeli Palestinian youth have been able to reestablish a sense of belonging to a larger Arab world and to reinforce pride in its own identity.

The Process in Acre

By 1951, the educational system in Acre had expanded to twenty kindergarten classes and fifty-five elementary and other classes. All of the trends were represented, and there were separate classes for Arab students, special education students, working youth, and continuing education students (table 5). As elsewhere in Israel, the Labor trend captured most of the student enrollments, with 51 percent in 1951 and 45 percent in 1952, compared to a national average of 43.4 percent in 1952–53 (national figures from Cohen 1992, 238). Teacher/pupil ratios varied from sixteen students per teacher in the Mizraḥi track to thirty-nine per teacher in the Minorities track. At the kindergarten (*gan*) level, teacher/pupil ratios actually worsened from 1951 to 1952 as classes were lost; the ratio varied from one teacher per thirty-two children for the Agudat kindergartens to one per fifty children in the Arab kindergarten. Expenditures on education were 47.5 percent of the expenses for public services in Acre from 1949–50 to 1952–53.[23]

In Acre, as elsewhere in Israel, immigrant children were enlisted in the process of educating their parents in new values and behaviors. As one educator emphatically put it, "Our influence on the surrounding can be great with the help of our faithful partners, the children, if only we will know how to inject into the home one common version of customs. . . . That is why we can hope that in the new assignment of the 'ingathering of the exiles' . . . the child will fulfill his mission and will not disappoint us" (Zanbank-Wilf 1958, 57). Thus, the municipality, members of the Education Department, and the Kūpāt Ḥōlīm (health clinic) decided to teach housekeeping to seventh- and eighth-grade girls from Shikūn Amidar, the immigrant neighborhood. In a memo dated 19 January 1956 from Mayor Gadish to Mr. Vind of the Sōkhnūt in Tel Aviv, Gadish indicated that they "see this as an effective way to educate the *olim* [immigrants] to arrange their apartments, to keep them clean, to care for their furnishings and clothing, and to live a way of life that we long for. We hope the girls will have a great influence on the level of cleanliness in their parents' homes."[24]

By the 1960s, the educational system in Acre had greatly expanded. Nursery schools and the secondary school were partially subsidized. Rubin (1974, 86–88) provides us with a glimpse of educational practices in Acre during this period. He lived there for much of 1965 and focused his investigations on the public and private lives of local residents. Arab students attended either the government school or Terra Sancta, the

TABLE 5.   School Enrollments in Acre, by Trend, 1951–52

Trend	Number of Students		Number of Classes		Number of Students per Class	
	1951	1952	1951	1952	1951	1952
Primary and secondary schools						
Labor	527	683	16	22	33	31
Mizraḥi	193	204	12	13	16	16
Agudat Israel	58	121	5	5	12	24
General	178	249	8	8	22	31
Minorities	443	552	13	14	34	39
Special education	—	12	—	1	—	12
Working youth	—	110	—	3	—	37
Continuing education	15	25	1	2	15	13
Total	1,414	1,956	55	68	26	29
Kindergartens						
Labor	200	209	7	5	29	42
Mizraḥi	110	117	4	3	28	39
Agudat Israel	42	63	1	2	42	32
General	105	204	6	5	18	41
Minorities	78	50	2	1	39	50
Total	535	643	20	16	28	40

Source: Baruch Noy, Mayor, Administrative Report on the Municipality's Activities for Fiscal Year 1951–52, Acre, Acre Municipal Archives.

only parochial school. Some Ashkenazi families chose to send their children to private schools in nearby Haifa. Others kept their children in the public schools of the city. In his composite portrait of a typical Jewish family (which was, it so happens, Ashkenazi), we meet the son, Danny, who entered secondary school on a partial scholarship because he received high scores on the qualifying exam. Danny, we are told, is an exception because he did almost as well on the exam as the children of white-collar and professional families in Acre. Most of the Mizrahi and many working-class Ashkenazi children scored poorly on these exams. Their poor scores meant that many of them would either not be placed in secondary school or would not be able to afford to attend (secondary education was not free and scholarships went to those who scored well on the *seker*).[25] These children would either leave school and get a job or learn a trade in a vocational program until called for military service. While Danny has Mizrahi friends from the neighborhood and youth groups, "lasting contact is reserved for those who have the ambition and the ability to accompany him into secondary school and the Gadna [high school paramilitary training group]" (Rubin 1974, 87).

Danny's younger sister, Miriam, prefers the schools in the central part of the city to those in the immigrant quarters because the immigrant students (many of whom are Mizrahi) are seen as less serious about their studies and less likely to attend secondary school. In these statements, we can see the prevalent stereotypes of Mizrahi children as less intelligent and less ambitious than Ashkenazi or Israeli-born children. Teachers encouraged students like Danny to further their education, while others (the Mizrahi and working-class Ashkenazi) were referred to evening training classes designed for working youth.

Although reforms were proposed for Acre in 1968, they were not implemented until 1975, when the junior and senior high schools were merged. Prior to the reforms, many Acre students went outside — to Haifa, the Qrayot, or Nahariyya — for their high school educations.[26] This was due to both the poor image of the local high school and the limited range of subjects it was able to offer, especially the lack of advanced mathematics courses and technical studies. In 1970, only 50 percent of the teachers employed in Acre lived in the city.[27] The municipality wanted to give discounts and grants to teachers to encourage them to settle in the community. It hoped that the teachers would be more concerned about the quality of the educational system if their own children were enrolled in it.[28] In his study of three development towns, Peres (1970) finds that teacher residence is an important factor in the quality of a community's educational system. Teachers who are also local residents are more involved in the community; they are likely to have contact with students and parents after school hours, which increases their feelings of personal responsibility for their students' welfare.

In 1988 and 1989, Acre's educational system was the largest in the Western Galilee, with more than 10,000 students in classes from kindergarten through grade twelve. The system included thirteen elementary schools (4,800 students), three upper-grade schools (2,750 students), and sixty-five kindergartens (2,250 students); this included more than 2,000 Arab students in eleven kindergarten, elementary, and upper-grade classes. The educational system employed seven hundred individuals as kindergarten, elementary, and upper-grade teachers, with an additional two hundred staff members employed as managers, secretaries, maintenance workers, and teacher's aides. Terra Sancta, the private Catholic school that offers prekindergarten through grade twelve, enrolled 730 students in 1988–89 and employed thirty teachers.[29] Jewish parents in Acre could send their children through twelve years of state secular or state religious education; Arab parents could choose between the state Arab system or Terra Sancta.

The Hebrew state secular system in Acre comprised seven elementary schools that fed into a single junior and senior high school. The seven elementary schools were scattered throughout the city: Weitzman and Ha'Tomer in the city center; Bialik, Ben-Tzvi, and Shazar in the north; and Gordon and Eshkol in the east. The junior high school — Qiryat Ha'Hinukh (Rose) — was located in the east, while the senior high school — ORT Darsky — was located slightly north of the central city. The Hebrew state religious system consisted of two elementary schools — Herzel in the city center and Rambam in the east — and a junior-senior high school, Kennedy, in the east. The Arab state system consisted of two elementary schools — Amal in the New City, outside the walls, and Arab Beit in the Old City, next to the Al-Jazzâr Mosque — and an Arab junior-senior high school located next to Amal.[30] In addition, Agudat Israel operated schools in Acre, in the city and the eastern neighborhoods.

Responsibility for the educational system in Israel is divided between the Ministry of Education and Culture, which provides all professional aspects (teacher licensing requirements, development and implementation of curriculum, and the hiring and firing of teachers), and the local authorities, who are responsible for building and maintaining the physical plants and providing equipment and furnishings. In Acre, the municipality must supply appropriate structures and furnishings for the state secular, state religious, and Arab school systems. In 1989, it spent NIS 600,000 (about $300,000) for school improvements (painting, carpentry, electrical and glass repairs, and gardening), NIS 60,000 ($30,000) for furnishings and equipment, and an additional NIS 200,000 ($100,000) to computerize some of the schools. Between a quarter to a third of the municipality's yearly budget has gone for educational expenses, but those monies have not been divided equitably between the school systems or even between the schools within a single system. The municipality's provision of "basic" services reflects the discrimination present in Israeli society. Nowhere is this more apparent than in comparing the educational facilities of the Jewish and Palestinian sectors (although differences also exist within the Jewish sector).

In developing Acre, municipal officials turned to outside sources of assistance, such as the Jewish Agency and private Jewish benefactors, to raise the monies necessary to build new schools or improve existing ones. Throughout 1987–89, a variety of proposals were in process to improve Acre's Hebrew school system. The upper-grade schools of the state secular system had already been integrated into the national ORT network (which stresses advanced technological education), which resulted in improvements in academic and technical studies and equipment.[31] More importantly, this transition removed the schools from municipal control and placed them under the management of the national ORT network. In August 1988, a committee composed of ORT and municipal representatives met to consider integrating the state religious comprehensive school, Kennedy, into the ORT network. That same month, Jewish Agency officials announced that Project Renewal would begin an exploratory project to renovate schools in Acre.[32] The required sum of NIS 160,000 would be divided between the municipality and Project Renewal and would be used to repair building facades, roofs, and fences at Gordon, Rambam, Eshkol, Kennedy, Ha'Torah, Eyal, and Maftan (all Jewish schools).[33]

In October 1988, the management of ORT Acre announced a new program to be launched in cooperation with the Technion (Israel's premier science and technology university) to advance "technological manpower" among students in grade nine. If the program was successful, they would later expand it to include students from Nahariyya, Karmi'el, Maʿalot, Kabri, and the Qrāyōt. During the 1989–90 school year, the Zehavi Association helped Jewish parents with four or more children pay the activity fees for grades seven to twelve (fees ranged from NIS 218 to 240 per child). In March 1990, officials announced that the Jewish Agency would invest in improving education in the comprehensive schools in Acre. To deal with the problem of "grey education" (private tutoring available to those students who could pay), the general director of the junior-senior high schools, Dr. Shmaryahu Biran, founded a Learning Center. The funding came from the municipality, Project Renewal, ORT, the Welfare Office, and the Parents' Committee; students paid a nominal fee of three to three and a half shekels per lesson. Teachers from the Jewish senior high school provided lessons in grammar, English, mathematics, physics, and accounting. While any student in Acre could take the classes, it is the students in the Hebrew sector who used the center — about three hundred of them.

In comparison, conditions in the Palestinian sector are bleak. The buildings in which students learn operate under substandard conditions. In January 1987, Education Minister Yitzchak Navon promised that money would be made available to begin building a new Arab elementary school, although he initially agreed to finance the construction of only twelve classrooms. As the principal, Abdallah Hamza, noted: "It hurts the Arab children when they see the modern and fully equipped buildings in which Jewish children study and compare them with the conditions in their schools."[34] By January 1988, Hamza had resigned his post to protest the "discrimination and deliberate contempt toward the school's population."[35] What had begun as leaks in the school's ceilings had turned into pools of water. Students had to bring umbrellas to use in their classrooms. Teachers were afraid to use electricity because of the water. When local reporters asked the mayor's office to respond to Hamza's charges, David Goraly, the municipal spokesperson, noted that the municipality does not differentiate between sectors in the allocation of resources. The work would be completed, he said, according to the timetable and the city's limited resources. The correspondent for *Tsafon 1* (the major regional newspaper) reported a different story. Apparently a senior clerk had instructed the city's maintenance team not to fix the roof. This was done because some of the Arab municipal workers had participated in a Day of Peace strike.

By the start of the 1988–89 school year, some elementary students had transferred to the new school, but new problems arose. Amal students spent their first two weeks of school on strike, protesting the fact that some of the classrooms were unfurnished and children were expected to sit on the floor. In addition, the municipal workmen still needed to lay water pipes for drinking fountains and bathrooms.[36] David Bar Lev, the deputy mayor responsible for education, denied culpability and blamed the school's principal, accusing him of misuse of funds. The school, however, received the support of the citywide Parents' Committee in pursuing its grievances, and the municipality eventually agreed to deal with matters in a timely fashion.

In January 1989, it was the senior high school's turn to endure strike. Again, the complaint involved water leaking into the building. Teachers of technological workshops had refused to allow students to use equipment since the beginning of the previous school year because of water in the electrical sockets. Broken windowpanes and doors also leaked.[37] The principal remarked that the school had to close periodically due to water and electrical problems.[38] He was negotiating with the ORT network in the hope that it would agree to take over the Arab school as it had the Jewish high school. The transition would mean a great improvement in both physical conditions and equipment.

Tracking exists in both the Hebrew and the Arab state systems in Acre.[39] In the Arab system, three tracks exist at the high school level—one for the *bagrūt,* one for the *teʿudāt gemer,* and one for vocations. In the Hebrew system, tracking begins in junior high school, where students in grades seven and eight are placed in one of three tracks in accordance with their ability levels in different subjects.[40] In the ninth grade, students are tracked at the same level for all subjects (*aleph,* 2 *aleph, beit,* 2 *beit,* or *gimel*), with their level determined by their grades and their teachers' recommendations. In the high school, there are two basic tracks—*bagrūt* and non-*bagrūt*—and students are placed according to their level in grade nine. *Aleph*-level students will be on the *bagrūt* track; *beit* students may be included if their grades are good; and all other students are directed into non-*bagrūt* tracks.[41] Both systems compete for students with other nearby school systems. Many good Arab students attend private schools like El Mutannabe in Haifa, while Jewish students may choose to attend the ORT high school in Qiryat Bialik because it offers professional training not available in Acre.

The students in the Arab junior-senior high school are all Acre residents except for twenty who travel from Makr, a village five kilometers east. Both the principal and teachers reported that many students who live in the Old City experience real problems that affect their learning experiences—parents who cannot afford to purchase schoolbooks, problems with drug abuse at home, and dwellings so crowded or dilapidated that students have no fit place to study. According to the high school principal, 70 percent of his students come from poor families. Teachers were more likely to blame structural factors (poverty or inadequate school facilities) than lack of ability for their students' problems in learning. Three Arab students study in the Hebrew state system. Such students are seen by Jewish educators as problematic. During a discussion with one Jewish teacher and her husband, a young Arab neighbor came over to visit with their son. The husband, a municipal official, told me that this was the real problem—this young Arab boy was growing up in Jewish society and attending Hebrew schools, and he had no real sense of who he was. He thought of himself as being like everyone else. While they had no problems with this boy associating with their son, they both felt that it was unfair to him to act as if being Arab meant nothing.

Within the Hebrew state system, both teachers and principals insisted that not much attention is paid to the ethnic background of the students, although at one point they had to check to make sure the schools were integrated. At the senior high school, the principal did remark that the Ashkenazi children were usually to be found in the upper levels of each class, while the lower levels mostly held Mizraḥi children. In checking the distributions by father's country of origin for grades ten and twelve for 1988–89, I found her observation confirmed. In grade ten, 74 percent of Ashkenazi and 49 percent of Mizraḥi children were studying for the *bagrūt;* in grade twelve, 77 percent of Ashkenazi and 55 percent of Mizraḥi children were studying for the *bagrūt* (table 6). Some teachers spontaneously volunteered the opinion that the whole integration experiment had been a failure. Both teachers and administrators reported problems in the schools because 60 to 70 percent of Acre's population was *ḥalāsh* (weak). One informant put it quite bluntly: 40 percent of the students were human and the other 60 percent were not. *Bagrūt* scores appear to reinforce the teachers' assessments of their students. In 1989, the rate of success on the *bagrūt* in the Western Galilee was the lowest in Israel—less than 50 percent of twelfth-grade Jewish students and only one-third of Arab students had passed the theoretical track. For the technological track, passing rates were even poorer—less than 20 percent of Jewish and only 7 percent of Arab students. Most of those who passed the theoretical track *bagrūt* were Ashkenazim; for the technological track, 54 percent of Ashkenazim succeeded versus 39 percent of Mizraḥim.[42]

Because the teacher is the central figure in the Israeli educational system, being responsible for what actually goes on in the classroom, I interviewed teachers in the Hebrew state secular and Arab state tracks

TABLE 6. Enrollments in Acre's Jewish High School (grades ten and twelve) according to Track and Father's Country of Origin, 1988–89

Father's Country of Origin	*Bagrut* Track		Non-*Bagrut* Track		Total Number of Students
	Number of Students	(%)	Number of Students	(%)	
Grade ten					
Ashkenazi	35	(74)	12	(26)	47
Mizraḥi	84	(49)	86	(51)	170
Israeli	17	(52)	16	(48)	33
Grade twelve					
Ashkenazi	33	(77)	10	(23)	43
Mizraḥi	85	(55)	69	(45)	154
Israeli	9	(53)	8	(47)	17

Source: School registration records, Acre, 1988–89.

in order to learn more about the identity-defining aspects of curriculum content and how they perceive that content. Most of the Jewish teachers believed that the material they taught was only indirectly related to defining the Israeli identity or national values. This perception may be due to the fact that, while a number of special programs have been developed to improve the transmission of national values, most of these have removed the topic from the purview of literature, history, and geography teachers and placed responsibility on the *meḥanekh* (an instructor similar to the American homeroom teacher) (Gordon 1984, 164). This teacher, during the weekly "social hour" and in special short-term projects, is expected to transmit the necessary values.

While teachers may no longer see the curriculum as transmitting national values, analysis of the curriculum clearly indicates that it meets the goal of promoting loyalty to and identification with the Jewish people. Consider the Jewish history curriculum for grades seven through nine. In grade seven, students learn about the Roman Empire and Jewish life under it. The history coordinator explained that in this unit teachers establish the right of the Jewish people to return to Israel. In grade eight, students cover world history, but the teacher uses it as background material to help students understand Jewish life in the diaspora under both Christian and Muslim rule. Here students also learn that Jews have long been returning to Israel. This prepares the way for studies in grade nine that focus on Zionism and its origins and development prior to 1948, from the beginning to Herzel (founder of the World Zionist Organization). Students also learn about the Holocaust in these units.

This pattern is repeated in other subject areas. In teaching *Tanakh* (the Old Testament), besides introducing students to the book and the ideas advanced within it, teachers want to convey the connection between the people and the land—the Jewish right to Israel. They also want students to learn how and why Jewish society is different from others in terms of its moral and religious beliefs — that Jews are indeed a chosen people. In geography, students learn *'ahavāt ha'aretz* (love of the land) along with more general knowledge about the world and general geographical skills like reading maps and charts. Grades seven to nine deal with different aspects of Israeli geography — the coast, the Negev, general features. In grade ten, the curriculum is divided between Israeli geography (50 percent) and the physical and human geography of the rest of the world (50 percent). Students may take class trips to different parts of Israel. These trips are used, in the words of one teacher, to get students to feel that "this place is ours." She added, "It's important that students feel they are part of the land and to strengthen their ties to the land." Class trips often involve re-creating the battles that were waged to gain a particular piece of land so that the students will realize how hard it was to obtain.

Arab teachers, not surprisingly, were much more conscious of the effects curriculum material had on their students' identities. As Mar'i noted, the Arab curriculum gives students no sense of an Arab or Palestinian national identity. Consider the history curriculum for grades seven through nine. In grade seven, students learn about the Middle Ages in Europe (the Roman Empire, the development and influence of the Catholic Church, and the Ottoman Empire). In grade eight, they deal with the "New Age" — the Industrial Revolution, the French Revolution, and World Wars I and II. This section includes units on imperialism and events in the Middle East at this time and a large unit on the Holocaust. In grade nine, they return to ancient history — the Egyptians, Phoenicians, Greeks, and Romans. Approximately 70 percent of the material in the history curriculum deals with Europe, with the remaining 30 percent split evenly between Arab and Jewish history. They teach using outdated books written in the 1950s and 1960s.

In geography for grades seven to nine, Israeli Palestinian students spend one year learning about world climate and general processes of land formation, another year learning European geography, and their final year learning U.S. and agricultural geography. No Israeli geography is taught during junior high.[43] These teachers are sensitive to "hidden" messages in the material that students learn. In the book on U.S. geography (written in 1987), they pointed out that students learn in depth about the procedures required to obtain green cards and American citizenship. They see this as encouraging students to think about leaving Israel and settling in the United States. A unit about the European Common Market (from a 1984 text) is accompanied by pointed questions about cooperation between Israel and Arab countries in markets. Students are asked to think about who promotes such cooperation and who opposes it (and teachers note that Israel is the first answer, the Arab countries the second). The book used to teach citizenship (written in 1962 by a Druze superintendent) calls Arab nationalists *ḥablānim* (saboteurs, a word usually used to mean terrorists). When referring to geographical places in Israel, the Arabic textbooks use Hebrew rather than Arabic names for locations such as Yerushalayim (not El Quds), Shekhem (not Nablus), and 'Akko (not 'Akkā).[44] Several teachers summed up what students learned about Arab culture as "horses and love" because these are the only type of stories or poems they are allowed to read in literature classes.

While the curriculum provides little in terms of lessons regarding Palestinian identity, the students make connections between what they learn in class and the real world. Several instructors noted that when they were teaching units on the Holocaust students drew comparisons between what happened to the Jews under the Nazis and events that were occurring in the West Bank and Gaza Strip. They likened the special badges that some Jewish settlements made workers from Gaza wear to the yellow star that Jews wore. Arab teachers have been forbidden to discuss politics in their classrooms until recently, when the education minister explicitly issued a new directive that frees teachers to direct and listen to students' opinions on current affairs. This directive was issued in an attempt to manage the effects of the *intifada* on Arab youth. Many teachers are suspicious of the sudden freedom they have been granted and fear that if they use this opportunity to introduce current affairs and political discussions into their classrooms, in another two to three years they will have to deal with visits from security personnel. All Arab teachers are reviewed by the Prime Minister's Adviser on Arab Affairs before being hired by their schools. As Mar'i (1978, 37) notes, one young teacher told him: "I am absolutely going mad. . . . When I educate my pupils towards loyalty to the state I am considered a traitor [to my people] . . . and when I emphasize the national character of my pupils and try to nurture in them a sense of national pride, I am told I am a traitor [to the state]."

"Educating for Democracy": Teaching Tolerance

The decade of the 1980s brought new challenges to Israeli society. The Israeli army was mired in Lebanon in the disastrous Operation Peace for the Galilee (often called Israel's Vietnam) from 1982 to 1985.[45] The Sabra and Shatila massacre in September 1982 severely tarnished the moral image of the Israel Defense Forces and roused massive public outrage.[46] As the Lebanese conflict dragged on, confrontations increased between the newly active peace movement (led by Peace Now)[47] and loyal followers of the Likud government's hawkish policies. It was only with the election of Rabbi Meir Kahane to the Knesset in 1984 that Israelis began to recognize and fear the growth of racism within their society.[48] Reports by the Jerusalem Van Leer Institute that Israelis, particularly adolescents, were expressing increased levels of support for Kahane's virulent anti-Arab views prompted the Ministry of Education and Culture to act to counter what it called antidemocratic attitudes on the part of Israeli youth.[49] "Education for Democracy" (a euphemism for antiracism education) thus became a top priority for the entire educational system, and the ministry solicited the development of "coexistence curricula" and in-service training programs for teachers.[50]

Organized encounters between Israeli Jews and Palestinians are not a new feature of Israeli life. In Acre, for example, the Ministry of Education and Culture ran summer day camps that attracted both Jewish and Palestinian students (Rubin 1974, 72). In 1962, eighty Jewish secondary students came to Acre for ten days to study in Arab schools and learn trades with local residents.[51] Beit Kedem, an Arab-Jewish community center in Acre, opened in 1973 and remained in operation until 1983 (when it was forced to close due to lack of funding). In Haifa, Beit Hagefen, another Arab-Jewish community center, has worked since 1963 on community involvement and coexistence. Shūtāfūt (Partnership), another Haifa-based group that formed in 1976, attempts to integrate educational, social, and community development in its initiatives for grassroots development and Arab-Jewish social action and change. Neve Shalom/Wahat Al-Salam, conceived in 1972 as an interfaith (Christian, Muslim, Jewish) community whose residents would break through the barriers of distrust by living together, established its School for Peace with the aim of building mutual trust. By 1987, more than eight thousand adolescents and one thousand adults (almost equally divided between the two peoples) had participated in educational activities, courses, or workshops offered by the school. Other organizations include Interns for Peace, Ulpan ʿAkiva, the Institute for Jewish-Arab Coexistence, the Israel Interfaith Committee, the Education for Peace Project, the International Centre for Peace in the Middle East, and Circle for Nazareth–Upper Nazareth Cooperation (for a more complete listing, see Hall-Cathala 1990).

Many of these programs operated on limited budgets and provided services to their local communities or to a select population. They were not integrated into the national educational system in any systematic fashion. The impetus for national curriculum reform was conceived in 1981 by researchers at the Jerusalem Van Leer Institute[52] who were concerned about the increasing levels of bigotry seen in Israeli schools; they received the Ministry of Education and Culture's formal endorsement in 1983. Under the direction of Alouph Hareven, the Van Leer program had as its goals removing negative stereotypes from textbooks, exposing Jewish pupils to Arab literature and culture, educating both Jews and Arabs in the democratic principles of civic equality, and beginning a dialogue about Arab-Jewish relations in Israel in the schools. In Hareven's words, "For thirty-five preceding years, there has been no education at all. Pupils would go through twelve years without a single hour devoted to the question that every sixth Israeli is an Arab and that we live in a region where our historical destiny is to live with Arabs" (Shipler 1986, 520). By 1985, the Van Leer program had been field-tested in several hundred classrooms.[53] With the adoption of "Education for Democracy" as the theme for the 1987–88 school year, "coexistence" curricula flourished. By 1989, when I conducted my research, there were more than thirty organizations working in this area with forty different programs, yet less than one half of 1 percent — only three to four thousand students per year out of one million Israeli schoolchildren — were actually involved in some sort of Arab-Jewish coexistence program (Hertz-Lazarowitz et al. 1989).

All Israeli students take classes in citizenship. In the Hebrew system, they learn about the general elements of the system of government (democracy, the political parties, the Knesset, the judiciary, and so on), the status of the Arab population in Israel, general problems in Israeli society (economic, political, and social), and current events (new economic policies, changes in the government, and more recently the *intifada*). The curriculum in the Arab system covered three main areas — the system of rule, the society, and the economy — until 1988, when a revised curriculum was introduced in a small number of schools. The revised curriculum added a unit called "Arab Citizens in Israel" that deals with the connection of Arabs to the system of rule in Israel. It includes such topics as educational levels pre- and post-1948, modernization and the *hamulōt,* the economy pre- and post-1948, the political structure, and voting patterns. The unit directly addresses the issue of identity by using a psychological definition that divides it into internal and external.

How have Israeli instructors approached educating for democracy? Most curricula in Israel are based on a "contact hypothesis" approach or some variant of it.[54] In brief, this approach relies on intergroup contact to begin to break down negative stereotypes. Groups are provided with joint positive experiences that challenge their perceptions and opinions of the other group. This approach is often combined with a majority-minority relations emphasis that stresses the responsibilities of the dominant majority toward the subordinate minority and the duties of the minority to accept their position and be loyal citizens. A few examples will illustrate the approach.

The School of Education at Tel Aviv University conducted a four-year project in 1984–88 to train teachers for Jewish-Arab coexistence in Israel. Their in-service training focused on acquisition of knowledge as one way to break down stereotypes. The program of eighteen weeks for both Arab and Jewish teachers had as its intention "changing Jews' discriminatory beliefs against Arabs" (Ben-Gal and Bar-Tal 1989, 2). The program, according to Ben-Gal and Bar-Tal, included a series of lectures on Arab society in Israel — "its political and social structure, religious principles, Israeli-Arab literature, educational system and also legal and social aspects of their minority status" — but "few lectures were given about Jewish society" (4–5). In reviewing the outline of this training program, I was struck by its overwhelming focus on Jewish life: lectures on Jews as a minority, Jewish history and current opinions, Israel in the Middle East, Judaism and democracy, Israel and democracy, and pluralism and majority-minority relations in Israel. Arab life appears in a session on Arab society, single lectures on Arab literature and Arabs as citizens of Israel, and a session devoted to the "Palestinian problem."[55]

The second example, the Neve Shalom/Wahat Al-Salam School for Peace, has provided joint Arab-Jewish encounters since 1980. In its earliest programs, the major focus was on the encouragement of closer ties and more contact between the two groups during and after every encounter. More recently, the program has shifted its goals to focus on "an awareness of the situation, on skills to live amidst the conflict, and on one's natural affinity for and acquaintance with oneself, one's group, and the other national group" (Eady 1988, 3). Beginning with the 1986–87 academic year, the school has worked with small groups of students from ten high schools throughout the country, five from each national group. The students, all juniors, were chosen for their ability to influence those around them (both within and outside of school). Two program models are used, one designed for participants who need to work through emotional and cognitive issues in a uninational group before moving on to a binational meeting (model A) and one designed for participants who are cognitively and emotionally ready for immediate binational meetings (model B). The goal of these programs is to improve students' ability to "live with the conflict": "including familiarity with the conflict, development of a certain measure of mutual trust, assessment of relations between the peoples, recognition of solutions to the conflict as perceived by each of the peoples, and strengthening of personal and national identity" (Bairey 1988–89b, 2).

Giroux argues that schooling for democracy must reclaim the idea of citizenship: "[C]itizenship affirms and articulates between various public spaces and communities whose representations and differences come together around a democratic tradition that puts equality and the value of human life at the center of its discourse and social practices" (1989, 7). In Giroux's model, students are encouraged to explore how particular communities construct their visions of democracy out of their own experiences and how people struggle in the public sphere in support of these different visions. The contact model provides only limited opportunities for such an exploration. Research has indicated that contact leads to improved relations only under specific conditions: (1) equal status within the situation, (2) opportunity to disconfirm stereotypes about the other group, (3) mutual interdependence in achieving group goals, and (4) social norms that favor group equality (Miller and Brewer

1984). The minority-majority approach, in highlighting the unequal status of Palestinians, would thus seem to compromise any benefits that might accrue from contact situations. Thus, the dominant model used in Israeli programs is problematic as a teaching methodology for educating for democracy (or combating racism).

In reporting on problems in the Tel Aviv training program at a conference, Dr. Daniel Bar-Tal singled out the Arab teachers (about 30 percent of participants) and noted that they had negative attitudes toward Jews. The Arab teachers saw themselves as "missionaries" whose job was to "enlighten" the Jewish participants about the situation of Arabs in Israel.[56] Rather than exploring the reasons why Arab participants felt this way or what this implied about their understandings of democracy or coexistence in Israel, the program's organizers viewed the Arab teachers as posing a "problem" that had to be solved. To solve it, they added two new sections to the training, psychological foundations of Israeli politics and Jews as a minority group. Then "the Arab teachers began to understand Israeli problems." Notice that the term *Israeli* here refers only to Israeli Jews. This glossing of *Israeli* as referring only to the Jewish sector of society is common. The problem that program organizers "solved" was a problem of parity in victimization—Arab teachers had to be taught that Israeli Jews have also been victims so they would come to "understand" why Israeli Jews now act as they do. Rather than using this opportunity to explore the relationship of power illuminated in this encounter, the organizers masked the contradictions inherent in the victim becoming the victimizer. Past history was mobilized to justify current realities.

Ariela Bairey, educational director of the Neve Shalom/Wahat Al-Salam School for Peace, discussed the adjustments needed in the program in response to the *intifada:* "For the Jews, the uprising generated a stronger need than in the past to work through their fears. It became more important for them to develop tolerance and acceptance of different views, and *to understand the special problems of a Palestinian national minority living amidst a Jewish majority* and their connection to the problems of the Palestinians as a people." She continues: "[An] effort was made to create an opportunity to work through questions of personal identity as an adolescent; identity as part of a *traditional society coming into contact with an open and modern one;* and identity as a *member of the Palestinian minority living in a state with a Jewish majority*" (1988–89a, 5; emphasis added). Palestinian identity is here presented as problematic, Palestinian society as a traditional society that must be understood by the (Jewish) members of the more modern and open (Israeli) society. A number of students in this program are Mizraḥim, but program organizers do not see it as necessary to explore the special problems of a Mizraḥi Jewish majority living amid an Ashkenazi minority, even though Mizraḥi identity is just as problematic in Israel. There is an implicit assumption that all Jews are the same: they experience the same fears, understand the *intifada* in the same way, and need to develop the same levels of tolerance. "Living with the conflict" does not mean analyzing and critiquing the institutions, policies, or structures within Israeli society that support and promote the subordinate status of Palestinians (or Mizraḥim).

School and Coexistence in Acre

Most of the programs that bring students together to learn about coexistence work by matching an Arab and a Jewish school. The students in these schools generally live in segregated communities. Students from an Arab village are matched with students from an exclusively Jewish kibbutz, town, or city. For some of these children, this is literally the first time they experience persons on the other side as human beings (not as images on the television screen or in children's books or as invisible servants or restaurant workers). In Acre, however, Palestinian and Jewish residents interact on a daily basis; they mingle in shops, banks, the post office, municipal offices, buses, health clinics, apartment blocks, parks, and playgrounds. Thus, when Palestinian and Jewish students there participate in "coexistence" courses, they bring with them their own lived experiences of what coexistence in Acre means.

Three types of coexistence programs were operating in Acre's schools during the 1987–88 and 1988–89 school years. Since "Education for Democracy" was the school theme for 1987–88, a two and a half month segment was set aside in the Hebrew curriculum for teaching students about democracy and citizens' rights. One of the programs was developed by Shūtāfūt (the Haifa-based Arab-Jewish social action group). Activists prepared their program as a yearlong project that involved about one hundred tenth-grade students from Amal and ORT-Darsky. The Jewish students chosen to participate by the school were from classes whose socioeconomic status indicated that they would be favorably inclined to the idea of coexistence meetings. Shūtāfūt coordinators met with the students from the two schools separately over a two-month period to prepare them for a two-day joint meeting to be held at a youth hostel next to Qiryāt Ata (about ten kilometers south of Acre).

The joint meeting, held at the end of March 1988, "exploded and ended before the scheduled time."[57] Jewish students alleged that the Amal students refused to participate in discussions, demonstrated an identification with the PLO and its goals, and compared events occurring in the occupied territories with the Holocaust. There were also allegations that some Amal students refused to speak Hebrew and that in groups they were more radical than they were by themselves. Countering these allegations, one of the Palestinian counselors noted that the Jewish students were provocative. They talked loudly and did not allow the Amal students to freely express themselves. At the dance party the first evening, the Jewish students refused to listen to Arab music and put out the light. The Jewish boys began to bully Amal girls. They insulted other students and even tossed a stink bomb into the Amal sleeping quarters. One counselor claimed that some of the Jewish students were Kahane supporters who had been deliberately placed there to disrupt the meeting.

The charges and countercharges are not surprising when one considers that this meeting was an attempt to deal with issues that are extremely sensitive to most Israeli Palestinians and Jews. What was surprising was the reaction of Jewish school officials. They branded the meeting a failure (even though a group of Jewish students expressed an interest in continuing) and halted the project midyear. At the start of the next school year, Darsky's principal, Batya Bruner, said: "Today, after the intifada's outbreak, the considerations are different. We won't renew the activities and we won't engage in meetings between Jews and Arabs."[58] When relations were most likely to be tense and strained between the Palestinian and Jewish populations of Acre, therefore, school officials refused to continue participating in coexistence programs. Bruner's statements mirrored those of the students themselves: "We're not willing, in any way or form, for any form of meeting between Jews and Arabs."[59]

Jewish students' comments to a journalist about the coexistence programs are enlightening:[60] "You wish [that I'll change my opinion when I enter the army]. In the army, I'll liquidate every Arab who raises a stone," one youth asserted. Another added, "They're everywhere. We don't enter their villages and they come to our house." A third student noted, "Also Israeli Arabs are terrorists. There's no chance for peace. I worked on vacation at Tambour [a local industrial plant] and there the Arab workers tried to provoke us." Arab students held more favorable views about the programs. "I'm for meetings between Jews and Arabs. I live in a neighborhood with Jews on Ha'Oren Street in (North) Acre and there's friendship between us, I think these connections are healthy." Another student commented, "I think that it's advisable to sit with students and to clarify problems. When I walk around on the street, Jews curse me without a reason. 'Son of a whore' they call me. We're interested in peace. I myself support my brothers in the territories and I support the intifada and together with this, I'm interested in the establishment of a Palestinian state. Only thus will there be peace."

The second program, Shkhenīm (Neighbors), was developed by the Unit for Democratic Education of the Ministry of Education and Culture. During the 1988–89 school year, Shkhenīm was being used at Rose (the Jewish junior high school) in four classes (chosen randomly) with a special coordinator. At Amal, the program was in its third year. The Hebrew workbook for students begins with lessons on groups and subgroups that explore the issue of difference and similarity and which is more important when.[61] Students are given a simulation exercise on conflict resolution that deals with an argument over a neighborhood playing field. Four scenarios are presented: the first ends in a fight with all sides losing, the second involves the dominant group agreeing to allow the newcomers to play with them but only if they accept status as guests, the third has the newcomers scaring off the neighborhood group temporarily but facing the threat of a greater show of strength the next time, and the fourth introduces a mediator (a neighborhood counselor) who assists the groups in developing a plan to play together twice and split the remaining days.

Students then move on to an excerpt from A. B. Yehoshua's *The Lover,* wherein Dafi, the Jewish daughter of the house, laughs at Naʿim, the young Arab employed by her father, who has changed from wet clothing into a pair of fancy pajamas. Naʿim is quizzed about his family, their history, life in his village, and what he knows about Jews and Zionism. In the course of the conversation, it becomes clear to him the Jewish family knows nothing about Arabs. To please his hosts, he recites the poetry of Bialik, which he had learned in school. Next there is a lengthy section on the historical background: the Jewish people's move from minority to majority, the 1947 UN decision, Israel's 1949 admission to the United Nations, the *Megilāt Ha ʿAtsmā'ūt* (Proclamation of Independence), newspaper clippings, poetry, and Arab and Jewish proverbs. The clippings from Hebrew newspapers stress the theme of coexistence: "An Arab scientist would be welcomed at the Weitzman Institute" (*Yediʿot Aharonot,* May 1986); "Arab Teachers Plant Trees" and "Arabs and Jews at the Synagogue" (*Yediʿot Aharonot,* March 1988); and "A Police Captain to the Supreme Court: They Won't Let Me Live in a Bedouin Settlement" (*Yediʿot Aharonot,* 1988 [no month listed]).

Jewish teachers, when questioned, said that the program was not going well — it was like "walking on eggs." The junior high school history teachers felt that it was particularly difficult to teach at that moment (May 1989) because of the "hot" atmosphere in the city.[62] Palestinian teachers were incensed about the material on stereotypes included in the program: Jews say Arabs are dirty and primitive, while Arabs say Jews are lazy and liars. They questioned why their students needed to be exposed to such stereotypes and why this was important in a course on coexistence. They charged that the materials have little or no meaning for, or connection to, the daily lives of Palestinian students. These students live in a reality not presented in the coexistence materials, where they face discrimination and harassment and little chance of upward mobility. Jewish teachers also felt that the reality in which their students live will persuade them to behave differently. Noble-minded students stay that way until they enter the army and have stones thrown on them. The program, which had worked well in Amal for the past two years, was a disaster in 1988–89. The Amal students visited Rose Junior High School, but the meeting was a failure. The Amal coordinator summed the situation up with the following illustration, a synopsis of a short film used in Shkhenīm: A flower grows on a border between two neighbors' homes. The neighbors fight back and forth over to whom the flower belongs, while the flower continues to grow. In the end, the neighbors kill each other. The flower continues to grow, and eventually it blooms on the graves of both of the neighbors.

Interns for Peace also worked in Acre's schools in 1987–88. After several preparation sessions with students, it was able to hold a one-day joint meeting that ended successfully. By the time its workers began to prepare for the 1988–89 school year, however, the atmosphere had changed. Jewish parents were expressing increased hostility toward the meetings, and Jewish teachers began to postpone and then cancel them. In the face of stiff opposition, the two American interns canceled the program before the school year began.

By May 1989, almost a quarter of the students at the Hebrew junior high school supported the idea of transferring Acre's Arab population out of the city (a possibility first raised by the Likud candidate during a municipal election campaign). Students claimed that the Arabs wanted to dispossess the Jews of New Acre. While some students supported the idea of forcible removal, others wanted it done in a "cultured way" or with their voluntary cooperation. According to students, a local supporter of the Moledet Party (which supports transferring Arabs from the territories) was distributing its news sheet in the school and a number of students were reading it. When asked how the teachers should react to this, Dani Koran, the principal, said that the idea was political propaganda, so teachers were not responsible for dealing with it.[63] Yet in June of that same year the local Histadrut council sponsored a seminar for thirty-five teachers and their spouses, through the framework of Values Education, entitled "Political Education in the School, the Arab-Jewish Problem, and the Reasons for the Outbreak of Riots in the Territories." The program, which "teaches the work ethic, the mutual aid ethic, equality, and so on," started with two classes and was expanding to four. Workers hoped that even more would be added.[64]

This style of "Education for Democracy" cannot begin to address the fundamental issue of an increase in racist or antidemocratic attitudes because nowhere does it confront the issue directly. Both Palestinian and Jewish students learn about stereotypes, group relations, the process of differentiating one's group from others, general human rights, and the course of democracy in Israel. Students do not learn to analyze critically the underlying structures that create, reproduce, and benefit from the process of "racializing" (or polarizing) relations between Israeli Palestinians and Israeli Jews. Yet it is this process of deconstructing the practices and procedures that generate and perpetuate racism that is essential for a truly effective antiracist pedagogy, as Brandt (1986) illustrates with examples of such efforts in Great Britain. Giroux introduces the idea of "border pedagogy," by which he means "educating students to both read these [different cultural] codes historically and critically while simultaneously learning the limits of such codes, *including the ones they use to construct their own narratives and histories*" (1992, 29; emphasis added). Educational interventions that provide justification for or attempt to legitimate the current structure of the Israeli state cannot also be used to guide students to explore the partial, limited, and particular construction of their own values and politics.

Radical critics in Israel charge that programs that promote Arab-Jewish coexistence within the framework of a Jewish state are simply trying to make Zionism more palatable for Palestinians. These programs are intervening at the microlevel to produce changes in knowledge, tolerance, or understanding. Their interventions do not address the root causes of these problems, which can be found in macrolevel problems of war, occupation, denial of Palestinian self-determination, and the minority position of Palestinians in a Jewish state (Hall-Cathala 1990, 133). Even within these interventions, Jewish educators often resort to particular control mechanisms such as assuming that Hebrew will be the language of use or demanding that politics be kept out of discussions as a way to subvert or divert them (Lemish 1993). These critics emphasize that dialogue alone is doomed to failure unless attempts are made to solve the larger problems. Yet such dialogue is possible only when the status quo remains unchallenged.

It is clear from the experience in Acre that coexistence programs like those used there cannot cope when larger issues suddenly flare up and threaten to rupture the accepted order of things. Such programs cannot change students' attitudes and understandings when the rest of the curriculum promotes different notions of identity and coexistence. Israeli Jewish students go from a single course in coexistence to courses in geography, where they are taught that the coastal lands were unproductive swamps until the Jewish pioneers reclaimed them; to courses in world history, where they are taught that history as background material for understanding Jewish life in the diaspora; to courses in the *Tanakh,* where they learn "love of the land" and how Judaism as a religion is better and more moral than other belief systems. Israeli Palestinian students go from courses in coexistence to courses in history, where they learn about the Israeli people from the Second Temple period to the founding of the state; to courses in geography, where they learn about agriculture and about how to get U.S. citizenship; to courses in Hebrew literature, where they read from the *Tanakh, Mishna,* and *Agada* (all Jewish religious texts). This curricular foregrounding of the Jewish experience (for both Jewish and Palestinian students) represents what Dominguez calls the paradox of creating "oneness" in Israeli Jewish society; the process produces a population that is "self-absorbed, uninterested in others, except when it perceives it must be interested in them — for reasons of security, international relations, trade, or finance" (1989, 153). Even within the small sample of students who were exposed to coexistence programs, mutual relations took a severe blow with the mounting toll of dead and wounded Palestinians and Jews as the *intifada* entered its second and third years. By the end of the 1988–89 school year, a number of these programs had ceased functioning in the schools and were not scheduled to be continued.

When the Ministry of Education and Culture integrated the schools, it did not do away with the separate Arab school system and place Arab and Jewish students together. Had it done so, it is possible that it would have created the space for a more radical critique of racism and discrimination than one currently finds in Israeli schools. Consider one geography teacher in Acre, who spoke about lessons on Jewish settlement in Palestine in the 1920s and 1930s in which students learn that the Jews were sold coastal swamps that they turned into productive farmland. These are, she insisted, the historical facts. Nevertheless, she admitted that she would feel uncomfortable about presenting such things if she had Arab children in the class because she is aware of their feelings, although she continued to insist that what she presents is historically accurate.[65] Where Arabs and Jews do study together, as at the universities, the Arab students can be placed in the position of either uncritically accepting the party line or speaking out and challenging the received wisdom. Those who challenge may suffer the consequences.[66] This ability to challenge the official discourse does not exist at the lower levels — neither Arab students nor Arab teachers interact in the Hebrew school system (except as topics within units in which Israeli Jewish teachers tell Israeli Jewish students about how Arabs live). The one area in which some small interaction does occur is that of the programs for coexistence. This is what makes them so important in examining the context of teaching democratic (antiracist) principles.

The question arises as to who are the target audiences of the "Education for Democracy" classes. The pervasive stereotype in Israel is that people of oriental background are the ones who most hate the Arabs; therefore, they may also be seen as the target audience for such programs.[67] The Ashkenazi student may already be seen as possessing the ideals and behaviors suitable for democracy. When one considers the overwhelming absence of Mizraḥim in the mainline Israeli peace movements (particularly Peace Now),[68] it becomes clear that education for democracy may be viewed as another compensatory program for students who are culturally deficient. Israeli Palestinians who participate in the programs are educated to accept a democracy that relegates them to status as second-class citizens.

Even more interesting is the expression of antidemocratic attitudes in the religious sector. Liebman and Cohen note that "the most extreme expressions of racism and ethnocentrism are generally confined to religious Zionist spokesmen in Israel" (1990, 61). This is particularly revealing given that it was the Orthodox religious parties that opposed the initial draft of a 1986 law against racial incitement as posing serious problems for religious Jews. To gain the support of the religious bloc and pass the law, its framers had to insert a provision that specifically excludes the expression of religious doctrine from prosecution as racist incitement (Hall-Cathala 1990, 81; Sharkansky 1991, 89). It is in the religious schools that the Van Leer survey indicated strong anti-Arab prejudice. Ironically, coexistence curricula are not used in religious schools because such contact is seen as potentially polluting. Parents worry that their children may eat nonkosher food or form friendships (and possibly sexual liaisons) that could result in mixed marriages. Liebman and Cohen report that some religious Zionist high schools in Israel have revived ancient and medieval conceptions that attribute inferior biological characteristics to gentiles. "Thus students in some of these schools learn that the first two patriarchs, Abraham and Isaac, each had two sons so that the Jewish son might inherit pure genes whereas the corrupt, impure genes that Abraham inherited from his idolatrous ancestors could be passed on to the non-Jewish son. Only Jacob's sons — those of the third generation — inherited pure genes and were worthy of being Jewish" (1990, 60). Thus, the coexistence curricula are having the least influence in exactly those sectors where they are most needed.

Integration in Acre: Sharing the Preschools

Zionist educators during the period of the Mandate viewed *ganim* (singular *gan;* kindergartens or preschools) as sites for infusing the meaning of

Zionism in students and teaching them some sort of vague Israeli culture that, through the children, would also reach the parents (Shamgar-Handelman and Handelman 1986). The *gan* was a tool to achieve a national goal: transforming the child into a new Israeli person different from his parents. With statehood, this theme was retained. The child was cast as a partner in the process of assimilating new immigrants into Israeli society. Israeli educators see control of the child as crucial to the reproduction of the nation-state. *Gan* in Israel is the first stage in an educational process that gradually moves the child from his or her embeddedness in the family to an awareness of belonging to a larger national collectivity. It culminates when the child leaves school at age eighteen to enter the army (ibid., 72). Several studies of rituals and celebrations in Israeli Jewish *ganim* illustrate the importance of these schools as sites for planting ideas regarding the relationship between the child, his or her family, and the nation-state (Shamgar-Handelman and Handelman 1986; Weil 1986; Doleve-Gandelman 1987).

Israeli parents use the preschool services made available to them by their municipal authorities. By law, children aged five are required to register for *gan ḥōvāh* (the mandated kindergarten). Many municipal governments also provide services for three and four year olds (*gan tet-ḥōvāh*, literally "below the requirement," the equivalent of nursery schools or preschools). All three age groupings may not be included within the same framework. In 1988–89, more than 75 percent of Jewish children aged two and 96 percent aged three and four attended some form of preschool. Of Jewish children aged four, 94 percent were attending public preschool centers. Among Arab children, 25 percent of those aged three and 53 percent of those aged four attended preschool centers.[69]

In Acre, the municipal government has expanded the provision of free preschool education services to include children aged three and four. Besides the municipal centers, there are private ones run by women's organizations such as Na'amat and Wizo that serve the needs of working mothers. The Acre Arab Women's Association established its *gan* as a direct response to the problems their children faced as minorities in majority-Jewish frameworks.[70] Ideally, *ganim* are built to service a particular residential neighborhood so that children are within walking distance of their homes. Assignment of children to *ganim* is handled by municipal authorities, beginning with age five and moving down. They try to match children with the *gan* closest to their home, but allocation problems sometimes mean that a child is assigned to attend a distant *gan*. In Acre, integration exists at one level of the educational system—the *gan*. This was not a planned educational strategy but an unexpected outcome of housing patterns in the city. As Palestinian families began to move out of the Old City and into the central, eastern, and northern sections, they sought to have their children registered in programs close to their homes. As the Arab *ganim* in the Old City reached their capacity, the municipality had no choice but to place some Arab children in Jewish programs in the New City. By 1989, almost 160 Arab children were registered in *ganim* there.[71]

When Arab children are placed in majority-Jewish *ganim,* no effort is made to adjust the curriculum to accommodate them. These children receive a Jewish education. Along with the other children, they celebrate holidays like Purim and Lag B'Omer, take part in lighting Shabbat candles, and help carry out the Pesach seder. They begin to learn Hebrew. I heard little Palestinian girls singing in perfect Hebrew Pesach songs such as "Why is this night different? This night, this night, we only eat matzo" or the nationalist "My flag is blue and white." Some parents deliberately choose to place their child in a Jewish framework so that he or she will begin to learn the Hebrew language and assimilate Jewish culture at an early age. Since Arab parents do not view the schools as essential in helping to form their child's awareness of his or her Palestinian identity, sending their child to a Jewish *gan* was not perceived as a threat. Yet Jewish *ganim* impart certain experiential and emotional lessons regarding links between individuals, families, and the Jewish state. At an early stage of identity formation, Arab children in Jewish *ganim* are thus exposed to conflicting messages concerning their position in society. At the school, they participate as all the other children participate, but the lessons they learn are not necessarily reinforced at home. At home, they are immersed in a different culture and language , which stresses different values and expectations regarding proper behavior.

In 1990, the issue of mixed *ganim* exploded. Uri Mizraḥi, acting mayor, chairman of the Education Committee, and the National Religious Party representative on the municipal council, decided that "joint centers for Jews and Arabs spoil the spirit of Jewish youth and especially young Jewish girls, something that could cause mixed marriages in the future." His proposed solution: to "separate them while they're still young."[72] Jewish municipal officials who supported separation claimed that the change was due to pressure from the Arab sector. Arab leaders claimed that because the education in mixed *ganim* was based on Jewish culture Arab children in those schools lost their connection to Arab traditions. Some Jewish parents in Acre supported the decision as well. As one mother said, "I'm not willing that my children study in *gan* with an Arab child. The Arab children speak Arabic among themselves and this angers me. It's not enough that they live with us in the same building, my child needs to suffer them also in *gan*."[73]

Local Arab and Jewish residents and officials who opposed the decision saw this as the failure of coexistence in Acre. Yossi Fitosi, a member of the municipal council, opposed the decision because he saw it as beginning a process of dividing the city into separate Arab and Jewish enclaves.[74] He warned that this would accelerate the process of Jewish residents leaving the city, urge Arabs from elsewhere to move to Acre, and strengthen the "appetites" of people in the city who wanted to convert it into "a single-nationality city, like Nazareth and Sakhnin." One local paper reported: "In Acre, they're cleansing the mixed *ganim.*"[75] Several people wrote letters to the editor in which they drew comparisons between the decision to separate the children and Hitler's actions against the Jews. They condemned the decision as subverting Jewish religious traditions, which teach respect for others. One mother recommended that parents who opposed Arab children participating in Jewish holidays study the *Tanakh* themselves. In Deut. 16:14, she noted, "God commanded us: 'You shall make merry at your festival, you and your sons and daughters, your male and female slave, the Levite, the alien, the orphan, and the widow that are within your gates."

The conflict over the mixed *ganim* erupted after a bitter municipal election campaign (see chapter 5) in which the Likud candidate stoked the fears of Jewish residents that Acre could become an Arab city. Tensions in the city did not dissipate in the aftermath of the elections because the losing Likud faction continued to agitate against the Arab residents of the city. The election campaign and its aftermath provided the context within which the religious council member could realize his goal of separating Arab and Jewish children in the *ganim*. This same official had expressed opposition to the coexistence programs in the local high school. The tense local situation may also explain why some Arab residents were willing to push for separate *ganim*. They probably feared for their children's well-being at school. Jewish children, infected with their parents' anti-Arab attitudes, might be more likely to harm the Arab children in their schools. For Arab political leaders, the situation provided an opportunity to gain some additional benefits for their constituency. For some Jewish parents, the mixed *ganim* were just another instance of contamination. Some Jewish officials saw this as an opportunity for the municipality to cut its expenses because the Arab children could be moved to other existing facilities.

Were the *ganim* indeed separated? The answer is no for a variety of reasons. The municipality was not willing to build Arab *ganim* in the New City. Palestinian parents living in the New City were not willing to send their children far from home to *ganim* in the Old City. Considerable pressure was exerted to maintain the status quo. Ironically, the influx of new immigrants to the city was the final factor that operated to end the idea of separation. Almost eight thousand Soviet and three thousand Ethiopian Jews have been settled in or near Acre since 1990, accounting for almost one-quarter of the city's population. The local school system must cope with absorbing their children. The presence of the Palestinian children in the mixed *ganim* has helped to maintain the Israeli character of the *gan,* which would otherwise have been swamped by the new Russian and Ethiopian cultural elements.[76]

The case of the integrated preschools provides a number of insights into the complexities of Palestinian-Jewish coexistence. Like the coexistence curriculum, the mixed *ganim* reinforce the minority-majority framework of relations between the two communities. The Palestinian children, as the minority, may attend mixed *ganim,* but the education they receive will be that of the Jewish majority. Coexistence comes to mean that the minority group must learn to adjust to and accept its minority status. The mixed *ganim,* therefore, can be used to publicly symbolize that Palestinian and Jewish Israelis can live together in harmony, without policymakers having to examine what this accommodation costs the Palestinian children in terms of stable and secure personal and group identities.

At the same time, Palestinian children in mixed centers are also being socialized into an Israeli Jewish framework of social relations. Israeli Jewish children who play with Palestinian children see a different face of "the Arabs" that is at odds with the images presented on the television screens. The assumed boundary that divides Palestinian and Jewish Israelis fades when new Jewish immigrants are added to the local community. It is the Palestinian children who help to maintain the Israeli character of the schools. For a brief period of time, the borders are effaced, until the new immigrants are absorbed as Israelis and the boundary markers are once again firmly established.

Elite Israelis are very worried about the increase in Israeli Jewish intolerance toward Arabs. Outsiders — other governments and Jews who live in the United States and other countries — do not accept this intolerance as simple bigotry. Even now, cultural explanations are advanced for why "those" people are becoming more intolerant. We are told that most Israelis immigrated from nondemocratic countries (in the Middle East) and that the control that Orthodox Judaism exercises over public life allows certain rights to be curtailed. Once again, Israeli (read Western) culture is not to blame for the intolerance, in what Shohat (1988, 27) calls a "self-celebratory We-of-the-liberal-West image before international public opinion." Were the Israeli political elite to champion educational programs that truly encouraged Jewish students to examine notions about identity and democracy in Israeli society, it might have to explain the contradiction between a national ideology that stresses the unity of the Jewish people and the primacy of their rights and well-being and a national reality in which equality is available only to certain groups of Jews. Israelis are trapped in a siege mentality, a product of the Holocaust, that does not allow them to recognize the other.[77] There are signs that some individuals in Israel are beginning to recognize the workings of this process. In June of 1990, at the conference "Education against Hatred," Sammy Smooha was subjected to a storm of opposition from conference attendees for his recognition that "intolerance in Israel is caused by the structure of the state. Intolerance proceeds from the central forces in the system, not from the margins."[78] The recent flood of Russian Ashkenazi immigrants to Israel has exacerbated tensions within the country, and for the first time Mizraḥim and Palestinians share a common cause in their opposition to government policies that favor the new arrivals. While the new immigrants are being housed, educated, and employed at the state's expense, Mizraḥim must live with record unemployment, skyrocketing housing costs, and further reductions in the school day. The facade of Israeli Jewish unity has begun to fracture; it remains to be seen whether Palestinian and Mizraḥi Israelis will be able to stitch together a new fabric that is truly revolutionary, a borderland that remaps difference and decenters power.

CHAPTER 4

Living Together in
Shkhūnāt Wolfson

If Acre is a border zone within Israel, then Shkhūnāt Wolfson represents a border zone within a border zone. Squatting next to the central bus station, the neighborhood presents a tired, worn face to passersby. A triangular area of approximately fifty dunams (twelve and a half acres), it is bounded by the bus station and municipal market, what was the main Haifa-Nahariyya highway until a few years ago, the railroad station, and a major city street, Rehov Ha'Arbʿa. The concrete walls of the buildings have turned a dingy brown with the passage of time. Lawns and walkways are littered with bits of paper and other trash blown over from the nearby highway. Laundry and bedding are draped out of apartment windows (fig. 6). The Wolfson of 1988–89 was an unkempt shell of the once select, high-class neighborhood that opened its doors to residents in the 1960s. The story of the neighborhood's fall from grace parallels the saga of the city's struggle to maintain its status and continue to develop, a story repeated over and over in many of Israel's development towns.[1] The residents of Shkhūnāt Wolfson live out in their daily activities many of the implications of the identity politics of Israel. By analyzing how the residents of Wolfson construct their desires for recognition, security, and affiliation, and thus their senses of themselves and others, a great deal can be learned about the politics of identity in Israel.

The Experiment Begins

Between 1948 and 1961, Acre's population grew from 4,000 (3,100 Arabs, 900 Jews) to 25,200 (6,200 Arabs, 19,000 Jews).[2] Additional stock had to be built to house the new immigrants who were being directed to the city. The municipality was also under considerable pressure to liquidate the transit camps and provide housing opportunities for young couples. With assistance from a British philanthropist, Keren HaYesod (the National Fund), and the housing ministry, Shkhūnāt Wolfson took shape on a plot of former swampland containing a small number of

FIG. 6.   One of the apartment blocks in Wolfson. (Photo by author.)

Arab, privately owned, stone dwellings built before 1948 and uninhabited since the conquest of the city in 1948.

Sir Isaac Wolfson, a Zionist British industrialist, donated seven
hundred thousand pounds to the Special Programmes section of Keren
HaYesod to help build housing for immigrants who arrived without
means.[3] The apartment complex was planned to include 520 units, a
kindergarten, a business center, playgrounds, and a synagogue. The

apartments were spacious by the standards of the day—a living salon, kitchen, two bedrooms, and bath, all in all about fifty-four square meters. The planners even included parking spaces for cars that the residents might one day be able to afford.[4] The quarter was actually built by the Ministry of Housing, at a total cost of eight million Israeli līrōt (IL). The new residents would purchase their homes, but all public facilities were paid for by the Keren HaYesod. Ground was broken in 1963, and on 20 April 1966 the municipality staged a festive naming ceremony at which Sir Isaac and Lady Edith were honored guests. By this point, more than five hundred homes had been or were being built and two-thirds of the residents had moved in. It was estimated that the quarter would be completed before year's end.

Inhabitants of the quarter were labeled the "typical Israeli medley," namely, new immigrants and young couples who either were born in Israel or were very young on arrival.[5] In the words of Mayor Yosef Katran at the dedication, "This neighborhood is at heart like all of the city's neighborhoods. It is a miniature picture of the country that is absorbing her returning children within her border: new immigrants from many countries, old-timers, the native-born, young couples all living under one roof, living and supporting themselves and working to develop their cities."[6] About 120 young couples were provided with apartments in Wolfson on easy financial terms.[7] With the liquidation of some of the transit camps (particularly Mishmar Ha'am, whose land was slated for industrial development), Amidar allocated apartments in the complex to a number of Mizraḥi families, mostly from Morocco. The Wolfson neighborhood, with its spacious apartments and central location, also attracted the elite of the city—doctors, lawyers, teachers, and even the mayor and deputy mayor—who abandoned lower-quality housing in the eastern neighborhoods for the convenience of life in the city's center.

In 1965, when the Wolfson quarter was half built, a house collapsed in the Old City, killing an elderly occupant and injuring others. The family took refuge in the al-Jazzâr Mosque, and there was a national outcry about housing conditions in the Old City.[8] Communists fought with Labor Party supporters within the mosque's courtyard as they pressed for a solution to the housing problems of Acre's Arab residents.[9] To deal with the crisis, the municipality pressured the Ministry of Housing to allocate one apartment per residential block in the Wolfson quarter to young Arab families. Some families were evacuated directly from unsafe housing to the new neighborhood. Most, however, were carefully selected; they were middle class, often young couples who worked for the municipal or national government or as teachers (Cohen 1973, 10). Forty Arab families moved into the Wolfson estate, where they were concentrated in a few sections of several blocks rather than being dispersed. The municipality turned their apartments in the Old City over to other Arab families who lived in unsafe structures. The dangerous houses were demolished, and the rubble was carted away to create more open space in the Old City.

Although some of the Mizraḥi residents of the neighborhood opposed living with Arabs, the families moved into their new residences without encountering any problems. Cohen reports that while there were occasional fights between children and tensions between adults no serious ethnic clashes occurred in the neighborhood during the first five years (1973, 10). This is significant when one considers that this period included the 1967 Six Day War and the 1969 discovery of a terrorist cell operating in the city. During the 1967 war, the Arab residents of Wolfson felt isolated in the new housing quarter. Many of them returned to the shelter of the Old City's walls or to relatives' homes in the city or nearby villages. Those who remained in the neighborhood, however, assisted the women and children whose husbands were away on battle lines. As a current Arab resident reported, when asked to describe the development of Arab-Jewish relations in the neighborhood, "The two sides cooperated and helped each other. We used to close the gas cylinders together and go down to the shelter together when there was an air raid."[10] A Jewish man said, "During the Six Day War, they helped the women put the children in the bomb shelters, encouraged and cooperated, or so we were told by the women. We were on the lines." Another Jewish resident reported that "in 1967, after one year of living here, there were very few Arabs, but they helped us to enter the bomb shelters and behaved in a model fashion."

With cooperation, however, there were also feelings of resentment and anger. A Jewish resident captured more of the ambiguity of integrated living: "At first there were good relations. But since the Six Day War we've been in the bomb shelter. In the Six Day War, when Jews were happy that we had conquered Jerusalem, the Arabs were angry that we danced and sang. We wrote a letter to the government that during the war we didn't enjoy being together [with Arabs] in the shelter; they agreed, and gave us a shelter alone." It was an extremely tense time, with Arab neighbors not appreciating the joy shown by their Jewish neighbors, and Jews not understanding the Arabs' feelings of anger and humiliation. One Arab resident said that he felt despised by the Jewish residents in 1967 (a result of the short duration of the war and Israel's overwhelming success in seizing territory). Several Arab residents reported that Jewish children who used to play with them threw eggs at them instead.

During the 1970s, Acre continued to grow. In September of 1974, the new Egged Bus Terminal, located next to the Wolfson development, opened for business.[11] This terminal replaced the clogged, open-air station located in the center of the city on Rehov Ben Ami, ten or so blocks west of the quarter. Behind the new Egged station, a municipal market, which included an open-air vegetable market as well as a number of small shops, opened for business. Wolfson residents could now do their shopping closer to home. In September 1973, it was announced that Maʿabārāh Napoleon would be liquidated over the next four years and the two hundred families living there would be housed elsewhere.[12] By December of 1976, a new housing quarter of five hundred apartments had been constructed in the northern section of the city.[13] Changes in construction standards meant that these apartments were larger than those in Wolfson—seventy-four and seventy-nine square meters compared to Wolfson's fifty-four. The apartments cost IL 145,000 and IL 185,000, but tenants (including newly married couples, who were most affected by the housing shortage) were required to pay only IL 30,000 to IL 45,000 in cash.

In the fall of 1979, when Avitsour and Deutsch carried out their study of interethnic social relationships in the neighborhood, there were 430 Jewish and 70 Arab families living in Shkhūnāt Wolfson.[14] They interviewed all sixty-three Arab family heads who lived in the same apartment block as Jews, as well as ninety-two Jewish household heads who lived in blocks with Arabs.[15] Forty-two percent of the Jewish family heads were under forty-two years of age, compared to almost 68 percent of Arab family heads. The majority of the Jews were of Asian-African origin and could communicate in Arabic, while all of the Arabs had been born in Palestine and could communicate in Hebrew. About half of each group had only completed elementary school (eight years), while the other half had secondary or technical education. In terms of occupations, almost 43 percent of the Jews and 32 percent of the Arabs were blue-collar workers (mostly in industry), 40 percent of the Jews and 57 percent of the Arabs were civil and public servants, and the rest of each group were merchants. The majority of respondents had lived in Wolfson for at least five years, and about two-thirds had purchased their homes (while less than a third were renting). Apartments were similarly furnished with radio, television, refrigerator, washing machine, stove, and oven, although more Jewish homes (73 percent) than Arab homes (20 percent) had telephones.

Avitsour and Deutsch were interested in the impact of shared living and daily contact on the quality of social relationships between Arabs and Jews.[16] On the basis of their survey results, they concluded that "Arabs and Jews perceive their mutual relationships and daily contacts as stable, satisfying, and generally free of political tension (although they affirm that relations might be affected by political events)" (Deutsch 1988, 73). When asked if they intended to remain in Shkhūnāt Wolfson, most of the family heads said yes (80 percent of Arabs, 60 percent of Jews). Of those who indicated that they would prefer to move, 50 percent of Jews and 76 percent of Arabs gave as their reason "improving living conditions."

Closer examination of their data, however, yields a more ambiguous reading of the nature of social relationships between Arab and Jewish residents.[17] When asked, "Do you feel uncomfortable in the company of Israeli Jews/Arabs?" 50 percent of the Jewish family heads responded affirmatively, compared to only 23 percent of Arab family heads. When asked with which nationality of neighbors they had the friendliest relations, 72 percent of Jewish respondents said all were Jews and 16 percent said most were Jews; among the Arab respondents, only 20 percent responded all Arabs, with 31 percent saying most were Arabs. When asked to characterize their relationship with neighbors of the opposite national group, 37 percent of Jews and 78 percent of Arabs answered "cooperative," 24 percent of Jews and 9 percent of Arabs said there was no relationship, 10 percent of Jews and 5 percent of Arabs called it "formal," and 23 percent of Jews and 2 percent of Arabs classed it as "indifference." A question concerning whether Israeli Jews and Israeli Arabs have common goals elicited a negative response from 59 percent of Jewish family heads, while 82 percent of Arab family heads responded in the affirmative.

Jewish men were as likely to say that they were uncomfortable in the presence of Arabs as that they were at ease. Only a minority saw intergroup relations as cooperative, not so surprising since many believed there were no common goals for Arabs and Jews. It is clear from the responses that most of these men preferred to establish close friendships with other Jewish men. The level of discomfort and lack of willingness to establish relationships are even more striking when one considers the fact that most of the Jewish respondents were from Mizraḥi cultural backgrounds.[18] Their responses highlight a critical dilemma for Mizraḥi Israelis. They have been placed between the proverbial rock and a hard place: to be Israelis, they must negate their Arab cultural background and stress their common Jewish heritage; negating their Arabness, however, does not provide them with an equal share of Israel's economic, political, and social benefits. Ashkenazi Israeli society, while demanding that Mizraḥim deny their Arab cultural heritage, at the same time uses that heritage to discredit and deny their claims for full and equal participation in economic and political power.

Arab men were likely to report feeling comfortable in the presence of Jews, to see relations as cooperative, and to recognize common goals.

Given the responses of Jewish men, one could question whether the Arab men really felt this way or whether they were instead presenting the interviewer with an idealized image of how they wished relationships were between the two groups. Generally speaking, in similar types of surveys Arab respondents often express more desire for intergroup contacts and cooperation than do Jewish respondents.[19] Their responses, like those of the Mizraḥim, reflect the broader social and political context within which they live. As a minority population, they are very aware of their dependence on the good graces of the Jewish majority.

With increased availability of other housing choices, such as the new apartments in the north of the city, some Wolfson residents began to sell their apartments and leave. What started as a trickle became a flood. Between 1978 and 1983, one-quarter of the neighborhood's residents moved out and new families moved in, many of them Arab households seeking better housing stock than that available in the Old City (Frey and Assadi 1986, 12). By 1986, when the Project Van Leer team conducted a neighborhood household survey, Shkhūnāt Wolfson was home to 2,040 people, 912 Jews (45 percent) and 1,128 Arabs (55 percent).[20] The Arab population was composed predominantly of young couples with large numbers of children and very few older adults. The Jewish population was the converse — large numbers of elderly (about one-third of Jewish household heads were sixty-five or older) and far fewer young couples with children. The Van Leer team found that most household heads were employed in low-paid, light industry jobs and that educational levels for the entire population were low. It also reported that the neighborhood contained a high-percentage social disability population — people who were temporarily unemployed, the aged, pensioners, invalids, the chronically ill, and single-parent families. Over a twenty-year period, this elite, prestigious neighborhood had been transformed into a derelict, neglected residential quarter with an extremely negative image.

Three processes appear to have been at work in transforming the neighborhood's demographic and economic structure. Residents themselves recognize two of them: the exit of young Jewish families and the influx of Arabs. As one resident explained, "At first, everyone were Jews. It was good to live here. There were many young couples, their families grew, they left and sold their apartments, and so the Arabs began to enter and now everything is full." Young couples who had moved to Wolfson when they were first married found that as their families grew their apartments began to seem cramped and crowded. Those families who were financially secure solved their housing problems by moving to larger ones, either elsewhere in Acre or in nearby settlements such as Nahariyya or the Qrayōt suburbs of Haifa.[21] As the more established families (both Jewish and Arab) left the neighborhood, its character began to shift since a number of the residents who remained belonged to a lower socioeconomic class.[22]

Arab residents of Acre had extremely limited housing choices. Originally concentrated in the Old City, they gradually began to move into apartments in Mandate Acre, near the Old City, as apartments became available. Major housing developments during the 1950s, 1960s, and 1970s were intended for the Jewish sector of the population or for new Jewish immigrants. While a few Arab families had been given apartments in the Wolfson development, this was an ad hoc solution to the very real housing crisis in the Old City. In a sample of needy families there, Ben Yitzhak (1981) found that 65.1 percent of the houses had sanitation problems, 87.2 percent had problems with seepage, and 60.4 percent had problems with flooding.[23] Rather than constructing a new Arab neighborhood within the city's limits, the housing ministry poured money into Makr, five kilometers east of Acre. Arab residents of the Old City who wanted to improve their living conditions were encouraged to purchase apartments in Makr. They were offered attractive terms for mortgages. The housing itself was modern and appealing, compared to the half-open, one- or two-room shells that had been home to some families. As noted in chapter 2, this plan served two additional purposes. Jewish municipal leaders were very worried about the increasing Arab and decreasing Jewish population in the city. By not building within Acre's municipal boundaries, they hoped to siphon off some of the Arab population of the city. In addition, by reducing the Arab population of the Old City, officials could implement their plans for developing the tourist potential of that quarter. Arab leaders and residents of the Old City did not support the proposed housing solution, and a number of people refused to leave Acre. Those Arab families who had the resources, therefore, began to move into Shkhūnāt Wolfson.

The forty established Arab families in Wolfson provided a core that drew additional households. Wolfson was not completely alien territory. It was centrally located, with medical facilities, transportation services, and shops within walking distance. As Jewish families sold, Arab families bought. The Arab families were willing to pay higher purchase prices for the property than potential Jewish buyers. Many Jewish residents bitterly opposed the initial sales by Jews to Arabs. One resident reported that "quarrels broke out between Jews. Why were they selling their apartments to Arabs? The neighborhood's reputation was destroyed." Another resident declared, "When the selling began to Arabs, we convinced the Jews not to sell. The Jews really begged the neighbors not to sell. It caused tension and arguments. The Jewish neighbors told the new Arab neighbor they would cause him trouble until he left, and he, of course, laughed and said, 'You don't understand anything. We have a plan to take control of the neighborhood.' " The turning point appears to have been 1979. At least 10 families from our survey of 109 Arab families in the neighborhood had moved there that year, equal to the number of families that had purchased there during the preceding ten years. An additional 27 families had moved into the neighborhood during 1980–84, and 45 had moved there in 1985–89. The trickle had become a torrent and then a flood.

Rabinowitz (1990, 1997) looks at a similar process in the Jewish development town of Upper Nazareth, which overlooks the Arab city of Nazareth. He finds that the Jewish residents of Upper Nazareth rationalize selling apartments to Arab families in one of several ways. They maintain that the practice is wrong but recognize that due to economic hardship some families have no choice but to sell to Arabs. Where some families have already sold to Arabs and moved, other residents may present their decision to sell to Arabs as motivated by their desire to live among Jews. Finally, they describe the Arabs' presence as detrimental to the town, when in fact the incoming money has had a positive effect on Upper Nazareth's economy. Like the residents of Wolfson, people in Upper Nazareth blame the government for not intervening to prevent this situation. Jews in Upper Nazareth continue to sell to Arabs while at the same time lamenting the loss of their town. There are remarkable similarities between the Jewish residents of Wolfson and those of Upper Nazareth. Some residents of Wolfson believe that the Arab presence in the quarter is part of a Palestinian master plan to take over the city. In Wolfson, however, there is no longer any pressure on Jewish families not to sell. In fact, Arab demand has tapered off and Jewish residents who want to sell have to settle for lower prices. As one Jewish resident bitterly notes, "The Arabs themselves don't buy quickly today; they know that the Jews want to leave and they don't buy until a person is pressed and sells also to an Arab cheaply." This person's solution is for Jewish agents (e.g., religious groups such as Shas) to buy the houses and give them to young Jewish couples, "but that they'll give a high price like the Arabs."

In addition to these processes (exit of Jewish families to better housing and entrance of Arab families for the same purpose), Amidar, the national housing authority, played a major role in the neighborhood's decline. Amidar held 36 percent of the housing stock in Wolfson, which it made available to Jewish immigrant families or Jewish families dependent on government social services. Amidar did not rent housing to Arab families in Wolfson (on a similar policy for Upper Nazareth, see Rabinowitz 1997, 54–55). These Jewish families were of a lower social class than the other residents of the development. Many of them had large families (five or more children), which meant severe overcrowding in the apartments. Many of these families were unable or unwilling to purchase their apartments and rented. They were extremely dependent on Amidar, demanding that it improve the quality of the housing so that there was no real sense of tenant responsibility for upkeep. As the reputation of the neighborhood worsened, of course, middle-class Jewish families were less willing to move there. A similar movement to the American phenomenon of white flight developed: the upper- and middle-class Jewish families moved out and lower-class Jewish families moved in.

By the early 1980s, the demographic balance in Wolfson had dramatically shifted.[24] By the mid-1980s, the neighborhood, which was once majority Jewish, was majority Arab. Instead of being seen as a mixed neighborhood, Shkhūnāt Wolfson was known to other residents of Acre as an Arab neighborhood — some called it Mohammed's Way. The physical condition of the neighborhood had deteriorated. Its buildings were in disrepair, with trash from the nearby Haifa-Nahariyya highway littering the lawns and playgrounds. Periodically, large pools of water would form in ditches that were not separated from children's play areas by fences. The water, besides being deep enough to drown a small child, bred mosquitoes and other pests. The neighborhood was noisy, with both children and some adults ignoring rest hours from two to four in the afternoon. A number of apartments that belonged to Amidar sat empty because Jewish families were unwilling to move there. The neighborhood had attracted some of the less desirable elements of Acre's society — prostitutes, drug addicts, and criminals — who based their activities out of apartments there.[25]

Given all this, however, there still remained a core of middle-class, moderately successful Arab families that liked the neighborhood and its central location as well as a core of older middle-class Jewish families that had lived in the neighborhood for years and were unwilling or unable to move. Several families purchased additional apartments in order to knock out walls, renovate, and double the size of the original living space. The neighborhood was not a complete loss, and it was at this point in time that two local activists (one Jewish, one Palestinian) were approached by the Dutch Van Leer Foundation to establish a community development project that would deal with both the social and educational needs of the neighborhood. This was the birth of Project Van Leer, which worked to build neighborhood identity and responsibility and improve living conditions for Wolfson residents from 1986 to 1993.

Project Van Leer operated as an external catalyst to neighborhood change in Wolfson from 1986 to 1989. Its principal goals were to organize neighborhood residents, develop local Arab and Jewish leadership, and initiate a wide range of innovative early childhood programs with a community base.[26] Its early childhood programs included joint para-professional training courses for Arab and Jewish women, the establishment of a neighborhood resource center, parents' groups, summer activities for Arab and Jewish neighborhood children, and a variety of other educational enrichment programs. What made the project unique was its insistence on a model of joint Arab-Jewish effort to achieve a set of common goals. In its own structure, the project presented a different model to local residents — one in which Arab and Jewish directors (Mohammed Assadi and Harry Frey), staff, and residents worked together as equal partners in implementing changes in the neighborhood. By 1990, the directors of the project were ready to expand their base of operations to other parts of Acre. That same year, in April, residents of the neighborhood formed their own fledgling organization — the Jewish-Arab Community Association (JACA)-Wolfson Neighborhood — and they began lobbying to take over management of the soon-to-be-constructed neighborhood center.

Those Who Remain

In 1989, at the time of my research in the neighborhood,[27] there were 459 housing units in twelve apartment blocks.[28] One hundred and eighty-eight apartments were occupied by Jewish households (41 percent), 233 were occupied by Arab households (51 percent), 6 were occupied by mixed Arab-Jewish households (1 percent), and 28 were empty (6 percent).[29] The apartments themselves varied in size: fifty-four square meters (60 percent), sixty-four square meters (15 percent), seventy-eight square meters (22 percent), and ninety-two square meters (3 percent) (Rechman 1990, 6).[30] In addition to the apartment blocks, there were two bomb shelters and a central block of buildings that housed a kindergarten, a grocery shop, the Project Van Leer offices, and its associated children's center (fig. 7). All of the apartment blocks were inhabited by both Jews and Arabs, although to varying degrees (table 7).[31] Most of Wolfson's buildings had multiple entrances, which served to break these large buildings up into smaller units based around the entrance. Entrances are important in Israel because housing committees, which are responsible for maintenance of shared facilities such as water heaters as well as external cleanliness, are usually organized around entrances. Not all entrances were mixed. Some Arab families, while living in a mixed building, had a nonmixed entrance. All Jewish families lived in mixed entrances.

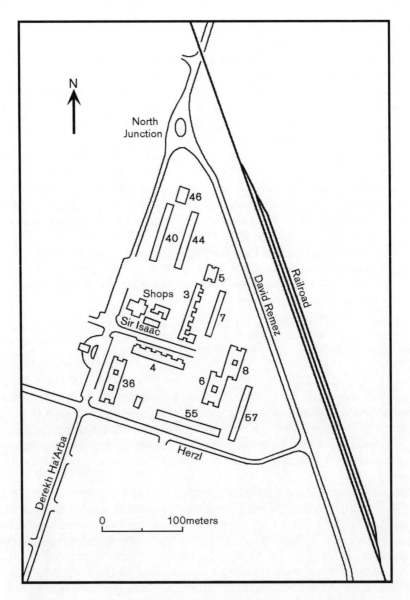

FIG. 7.   Shkhūnāt Wolfson (1987–89). (Map by Ardeth Abrams.)

So who were the residents of Wolfson in 1989? Were they still that "miniature picture of the country" of which Mayor Katran was so proud when he dedicated the neighborhood in 1965? Were they closer to local stereotypes — lower class, welfare recipients, and *kafrīīm* (literally "villagers," with a connotation of primitive)? Or is the reality more complex?

We interviewed the male or female head of 96 Jewish and 109 Arab households, which comprised approximately half of the residents of the neighborhood (see table 7 for the breakdown by group and building).[32] Of the 96 Jewish respondents, 26 (27 percent) were Ashkenazi, mainly from Poland (6 people) and Romania (13), while 69 (72 percent) were Mizraḥi, mainly from Morocco (43 people) and Tunisia (10). The 109 Arab households were Muslim except for four Christian families. Fifty-one percent of the Jewish respondents were men (*n* = 49) and 49 percent were women (*n* = 47), while only 35 percent of Arab respondents were men (*n* = 38) and 65 percent were women (*n* = 71). The disparity is due to the fact that it was extremely difficult for the Arab interviewers to catch male household heads at home. A key difference between the two populations was the age structure. The Arab population was young — 69

TABLE 7.   **Residential Patterns of Shkhūnāt Wolfson and the Distribution of Interviews**

Block	Arab Residents	Arab Residents Interviewed	Jewish Residents	Jewish Residents Interviewed	Empty	Mixed Couple	Total
3	23	6	16	8	8	2	53
4	29	11	9	7	1	1	40
5	8	4	7	0[a]	1	—	16
6	25	14	3	3	—	—	28
7	17	8	15	9	6	1	39
8	21	10	7	6	—	—	28
36	11	11	31	16	—	—	42
40	18	10	25	11	3	—	46
44	23	11	17	8	6	1	47
46	1	1	15	7	—	—	16
55	11	8	41	19	3	1	56
57	46	14	2	2	—	—	48
Unknown		1[b]					
Total	233	109	188	96			

Source: Wolfson neighborhood survey conducted by author and Oren Rechman.

[a]I was unable to arrange interviews with any of the Jewish residents of this building. One interview was conducted, but the respondent's understanding of Hebrew was so poor that it was excluded from the final analysis because many questions were unanswered. Several other residents were either mentally incapacitated or known drug addicts.

[b]One of the questionnaires lacks the building code, but it was included in the analysis anyway. It would have been from Block 4, 36, 40, or 44.

percent under forty, 25 percent between forty and fifty-nine, and only 6 percent over sixty. The Jewish population, by comparison, was elderly — only 23 percent under forty, 30 percent between forty and fifty-nine, and 47 percent over sixty (see table 8).

About 90 percent of the Arab respondents were married, with an average family size of three children. Widows or widowers accounted for only 6 percent of the respondents, while an additional 4 percent were divorced. Sixty-eight percent of Jewish respondents were married, with an average family size of four children. Widows or widowers accounted for 25 percent of respondents, while divorcees numbered 5 percent. About 53 percent of Arab children were under the age of 14 compared to only 18 percent of Jewish children. In both communities, it was common for children to remain at home until their middle to late twenties. Fifty-seven percent of Arab and 55 percent of Jewish respondents described themselves as preserving some traditions or customs regarding religious observance, while an additional 19 percent of Arab and 29 percent of Jewish respondents described themselves as religious, preserving all traditions.[33] Twenty percent of Arab and 22 percent of Jewish parents had tried to pass on strict religious observance to their children, while 54 percent of Arab and 63 percent of Jewish parents had tried do teach their children to preserve some traditions or customs. While 10 percent of Arab and 16 percent of Jewish respondents described themselves as secular or humanist, only 8 percent of Arab and 13 percent of Jewish parents wanted to transmit that orientation to their children.

Arab men were employed in four major occupational categories: professional/management (15 percent), skilled industry/crafts (19 percent), services/sales (28 percent), and unskilled labor (17 percent). Most of the Jewish men were retired (35 percent), a result of the greater relative proportion of Jewish neighborhood residents over sixty. Of those still employed, 11 percent were in services/sales, 8 percent in professional/management, and 9 percent each in skilled industry/crafts, clerical/public service, and unskilled labor. Seventeen percent of Jewish men were unemployed at the time of the survey, compared to 10 percent of Arab men. Most of the women were housewives — 72 percent of Arab and 69 percent of Jewish women. Eleven percent of the women in each group were employed in professional or management positions. In Acre as a whole, 33 percent of Jews and 40 percent of Arabs were employed in industrial occupations, while 18 percent of Jews and 11 percent of Arabs were employed in professional and managerial positions (for Israeli Jews as a whole the figures were 24 percent and 30 percent, respectively).[34] Two-career families were rare in both groups — only ten Jewish and fourteen Arab households.

In Acre overall, the average annual income of Arab households was

TABLE 8. Selected Characteristics of the Neighborhood Sample

	Arab		Jew	
	N	%	N	%
Age				
Over 60	7	6	45	47
40–59	27	25	29	30
Under 40	75	69	22	23
Occupation				
Men				
Professional/management	14	15	5	8
Skilled industries/crafts	18	19	6	9
Services/sales	26	28	7	11
Unskilled labor	16	17	6	9
Retired	2	2	23	35
Unemployed	9	10	11	17
Women				
Housewife	65	72	62	69
Professional/management	10	11	10	11
Annual Income				
More than NIS 24,000	11	10	5	5
NIS 18,001–24,000	18	17	7	7
NIS 12,001–18,000	37	34	16	17
NIS 6,001–12,000	38	35	48	50
Under NIS 6,000	4	4	20	21
Education				
Men				
Some higher education	7	7	6	9
9–12 years	49	50	32	47
0–8 years	41	42	31	44
Women				
Some higher education	7	7	9	9
9–12 years	58	54	37	40
0–8 years	41	39	45	49
Home ownership				
Own home	95	87	50	52
Rent privately	12	11	2	2
Rent from Amidar	2	2	44	46
Home satisfies own/family's needs				
Yes	62	56	73	76
No	46	42	23	24
Prefer to stay	57	52	15	16
Prefer to leave	38	35	79	82
Neighborhood as a place to live				
Good	87	80	23	23
Bad/horrible	18	16	67	70

Source: Wolfson neighborhood survey conducted by author and Oren Rechman.

NIS 6,700, while for Jewish households annual income averaged NIS 11,800 (compared to a national Jewish average of NIS 14,100).[35] Jewish families living in Wolfson fared worse than the average Jewish household in Acre, with 21 percent earning less than NIS 6,000 annually, another 50 percent earning NIS 6,001 to 12,000, and 17 percent earning NIS 12,001 to 18,000. Arab households, in contrast, fared better than both the average Arab household in Acre and their Jewish neighbors in Wolfson, with 35 percent earning NIS 6,001 to 12,000 annually, 34 percent earning NIS 12,001 to 18,000, and an additional 17 percent earning NIS 18,001 to 24,000.

Educational levels were similar for the two populations. Of the Arab men, 42 percent had zero to eight years of schooling, 50 percent had nine to twelve years, and 7 percent had some form of higher education. Forty-four percent of Jewish men had zero to eight years of schooling, 47 percent had nine to twelve years, and 9 percent had some higher education. For women, the younger age of Arab women was reflected in their greater rate of secondary education. Thirty-nine percent had zero to eight years of schooling, 54 percent had nine to twelve years, and 7 percent had some form of higher education. Among Jewish women, 49 percent had zero to eight years, 40 percent had nine to twelve years, and 9 percent had some higher education.

Most of the Jewish respondents had immigrated to Israel between 1946 and 1965, with 23 percent arriving between 1951 and 1955 and 36 percent between 1961 and 1965.[36] Fifty-two percent of them came directly to Acre to live upon their arrival in Israel. About 24 percent remained in Haifa or were sent elsewhere in the north of the country prior to their move to Acre. The remainder were sent to either the central or south region upon arrival and moved to Acre later. Most of the Jewish households moved to Acre between 1948 and 1967 (87 percent), a period that coincided with the major waves of immigration. Only seven households out of ninety-four had moved to Acre in the 1980s.[37] About 30 percent of the Jewish respondents were housed initially in one of the three transit camps, 19 percent had found housing in Mandate Acre, and 25 percent had lived in the eastern neighborhoods; only 7 percent reported living in the Old City. Fifty-eight percent of respondents had moved to Wolfson in the 1960s, 19 percent in the 1970s, and 22 percent in the 1980s.

Jewish respondents who came to Wolfson during the 1960s reported a variety of reasons for their move. Some had no choice, for the transit camp at Mishmar Ha'Yam was torn down to make way for a light industry zone. As one respondent noted, "They dismantled the neighborhood in order to build factories." Others moved to Wolfson because of the quality of the housing available there. "It was the most prestigious neighborhood in Acre, so it was an honor to come to live in Wolfson," one woman explained. Others were interested in leaving the Old City. "All the Jews left the Old City. I remained the solitary Jew, so I moved," a Mizraḥi woman stated. For those who were living in the huts in the eastern neighborhoods, Wolfson was a major improvement in living conditions. A Mizraḥi man reported that he and his family were living in a shack of thirty-six square meters. He made an agreement with Amidar to move to Wolfson in order to increase his living space. For many residents, the move to Wolfson occurred because that was the housing Amidar assigned to them.

Those who had moved to Wolfson during the 1970s were still drawn by the quality of the housing stock. "It was a prestigious, pretty, central neighborhood, comfortable apartments," stated a Mizraḥi woman. Others described it as a wonderful place or reported that they liked the apartments. Some families that had lived in Mandate Acre changed apartments in order to increase their living space and gain newer housing. Most of the residents who reported moving to Wolfson in the 1980s did so because they were given housing there by Amidar. A few respondents reported that they had either purchased an apartment from their parents at half price or were living there for free because the apartment belonged to a parent or in-law.

Almost 63 percent of the Palestinian respondents were born in Acre. Of the remainder, 13 percent had moved to Acre during the 1940s, 3 percent during the 1950s, 3 percent during the 1960s, 7 percent during the 1970s, and 12 percent during the 1980s. Those not born in Acre had come from Haifa and its environs, Kufr Yassif, ShefarʿAm, or another village in the north. The arrival of Arabs in Shkhūnāt Wolfson was relatively late: 16 percent had moved to Wolfson in the 1960s, 17 percent in the 1970s, and 67 percent in the 1980s. Most of the Arab respondents had moved from the Old City to Wolfson. A few people had come from the Mandate City, the northern neighborhoods, or Makr, a village five kilometers east of Acre.

The families who came to the neighborhood in the 1960s often cited housing collapse as their reason for moving. "We had a house in Old Acre, but the house collapsed and we escaped from the danger to Wolfson," reported one man. "The houses collapsed. It was the first block that was built, there was no electricity, no water, and no Jews and no Arabs, just us," an Arab woman remembered. Others moved to the neighborhood because of special opportunities made available by the municipal authorities. "They gave homes in Wolfson to teachers at low prices, and I'm a teacher," declared one woman. Another volunteered, "It was the municipality's idea. They presented to young couples the possibility of living outside the Old City. The municipality took their homes, including my parents' place, and that is how they got the Khan al Umdan."[38]

Of those respondents who came to Wolfson during the 1970s and 1980s, the most commonly cited reason for the move was marriage. It remains the norm for young Arab couples to live with the groom's parents for several years after marriage. In the villages, an additional set of rooms or a floor may be added to the parents' home or the young couple will build their own structure on the same plot of family land. In the Old City, however, Arab residents are not allowed to add onto existing homes; in fact, it is almost impossible to get building permits to make needed repairs on fallen walls and roofs. There is no available land for new building. Thus, young couples have few choices — live in what are usually overcrowded family quarters or move out of the Old City and rent or purchase housing elsewhere in Acre. Other individuals mentioned the poor conditions and crowding in the Old City. "The only reason was the sewage in the Old City, which caused disturbance despite the fact that the house there was much more beautiful and spacious than here," notes a woman. Others purchased in Wolfson because they could afford the price of the apartments. The municipality continued to "encourage" certain families to vacate historic buildings in the Old City. "Our house was the 'Ajun palace, and they took it in return for us living somewhere other than the 'Ajun palace," an Arab man reported.

Eighty-seven percent of Arab respondents owned their apartments, and an additional 11 percent rented from private owners. Fifty-two percent of Jewish respondents owned their apartments, while 45 percent rented from Amidar, the national housing authority. When asked if their home satisfied their needs and those of their families, 56 percent of Arabs and 76 percent of Jews responded affirmatively, while 42 percent of Arabs and 24 percent of Jews responded that it did not satisfy at all. Yet, when asked which they would prefer, to leave or stay in the neighborhood, 52 percent of Arabs preferred to stay and 35 percent preferred to leave, compared to 16 percent of Jews who would stay and 82 percent who would leave. Only 23 percent of Jewish respondents saw Shkhūnāt Wolfson as a good place to live, compared to 80 percent of Arab respondents. Fully 70 percent of Jewish respondents saw the neighborhood as a bad or horrible place to live (compared to only 16 percent of Arab respondents).

Part of the reason why Jewish residents felt so negative about the neighborhood may relate to their relative lack of family and friendship connections with other residents. Eighty percent of the Jewish respondents had no members of either their family or their spouse's family living in the neighborhood. Of those who had family living elsewhere in

Acre, it was usually either children only (32 percent) or siblings only (18 percent). Twenty-five percent of Jewish respondents had no family members or in-laws living in Acre. When asked how many of their friends live in the neighborhood, 65 percent of Jewish respondents reported none. Jewish respondents knew fewer neighborhood residents by name — 39 percent knew one to ten people, 17 percent knew eleven to thirty people, and 14 percent knew the names of all their neighbors. Concerning when they were in need of help, 39.5 percent of Jewish respondents reported that they did not seek assistance from any of their neighbors, 25 percent reported turning sometimes to Jewish and sometimes to Arab neighbors, and 27 percent turned usually to Jewish neighbors.

The Arab residents reported rich and varied family connections in the neighborhood. Only 17 percent had no family or in-laws living there. Others reported siblings, parents, aunts, uncles, and cousins. The same held true for family members living elsewhere in Acre. Only 10 percent of Arab respondents had no family or in-laws living in Acre. With regard to friends in the neighborhood, only 23 percent said that none of their friends lived there. Fifty-seven percent had half or fewer of their friends in Wolfson, while 12 percent had more than half and 7 percent reported that all of their friends lived in Wolfson. Arab respondents knew many more neighborhood residents by name. Fifteen percent reported knowing 11 to 30 people, 15 percent knew 31 to 60 people, 12 percent knew 101 to 200 people, 12 percent knew more than 500 people, and 15 percent knew many or the majority of residents. Concerning when they were in need of assistance, only 19 percent of Arab respondents said that they never turned to neighbors for help. Forty-seven percent reported that they usually turned to Arab neighbors, while another 22 percent responded that they sometimes turned to Jewish and sometimes to Arab neighbors.

When asked whether they initiate joint activities with other Wolfson residents, 64 percent of Arab and 85 percent of Jewish respondents said never, 17 percent of Arab and 6 percent of Jewish respondents answered seldom, and 16 percent of Arab and 7 percent of Jewish respondents reported often. Arab respondents reported participating in activities such as sharing child care, helping with household repairs, caring for the sick or elderly, and attending family meetings. For Jewish respondents, helping with household repairs was the only area with any significant level of joint participation. When asked if they would be interested in participating in joint activities with the Arab residents in the neighborhood, no Jewish respondent was very interested, 4 percent were sometimes interested, 16 percent were not much interested, and 79.5 percent were not at all interested. This contrasts with 21.1 percent of Arab respondents who were very interested, 26 percent who were sometimes interested, 15 percent who were not much interested, and 34 percent

who were not at all interested in participating in joint activities with
Jewish neighborhood residents.

Wolfson residents, both Arab and Jewish, were unanimous in feeling that their neighborhood's needs and interests were not being represented by the major political actors — the mayor, the municipal council,
the Workers' Council (Histadrut), and the MATNAS (cultural center) —
in the community (see table 9). Arab residents conceded that the municipal council represents the neighborhood a little (32 percent of responses
compared to 3 percent of Jewish responses). While Jewish residents
believed that Project Van Leer did not represent them (46 percent said

TABLE 9. Perceptions of Problems in Wolfson and the Locus for Change

	Arab		Jew	
	N	(%)	N	(%)
Reasons for problems				
Mixed neighborhood	1	1	22	23
Resident neglect	21	21	10	11
Municipal neglect	18	18	2	2
Resident and municipal neglect	31	30	2	3
Mixed neighborhood and other	8	8	45	48
Represents neighborhood's needs and interests				
Mayor				
None or little	96	95	83	91
Good or most	5	5	8	9
Municipal council				
None or little	95	95	87	97
Good or most	5	5	3	3
Workers' Council				
None or little	89	96	89	99
Good or most	4	4	1	1
MATNAS				
None or little	94	100	91	100
Good or most	0	0	0	0
Project Van Leer				
None or little	29	28	44	72
Good or most	75	72	15	25
Who must initiate change				
Municipality	18	17	39	41
Residents	16	15	6	6
Municipality and other agents	58	53	44	47

Source: Wolfson neighborhood survey conducted by author and Oren Rechman.

not at all and 26 percent said a little), Arab residents felt the opposite, with 46 percent saying that it represented them a good deal and 26 percent saying that it represented them the most. When asked why the neighborhood had problems, Jewish residents overwhelmingly pointed to it being a mixed neighborhood (71 percent included this in their responses), thus implicitly blaming their Arab neighbors, while Arab residents were more likely to point to neglect by residents (21 percent), neglect by the municipality (18 percent), or both (30 percent). When asked who must initiate change to improve the neighborhood, 41 percent of Jewish respondents said the municipality, compared to only 17 percent of Arab respondents. Arab respondents were more likely to see combined resident and municipality action as required (36 percent).

The decision to mix Arab and Jewish residents was taken initially by the municipality. It comes as no surprise, therefore, that Jewish residents blamed the municipality for the current situation in Wolfson. Furthermore, the emphasis on the municipality can be understood better when one considers how it was making use of the neighborhood in its efforts to attract investment opportunities to Acre. Shkhūnāt Wolfson was a useful symbol of *dū-qīyūm* (coexistence) that local officials could parade before visiting foreign dignitaries and potential benefactors. As one resident rather cynically noted when commenting on a neighborhood fight: "And the mayor tried to close the matter so they wouldn't say there's quarreling here in the neighborhood. They want to show that we live in peace."

Neighborhood Encounters

> Demographer's defeat: invisibility powder. Rubbed into the skin of a million Ahmeds bussed in from the Territories. Into the skin, the hair, the kefiya, the shirt. For Arabs should be worked but not seen. And not too thrifty with the powder, please. Do you want an Arab button or shirtsleeve molesting a Jewish street? Not a sleeve not a sleeve not a sleeve — that's the new song of the irredentists. (Silk 1988)

For many Israeli Jews, their experience of the Palestinian other is not direct. They learn about Palestinians secondhand through the newspapers, the television, radio reports, or school presentations. Residential segregation throughout the country helps create distance and otherness and prevents recognition. With separate school systems, Israeli Jews may have their first contact with a Palestinian when they are adults at a university or workplace. Palestinian construction workers, mechanics, domestic help, and restaurant workers might as well be invisible. The Palestinians encountered while waiting for buses, in lines at banks, or in offices are to be ignored or avoided. Army service may provide direct contact, but it is a contact steeped in violence that more often than not dehumanizes the other instead of making her or him human. Working for the same employer may bring Jews into direct contact with Palestinians, but it is uneasy contact at best. Weingrod finds in his study of a Jerusalem factory that "talking politics" was avoided at work because it damages or destroys cooperation between workers (Romann and Weingrod 1991, 138). Even when closer relations develop between coworkers, asymmetry exists. Jewish workers may visit the homes of their Palestinian friends, but Palestinians visiting Jewish homes might raise questions on the part of family and neighbors and usually is not acceptable.

For many Israeli Palestinians, their experience of the Jewish other is usually more direct. While their villages and schools are detached from Israeli Jewish society, they still confront the power of the Israeli state in their daily lives. They learn about Jews through encounters with policemen, General Security Service (GSS) agents, and government officials who often hinder more than they help. Working for the same employer (usually Jewish) for them means slower advancement, less job security, and having to endure the sniping and insults of Jewish workers. When there is an "incident," they are automatically under suspicion if they are nearby and they will be picked up and questioned by police. Standing in line for buses, banking services, or bill paying at government offices, they must endure the stares and sometimes open hostility of the Jewish people around them.[39] Arab students learn either to forget about careers in defense-related industries (for which they will not be granted security clearances) or to plan on emigration in order to pursue their interests in a foreign country. Traveling out of the country involves extensive searches (including a body search) at airports or border crossings, while around them Israeli (and non-Israeli) Jews are asked a few questions and waved through. As Shipler (1986, 429) notes:

> Just being an Arab in appearance is to wear a badge that commands the attention of the security services. Showing the official ID card with "Arab" written in the space labeled "Nationality" is to announce, "Suspect me. Watch me. Check me. Search me. Question me."

These experiences of otherness are underscored in the "public transcript" of Israeli Jews and the "hidden transcript" of Israeli Palestinians (using Scott's [1990] terms). In the public transcript, Arabs only understand force: they are "guests" and must learn how to behave properly; they cannot be trusted; they are primitive and violent people who will serve you coffee and then stab you in the back.[40] "Arab work" is work done poorly or dirty, boring work no one wants to do. Children may be told not to do things "like an Arab." In the hidden transcript, Jews are aliens and outsiders who don't belong and never will. They are interlopers who will disappear in time as other conquerors did. They lack values and behave immorally. They are cold and inhospitable and cannot be trusted. They are all soldiers, violent and brutal, and racists.

The popular images of Palestinians harbored by Jews and of Jews by Palestinians are largely based on situations of residential and educational segregation. The Wolfson quarter, however, is integrated — Jews and Palestinians live in the same buildings, share the same entrances, and dwell on the same floors. In addition, their children may attend integrated kindergarten facilities, participate in integrated courses through Project Van Leer, or play together at the children's resource center or outdoors in the open spaces of the neighborhood. They live a much more complex reality than other Israelis and Palestinians, whose contact with members of the other group may be extremely limited. While contact in and of itself does not mitigate stereotypes, the Jewish and Palestinian residents of Wolfson could see themselves as a community vis-à-vis other neighborhoods in Acre and the municipality. All residents suffer from the municipality's neglect of the quarter and from the quarter's negative image in Acre. Yet the experience of otherness often outweighs the similarities between the communities and precludes recognition of common goals and interests.

The local community has been an important focal point in constructing identity for both Israeli Jews and Palestinians. Jewish life in the *shtetls* (ghettos) of Eastern Europe and the *mellahs* (Jewish quarters) of North Africa provided a measure of autonomy and recognition in the face of problematic interactions with the surrounding non-Jewish population. For Palestinians, the village has been important in framing their identity within the constraints imposed by the Israeli state (Haberer 1985, 203–4). Israeli Palestinians whose villages were destroyed in 1948 still identify themselves as being from that place — Sukhmata, Ikrit, BirʿAm — and these identities are passed on to children and even grandchildren. The neighborhood is home, a territory to be secured and protected against outsiders. It is a space in which people want to feel comfortable and accepted. What happens to notions of security, autonomy, and recognition when the home space is shared with members of a group that is perceived as the enemy, as is the case with the Wolfson neighborhood?

Some Jewish residents of Wolfson echo their fellow countrymen in their images of and complaints about Arabs. Plotkin (1991) calls this "enclave consciousness," a sense of group solidarity through which the community becomes estranged and alienated from other communities. People see their neighborhood as home territory, a space that has to be defended from the alien threats that surround it. For Jewish residents of

Wolfson, their home space has been invaded; they are living in a no-man's-land where home is no longer safe and secure. Two Mizraḥi men who had lived in the Wolfson neighborhood since the 1960s expressed their feelings as follows:

The Arab smiles in your face and is willing to stab you with a knife in the back. The Jews are a masochistic people — only with blows do they understand. Once Pharaoh, once Holocaust, and today we're returning to hard times. It hurts that a soldier stands trial after he tried to defend himself. My son grew up with an Arab child (they're the same age). My son went to the army, returned, and has no work. The Arab child worked, saved money, and traveled overseas to study medicine.

In my opinion, if you give more, more will be demanded. I read the newspaper and I can't look at them. It hurts what they do and more come with complaints. . . . It's *our* block. The Arabs say that Acre is a holy place for them, therefore they need to conquer and buy it. To buy house by house in Acre and so to fulfill a holy commandment. Pay attention. They buy stores for clothing, shoes, for food, restaurants, barbers, house-hold goods, whatnot? Doctors, lawyers, teachers. Where will you find a country with democracy like this?

In these narratives, Arabs are violent and untrustworthy; they hate Jews and would kill them if they could. The right of Jewish privilege is unequivocal — it's "our block, our neighborhood, our country." Many residents reported being very upset that their Arab neighbors would grill outdoors, make noise, or listen to the radio on Shabbat or Jewish holidays.[41] What Jewish residents object to is that such activities by their Arab neighbors, formerly done indoors and quietly, are now done openly and outdoors, publicly marking their neighborhood space as "not Jewish." Paternalism is evident in the notion that Jews give to Arabs, while Arabs are represented as ungrateful, constantly demanding more, and complaining (much like an ungrateful child). Jewish residents reported that it hurt them that Arabs don't serve in the Israeli army.[42] The Arabs are perceived as benefiting from nonservice; they advance more rapidly in Israeli society than do Jewish youths who lose time to army service.[43] Jewish fears of Arabs are on the surface, not hidden away. The Arabs are overwhelming the Jews, slowly and insidiously; they are conquering, taking back the land. In Acre, especially, Jewish residents are very worried about the "Arabization" of the city. Their fears for their city are reflections of government fears about the Galilee region as a whole — fears that spawned the intensified "Judaize the Galilee" settlement campaign in the late 1970s. The Jewish residents present themselves as victims again — of their refusal to be a people of blows, of their adherence to the standards of democracy.

For about half of the Jewish respondents, one of the most important problems with their neighborhood was the Arabs. A Mizraḥi man said, "The Arabs aren't considerate; they grill meat on Shabbat and holidays." Another person reported, "The Arabs, they come in masses. Someone needs to solve that problem." For a third, the problem was "the Arabs' behavior. There need to be laws that forbid them to make prayers outside." A Mizraḥi woman blamed the municipality's neglect on the Arabs. "Because Arabs live here, they [the municipal authorities] don't take care of the neighborhood. They know Arabs live in filth, they're used to it." For more than half the residents, it mattered a great deal that their neighborhood was mixed. Residents were split between seeing integrated living as having little influence on their lives and seeing it as the cause of many problems and tensions.

The Arab residents of the neighborhood were often described by Jewish residents as *kafrīm* (villagers) who had come to the neighborhood in *hamūlōt* (clans).[44] They were presented as uncultured people who needed to learn basic urban life skills. Jewish residents complained about the traditional wedding ceremonies that are still held, with the groom brought on horseback and several days of feasting, visiting, and celebration. A Mizraḥi man commented, "They should get married modestly. They should integrate to an urban mentality about life." A Mizraḥi woman complained:

> A village mentality. *Hamūlōt* sit on the grass, nuts, noise, roasting coffee, choking smoke, smell. . . . If you go to them, they say, 'Do what you want.' Radio, music in loud tones. They pour water and dirt on the laundry and the baby's diapers. I turned to the head of the *va'ad* [building committee] and he told me: 'We'll do death to you until you leave.' They go down the stairs in clogs — noise to disgust the soul. At wedding times, the noise of *hamūlōt* drumming. A horrible mentality!

According to the Jewish residents, the Arabs were the ones who hung laundry outside to dry, spoiling the block's outward appearance. They were the ones who didn't properly dispose of their garbage. They sometimes threw the garbage from the windows. Their children would play outside on the grass and make noise and break windows. When asked what they would like to better understand about their Arab neighbors, many residents responded "nothing," but some said that they already knew the Arabs from Morocco, or Tunis, or Iraq, or Egypt — all Arabs were the same. This statement reflects the Israeli government's stubborn insistence on nonrecognition of the Palestinians and its continued attempts to lump them into the larger category of Arabs in its political dealings.[45] It also reflects the speaker's own experience of the ideology of absorption in Israel, where all Jews theoretically are equal (but in fact are not).

While a number of residents used stereotypical images of Arabs to frame their protests, other Jewish residents did not like their new Arab neighbors because they saw them as different in terms of their class status. As one young woman, born in Israel, explained, "With the very first Arabs, there was no hatred because they were more cultured and also there wasn't as much tension in Israel as now. Now the first Arabs sold, and in their places other Arabs came who lack culture, and correspondingly the building tension in Israel caused tension and relations of hatred." A Mizraḥi man commented, "The Arabs aren't happy with the situation that's formed, that uncultured Arabs and delinquent Jews are coming." A Mizraḥi woman noted, "At first a small number of Arabs came, but cultured intellectuals. Afterward Amidar began to evict Arabs from the Old City to the neighborhood. In their footsteps came family hamūlas from the villages. The educated Arabs fled, the Jews began to leave, quarrels broke out between Jews." From this last explanation, it becomes clear that both upper-class Arab and Jewish families began to leave Wolfson because they did not want to live with Arab (and Jewish) families of lower-class status. Smooha (1992, 34) notes that most Israelis—76 percent of his Arab and 89 percent of his Jewish respondents—assigned themselves to the middle or upper classes when asked to choose where they belong. Even people who belong to the lowest occupational strata see themselves as being middle or upper class. The Jewish residents of Wolfson, however, are viewed by other residents of Acre as being lower class. The Arab presence in the neighborhood allows those Jewish residents who remain to blame their lowered living standards on the Arabs rather than recognizing the contradiction between the status they aspire to and their actual living conditions.

Jewish immigrants to Israel were promised by the government that they at last would be secure from persecution and harm. Israel was the Jewish state and the ancestral homeland. Many immigrants believed that their lives in Israel would be lived in a Jewish atmosphere. The structures of the state were intended to favor its Jewish citizens. The immigrants' desires for security, affiliation, recognition, and autonomy were all to be fulfilled by the Jewish state. The reality for the Jewish residents of Wolfson is a far cry from what they were promised. The Jewish atmosphere they should be able to enjoy is marred by the smells of grilling meat, by the sounds of Arabic music, conversation, and merriment. As a Mizraḥi woman complained, "At holidays, they don't think (and maybe it's not on purpose). They light fires, radio, a lot of commotion. Guests come—close family members from the villages—noise, they think the neighborhood is theirs, they feel safe, they sing, they drum until late." The space of the neighborhood is supposed to be a Jewish space. As one Ashkenazi man said, "Wolfson gave the money to Jews. Why did they give to Arabs? The Sōkhnūt [Jewish Agency] could have bought the apartments to give to new immigrants." A Mizraḥi woman who had lived in Wolfson since the 1960s declared, "In Wolfson, you feel like in the diaspora. You really don't feel here like in the country of Israel. There's nowhere to go out to, no society, a most primitive neighborhood with regard to lifestyle." Another Ashkenazi man, however, noted that not all the Jewish residents disliked the neighborhood, with an oblique reference to "certain" Jews (Mizraḥim). "I personally don't speak, don't argue, but there are Jews for whom it's very communal here. You feel here in the neighborhood like in a refugee camp."

Many Jewish residents express anger that the Arab residents of the neighborhood are heard and seen. In this, they reflect what they have learned from the public transcript regarding Arabs: they should be silent and invisible. Subordinate, minority populations are not supposed to be active and vocal; they should not attract attention. In these notions of what it means to be subordinate, one can see reflections of the Jewish experience in the diaspora, where it was better not to draw attention to oneself. One Mizraḥi man proposed the following solution to the problem of "filth" in the neighborhood: "They [the authorities] should bring ten trucks to load the Arabs and evacuate them." While on the surface this remark appears intolerant and racist, there is a deeper level of irony in his comment. Mizraḥi Jews themselves were loaded onto trucks at the Haifa port, without being asked where they wanted to live, and driven to the *mōshāvīm* (a collective agricultural settlement), where they were, in some cases, unceremoniously dumped and left to fend for themselves.[46] If Arab Jews (the Mizraḥim) are deserving of such treatment, then so too are other Arabs.

Integrated living baldly exposes the dilemma of the Mizraḥi Jew in Israel. To be accepted as fully Israeli, he must leave his Arab culture and language behind and adopt Western values and behaviors. The promised reward for making the transition is full participation in the political and economic system. The Mizraḥi Jewish residents of Wolfson have done part of this — very few of them reported being able to speak Arabic. They complained bitterly about the lack of culture and education among their Arab neighbors. Yet, the Mizraḥi residents of Wolfson are not being rewarded. They live in a neighborhood that is now majority Arab, in a city that is mixed. They work in low-level positions in local industries that are prone to layoffs and closures. Their children will never study at the university or become professionals. They look around them and perceive their

Arab neighbors benefiting more from the state than they do. As one
Mizraḥi woman saw it:

> In our time there was no project [Van Leer], they didn't build
> us games, they didn't help our children. To Arabs they do it all.
> They raise up their heads for them. . . . They receive chil-
> dren's allowances. They live only from the children's allow-
> ances. . . . The hard situation in the country caused people to
> reduce their families, but the Arabs continue to give birth. And
> it comes out that really they wanted to help Jews with children
> and they help Arabs. They give them money to raise children,
> and those children come out terrorists. To Jews, there's fewer
> children. If one is killed, they're alone, not like the Arabs who
> have numerous [children].

A Mizraḥi man noted that it hurt him that Arabs were given so many
opportunities. Overseas no one provided opportunities for him, so why
should his government now do that for others? Another man complained, "Jewish factory owners [mostly Ashkenazim] themselves say it's
preferable to employ Arabs. They're cheap and they don't stick you with
a month of them leaving for reserve duty." Shipler notes that Israeli
Jews, when referring to Israeli Arabs, often couple rights as citizens with
obligations, implying that Arabs must earn the rights of citizenship
(1986, 443). The Jewish residents of Wolfson echo this sentiment. Their
children serve in the army; they have fought for the country — what have
the Arab residents done to deserve any rights?

The Palestinian residents counter these Jewish perceptions with
their own reflections on the other, reflections that echo those of their
fellow countrymen as well. The Jews are conquerors, who "ravish" and
"slaughter."

> The Lebanon War — it was the beginning of racism on both
> sides. It was a period of taking away the blindfold and reveal-
> ing what was hidden in hearts. When the Lebanon War started,
> volcanoes of blind hatred and racism erupted from people's
> hearts. The Arabs want to defend the land because it's theirs —
> and the Jews want to conquer it with all their strength. The
> intifada — a spirit of defense and pain for the Arabs, and [in]
> the Jews in a spirit of conquering and repression and ravishing
> and slaughtering. Assassination incidents, killings, and rape
> between the two sides: we hear, see, and read about it every
> day. The situation is very difficult, and something must be done
> to live in greater peace because we want peace and nothing
> else. (Palestinian woman, resident since the 1980s)
>
> Racial prejudice did not exist among Jews but was instilled in
> schools . . . but the intifada affects this because government

policy reflects a people's attitudes so they treat the Arabs by the same logic as the government. (Palestinian man, resident since the 1980s)

War takes away the facade and reveals what is hidden in hearts. The Palestinian residents of Wolfson are aware that they exist in ambiguity — the apparent peace of today can easily shift on the morrow to hatred and hostility. Relationships with Jews that have been slowly built into friendships may vanish overnight if there is a war, a terrorist attack, an incident. The Palestinian speakers noted the influence of both the media and government policy on the ideas and actions of ordinary Israeli Jews. Rather than blaming the Jewish people for their troubles, these residents faulted the government and the media. The state is not a protector of its Palestinian citizens but is itself the source of their difficulties. Killing, rape, and assassination are things people hear, see, and read about every day. Racial prejudice is instilled in school — Jews are using the same logic as their government in how they treat Arabs. For many Palestinians, what was happening in the territories in 1987–89 recalled the events of 1948. The Palestinians are the "defenders" of the land; the Jews are conquerors who repress, ravish, and slaughter. The Palestinian speakers are struggling to change the level of awareness about the conflict in order to prevent a catastrophe like that of 1948. The events of 1948 are mythic, shrouded in the past and in memories. The killings and hatred of 1987–89 were more immediate, beamed into living rooms each evening on the nightly news program. The immediacy of the daily news coverage of the uprising blunted the emotional impact of homes being blown up, people teargassed, and children shot or arrested.

For the Palestinian residents of the neighborhood, the problem was not the Jews but prejudice and discrimination. A woman who had lived in the neighborhood since the 1970s explained, "In my opinion, there are problems between Arabs and Jews because the Jews especially are naturally prejudiced toward Arabs. You can observe this in the simplest problem where they gave us epithets straightaway, calling us Arabs as if this were a swear word." Another woman commented, "Jews feel that an Arab is a stranger or guest, undesired. In every event that happens, a Jewish person says to an Arab, 'Go the Old City,' or he makes noisy steps on the roof at two in the morning." A man noted, "Some Jewish families openly manifest their racial prejudice — 'underworld' [engage in criminal activity] to disturb Arabs." The Palestinian residents do not reject the presence of Jews in the neighborhood in the way that Jewish residents reject the presence of Arabs. The Palestinians are well aware that the neighborhood was better cared for by the municipal authorities when more Jews lived there. One man commented, "If there were 60 percent Jews and 40 percent Arabs, services would be adequate, so I'd prefer there to be a Jewish majority." Another said, "When there were

more Jews in the neighborhood, the municipality looked after it more."
Were the remaining Jewish residents to leave Wolfson, Arab residents
believe the municipality would totally neglect the quarter, similar to the
lack of attention given to the Old City. More than 80 percent of Palestinian residents reported that it didn't matter to them that the neighborhood was mixed. Forty percent saw integrated living as having no influence for the most part on their lives, while more than 38 percent thought
it was causing some problems but also made possible better understanding and cooperation between Arabs and Jews.

A number of Arab residents saw their Jewish neighbors as racists
who teach their children to hate. "The problems spring more from Jewish residents because they have a current of racism in their blood. They
bring up their children from an early age on discrimination, racism, and
hatred of Arabs however they are," one woman commented. A woman
who had lived in the neighborhood since the 1960s declared, "A Jew
does not respect or appreciate an Arab." This lack of respect on the part
of the Jewish residents is felt deeply. One man indicated that he was
willing to respect his Jewish neighbors' lifestyle "on the condition that
there's respect from them, for example, for them not to talk about
stories when he was at war and how many victims were killed and how
the battle was." An Arab man, also a veteran of the 1960s, put the
blame on politicians: "Jews are slaves of propaganda. . . . Therefore the
cause of these problems and conflicts and suspicions is the extreme right
wing Jewish leadership." Another man noted, "Given that a Jew is in his
state, an Arab is a servant to him; even if he be an engineer or doctor,
this is the Jewish perception of him." The Jewish residents are perceived
as bullies, who curse and threaten their Arab neighbors when conflicts
arise. One woman reported that Jewish children (and some mothers)
beat Arab children on the playground. The Jewish neighbors were quick
to call the police on Arabs.

The Israeli state has promised its Arab residents that they have all
the rights and protections of citizenship. The Proclamation of Independence states that the state of Israel "will uphold the full social and
political equality of all its citizens, without distinction of religion, race,
or sex" (Laqueur and Rubin 1984, 127). Yet the Palestinian residents of
Wolfson do not feel like full and equal citizens. They are not secure
because the state apparatus favors its Jewish over its Arab citizens.
"When they [Jews] make disturbances it makes me cry because I don't
know what to do. When I see them through the window beating my child
and I can't protect him, I cry. They always say "Dirty Arab! Stupid
Arab!" and other bad words like *whore*. I can't answer back, so I cry,"
one mother related. Some Palestinian mothers in the neighborhood fear
for their children: "I explain to him [her child] that the state is Jewish

and not ours, and I fear for him about Jews and I don't like him playing with them." Other residents pointed out that the promised equality does not in fact exist. "But there isn't equality in the position of Arabs and Jews. Jews, for instance, receive much more assistance in loans, work positions, education." One man focused on the police and the preferential treatment that the Jewish residents receive: "If an Arab calls the police for whatever reason it takes them about another two hours at least. While, on the other hand, if a Jew calls them up for any reason, the police arrive immediately, with special units to investigate and disturb Arabs as if everything that happens somehow stems from Arabs." Several residents made a connection between army service and the treatment they receive in the neighborhood. A Palestinian man commented: "Because their fathers serve in the army, Jewish children attack Arabs in pretense of the *intifada.*"

The Palestinian residents emphasized the outsider status of the Jews when they reflected on who has rights to the land. "Although the land is our land, and we have a right to it more than all the Jews, they are just refugees in this land," a Palestinian woman declared. Another woman reiterated this theme and linked it to inequality: "They even have greater rights to the land because it's our land and they plundered it. . . . We are the original residents and they are refugees from all over the world." These women inverted the Israeli state's formula that the Jews are the original owners of the land and the Arabs are refugees or migratory peoples who moved into Palestine because of the prosperity the Jews brought.[47] Palestinian residents were upset about the treatment they habitually received at the hands of such state representatives as the Special Units of the police. The Special Unit "treats the Arabs inhumanly and in a bestial fashion without any cause for a problem of any legal infringement. For example, when there's a small fight or disagreement, they round up all the Arabs, even if they are passersby or onlookers, and they book them — penal or civil or warnings — or they create reasons from nothing," one woman reported.

Integrated living also exposes the dilemma of Israeli Palestinians. As non-Jews, they are second-class citizens. If they were living in one of the villages or the Old City, they would not necessarily be reminded on a daily basis of this situation. Living with Jews, however, means that they are confronted daily with their lower status. Their awareness of and sensitivity to the religious beliefs of their Jewish neighbors (such as not grilling or turning on the radio on Yom Kippur) is not rewarded with an equal attention to their religious beliefs and customs. "They should understand that we are like them, and when they were fasting they didn't allow us to turn on the radio, but during our fast, and when we'd turn on to the prayers, they tried once to prevent us by calling a policeman," one woman reported. As Israeli citizens, like all others, Israeli Palestinians feel that they should be free to express their own culture, advance economically, and express their opinions, personal or political. They want to live in peace, to know that every quarrel between children will not escalate into a nationalist struggle between adults. Attalah Mansour, an Israeli Palestinian writer, captured the quandary of Israeli Jews vis-à-vis Israeli Palestinians: "Instead of stepping on the snake that threatened them, they swallowed it. Now they have to live with it, or die from it" (quoted in Elon 1971, 31). The Palestinian residents would like their Jewish neighbors to learn to live with them — to accord them equal treatment, respect, and peace.

Remembering Violence to Maintain Boundaries

> To the Israeli Jews, the Palestinians threaten to take away the present; to the Palestinians, the Israeli Jews have taken away the past. (Xenos 1989, 233)

Here they're raising new terrorists. Today they're fighting on the border. Tomorrow we'll need to fight in the midst of Israel. I'm for transfer. I came from Romania because there they yelled, "You're Jews." For what do I need to live here with Arabs? So they will call me "Jew! Jew!" I fought and I was wounded for the country — so I could arrive at a situation like this? This is our country. Move them all [the Arabs] and so the Jewish unemployed will know there's no Muhammed who will do the work. Everyone will begin to work. You can't flee from reality, those who hate Israel. You need to make order in the country once for always. I've passed so much in my life. I've seen many different things, but this atrocity I've never seen. I've suffered enough in my life — so Arabs will call me "Jew"??? (Ashkenazi man, resident since the 1960s)

This man clearly states that Israel belongs only to the Jews: "This is our country." He personally fought and was wounded for this land, thus proving his right to ownership. For him, the Jews are active appropriators of the land, independent, omnipotent selves. The Arabs may do all the work, but work alone does not translate into a claim on the land. Arabs, as obstacles, can (and should) be removed; they will be replaced with Jews who will work once there's no "Muhammed." Jews are the masters, while the Arabs as workers are dependent on the goodwill of these masters for their continued existence on this land. Arabs as a category are other, those who hate Israel, terrorists who will strike from "the midst of Israel" at the rightful occupants of the land, who are already fighting on the borders. This fear of being engulfed from within (and thus losing an independent existence) is echoed in the speaker's anger about being called "Jew." He remembers his previous experience in Romania, where he was objectified and named "Jew" by more powerful others. In his country, it is an atrocity that Arabs — the powerless — would dare to "name" him.

> Tensions began before 1948. Then the 1948 war, the Israeli occupation. [Then] 1982 — the Lebanon War; the inhabitants of Lebanon are pretty much all people who were expelled from Palestine [Israel]. These and other events led to: lack of respect — Jews slag off at Arabs about everything; lack of understanding of customs and traditions; blind hatred; from the days of Ben Gurion, racial prejudice — he didn't want to carry an ID card with Arabic written on it. The *intifada* has led to the deterioration of the national economy . . . and has increased the blind hatred and tensions between the two sides. However, the Jews forget that we are good citizens. We didn't take part in demonstrations or wars which are directed against our brothers and on a racist basis. (Palestinian man, resident since the 1960s)

This man has no need to establish his claims to the land; his knowledge of the land and its history demonstrate that he has lived here and had ownership. He knows that tensions between Arabs and Jews began before 1948, before there was such a thing as Israel. The Israeli war in 1948 brought not a Jewish return to the homeland but occupation — an occupation that was taken even further in 1982 when those who were expelled from Palestine again bore the brunt of attacks in Lebanon. He catalogs the sufferings of the dominated: lack of respect, lack of understanding of culture and traditions, blind hatred, and racial prejudice. His is the moral high ground; it is the Jews who are racist. Ben-Gurion himself (to some the revered founding father) wanted to erase Arabness from Israeli society. The Arabs, however, persevere; they remain steadfast. "The Jews forget that we are good citizens." "We" did not take part in "demonstrations or wars which are directed against our brothers and on a racist basis." Implicit in these statements is censure of Israeli society — which claims to be democratic but in practice is not.

Israeli political elites have developed security nationalism as a narrative in which a Jewish self faces off against the Arab other. In this narrative, the Holocaust Jew — embattled victim, martyr, sufferer — has become the trope through which the present experiences of Israelis are comprehended and represented. A narrative is woven in which Jews are only seeking to recover that which they lost thousands of years ago, national sovereignty, a return to the promised land, and thus a return to history. Returning to history, however, is a return to notions of time that are secular and linear, not ritual and sacred. Modern nation-states require notions of secular time. In the drive toward progress and the future, historical narratives and imperatives change. Old enemies may become allies, and old allies may become enemies. Secular time requires a certain ability to forget, an ability that ritual time would deny. The renewed significance of the Holocaust and its associated imagery within Israeli society since 1967 sets up a conflict in the drive toward the future. The Likud governments of Begin and Shamir used the events and experiences of sacred time — Amalek (the original biblical enemy tribe) and the Holocaust — as the lens through which political actions can be understood in the present.[48] Security nationalism came to be grounded in ritual time. New events are interpreted as repetitions of the old history of persecution. Thus, "never again," the notion that Israelis can move to a status wherein they can exist as a nation like all others, has been subverted from within. Linear time, and thus Israel's development as a modern state, have been arrested as sacred time has come to dominate people's understanding of the present and the future. Remembering the future for Israelis is an act of denial, not of affirmation. Yehuda Elkana, himself a survivor of Auschwitz, stated there is "no greater danger for Israel's future than a situation where the Holocaust penetrates the consciousness of the whole Israeli population — including the consciousness of most of the younger generation who have not experienced it." While the whole world "should remember in the future," Israelis "must forget."[49]

Many Israelis have internalized the self/other narrative of Israeli security nationalism. In this narrative of "a land without people, for a people without land," Jewish rights to repossess the land are rooted in the historical moment of their forced expulsion from it two thousand years ago. The Zionist narrative is built on a series of dichotomies: Arab/Jew, East/West, Third World/First World, other/self.[50] In the drive toward state autonomy, there could be no recognition of the Arab other because such recognition would threaten the independence of the new Jewish state. Israeli state elites tried to impose a new hegemonic collective identity on the Jewish immigrants streaming into the country, while the elites conversely worked to fracture the collective Palestinian identity of its Arab citizens. The collective memories, practices, and cultures that sustained Jewish communities through thousands of years were stripped away and replaced with Western notions of secular progress and an ideology of the land; the territory was Judaized, the people de-Judaized (Boyarin 1992, 126). Violence resulted from the clash between the state's attempts to impose a new mode of practice and identity and the attempts by members of different communities to retain older, more fragmented identities and lived experiences. As Connerton notes, the struggle of citizens against state power may involve the "struggle of their memory against forced forgetting" (1989, 15).

In Wolfson, relationships between Palestinian and Jewish residents were generally framed in terms of remembrances of violence. When asked to describe the most significant incidents that had influenced their relations, both groups mentioned wars, the killing of children or soldiers, the *intifada,* and acts of sabotage. The content and context of the remembrances varied, however. When Jewish residents spoke of the killing of children or soldiers, it was in an abstract sense. They did not mention a specific incident. "Now when they hear that soldiers are murdered, they are even happy." "When there is a murder of children and soldiers, it causes them to be happy and celebrate and afterward quarrels develop with Jews." "If a Jew dies or a soldier, they put on music." Only one Jewish resident mentioned the 1989 murder of an Arab youth in the nearby municipal market at the hands of a Jewish man. No mention was made of any effects of Arab deaths at the hands of Israeli soldiers. For the Palestinian residents, remembrances were more specific and localized, although a number of people mentioned the Lebanon War (particularly the Sabra-Shatilla massacre) as the beginning of the deterioration in relations and the *intifada* as the most recent source of tension. Several residents remembered the events of 1970: "the day that Jamal ʿabd al Nasser died there were demonstrations and expressions of mourning in the Old City of Acre and Jewish residents of New Acre performed many provocative acts directed at the Arab residents of the Old City." "When ʿAbd al Nasser died, the Jewish residents were happy and danced. Despite this, I took them refreshments." Others remembered returning to the Old City during the wars of 1967 and 1973 because of neighborhood tensions. Several people mentioned the murder of the Arab youth in the municipal market and said they had feared for their own lives.

One Mizraḥi woman, in detailing the obstacles to friendship between the Jewish and Palestinian residents, stated simply, "Look, it's known they were enemies to Jacob. There is no possibility of joint living. Always Jews hated Arabs and the reverse." The conflict was often presented by Israeli Jews as mythic in proportion, an age-old "war of brothers." A Mizraḥi man explained, "The Talmud tells us there is no trusting in *goyim* (a derogatory Yiddish term for non-Jews), therefore there are discussions and quarrels. Different opinions. With all respect to the desire to live together, it's known always and forever that Jew and Arab hate." In these explanations, violence is naturalized and unavoidable. It is beyond the capacity of individuals to create a different lived experience because the hatred has always existed and always will. Such statements, however, overlook the historical reality that Mizraḥi Jews and

Arabs lived together for thousands of years in relative peace. The creation of the state of Israel broke that pattern of coexistence and produced tensions in Arab countries that resulted in many Mizraḥi Jews being forced to leave their homes and immigrate under duress to Israel.[51] Ammiel Alcalay finds that the more knowledge Mizraḥim have about their past history in their countries of origin the more willing they are to compromise with Palestinians.[52] The anti-Arab attitudes of children in such households are products of their socialization into Israeli society — exposure to the media, schools, and public life — not the outcome of any family history of persecution.

Palestinian residents also spoke of hatred for some Jews, but their narrative of where this hatred comes from is grounded in the specific historical experience of losing their homeland to the Jewish outsiders. It is reinforced by the treatment they have received at the hands of state bureaucracies and authorities. Special police units "hit without cause — they are aggressive toward people in the street without cause, and confrontations without cause. Their behavior is usually in an ugly and inhuman vein." Palestinian residents claimed to be better able to separate the acts of the few from the characterization of the many. "However, when something happens in the West Bank, for example, when many Arabs are killed, we don't pay attention, but when a Jew is killed they hate us as if we were the cause," one man commented. Most important, however, is the profound state of ambivalence in which Palestinians live, torn between loyalty to a state that does not accord them equality and loyalty to their people, to relatives and friends. "The Jews feel that we support those people in the West Bank and that the Arabs are traitors of the state. But the reality is that we are confused to be honest to the state or to our relatives in the West Bank and Lebanon. Here there is a kind of conflict," a woman explained.

Violence in this context plays an important role in maintaining the boundaries and power relationships between the two communities. The dual memory of the Holocaust Jew as victim and hero fractures the state's self/other narrative for some Israelis because "that same figure of victimization that motivates him as a soldier also compels extraordinary sympathy for his defeated enemies, now grasped in the figure of his own people's defeats" (Young 1988, 136).[53] Some Israeli Jews are not comfortable with the reversal of their fortunes from victim to master. By defining Arabs generally and Palestinians specifically as prone to violence and ready to murder any and all Jews without provocation, many Israeli Jews can validate their government's use of force against a subordinate population. In its implementation of policies based on the ideology of security nationalism, the Israeli state is attempting to master violence, to eliminate the unpredictability and accidental character of it. Violence is used against Israeli Palestinians in order to eradicate the possibility of violence against Israeli Jews. Such a strategy can never work, as events in Israel have proven. Despite a pervasive policy of control, individual Palestinians still react to the violence of Israeli policies with their own acts of violence. When the dominant order is based on a system of violence, violence may be seized upon by subordinate groups in their challenges to the accepted frameworks.

For Israeli Palestinians, the violence against them is an affirmation of the rightness of their cause, almost a form of recognition of their existence. In the face of this violence, they can unite. "Jewish people attacked Arabs in the Old City in an attempt supported by the authorities to disperse and dominate them. Despite all this, the dreams of the Jews have dissolved with the unity of the Arabs," one man stated. "The authorities tried to bring in the Special Unit, which is trained to beat, destroy, and dominate. They entered Acre and with all their power set up strict rules affecting the day-to-day life of the people [military rule]. Then we were indeed like the West Bank and Gaza, and we felt that we were not Israelis. Life has become unbearable in the face of the oppression by our brother Jews." The arbitrariness of the violence in their lives produces what Laclau and Mouffe (1985) have called total equivalence, a situation in which all agents of antagonism are rendered equivalent. Individuals who suffer the effects of these antagonisms are rendered the same, regardless of the other elements of their identities. Thus, Israeli Palestinians can come to identify with the Palestinians of the territories because they both are suffering at the hands of Israeli soldiers or police.

Crossing the Border Zone: Can the Walls Come Down?

Crapanzano, in his study of whites in South Africa (1985, xxii), points out that through "waiting in fear" people lose what Keats (in another context) called negative capability, the ability of so negating their own identity that they are open to the complex and shifting reality around them. Instead, they close themselves off, creating circumstances in which the other is not recognized, where he or she becomes both an object to be manipulated and an object to be feared. In Wolfson, many Jewish residents do indeed close themselves off in fear. An Ashkenazi woman reported, "I have never been afraid in Israel even in wartime. But today I am very, very afraid. To be alone. All of the part [of the block] after me is *hamūlōt* of Arab families." If Jews see on television or read in the paper that a Jew was killed in Hebron or Gaza, they believe that tomorrow the killing may take place in their own neighborhood. A

Mizraḥi woman worried, "There is anxiety that in wartime, what will we do, to what shelter will we go? They'll [the Arab residents] still butcher us in the shelter, and no one will feel it." Jews are closer in kinship to that distant Jewish victim than they are to their Arab neighbor. They may create a stylized universal reality in which each Jewish death becomes their potential death and each Jewish victim is them. They may represent reality as a mythic struggle between the archetypal good Jew and the archetypal evil Arab. The fear does not, however, overshadow the fact that the Jewish residents of Wolfson are in this position because of actions taken (or not taken) by the Israeli government. One Mizraḥi woman, while expressing her fear, put the blame for her situation on the government: "We live in fear. . . . We left Morocco, happiness, and wealth, and they buried us with Arabs in Wolfson."

Some Arab residents also retreat in fear and choose to remain in isolation from the reality of their neighborhood. They cannot close out the Jews completely (any more than the Jews can shut out the Arabs), but they can limit the perceived contagion that contact with Jewish society brings, with its sexual freedom, immorality, racism, and disregard of honor. They, too, may create a stylized universal reality in which every Jew is a soldier who may kill or rape and every Palestinian is a victim. One woman explained, "The Israeli soldiers attack Arab youths without reason, just to put inside us fear and defeat—for domination." Others choose to shut out their Jewish neighbors in order to protect their dignity and traditional way of life. One man wanted the Jews in the neighborhood "to understand the Arab as a person, an individual, whatever his education, nationality, or political stance, and to treat him on the basis of respect."

On some occasions, however, Israeli Jews and Palestinians in the neighborhood suddenly burst upon each other, seeing not a stereotype but another human being with similar fears, worries, and joys. Jewish and Arab residents appreciate similar features of the neighborhood. They like its location close to the market, the city center, and transportation. Some residents also reported that the apartments were nice and spacious. A number of Jewish and Arab residents mentioned that they had good neighbors. Finally, for a few Jewish and many Arab residents the fact that the neighborhood was mixed was positive. As an Arab man noted, "A mixed neighborhood—it helps in learning manners, values, language, and lifestyles of both sides." When mutual recognition occurs, both transcripts (those of the powerful and the powerless) are challenged.

> Once there was more respect; to love there was a place, to sleep a place—today it's all a big mess. So what is there to demand from others, from Arabs. Even we aren't better. They [Arabs] relate to me nicely. I wish that the Jews would behave

to older people like the Arabs; they respect elders. (Ashkenazi man, aged sixty-eight, resident since the 1960s)

I don't like politics. I don't even like watching violence and death on TV, and I don't like hearing it on the radio either because I love living peacefully and I don't like watching or hearing about dead people in wars. (Palestinian man, aged twenty-six, resident since the 1980s)

The Jewish speaker remembered a past when the world was organized as it should be—a place for love and sleep, respect for elders. Young Israeli Jews, with their modern ways, had made a mess of the society and lost their claim to moral superiority. The Arab residents of the neighborhood allowed this man to recover a little of the past with the respect they accorded him. They had not turned their backs on traditional values; they knew how to behave toward their elders. They could educate his generation in such matters. The Palestinian speaker represents a response of the younger generation. He rejects the past and even the present; he does not want to know the history, the legacy of violence. To know it is to be entrapped within it. Watching and hearing violence prevents one from leading a peaceful life. It is better to close the eyes and ears and live in peace with one's neighbors.

I'm afraid to sleep at night, alone; among the Jews, I wasn't afraid. Because Arabs have anger at Jews, and when they want revenge, they search out the weak who can't defend themselves. In this neighborhood, it's not a problem because they're used to being together. And they respect each other. (Mizraḥi woman, resident since the 1980s)

Whatever happens in the West Bank and however severe the Jews are in the West Bank, we Arabs here preserve our relations with them, but they, in contrast, are affected by whatever happens, for instance, in the West Bank. But are we guilty for that? Of course not. (Palestinian woman, resident since the 1980s)

The Jewish woman began by universalizing—all Arabs are angry at all Jews and will take out that anger on weak Jews (like women alone) who are defenseless—but then she temporized her story by examining the specificity of life in this mixed neighborhood. In Wolfson, something different occurs—Jews and Arabs are used to being together; they respect each other. In other words, they have moved past the level of Jewish subject interacting with Arab object to one of mutual recognition and accommodation. The Palestinian woman began by highlighting specificity—no matter what the Jews (universal) do in the West Bank, the Arabs in Wolfson preserve relations with their (particular) Jewish neighbors. She chided the Jewish residents of the neighborhood for their inability to make this crucial distinction: were their neighbors guilty for the actions of Arab people on the West Bank? Of course not. This woman wanted to be recognized as an individual, not a faceless, generic member of a feared and hated other.

> At first, it bothered us [that Arabs voted more than before in the last municipal election], but afterward I understood that it's natural that they have the right to vote and they try to realize their right on the best side for their own welfare. (Mizrahi woman, resident since the 1960s)

> In the beginning, when we came here fourteen years ago, the Jews used to fear us because we had many children. Later they started to like us because they knew us in reality and not what they thought about us. (Palestinian woman, resident since the 1970s)

The Jewish woman admitted that she was bothered by Arabs voting and thus affecting the outcome of the municipal elections. Once again, we hear the echoes of the belief that since the state is Jewish, Jews should determine the outcomes and contours of government. This woman, however, had moved beyond the notion of her own rights to realize that Palestinians, too, have rights in the state as citizens. Further, she was able to recognize that they were exercising their right to provide for their own benefit, not to cause harm to Jews. The Palestinian woman also pointed out that it is possible to move beyond stereotypes and accept people for their real characteristics rather than those imagined in fear. Wolfson, as an integrated neighborhood, provides the space within which Jews and Palestinians can lay aside their fears and come to know the reality. In that process, true friendship and cooperation can develop.

> It's true that we agreed to remain living with Arabs, but they don't understand that Israeli Arabs are different. . . . I explained to Itzik that I'm ready to kill Arabs from the territories but I really respect Arabs from the neighborhood. (Mizrahi woman, resident since the 1960s)

> Since the *intifada,* there are suspicions and tension between the two sides and at the same time there are relations. (Palestinian woman, resident since the 1980s)

Living in tension. Balancing between fear and suspicion and acknowledgment of and respect for the other. These last two women captured best the contradiction of integrated living in the city of Acre. Residents of the neighborhood are sometimes able to move beyond the stereotyped images and interact as equals: the Palestinians who watch their Jewish neighbors' apartment when they are away on vacation; the women who provide help to each other — showers and the washing machine when the water is turned off, invitations to come and spend time rather than be alone, expressions of concern about soldier children. They provide some seeds of hope that an end to relationships based on domination is possible. Throughout Israel, face-to-face meetings are in progress between Israeli Jews and Palestinians (both Israeli and those living in the West Bank and Gaza Strip). There are women meeting together as mothers, sisters, and daughters to discuss common concerns. Mental health professionals who share grave misgivings about the implications for future generations of the ongoing violence hold joint talks. Ordinary people who are tired of living in a war zone are reaching out to those on the other side. In their study of relations between Israeli Jews and noncitizen Arabs in Jerusalem, Romann and Weingrod (1991) demonstrated how Israeli domination largely precluded the establishment of crosscutting ties. Acre's Arab residents, however, are Israeli citizens and as such operate within the system. They frame their demands in the terms of the dominant discourse, using the "symbolic tools" (Scott 1985) provided by Israeli democracy and claiming the rights accorded them in Israel's Declaration of Independence. Israeli Palestinians cannot be simply excluded, transferred, or ignored. Living together in Acre may be fostering the beginnings of a movement toward mutual Palestinian-Jewish recognition and the restoration of that tension between the needs for autonomy and recognition that comprise the paradox of their and our lives.

CHAPTER 5

The "Conquest" of Acre:
Whose City Is It?

Palestine and Israel occupy the same space but they are different places. What is familiar to one is an erasure of the familiar
to the other. (Xenos 1989, 233)

For both Israeli Jews and Israeli Palestinians, land is an important
focus of identity. For Jews, Israel is the Promised Land, the home of
prosperity given to them in fulfillment of their covenant with their
deity. This land, however, is not an abstract vision; the scriptures are
full of concrete, topographical details. For Palestinians, Palestine is a
concrete and historical place; olive trees, almond groves, oranges, jas-
mine, thyme, rocks, and hills are the images celebrated in their poetry
and literature. The olive grove that for an Israeli Jew conjures up
images of his or her biblical forefathers, for the Israeli Palestinian
brings memories of the grandfather, father, or uncle who planted the
trees. The Israeli-Palestinian conflict has been described as a clash
between two nationalisms claiming the same territory. Yet, this piece of
land has a rich history of conquest and expropriation, as Said notes.
"Cover a map of Palestine with the legends, insignia, icons, and routes
of all the peoples who have lived there, and you will have no space left
for terrain" (1985, 61–62). Implicit in the claim of nationalisms battling
over territory is the assumption that only one can realize its claims at
any given point in time. Land and identity become intertwined; the
struggle to protect the national territory is inextricably linked to pro-
tecting the national identity.[1] As Raja Shehadeh, a Palestinian lawyer
and himself a refugee, puts it, "I finally began thinking of this land as
seducing us all into war—calling us into its lap to fall bleeding—a
vampire that will suck our blood as we fight for it. You, who were only
a temporary camp for us—now we will die for you—you have pulled
these boys here as Jaffa pulled them—again we shall die for our land"
(1982, 124).

The battle over naming space, over nationalizing territory has been
fought in Acre. The Israeli conquest of the city in 1948 is now remembered officially in Independence Day celebrations as the town's "liberation." The Arab village of Al-Manshiyya was obliterated to be replaced

with the Jewish homes of East Acre. Acre, which should have been part of a Palestinian state, is now an integral part of the Jewish state. There can be no return for the Palestinian former residents of the city who fled its walls in 1948. The battle for control over Acre, however, is not over. Throughout its fifty years as an Israeli city, officials have warred against its Arab elements and struggled to Judaize the city and its inhabitants. In this chapter, I examine the ongoing battle over the city. The municipal election campaign of 1989 was only the latest episode in the series of struggles over the city's affiliation and identity. Would it be an Arab or a Jewish city? That it could continue as a mixed city was not conceived as likely or desirable. Acre's existence as a mixed city threatens the continued hegemony of nationalisms since it fractures the unity of place and identity for both its Jewish and Palestinian inhabitants.

"Reclaiming" the Land: Acre as a Jewish City

> And there was no life in her [Acre], only silent walls sprouting out of the deserted houses, with no living thing to be seen there. And a healing spirit will blow on the walls of the empty city and a deathly silence will rule in every corner. . . . And a man said to his wife: We are the exiled of Israel, who came out of exile from the four corners of the land. With the help of Adonai, Lord of Hosts, and the spirit of redemption of the land and people, we will rise as one man, we will build a city and settle in it, plant gardens and eat their fruits, and we will be one people in our city, new Acre. (Moshe Norman, "Legend of the City's Beginning," Acre Municipal Archives)

In this way, Moshe Norman reworked the Zionist slogan "A land without people, for a people without land" in framing his understanding of how Acre became a Jewish city. Acre was not, however, an empty city. The Israeli government had to make a considerable investment in erasing the Arab presence from the land it held after the war of 1948. This process was accomplished through both ad hoc policies and legal measures.

One example of an ad hoc policy was the decision to consolidate the remaining Arab population within the walls of the Old City after Acre's surrender in May 1948. Concentrating the population made sense from a military perspective. The Old City was blocked off, and its Arab population was not allowed to circulate freely. Arab residents who owned property outside were forced to move to the Old City, where they were relocated into housing that had not been demolished during the fighting. Their unprotected homes in the New City became prime targets for looting, both by soldiers and by new immigrants. The homes were then commandeered by new immigrants, who often simply squatted in them. As Segev (1986, 68–91) notes, looting and seizures of Arab property were occurring throughout Israel, so events in Acre were not unusual.

Legal measures such as the Absentees' Property Law of 1950 were also used to expropriate Arab land. "Abandoned" property was initially placed under the control of the Committee for Arab Property (established by the army), which was later replaced by the Custodian of Absentee Property. As described in chapter 2, during 1948–50 the Custodian's office in Acre carried out a number of sweeps to confiscate abandoned goods, which were placed in its warehouses. Under the 1950 law, the Custodian was able to transfer the property under his control to the newly created Development Authority. On 29 September 1953, an agreement was made between the Custodian and the Development Authority under which all the property under the Custodian's control passed to the authority (Kretzmer 1990, 58). The Development Authority could legally sell land to one of four bodies: the state, the Jewish National Fund (JNF), local authorities (restricted to urban land), or an institution for settling landless Arabs (which was never established). The bulk of the land was sold to the JNF. By the late 1950s, more than 90 percent of all land in Israel was held either by the JNF or the state. According to the charter of the JNF, land they acquired could never be sold to a non-Jew, which effectively prevented Arabs from retaining the right to make future land purchases. In Acre, more than 90 percent of the housing stock in the Old City was transferred from the Custodian to Amidar, the national housing authority. While a few Arab residents of Acre retained title to their urban holdings (in the Mandate and Old Cities), they sometimes lost title to rural land under the provisions of the Land Acquisition Law of 1953. The government-appointed minister who administered the 1953 law had the power to expropriate land if on 1 April 1952 it was not in the possession of its owners; if between 14 May 1948 and 1 April 1952 it had been used for purposes of essential development, settlement, or security; and if it was still required for any of those purposes. Until 1951, the military government restricted the movements of the Arab residents of Acre. Those who owned olive trees in nearby villages received some compensation for their 1949 harvests, but they stood to lose their rights to those groves because they were not tending them personally. In addition, many people then resident in Acre were refugees from villages, some of which had been destroyed by the Israeli military.

The government quickly moved to set up new communities and construct factories and housing on the seized lands. In Acre, for example, the housing constructed in the east during 1949 and 1950 was built on the remains of the Arab village of Al Manshiyya. What remains today is a mosque, which has been turned into a private home by a Jewish family, and several other old stone buildings that border the gardens of the Bahai. Throughout the Galilee, an observant traveler might note clumps of cactus, olive or fig trees, and crumbled stone walls that are all that remain of more than 350 Arab villages that were destroyed in 1948–49.[2] Arab houses in the Mandate City were divided into apartments or used as schools, government offices, or shops. Housing construction in the 1960s and 1970s completely altered the face of the city. In the Old City, families were vacated from historic properties, some of which were converted into tourist facilities and others of which continue to sit vacant, awaiting transformation at the hands of outside investors. The Turkish bathhouse became the Municipal Museum, and the Turkish citadel was converted into the Museum of Heroism in honor of members of the Mandate-period Jewish underground who were interned or executed there (with no mention of the Palestinian prisoners who met their fates within its walls).[3] New housing construction sprouted north of the Mandate City in an area of drained swampland.

Reclaiming Acre also necessitated reworking the city's history. The immediate past was forgotten in favor of a more distant past that had closer ties to a Jewish presence in the city. The municipal emblem, which resulted from a national competition held in 1949, is a graphic depiction of how local officials decided the city's history is to be remembered. A number of the entries in the competition attempted to combine Arab and Jewish elements in their designs—mosques with synagogues, mosques with modern buildings and Israeli flags, interlocked hands, Arab and Jewish figures.[4] The winning design was a shield divided into four quadrants. Each quadrant contained an image—a Phoenician sailing ship, a factory symbol, a stylized modern building with palm trees, and a wall with battlements. The emblem unites the modern (factories and apartments) with the ancient (the Phoenicians and the Crusaders). Arab Acre has no place in this portrayal.

Excavating the city's past also helps in reclaiming Acre as a Jewish city. Indeed, Nadia Abu El-Haj assets that "the work of archaeology does not simply reflect or legitimize specific regimes of rule. Rather, it can help to *produce* them" (1998, 179). As Elon notes, "Israeli archeologists, professionals and amateurs, are not merely digging for knowledge and objects, but for the reassurance of roots, which they find in the ancient Israelite remains scattered throughout the country" (1971, 280). Archaeological excavations in the city have concentrated on two major locations: Tel Napoleon, believed to be the original site of the city; and the Crusader city, which lies under the modern Old City. Besides its importance as the original site, Tel Napoleon is significant because it was from there that Richard the Lion-Hearted launched his attack on the city in 1191 (when it was recaptured by the Crusaders), as did Napoleon Bonaparte in 1799 and the Israeli army in 1948. Tel Napoleon has been excavated by archaeologists from Haifa University for more than eleven seasons. The site contains remains from the Canaanite and Israelite periods. During 1989, the municipality uncovered a number of Hellenistic grave sites while digging a new sewage canal on the northern beach. Within a few days of the discovery, the graves had been looted. Local residents had easy access to the site and could literally stroll along the trench and peer into the empty chambers. No guards were present to keep people away from an important archaeological find. Had the remains been from the Israelite period, it is safe to speculate that the find would have been heralded as a national treasure and an archaeological team would have been dispatched immediately to begin excavating. Elon notes that Israeli archaeology is most interested in "the country's Israelite past, often to the exclusion of other rich and fascinating periods, Hellenistic, Roman, Byzantine, Moslem, and Crusader" (1971, 281).

The Crusader city is unique in Israel. When Shaikh Ẓāhir al-Umar began to rebuild Acre in the mid–eighteenth century, he had his workers build on top of the structures that were still standing by covering them over with dirt. Thus, the Crusader city was preserved until its excavation by Israeli authorities beginning in the 1960s. The Kesten Report of 1963 outlined a restoration program that would take five to ten years and cost five to ten million Israeli pounds.[5] Preserving Acre as a museum city has its roots in the establishment of the Acre Development Corporation in 1965. Crusader remains, however, are not a priority in terms of national archaeology. In 1979, Sa'adia Mandel, the architect responsible for the development of Old Jaffa, said, "People who should know say that Acre is the country's finest historic plum after Jerusalem. But nothing is done about it. Here you have two complete and largely intact towns, one on top of the other. And there is more to Acre than Crusaders and Moslems."[6] The Crusader ruins in the city are one of its tourist attractions, and municipal officials have acted to preserve and reinforce this part of its heritage. Thus, squares in the Old City were renamed Pisa, Venice, and Genoa, while streets were named after Marco Polo and Benjamin of Tudela. The Arab names of Old City quarters do not appear on municipal maps. The authorities have renewed connections to the cities of Venice, Genoa, Pisa, and Amalfi by organizing youth and cultural exchanges. The Crusader heritage of the city is remembered so as to emphasize connections to the Christian West rather than the Muslim East. Thus, the Crusader remains are also used to obliterate the city's Arab heritage.

The Independence Day celebration in 1988 aptly illustrates the way in which Acre's history is reworked to highlight its Jewish and Western heritage and suppress its Arab past. Municipal officials staged a locally produced theatrical extravaganza to celebrate Israel's fortieth year of independence. The subject of this production was Acre's rich and colorful history, which spans at least five thousand years The result was an oriental-flavored epic of "five thousand years and another forty" of the city's existence. Crowded onto the grass around the soccer field, residents of the city were regaled with song, dance, and video images of their city and its history. As Acre's guardian angel shared his memories of key events in the city's past, we, the audience, saw reenactments of the Crusaders' final battle, al-Jazzar Pasha (the "butcher" of Acre), Napoleon's abortive attempt to capture the city, and Moshe Carmel and the conquest of 1948. Fireworks, parachutists carrying Israeli and municipal flags, physical fitness demonstrations, folk dancing, songs about peace and coexistence, and an elaborate video on the city's development since 1948 rounded out the program.

In this celebration, historical events were remembered in such a way that a central Arab presence and an absent or marginal Jewish one were reworked to reach a present moment in which the Jewish presence is central and the Arab marginal or absent. The Arabs who resided in Acre for more than a thousand years were reduced to the role of others who drove the Crusaders away and devastated the city in 1291 and the oriental despot who, although he rebuilt the city, did so by terrorizing his people. Juxtaposed with these images of destruction, Moshe Carmel's conquest of the city was described as its liberation. Development since 1948 was portrayed as miraculous, a product and proof of Zionism's promise to make the desert bloom. Arab residents figured in this development as beneficiaries of municipal officials' commitment to Arab-Jewish coexistence. The Jewish residents present at this celebration could leave satisfied that Acre was indeed a Jewish city.

The Demographic Danger

One of the main paradoxes of Israeli nationalism is the claim that Israel is both a democratic and a Jewish state.[7] Prior to 1967, the Israeli state could comfortably accord rights to its Arab citizens since they accounted for only 15 to 17 percent of the population. Since 1967, however, the Israeli state has exercised control over an additional one and a half million Palestinians. As long as the majority of Israel's citizens are Jewish, its existence as a Jewish state will not be threatened and it can continue to allow non-Jewish citizens the right to vote and participate in national government. Had Israel annexed the West Bank and Gaza Strip, Palestinians would have accounted for about 40 percent of the population. Demographic change threatens to break the precarious balance between Israel's existence as the state of its citizenry and as the state of the Jews. As Yuval-Davis notes, a " 'demographic race' between Jews and Arabs in Israel is seen as crucial to the survival of Israel, not only as the state apparatus of the population living in it, but as the state for Jews everywhere" (1989, 92).

Demographics became a central consideration in Zionist planning for the Jewish state when it became apparent to the early Zionists that the Palestinians opposed their intentions. Masalha (1992) traces the persistence and prominence of the concept of "transfer" in Zionist political thought from 1882 to 1948. In 1937, the Peel Commission considered the possibility of a population exchange as part of its proposal to partition Palestine into an Arab and a Jewish state (Morris 1987, 25). Between 1938 and 1942, a number of Yishuv (the pre-state Jewish community in Palestine) committees considered aspects of the transfer proposal such as how to implement it, how to finance it, how many refugees neighboring countries could absorb, and so on (27). The issue of population transfer was raised again during the debate by Zionist factions over the Biltmore Program in 1942.[8] Those who favored the idea cited the example of the population exchange between Turkey and Greece after World War I, which was generally viewed as a positive experience. Other factions, such as HaShomer HaTsair, viewed the idea of transfer as morally unacceptable (Shapira 1992, 285). Transfer proposals were matters for private discussion and consideration; they were not to be aired publicly. While publicly remaining silent or disavowing interest in transferring Arabs from the Jewish state, however, Ben-Gurion had a different message for his own supporters. On 3 December 1947, four days after the United Nations voted to partition Palestine into two states, he outlined the new state's main problem: it would contain a non-Jewish population of 40 percent.

> This fact must be viewed in all its clarity and sharpness. With
> such a composition, there cannot even be complete certainty
> that the government will be held by a Jewish majority. . . .
> There can be no stable and strong Jewish state so long as it has
> a Jewish majority of only 60%. (quoted in Morris 1987, 28)

A de facto population transfer occurred during the 1948 war over Palestine. Palestinians left their residences for a variety of reasons: Israeli attacks on villages, fears of atrocities like that of Deir Yassin (where more than two hundred villagers were killed by Israeli forces), friendly warnings to leave, forcible expulsions, and the fact that many who left were prevented from returning.[9] The unofficial Transfer Committee of Yosef Weitz moved to prevent the return of refugees by destroying their villages and settling Jewish immigrants on their lands (Morris 1986; Masalha

1992). By 1949, almost eight hundred thousand Palestinians were home-less and registered as refugees in neighboring countries with the United Nations Relief and Works Agency.

Transfer, now the removal of the Palestinians of the West Bank and Gaza Strip for resettlement in neighboring countries, was again raised as a potential solution to the demographic problem by Rehavam Ze'evi in 1987 in response to the *intifada*. Ze'evi was a major general in the IDF and served as the adviser to the prime minister in the fight against terrorism from 1974 to 1978. Ze'evi's position differed from Meir Kahane's call to evict all Palestinians in that Ze'evi referred to "an agreed-upon" transfer, implying that they would not be unilaterally ex-pelled. He argued that the old idea of transfer from the debates in the 1930s was an appropriate resolution to the current situation in the occu-pied territories. He formed a new list, Moledet (Homeland), to run for the Knesset in 1988 on a transfer platform. Moledet received enough votes to send two representatives to the 1988 Knesset, indicating that Ze'evi had been correct in his analysis of trends in Israeli society.[10]

With the founding of the state in 1948, barriers to Jewish immigra-tion were lifted. During 1948–51, Israel's Jewish population doubled. Additional waves of mass immigration occurred in 1955–57 (from Mo-rocco), 1961–64 (from Morocco and Romania), and 1969–79 (from the Soviet Union and Romania). Even with an overwhelming Jewish major-ity, Israeli leaders continued to pursue demographic policies that sought to further increase Jewish numerical superiority. Attention shifted from transfer of the Arab population to augmentation of the Jewish popu-lation through pro-natalist policies. In the early 1950s, Ben-Gurion im-plemented a program of rewards to mothers of ten children or more — so-called heroine mothers (Yuval-Davis 1989, 95).[11] From 1958 to 1960, immigration occurred at one-half to one-third the rate of the previous three years. In the early 1960s, government attention again focused on the issue of Jewish and Arab birthrates. Efrat, the Committee for the Encouragement of a Jewish Birth Rate in Israel, was established (Yuval-Davis 1987, 77). By 1967, the government had established the Centre for Demography. After the 1967 war, with the addition of the Palestinian population of the occupied territories, the "war on the baby front" became an important political issue.[12]

The Centre for Demography has promoted various pro-natalist poli-cies since its inception, including the Fund for Encouraging Birth set up by the housing ministry in 1968 to provide subsidies to families with more than three children whose household heads had served in the military. Child benefit allowances are paid to all Israeli citizens, although Jewish families receive larger benefits due to army service. In 1983, the Law on Families Blessed with Children was passed, which gives a range of benefits to families with more than three children, although once again eligibility for the program is limited to those who also qualify for assistance under the Veterans Benefit Law. Efrat, which had been inactive during the 1970s, resumed its activities and began to establish centers and branches all over the country during the 1980s. Israeli Jewish women were called upon to fulfill their national duty by bearing children to replenish the Jewish nation, children to replace those lost in the Nazi Holocaust and in the "demographic holocaust" (intermarriage and assimilation abroad). During 1986, the *Jerusalem Post* published articles entitled "The Demographic Danger," "Rating the Birthrate," and "A Need for Painful Rethinking," all of which focused on the issue of Arab-Jewish demographics. Portugese notes in her study of fertility policy in Israel that the government provides inadequate family-planning services due to the influence of Zionist, religious, and familist forces on policy (1998, 132). As of 1994, the government was paying for adequate services for only two groups of new immigrants — Russians (to forestall their use of abortion as a method of birth control at a higher cost to government health funds) and Ethiopians (because of the linkage, however unproven, in government eyes of these immigrants and AIDS) (Portugese 1998, 127).

Besides policies focused on increasing or suppressing birthrates, the Israeli government also made efforts to reshape the internal population distribution. The greatest concentration of Arab villages that remained was in the Galilee. Close to half of the Arab population lives in the Northern District of the country (which includes all of northern Israel except for an area surrounding Haifa). During the late 1950s and early 1960s, land was confiscated from Arab villages in the Galilee for the purpose of constructing new Jewish towns (such as Karmi'el) as part of a "Judaize the Galilee" policy effort. In 1973, the Jewish Agency prepared detailed plans for new Jewish settlements to be constructed in the Galilee also as a part of this effort (Zureik 1979, 109). When Jewish residents continued to leave the area, a new settlement effort — the *mitspīm* (fortresses) — was launched by the Jewish Agency. These settlements, located on the top of strategic peaks throughout the north, are reminiscent of the "stockade and watchtower" settlements of the pre-state period.[13] They are attractive to home buyers because they usually offer extremely reasonable mortgage packages and may entitle residents to claim tax exemptions and other government benefits.

Israeli elites feared another kind of demographic imbalance, that between the Ashkenazim and the Mizraḥim. Israel was established to solve the "Jewish problem" of Europe. Zionism was meant to bring about the liberation and salvation of European Jews; its message was not directed at Mizraḥi Jews (Chetrit 1992). Thus, Israel faced another demographic problem. In the words of David Ben-Gurion, "But more than

Hitler hurt the Jewish people, whom he knew and hated, he injured the Jewish state which he never anticipated. He had annihilated the carrier and the main and central constructive power of the Jewish state. The state was established and the people who longed for it were not there" (1954, 37).

Jewish immigration from North Africa and other Arab countries came to be viewed as a threat to the Ashkenazi community very early. In 1949, the Foreign Office was already warning its diplomats that "preservation of the country's cultural level demands a flow of immigration from the West, and not only from the backward Levantine countries" (Segev 1986, 156). Fears about being overwhelmed were also appearing in the national media. Arye Gelblum, a correspondent for *Ha'aretz,* wrote in 1949, "Obviously all these Jews [Mizraḥim] are entitled to come here no less than others, and they should be brought over and absorbed, but if it is carried out without consideration for our limited capacities and if it is not done gradually, they will 'absorb' us rather than we them." Gelblum went on to warn, prophetically, that Herut (later, Likud) was eager to bring these immigrants in because they could serve as raw material to eventually put the party in power. Fears about "Levantinization" did not recede as the Mizraḥi immigrants were integrated into Israeli society. In 1964, Kalman Katznelson published *The Ashkenazi Revolution,* in which he argued that Mizraḥim were genetically inferior and that Ashkenazi-Mizraḥi intermarriage was tainting the Ashkenazi race. He called on Ashkenazim to act to protect their interests in the face of an increasing Mizraḥi majority. As the Mizraḥim now constitute the majority of the Jewish population of Israel, Ashkenazi fears of being absorbed into Eastern culture have not disappeared. Consider the following statement, written by Amnon Dankner, also a columnist for *Ha'Aretz,* in 1983:

> This war [between Ashkenazim and Mizraḥim] is not going to be between brothers, not because there is not going to be war but because it won't be between brothers. Because if I am a partner in this war, which is imposed on me, I refuse to name the other side as my "brother." These are not my brothers, these are not my sisters, leave me alone, I have no sister. . . . They put the sticky blanket of the love of Israel over my head, and they ask me to be considerate of the cultural deficiencies of the authentic feelings of discrimination . . . they put me in the same cage with a hysterical baboon, and they tell me "OK, now you are together, so begin the dialogue." And I have no choice; the baboon is against me, and the guard is against me, and the prophets of the love of Israel stand aside and wink at me with a wise eye and tell me: "Speak to him nicely. Throw him a banana. After all, you people are brothers . . ."[14]

It is in the context of these fears of Arab and Mizraḥi birthrates that the Israeli government's enthusiastic support of massive immigration from the Soviet Union makes sense, coming as it does at a point in time when internally the country is suffering from major employment and housing difficulties. In 1990 alone, 181,759 Soviet Jews entered Israel. By 1998, total immigration from the former Soviet Union had reached more than 700,000. The Soviet Jews promise to solve both demographic problems at once — increasing the Jewish and the Ashkenazi populations. As Lavie notes, "One million [potential] Soviet Jews have the potential of smothering any indigenous Middle Eastern voices in Israeli culture" (1991, 11).

The national election campaign of 1988 prominently featured concerns over the demographic problem. Every political party had its platform on demography. For Tsomet, the right-wing party of Raful Eitan, a greater Jewish population could be achieved by attracting more Jewish immigration, encouraging a higher Jewish birthrate, and educating the Jewish population against emigration. He also wanted the state to facilitate the emigration of Arabs to any country they desired. Labor Party campaign literature noted that unfavorable demographic trends would only be reversed with massive Jewish immigration, a drop in Jewish emigration, a massive exit of Arabs, a rise in Jewish birthrates, and a drop in Arab birthrates. The impossibility of all these things being realized demonstrated the rightness of Labor's call for territorial compromise with the Palestinians: "The only way in which Israel can continue to hold on to the territories and improve the demographic ratio is by means of a forced transfer of Palestinians." Tehiya, the right-wing party of Geula Cohen, supported "birth incentives" in the Jewish sector by providing more government financial support (based on military service), a special fund through the World Zionist Organization, and an "adoption not abortion" policy. It proposed to execute a master plan for the immigration and absorption of one million Jewish immigrants over the next twelve years and to work against Jewish emigration. As for the Arabs living in the occupied territories, they would have resident status and could petition to become citizens, but "the right of citizen, as in all democratic countries, will be based on a rational demographic policy, that will protect the Jewish character of the state."[15]

Only the Likud seemed to reject concerns over demographics. It noted that the relationship between the Jewish and Arab populations of the state (including the territories) had changed by only 1.33 percent between 1967 and 1986. "So, who's afraid of demography?" a Likud brochure asked, and it claimed that the demographic problem has been exaggerated by the Labor Party so it could retreat from Judea and Samaria (the West Bank). The Likud appropriated the idea of transfer and used it in reverse imagery. On the front of one pamphlet appeared the words *Transfer: An Ugly Word* above a photo of an apprehensive young Ashkenazi girl who was obviously religiously Orthodox by her style of dress. Inside, the pamphlet noted, "Over 200,000 Jews live across the Green Line in Judea, Samaria, Jerusalem, Katif, and the Golan," and it queried, "How many will Shimon Peres transfer?"

The national preoccupation over too many Palestinian and too few Jewish bodies (and even fewer Jewish bodies of the right type) can also be seen at work in Acre. Throughout the 1950s and 1960s, the Jewish population of the city increased as new immigrants were settled there by the Jewish Agency. Municipal officials battled for the right type of immigrant — educated or skilled, young, and able-bodied. They were often sent families that ended up dependent on the welfare office because the parent was unfit to work or unable to locate suitable employment. Beginning in 1970, municipal officials began to warn the national government of a different demographic problem — a potential Arab-Jewish population imbalance. A confidential report was sent to the prime minister in July of that year by Acre's mayor, Israel Doron. In it, Doron warned of two trends in the city's population — small numbers of established Jewish families were leaving the city every year to be replaced with poorer Jewish people (many of whom were Mizraḥim). And the number of Arab residents in the city was increasing, while the Jewish population was remaining stable. Doron pointed out that the nine thousand Arab residents were three times the number present in 1948, and he claimed that the number of Arab residents was growing by two thousand every year due to births and immigration from the nearby villages. (Acre's Jewish population had increased twenty-eightfold since 1948, but this fact was not mentioned.) As a result of Doron's report, a public commission was appointed to look into the matter. Its members reached the same conclusion as Mayor Doron. They recommended that the government give Acre preferred area status for three years to help it revive. They also proposed the construction of higher-quality housing to attract new settlers while offering grants to young couples so they could purchase homes.

Acre got its new housing construction — a new quarter of five hundred apartments was completed by December of 1976. This housing attracted both new immigrants (who were arriving from the Soviet Union) and veteran Israelis from the suburbs of Haifa, who found the quality and price of the apartments appealing. The city absorbed another three thousand residents during the 1970s. The government also finally proposed a solution to the problem of unsafe housing in the Old City. The public commission appointed in 1970 proposed that an Arab development town be built on a site outside Acre's municipal jurisdiction. This recommendation was accepted by local leaders, who instructed the planners then developing a new master plan for the city to include the proposal in their design (Cohen 1971, 14). In 1974, the housing ministry announced that it would build a town for five thousand families on a site adjoining the village of Makr, five kilometers east of Acre. Arab families were induced to move from the Old City by means of financial incentives; special housing loans were made available to those who purchased in Makr.

Local authorities in Israel compete with each other for development funds from the national government and the Jewish Agency. Acre has been denied special development status (A+) for years, while such status has been granted to the nearby Jewish communities of Karmi'el, Nahariyya, and Shelomi. Using objective criteria, Acre should certainly also qualify for this status, but the Israeli government drew the boundaries of the "development" areas such that places with high concentrations of Arabs were excluded.[16] Municipal officials learned to use the one mechanism available to them to acquire financial concessions and preferential treatment from the government and the Jewish Agency — fear that Acre could become an Arab city. Thus, municipal reports of 1984, 1985, and 1989 warned that Acre could lose its Jewish character due to its shrinking Jewish population. Municipal officials proposed a number of initiatives to prevent that from occurring. Each time, the government responded to the crisis by providing a few additional benefits for a limited period. Thus, in the short run municipal officials realized both of their goals — increasing the Jewish population and attracting a better-quality Jewish resident. In the absence of any long-term development policy, however, such gains were temporary. Within five or ten years, municipal officials would again be sounding a warning bell. As one local politician noted, most Jewish residents of Acre saw it as a way station: "A man plants a walnut tree when his son is born because he knows that in thirty years his grandson will enjoy the use of the tree. In Acre, the grandfather does not plant the tree because he knows that his grandson will not be here to benefit from it. The Arab population, however, has roots in Acre (and strong ones at that)." In late 1988, as the municipal election campaign was beginning, the claim that Jews were leaving Acre captured both local and national attention once again.

The End of Coexistence? Municipal Elections in 1989

Local government (municipal, local, and regional councils) in Israel is still based for the most part on the system of district administration and local government established by the British during the Mandate period. Municipal authority is based on the Municipalities Act of 1934 and the Local Councils Act of 1941, although these have been amended to grant more power to the heads of local authorities (Al-Haj and Rosenfeld 1988, 24). Local government in Israel is limited to the provision of services such as education, health and sanitation, water, road maintenance, parks and recreation, and fire protection. Local authorities also levy and collect local taxes and fees, but income from these sources is generally limited, so most localities depend heavily on grants and loans from the central government. The Ministry of the Interior determines the budgets for local authorities and the number and/or type of employees they can hire, approves local bylaws, and reviews and approves building master plans for local or regional authorities. The ministry also determines the number of members of these councils in accordance with the size of the local population. Elections to such councils are like Knesset elections: residents vote for party lists, not individual candidates, and representation is general (at-large) and proportional. Until 1978, the chairman of the local authority was elected by the council members at their first meeting after election or appointment. Since 1978, heads of local authorities (mayors in municipalities) have been elected directly in a separate election held at the same time as the council contests.

In Acre, the first municipal council, appointed in 1949 by the minister of the interior, included equal numbers of Arab and Jewish residents as well as representatives of various government ministries. The first municipal elections were held in 1951. The thirteen-member council was dominated by a coalition between Mapai (Labor) and the Mizraḥi (religious), with Baruch Noy chosen as mayor. After Noy's resignation in October 1952, Yosef Gadish (Mapai) was selected to serve as mayor. In all of the succeeding elections for the municipal council, the Labor Alignment and its affiliated local lists (religious and Arab) won the majority of council seats, thus gaining the right to form a governing coalition and select the mayor. By 1965, the council had been increased to fifteen members (due to population increase). Arab council representation during these years ranged from two to five members, generally split between an independent Labor-affiliated list and Rakah (the Communist Party). Representatives of Herut, the Liberals, or the Gahal bloc (all of which eventually became the Likud) generally won between one and three seats on the council. When direct election of the mayor was introduced in 1978, the incumbent, Israel Doron (Labor), won the office. In the 1983 elections, Eli De Castro (Labor) was elected mayor with 45.7 percent of the vote compared to 25.5 percent for the Herut candidate, David Bar Lev. De Castro brought Bar Lev into his governing coalition by making him a deputy mayor and giving him the education portfolio. In addition to Bar Lev, De Castro had two other deputy mayors: Morris Ben Shoshan (Labor), who was in charge of health and engineering, and Hilmi Shafʿī (Labor affiliated), who was in charge of the Arab sector.

Municipal elections were scheduled for 28 February 1989. The campaign unfolded during a time of considerable stress for Acre. The liquidation suit against the Koor Group that was filed by Bankers Trust of New York in October 1988 was forcing Koor to cut wages, lay off workers, close factories, and sell off some of its affiliates. Koor factories were the core of Acre's industrial base. Earlier in the year, the city had lost 120 jobs at Tagal, 100 at Ilan Brothers, and 40 at Taʿashan.[17] In early November 1988, De Castro urged the managing director of Koor to keep further layoffs in Acre to a minimum.[18] The Koor-owned United Steel Mills plant had announced a layoff of 140 workers, while Koor's ceramics company, Na'aman, had debts of $1 million and planned to let 30 employees go. Many other Acre-based companies were experiencing difficulties. Miluot, the kibbutz-owned food-processing concern, had debts of $350 million, while Rafael, an armaments concern, had debts of $100 million and planned to fire 200 employees.

Unemployment rates rose rapidly in the city, as throughout the Western Galilee. In early November 1988, local papers reported that Acre had lost six hundred jobs. More than 350 people were laid off, with 960 individuals registered as seeking work, an increase of 170 people over the previous month.[19] By the end of the month, the number seeking employment had increased to 1,023, an increase of 20 percent in the number of laid-off workers. In the nearby cities of Nahariyya, Karmi'el, Shelomi, and Maʿalot, the work situation either improved slightly or remained the same.[20] Since the start of the year, the number seeking work in Acre had increased by 65 percent and the number receiving unemployment compensation had increased by 60 percent. To publicize the plight of the city's residents, the municipality and the local Workers' Council called for a strike by local residents for 4 January 1989. Over 1,000 people turned out for a march to Town Hall to protest layoffs and the lack of new jobs.[21] At the end of January, 200 residents traveled to Jerusalem to take part in a Histadrut demonstration at the prime minister's office to protest the employment situation in the country.[22]

The *intifada* was also having an effect. Many Israeli Jews were shocked when Israeli Palestinians participated in the Peace Day strike on 21 December 1987 to express solidarity with Palestinians in the territories. Yosef Goell, in an editorial in the *Jerusalem Post* on 25 December, expressed the views of many:

> What is needed, first and foremost, is to draw clear lines as to
> what is permissible and what is impermissible for a presumably
> loyal minority in an Israel which continues to be at war with an
> Arab world still intent on its destruction. It is, admittedly, an

especially poignant dilemma for the Israeli Arabs that the Palestinian national movement, as truly represented by the PLO, has placed itself at the spearhead of that war. The way in which every individual Israeli Arab, and the Arab community as a whole, choose to resolve that dilemma cannot but be seen as the test of their loyalty by a Jewish Israel.

In Acre, some municipal employees who participated in the strike were fired from their jobs. Throughout 1988, tensions increased in the community. In early September, Morris Ben Shoshan publicly charged that the PLO was financing Arab organizations in Acre through the Geneva Foundation.[23] The foundation had provided part of the financing for a teacher-training program organized by the Acre Arab Women's Organization in which women from Acre and the villages were trained as early childhood educators. The program's initiators were also involved in developing appropriate materials and curricula to teach Arab culture and values to young children. Ben Shoshan's charges were investigated by the local police. Local Arab leaders saw this as another form of government harassment and an attempt to stop autonomous development within the Arab sector. Ramzi Ḥouri commented, "Have I ever at any time opposed the support that is given to Jewish organizations by the Jewish Agency?"

On Sunday, 4 September, a Jewish shop owner in the Old City was attacked and beaten by a group of Arabs. In his report to the police, he said that they yelled at him, "Jew, get out of here." Because local officials viewed the beating as a nationalist incident, the Special Police Unit was called in to patrol the Old City and restore order. On Thursday, 8 September, Arab residents of the Old City, all of the Arab shop owners, and 80 percent of the Jewish shop owners there protested the police clampdown by staging a school and commercial strike for the day.[24] In reports published locally the following day, both Arab and Jewish merchants claimed that the beating incident had been a personal disagreement between buyer and seller that had been grossly exaggerated by the police.[25] Locally, rumors circulated that the whole affair was due to the Jewish man's underworld connections. Arab officials called on the government to investigate the Special Police Unit, which was, they claimed, unduly harassing and provoking Old City residents. Tensions remained high. The following week, two Jewish merchants found their shop windows smeared with eggs and feces when they arrived in the morning. Other Jewish shopkeepers reported that they had received threatening phone calls.[26] A week later, members of Kahane's Kach Party came to Acre in order to "strengthen the security in the Old City," given the recent incidents there.[27] Police units prevented them from entering.

Over the next few months, there were further incidents. In October, shops and houses in the Old City were plastered with stickers of the PLO flag. Police accused a print shop in the Old City of having produced the stickers. In November, residents of the Old City honored the Home Strike, which was called to protest the demolition of homes in the Arab sector. The previous week, the government had demolished fifteen homes in the Israeli village of Taibe that had been built without permits. Three days of rioting in Taibe followed the demolition. In December, another printer in Acre's Old City was accused by the police of printing seditious materials intended for distribution in the West Bank and Gaza Strip. That same month racist statements were painted on the walls of the Arab school, Amal. In the midst of the tensions created in the local community by these incidents, and by the growing economic crisis, local politicians embarked on their election campaigns.

On 2 December 1988, the local branch of the Herut Party published an announcement in the local broadside, Yedi'ot 'Akko,[28] that congratulated David Bar Lev on his selection as the Likud candidate for mayor in the forthcoming municipal elections. Bar Lev, who had served since 1957 in the Israeli police, was a senior officer when he retired from his job to enter politics in 1983. The announcement also provided details of the party's platform for the local campaign. "Judaize Acre Only by Positive Transfer," the headline read. The announcement spelled out the issue as Herut saw it: Acre had the image of an Arab city.

> In the last few years, the city of Acre has suffered from many
> Jews leaving it. And it has absorbed an Arab population even
> from remote places so hence the image of Acre as an Arab
> city.
>
> Together with the penetration of the Arab population within
> the city and among the Jewish population, this matter creates
> emotion in the area of the national interest and the cultural
> arena.
>
> In the national arena, the last strike that was declared in the
> Arab villages only, called upon the city of Acre despite it being
> a Jewish city, as if to tell us that Acre, too, is an Arab city, the

Arab nationalism in Acre is breaking out with greater vigor. Among the cultural problems, it cited parties on the grass in Jewish neighborhoods, loud music, opening businesses on Shabbat next to synagogues, the muezzin's loud calls at night and during the afternoon rest hours, and groups of Arab boys hassling Jewish girls out for an evening walk. To solve these problems, it proposed a series of measures:

1. Encourage the Arabs of the Old City to agree to live in the
   nearby villages, through a meaningful increase in the grants

from the housing ministry, with lenient and easy conditions or alternatively by building neighborhoods with low rents.

2. Make land available to the Arab residents outside the city, using Project Build Your Own Home, with subsidized prices.

3. Absorb strengthened Jewish immigration to the city of Acre.

4. Advertise the city of Acre as a city of Jewish settlement, to discharged soldiers and new immigrants, along with building a wide industrial base and selling land to investors.

It concluded by stating that the party would not allow Acre to become an Arab city: "Enough kneeling for the harlot's pay of votes, and enough of the PLO flag in Acre. A Positive Transfer Only Bar Lev Can Do."

On Sunday, 4 December 1988, Ramsi Houri, a member of the Acre municipal council (Rakah), responded to Bar Lev's proposal in *Al Ittihad,* the party's newspaper. Houri's response brought Bar Lev's transfer proposal into the national spotlight. The national media descended on Acre the following day, and by Tuesday, 6 December, the issue was the talk of the day — radio, television, and newspapers all reported and discussed the transfer idea. Local reaction ranged from support for Bar Lev, stressing that he spoke of a "voluntary, positive" transfer, to condemnation of his statements as inciting racism. Life in Acre was quiet, people noted, so why destroy the good relations with this nonsense?

Mayor Eli De Castro, seeking reelection, likened Bar Lev's idea of a "positive transfer" to asking someone sentenced to death to commit suicide.[29] He stated in a local paper, "The term 'transfer' awakens in all of us sickening associations, especially a few days after all the world marked the forty-ninth anniversary of 'Kristelnacht,' famous for disgrace, it's unnecessary to remind him what he opens."[30] De Castro pledged that Acre would continue to be a city of coexistence and that the good relations between its residents would be protected. The Arab members of the local council called for Bar Lev to be dismissed as deputy mayor and removed from all municipal responsibilities because of his racist statements. De Castro responded by noting that Bar Lev had the right to express his opinion because Israel is a democratic country. He said that Bar Lev worked with policies, not plans, so the request to dismiss him was irrelevant.

On 9 December 1988, *Yedi'ot 'Akko* included three manifestos, in Hebrew, by Arab residents of the city, all of which described Bar Lev's statements as racist. One said that Bar Lev's expressions had the power of blood libel against the Arab public: "The Arab population of Acre has the right to live in the city where they were born and where they grew up as equal citizens. And it's their right to express solidarity with the entire Arab population in Israel, and it's their right to manage their lives according to their traditions and customs." Another called on the "democratic public that values the coexistence and good neighborly relations in Acre not to stand with folded hands toward such transfer ideas because they are a gate to the most dangerous racism that today begins with Arabs and later with Jews." Members of the Labor Party also announced that they rejected the idea of transfer. They warned that such ideas could be used by fanatical elements to create further problems in the city. They expressed their desire to see "Acre develop as a city with a Jewish majority and a city of coexistence in peace like other mixed cities in the state of Israel."

Not everyone was upset by Bar Lev's statements. Morris Ben Shoshan had formed his own independent list, "For the Sake of Jewish Acre," three weeks prior to Bar Lev's call for a "positive transfer." Ben Shoshan requested the letter ט to represent his list, the same letter used by Moledet in the national elections.[31] Ben Shoshan claimed that Bar Lev had stolen the transfer idea from him.[32] Bar Lev, responding to the uproar of the previous week, stated that the problem was not his use of the word *transfer* but that he had called for Judaizing Acre: "The Arabs are aiming for Acre to be an Arab city and the uproar stems from this. Listen, in the preceding term, Mayor Doron moved more than 300 families to Makr. The difference is that I propose better conditions, but the method is the same. The Arab politicos who sit on the council today sat then also. Today, when someone from the Likud says this, he's a racist, and in my opinion, this is hypocrisy."[33]

In the elections for the Knesset, held 1 November 1988, the Likud and other national rightist parties such as Tehiya, Tsomet, and Moledet received about 44 percent of the votes cast in Acre. The Labor and other national leftist parties such as Mapam, Ratz, and the Progressive List for Peace accounted for only a little over 28 percent. The remainder of Acre's votes went to Arab-affiliated parties such as Hadash and the Arab Democratic Party (13 percent) or the religious parties — Shas, the National Religious Party, and Agudah (almost 11 percent). The remaining 4 percent was split among a number of small, single-issue or special-constituency parties. With the formation of a Labor-Likud-Shas "unity" coalition government in December 1988, each party held several of the ministries that played important roles in local government. Had either Labor or Likud been able to form a government without the other, its local branches could have used this as part of their campaign strategy since they could assert they would have better access to national officials than members of the opposing party. Going into the municipal elections, Bar Lev knew that if local residents voted as they had for the Knesset he was closer to polling a majority of voters in the city than De Castro. De Castro, however, had the advantage of being the incumbent. Bar Lev needed a campaign issue that would motivate a majority of local residents to support the Likud. "Yahud Acre" (Judaizing Acre) became that issue.

The Likud branch returned to the attack in the 9 December *Yedi'ot 'Akko,* proclaiming, "I accuse,"[34] and asking, "What's all the yelling about?" It made two points:

1. Eli De Castro promised to build an Arab neighborhood in Acre and a mosque in Shkhūnāt Wolfson. The Likud faction in the municipality prevented the realization of his scheme.
2. In the 1960s, Jews lived in the Old City who were vacated to the *ma'abarot* in disgraceful and inhuman conditions and all this for the purpose of improving the Old City.
   Is what was done to Jews forbidden to do to Arabs?

De Castro was lambasted for comparing Bar Lev's proposal to Judaize Acre to Kristelnacht, "a comparison that blasphemes Jews. Shame and insult." The Likud accused De Castro of having stopped the process of Arabs moving from the Old City to Makr. His promises to build an Arab neighborhood and a mosque in Shkhūnāt Wolfson had stopped Arabs from leaving the city, a process the party wished to renew. The election manifesto ended by noting that De Castro had publicly told the municipal council that "Acre was an Arab city before the founding of the state," which they concluded meant that he had reconciled himself to the fact that Acre was an Arab city.

These first manifestos provide early indications of how the election campaign in Acre would develop. Just as the national campaign had been seen by many Israelis as a critical turning point for Israel's future, Bar Lev and the Likud tried to introduce that same level of gravity into the municipal election. Acre's election was to be a referendum on the city's future: would Acre be an Arab or a Jewish city? The possibility that it could continue as a mixed city, admittedly a somewhat ambiguous existence often fraught with tension, was lost in the polarizing rhetoric of nationalism.

In the 16 December 1988 *Yedi'ot 'Akko,* the Likud's manifesto continued with the "I accuse" theme. This time De Castro was castigated for not having done enough to attract new immigrants to the city during his five years as mayor. The key event in this charge was his refusal to absorb Ethiopian immigrants in the city in 1984 and 1985. The Likud asserted that he had turned away Jewish immigrants so that the delicate balance between the Arab and Jewish residents of the city would not be destroyed. (A different local reading of his refusal suggested that he had refused the Ethiopians because they were black and so were often mistaken as Arabs. Their lack of education and skills and their dependence on government welfare payments were also cited as factors in his decision.) Because De Castro had refused to accept the Ethiopian immigrants, the Likud charged, Jewish homeowners who wanted to sell had to sell to Arabs. "For the massive penetration of Arabs to Jewish neighborhoods, you are guilty. For the lack of immigrant absorption, you are guilty. Judaizing Acre Only Bar-Lev Can Do."

The Labor branch responded to the Likud charges with a manifesto of its own. "We need lovers of our city, and not those who throw sticks in the wheels of others' hard work." The claim that De Castro had promised to build a mosque in Wolfson was dismissed as the product of a fertile imagination concocted by "distributors of lies and fabrications." The Labor branch stressed that what was needed to draw Jews to Acre was not speeches about "transfer," which only drove people away and slandered and shamed the city on every street of the country. The manifesto stressed that while Acre was a hard city to manage it was also a beautiful place full of challenges to those who loved it.

As the incumbent, De Castro fought his Likud challenger not only through words but by taking action to demonstrate he could solve Acre's problems. In this, he was aided by his contacts in national government ministries and agencies and his personal ties to important Labor Party officials and ministers. On 6 January 1989, it was announced that Acre would receive NIS 3.2 million for the development of tourism in the city.[35] At the end of January, Simha Dinitz, chairman of the Jewish Agency, announced during a visit to Acre that the entire city would now be included in the Project Renewal framework, previously limited to East Acre. The agency had already invested $15 million in projects in the city. It was considering allocating an additional $30 million for new projects and development.[36] In February, Uri Gordon, head of the Absorption Department of the Jewish Agency, announced that seventy families from France and South America would be settled in the city over the next year in order to halt the "Arabization" of the city. The agency was also budgeting $30 million to finance Project Renewal's cultural programs in Acre, and it called on the Israeli government to invest an equal sum in physical improvements.[37] De Castro called on the government to grant A+ status to the city (which would qualify local residents for special benefits and grants, the most important of which was a 15 percent reduction in income taxes), to encourage investment, and to provide financial assistance to beleaguered firms. At the end of February, Shimon Peres, then deputy prime minister and finance minister, visited Acre. He announced that he was willing to recognize it as "a single national model" and to grant it the same privileges accorded to areas designated A+ for national development purposes.[38]

The Likud and Labor Parties were joined in the race for council seats by a number of independent lists, all of which reflected concern over the city's future in the names they took for themselves. Morris Ben Shoshan's list, For the Sake of Jewish Acre, was joined by Uri Kaslasi's National Independent Faction (which had the support of Tsomet members in Acre). Kaslasi decided to form his own list after Our Acre, of which he was a member, disbanded to join with the Likud. Both Ben Shoshan and Kaslasi entered their names as candidates for mayor as well, only to withdraw later and throw their support behind the Likud candidate, David Bar Lev. Dov Kimche, a local Mapam member, formed One Acre (a united Arab-Jewish list) and also entered the mayoral race. Yossi Fitosi, who had not received a realistic spot on the Labor Party's list for the council, decided to run on an independent list, For Acre's Future. He received the endorsement and support of Israel Doron, who had served as mayor for thirteen years prior to De Castro's election. Fitosi's list decided not to endorse any of the candidates for the mayoral race.

Complaints came from veteran Ashkenazi politicians on both the right and the left that they had been pushed out of either the Labor Party or the Likud. Hanoch Hatzak, chairman for the Northern District of the National Workers Union, threw his support behind Kaslasi. His explanation, when challenged, of why he had previously supported Likud Party candidates was that Yosef Iluz, the Likud chairman in Acre, had pushed out all the old-timers and Ashkenazim.[39] Several longtime members of the Labor Party branch in Acre also resigned during the election, including Israel Doron, the former mayor. One member, Yehudah Ventura, gave as his reason that the party was ruled by family *hamūlōt,* making it impossible for him to contribute. Israel Doron gave his support in the mayoral election to David Bar Lev. In *Yedi'ot 'Akko* on 2 February 1989, Doron charged that the Labor branch was controlled by interests that had returned the city to feudal rule. He, too, complained that the party's Acre branch was ruled by family *hamūlōt* who were only interested in securing positions for themselves.

The local branches of Rakah and the Progressive List for Peace joined forces to form the United Acre List, while another independent Arab list ran under the name Sons of Acre. For the first time, no Arab candidate stood for the office of mayor. The Arab lists threw their support behind the Labor candidate, Eli De Castro. David Ben Shoshan, manager of the Legal Services office, formed an independent list, the Movement to Aid Everyone, which ran a slate of candidates for the municipal council. Two religious lists entered the elections — Shas and Mafdal (the National Religious Party).

The mayoral competition between David Bar Lev and Eli De Castro established the tone for the overall election campaign. Bar Lev and his supporters made "Judaizing Acre" the primary focus of their campaign. De Castro, however, also wanted to keep Acre a Jewish city, as his frequent calls for government assistance to prevent loss of Jewish residents proved. The right-wing faction needed to differentiate its platform from De Castro's concerns, which it did by taking a decidedly anti-Arab stance. Bar Lev made it clear that as mayor he would represent only Acre's Jewish citizens. In a similar fashion, Morris Ben Shoshan's slate listed its objectives as follows: to stop the Jewish emigration from the city, reduce Jewish unemployment, prevent intermarriage, cancel mixed Arab-Jewish school classrooms, stop the penetration of Arabs into Jewish neighborhoods, and provide housing and tax benefits only to discharged soldiers.[40] Acre's Arab citizens and their problems of unemployment, housing, and inadequate educational facilities were simply ignored.

The animosity of the election campaign carried over into meetings of the local council and the conduct of municipal business. At the meeting during the first week of January 1989, Bar Lev's transfer proposal was finally debated at great length. In an extremely tense session, the councillors spoke their minds about it. Bar Lev claimed that an Arabic notice circulating in the Old City, which had been signed by the Arab council members, called for him to be personally harmed because of his racist expressions. Ḥilmi Shafʿī and Mohammad Shaʿaban both pointed out that the Arab residents did not oppose or disturb the municipal council's efforts to Judaize the city or settle new Jewish immigrants. Razmi Ḥouri, for his part, said, "For me, the blood of Jew and Arab are equal and we need to educate the public this way. I don't accept Bar Lev's words." Morris Ben Shoshan said, "They ask who is a Jew. It's this way: a Jew is someone whose father is a Jew and who is holding an M-16." Shaʿaban asked Ben Shoshan how he could talk this way, seeing as "your wife raised my children."[41] The battle lines were clearly drawn. Needed repairs at the Arab high school to prevent water from leaking into the building were not being made, so the students went on strike that same month. The deputy mayor responsible for taking care of educational facilities was David Bar Lev. To the Arab residents of the city, the neglect of their schools reinforced their belief that he wished to expel them from the city and would use whatever means were at his disposal to accomplish that goal.

On 3 February 1989, in *Yediʿot ʿAkko,* both Shas and Mafdal announced that they supported David Bar Lev for mayor. Likud manifestos in the same issue repeated charges made in earlier notices — that De Castro had promised to build an Arab neighborhood and a mosque in

Shkhūnāt Wolfson and that he had said that Acre was and is an Arab city. The Likud branch then leveled a new accusation — that PLO supporters endorsed De Castro. The manifesto claimed that Rakah, the Progressive List for Peace, and the Sons of Acre had agreed to support De Castro in return for general promises that "are a danger to the Jewish future of the city of Acre." It noted that this was the first time since the state's founding that the Labor Party had signed an agreement with PLO supporters. "In signing this agreement, De Castro gives legitimacy to the representatives of Rakah, the Progressive List for Peace, the Sons of the Village, and all the nationalists in the Old City." It concluded by asking, "Will you allow Arabs to determine who will be mayor?"

The success of the Likud in setting the agenda for the elections can be seen in how other political slates adapted their rhetoric to the themes of the Likud campaign. The theme of Jews leaving Acre appeared in election advertisements run by Yossi Fitosi's slate. One featured an interview with Nurit and Dani, who were leaving the city, and focused on the reasons for their decision. Their complaints centered on the lack of attractions in the city, the quality of life, the lack of space for private homes, and unemployment problems. While Fitosi adopted the theme of Jews leaving Acre, he did not use the anti-Arab rhetoric of the Likud. In his notices, he remained silent on Arab-Jewish relations in the city, as did a number of other candidates for the municipal council such as Uri Kaslasi, David Ben Shoshan, and Dov Kimche.

In the 10 February *Yedi'ot 'Akko,* Bar Lev for the first time demonstrated to local residents that he, too, had connections with ministers at the national level who would provide assistance to Acre. The Likud manifesto announced that Bar Lev and the director general of industrial services had agreed to hold an industrial fair in Acre. In dealings with Ariel Sharon, minister of industry and trade, Bar Lev got an agreement to bring investors and high-technology factories to the city. The Likud brought a new set of charges against De Castro — that he had signed a surplus votes agreement with the Arabs so that "surplus Jewish votes are likely to enter an extra Arab representative to the council! Therefore, a vote for Labor is a vote to benefit an Arab slate! Only a vote for the Likud is a vote extended to Jews!" The Labor Party launched an attack of its own, "Lies, slanders, libels, untruth, and bloodshed! This is their way — and not our way! . . . Residents of Acre, they're throwing sand in your eyes!" their manifesto declared. The establishment of a new local association, of Acre residents who supported Mayor De Castro's reelection B.'A.D. (Ba'ad Acre De Castro, or For Acre De Castro), was announced. "I'm voting for De Castro because of tolerance," their manifesto asserted.

On 11 February, several hundred residents of the city (mostly

Arabs), as well as residents from nearby kibbutzim, made their views public on Bar Lev's transfer idea by staging a protest demonstration in Acre on Weitzman Street between the old and new parts of the city. Shūtāfūt and Qav 'Adōm (Red Line), a Galilee-based peace organization that opposes the Israeli occupation of the West Bank and Gaza Strip, organized the demonstration. Knesset members Charlie Biton (Ratz) and Hussein Faras (Mapam) attended along with local council members Ramzi Ḥouri, Shafʿī, and Dov Kimche. Participants carried signs in Hebrew, English, and Arabic with slogans opposing transfer such as "Arabs will stay in Acre." Speakers referred to transfer as an expression of racism (fig. 8). Knesset member Hussein Faras, himself from Acre, said that no matter how racist the government is the Arabs will remain and work against racism until they get peace. Josef Bourda, a Jewish resident of Acre for thirty-two years, said that in Acre there were no closed walls. Six boys and girls, Arab and Jewish, released doves during one part of the ceremony. At the end, an Arab and a Jewish man planted an olive tree next to the stage. All of the demonstrators were invited to link hands to form a human chain between the old and new cities. The demonstration ended quietly, the only incident occurring when a group of passersby shouted at the demonstrators that they did not need outsiders telling Acre residents what to do.

The demonstration itself became part of the political battle. On 17 February, a half-page advertisement appeared in *Tsafon 1*. "The price of the agreement between De Castro and the PLO supporters—no longer Jewish-Arab Acre but Arab-Jewish Acre" ran across the top in large letters. A picture of the stage at the demonstration, over which a banner had been draped that read "Acre—an Arab-Jewish city" in Arabic and Hebrew, was captioned, "Demonstration of PLO supporters that occurred last Shabbat in Acre." The advertisement was unsigned. In the meantime, however, the Labor Party had filed a formal complaint with the Central Election Committee about the Likud's charges that De Castro had PLO support. The committee's decision was announced in the 17 February issue of *Yediʿot ʿAkko*. Bar Lev and the Likud were ordered to remove statements regarding De Castro and PLO support from their publications and to refrain from making any future statements. In his investigations, the judge found the claim to be without basis and forbade its use.

Undaunted, the Likud changed its tactics only slightly. The manifesto for that week read, "Arab Supporters of De Castro Incite against Jews!" What followed claimed to be a Hebrew translation of an Arabic notice that "moderate Arabs" had distributed in the Old City. The moderates expressed their intention to remain in Acre no matter what happened: "It's their opinion that dry land in Acre is better in their

FIG. 8. Demonstration in Acre against transfer (1989). (Photo by author.)

eyes than a castle outside." The advertisement closed with the statement "If these are the moderates, it would be interesting what the
Arab fanatics think." In another advertisement, the Likud warned lo-
cal residents that they had to vote for Bar Lev in order to protect
Jewish Acre: "Jewish residents of Acre, you who are worried about the
Arabization of Acre, who are afraid of the intimacy of Jewish girls with
Arabs, who are opposed to mixed classrooms with Arabs. Now it's
already clear. In the coming elections the votes will be split between
the Arabs who support De Castro and the Jews who support Bar Lev.
De Castro is not leaving a choice."

On the last Friday before the elections, local papers were packed
with political advertisements and manifestos. *Yedi'ot 'Akko,* usually con-
sisting of only a page or two, expanded to thirteen pages on 24 February.
For the first time in the election campaign, Acre's Arab lists printed
manifestos (in Hebrew) in the broadsheet. The United Acre List called
on residents to vote for it, "For the sake of Jewish-Arab understanding,
for the sake of good neighborly relations and cooperation between Jews
and Arabs, . . . [and] for the sake of our city being an example of joint
living between Jews and Arabs that are destined to live together in one
city." The Acre branch of Hadash (Rakah and the Black Panthers)
published a manifesto against Yosef Israel. Israel was the centerpiece of
Likud charges about secret agreements made between De Castro and
the Arab slates. He claimed to be a Hadash Party member who was
present when the secret agreements were signed, as had been publicized
in local papers the previous week. The party had broken off contact with
him in October 1988 because he was seen as untrustworthy and willing to
do anything for money.

Charges and countercharges filled the pages. The Labor Party notices presented Bar Lev as a danger to the city: "Jew will speak about Jew
this way?" they asked, referring to his attacks on De Castro. They described Bar Lev's actions as aiding fanatics who were enemies of the city.
They once again denied the existence of a secret agreement with members of the Arab lists. A "concerned citizens" notice said of Bar Lev that
"if he realizes his policies, Acre will change from a quiet and calm city to
a cask of explosives. . . . [Bar Lev has] succeeded in entering hatred
freely between Jews and ideas of atrocities in the Arabs' hearts." Taking
a cue from the Likud notices, another concerned citizen announced that
Rakah supporters were with the party: "A Rakah man, the man who
shook the hand of Arafat — Yosef Israel — was received as an honored
member in the Likud branch in Acre. So who's doing everything to get
the seat?" Likud notices warned that De Castro was making it possible
for Acre to become Arabized: "You the voters will decide if Acre will
remain with a Jewish majority or an Arab majority." They again asserted

that De Castro was in league with the Arab lists. They presented the choice before the voters as between Bar Lev, supported by the Jewish Zionist parties, and De Castro, supported by Rakah, the PLP, and the Arab Sons of Acre.

Election day passed without incident, although at one polling place in the Old City swastikas in the colors of the PLO flag had been drawn on the voting slips of the Likud.[42] Likud election volunteers also complained that they had been treated like enemies while circulating in the Old City. Both Labor and Likud mobilized their volunteers to encourage people to vote. These volunteers went door to door in the neighborhoods, knocking and reminding residents that they should vote. Fleets of cars provided transportation for those who needed it. In the late afternoon, Minister David Levy arrived in Acre and made a tour of the city to aid the Likud campaign. His efforts, however, were in vain. When the results were tallied, as one local paper put it, "a blue and white mayor [a reference to the Israeli flag], a man of the national camp, wasn't chosen this time either."[43]

De Castro defeated Bar Lev for the mayor's seat by only 319 votes.[44] Overall voter turnout was 50 percent in the Jewish and 80 percent in the Arab sector. De Castro received 85 percent of the votes in the Old City compared to Bar Lev's less than 1 percent. De Castro also carried the majority in Mandate Acre and the southern parts of the city. Bar Lev received a majority of the votes cast in North and East Acre. Shkhūnāt Wolfson and the central area of the city (between the Mandate City and the new northern neighborhoods) split almost evenly for each candidate. Bar Lev received the majority of votes cast by soldiers. For the local council, the majority of the seats went to the small local lists, which accounted for ten of the seventeen seats. The Labor Party received four seats (an increase of one), while the Likud won three (no increase). Each of the religious parties (Shas and Mafdal) received one seat. The two Arab lists — United Acre List and Sons of Acre — each received two seats (an increase of one each). Ben Shoshan's list, For the Sake of Jewish Acre, won two seats, while Fitosi's For Acre's Future and Kaslasi's National Independent Faction each received one. Once the celebrations ceased, the new council members settled down to the business of drawing up the coalition that would govern Acre for the next five years.

Making an Intifada: *Boundaries in the Electorate*

Through Acre's municipal elections, local residents were made aware of and forced to frame the boundaries of their identity — as citizens and members of a national group. Kimmerling (1985) outlines two approaches to defining the Israeli collectivity — the state of Israel versus Eretz Israel. The first approach, that of a democratic state, grants membership in the collectivity to all citizens. As citizens, residents of the state have certain obligations and responsibilities toward that state, which must be fulfilled (military service, participation in governing, paying taxes, and obeying laws). The state, in return, will secure the safety and well-being of its citizens. It is important to remember, however, that in most cases the status of citizen initially applied only to the *male* members of society, so such models of citizenship are implicitly male oriented and do not guarantee that women's rights and needs will be addressed. The second approach, that of a Jewish state, grants full membership in the collectivity to Jews anywhere in the world. Non-Jews may reside there, but they cannot have status equivalent to that of Jewish citizens. Relations between individuals and the state in this conception resemble kinship ties in which all Jewish citizens are part of the same family (while non-Jewish citizens are excluded as outsiders). Obligations and responsibilities toward the state center on upholding a Jewish lifestyle. The state, in return, secures the well-being and safety of its Jewish citizens in a paternalistic fashion. Within this model, women's lives as citizens would be structured around notions of appropriate gender roles within the traditional Jewish family (i.e., women serve as the gatekeepers of the collective, both as the wombs that produce the nation and as the preservers of its cultural traditions).[45] Each of these approaches can be seen in the opposing political rhetoric and practices of the Labor and Likud factions during the municipal elections. Through its election campaign, the Likud conjured up an *intifada* in Acre and then asked voters to support them in dealing with it.

In its first manifesto, the Likud branch defined a particular collectivity upon which to draw for votes in the upcoming elections. The Likud established for its supporters the proper parameters of their desires for recognition, security, and affiliation. By stating that Acre had the image of an Arab city, they implicitly asserted that the Jewishness of the city went unrecognized, both locally and nationally. Since Arabs had penetrated into every part of the city, Jews could no longer avoid contact with them. The Jewish residents lacked a secure lifestyle. Arabs had parties on the grass in Jewish neighborhoods, they played loud music, they opened their businesses next to the synagogues on Shabbat, and groups of Arab boys hassled Jewish girls. The message to local residents was clear: only the Likud and its candidate, David Bar Lev, could restore the Jewish collectivity to its proper place of dominance. Bar Lev would accomplish that by reducing or removing the Arab presence in the city (positive transfer) and restoring and strengthening the Jewish presence, so that once again the Jewish residents could fulfill their desires to live a

Jewish lifestyle in a Jewish city in a Jewish state. If adherence to democratic principles poses a threat to the security of the Jewish state, then democracy must be circumvented in order to protect the Jewish people.

In responding to this first manifesto, the Labor branch and the Arab lists established a different definition of the collectivity and its desires. By linking transfer to Kristelnacht, De Castro made a universal appeal — the victimization that Jews experienced in the Holocaust was likened to the victimization that Arabs would experience were a transfer policy implemented. Jewish residents of the city were invited to look beyond the boundaries of their identity to recognize similarities with the other. De Castro used the rhetoric of coexistence and good relations that must be protected. Coexistence and tolerance of difference are considered essential values in a democratic state. Again residents were being urged to affiliate with a more diverse collectivity, membership in which was determined by rights of citizenship rather than birth to Jewish parents. De Castro, however, constructed notions about security in terms of coexistence in a city with a Jewish majority. Notions like transfer threatened the security of the Jewish residents because such ideas could be used by fanatical elements to create problems. He wanted Acre to be recognized as a Jewish city whose Jewish residents are able to coexist with the Arab minority. In this, he expressed the "democratic, but Jewish" paradox that has served as the centerpiece of Labor Party policy in Israel since the founding of the state. In this formulation, the Israeli state will be democratic as long as it remains unequivocally Jewish.

The Arab lists also appealed to a "democratic public that values coexistence and good neighborly relations." They emphasized the democratic status of the Israeli state. Like all citizens in a democratic state, Arabs have the right to live where they wish, express their opinions, and live according to their own customs and traditions. For them, what matters is that Israel is a *democratic* state. They privileged this side of the "democratic, but Jewish" paradox by demanding their right as citizens to make their own decisions about how their lives and identities would be constructed. They tried to draw a wider circle of recognition and affiliation, one that includes rather than excludes them, in warning that racism that begins with Arabs would eventually engulf the Jews.

The Likud Party came to power nationally in 1977 on the strength of the vote of Mizrahi Israelis, many of whom voted for the Likud to protest the treatment they had received at the hands of successive Labor governments. In Acre, however, Labor has retained control of the municipal government since its inception in 1951. Although both De Castro and Bar Lev are Mizrahim (De Castro was born in Egypt, Bar Lev in Morocco), De Castro represented the party that has been the stronghold of Ashkenazi power in Acre. Bar Lev played on Mizrahi experiences of discrimination. He painted a picture of Acre residents as suffering at the hands of a Labor government that moved Jewish residents to "disgraceful" transit camps but refused to move Arabs. He described a government that prevented Jewish residents from bettering their lives and fulfilling their Zionist duty through its refusal to accept Ethiopian immigrants, thus forcing local Jews to sell their homes to Arabs instead. De Castro was pictured as a man who loved Arabs, who put Arab before Jewish welfare in the city.

Bar Lev established in his campaign propaganda a series of equivalences (Laclau and Mouffe 1985) that link De Castro and the Arabs. De Castro promised to build an Arab neighborhood, he refused to treat Arab residents in the same way Jewish residents were treated, he publicly called Acre an Arab city, he turned away potential Jewish immigrants, he signed agreements with the Arabs, and finally he was supported by followers of the PLO. In Likud literature, De Castro stood for Arab neighborhoods, preferential treatment for Arabs, Acre as an Arab city, and an Arab leader. Bar Lev attempted to create a relation of total equivalence that would place De Castro outside the bounds of the Jewish collectivity in the minds of local residents and would produce an antagonism that would lead local residents to vote for the Likud.

Bar Lev created a similar relation of equivalence between the Arab residents of Acre and Palestinians (the PLO) through his campaign rhetoric. His proposal of positive transfer was the first link in the chain of equivalences. Up to that point, the term *transfer* had been used only when speaking of the Palestinian population of the territories. By extending its use to the Arab population of Acre, Bar Lev implied that they, too, have no rights to the land. By focusing on Arab penetration of Jewish neighborhoods, Bar Lev invoked the military image of the enemy who penetrates behind the lines to attack treacherously from within. Ḥilmi Shafʿī's moderate slate, Sons of Acre, was referred to as the Sons of the Village, thus linking it in Jewish residents' minds with the radical movement of that name (which was said to be linked to leftist factions within the PLO). The Arab members of Rakah and the Progressive List for Peace were labeled PLO supporters and likened to "all the nationalists in the Old City." Finally, Bar Lev reversed positions with the Arabs by charging that they were inciting against Jews, thus rousing Jewish fears of another potential holocaust.

Looked at from a gendered perspective, this election campaign was even more striking. Both the Labor and Likud slates included women as candidates (eight out of thirty-two for Labor, seven of twenty-eight for Likud), but only the Labor platform had a woman placed in a realistic slot on the list (number three). Ben Shoshan's platform included only one woman, placed thirteenth on the list of candidates. If this was a battle over the city's future, it was a battle that was being waged by the men (Jewish and Palestinian) of the city.

Bar Lev's political rhetoric was that of militarized masculinity, with its warnings about Arab penetration of Jewish neighborhoods and claims of Jewish girls being preyed upon by Arab youth or, even worse, intermarrying. Phrases like *ba'ḥădīrāh ha'masīvīt shel ha'ărāvīm lshikūnōt ha'yehūdīm* (in English, "the massive penetration of Arabs into Jewish neighborhoods") played on the Jewish sexual fear of Arabs. The image of the sexually aggressive Arab man is prevalent in Israeli society. Many Jewish parents I spoke with in Acre worried that their daughters might become involved with Arab youths (not knowing they were Arab) and would marry them. Residents claimed that there were a lot of mixed Arab-Jewish couples living in Shkhūnāt Wolfson, a result, they said, of integrated living.[46] When Ben Shoshan defined a Jew as someone holding an M-16, he reinforced the soldier as the ideal image to which all Israeli Jewish males should aspire. It is the duty of Israeli Jewish men to protect their homes (and by extension their wives and daughters) from sexual assaults by foreign (Palestinian) men.

What is striking here are the underlying notions about women's nature as revealed in the fear that Jewish women will marry Arab men if they are not kept separated. Recall that women in Israel function as the gatekeepers of the collective — one is Jewish if one is born to a Jewish mother. When parents worry that their daughters will marry Arab men "by mistake," they betray a vision of women's nature as driven by passion. Unless properly controlled and supervised, women can become involved with inappropriate others (however unknowingly); in the process, they will bring chaos to the Jewish collective. Women's sexuality is embroiled in the military conflict. Consider the folk narrative in which a Palestinian man, passing as Jewish, seduces an Israeli Jewish female soldier, only to reveal to her at the height of their sexual encounter that he is an Arab. It is not surprising, therefore, that within the collectivity as imagined by the Likud and its adherents women would have no real voice (consider the absence of women on the election lists as viable candidates). Women are not to be trusted.[47]

De Castro, in responding to Bar Lev, played into the gender stereotypes of Acre's residents. This was part of the problem with his campaign; by drawing comparisons with the victimization Jews experienced in the Holocaust, he was ironically calling forth a feminized image. Israeli masculinity was created in direct opposition to that of Jewish men in the diaspora, who were often portrayed as weak, impotent, and unable to defend themselves and their families, in other words as women. De Castro employed notions of peaceful coexistence and tolerance in his campaign rhetoric. He was the diplomat to Bar Lev's military soldier.

Unfortunately, the skills of diplomacy — an ability to listen, willingness to compromise, avoidance of force — are often seen as feminine attributes, further reinforcing the weak image of De Castro in the eyes of many community members.[48] Bar Lev's often repeated campaign phrase ("Only Bar Lev can . . .") portrayed his self-image as a man of action and force; De Castro had difficulty coming up with a comparable strong image for himself.

The Arab community of Acre recognized the danger of the Likud's rhetoric and came together in a united front to oppose his candidacy. For the first time, no Arab candidate stood for mayor. Internal political differences were submerged, and every party united behind De Castro. Volunteers worked to get every Arab resident who was eligible to vote registered before the election. Turnout in the Arab sector reached 80 percent. The Arab slates running for the municipal council also benefited from the high rate of voter turnout, and four Arab councillors won seats on the local council. The Arab residents of Acre did something in this election that the Arab citizens of Israel had never done — they voted as a bloc. Were Israeli Palestinians to vote as a bloc in the Knesset elections, they could account for as many as twenty seats, which would be a significant number.[49] It is possible that in the face of a threat similar to that which Bar Lev posed for the Palestinian residents of Acre, Israeli Palestinians would indeed unite and vote as a bloc. By uniting Acre's Arabs against him, Bar Lev brought about his own defeat.

De Castro was not as successful in combating the Likud's political rhetoric. He appealed to universal values — tolerance, coexistence, and love of the city. When he warned that Jewish extremism played into the hands of Arab fanatics who were the enemies of the city, he reinforced Bar Lev's characterization of Arabs as others who should be feared. De Castro's Acre embraced its Arab and its Jewish residents. His campaign notices stressed both his personal connections to national leaders and what he had accomplished for the city — building projects, the expansion of Project Renewal, and the development of education. While he asserted that talk about transfer slandered the city, this message was directed at those residents for whom such activities would be morally untenable, that is, the more educated and cultured residents of the city, those who valued democratic principles. He portrayed his opposition as liars, slanderers, and speakers of blood libel. He fought back by using the legal system when Bar Lev linked him in public notices to the PLO. Only in his last election advertisements did he question, "Jew will speak about Jew this way?" finally raising the specter of bloodshed and enmity between Jews (with reverberations going back to the founding days of the state when Ben-Gurion [Labor] decided to open fire on and sink an Irgun [later Likud] ship). De Castro stressed a democratic message rather than attempting to mobilize the support of Jewish residents as Jews. When both religious parties endorsed Bar Lev's candidacy, De Castro was even further removed from his Jewish constituency. In the end, the Arab voters of the city gave De Castro his victory. Bar Lev, however, had "made an *intifada*" in the city, the effects of which would be felt long after the election campaigns had ended.

The Aftermath of the Elections: Acre's Future

The animosities that became public during the election did not disappear when the voting ended. De Castro, personally insulted during the election campaign, was not going to forget the behavior of his opponents. "They called me 'Mahmoud De Castro' and said that my mother was an Arab. I won't rest until the truth is known, until all the residents of Acre know that their mayor does not lie." Bar Lev, for his part, continued to assert that "the Jews of Acre want me as their mayor."[50] On 10 March 1989, the secretary and council of the local Labor branch announced the formation of a new governing coalition in the city.[51] Headed by Labor and its affiliated Sons of Acre list, with six seats, it also included the Mafdal member Uri Mizraḥi, Yossi Fitosi of the Acre's Future list, and Uri Kaslasi of the National Independent Faction. Unofficially, the coalition also received the support of the two Rakah council members. The members of the coalition "promised cooperation on behalf of all the citizens of Acre with no difference" and continuation of the city's development as a place "that protects its Jewish majority and lives in peace with its Arab citizens." Uri Mizraḥi, Ḥilmi Shafʿī, and Uri Kaslasi were appointed deputy mayors, while Yossi Fitosi was named to head a committee to solve the problem of residents leaving the city. Fitosi said that he agreed to join the coalition because "We didn't want a coalition of eight mandates, that relied on Rakah. We think that the coalition needs to rely on a majority, and on a Jewish majority only."[52]

On 17 March 1989, the Likud published another notice in *Yedi ʿot ʿAkko* — their report on the election results. "Sixty-seven percent of the Jewish residents of Acre gave their trust to the Likud and only 33 percent of the Jewish residents gave their votes to Labor." They reported that they had tried to form a coalition with only Jewish council members; they had even been willing to give up the offices of deputy mayor, but De Castro refused. He had made it clear that he would not form a coalition with either the Likud or Morris Ben Shoshan's list because of the way they had personally attacked him during the election campaign. On 7 April, Ben Shoshan published a notice in *Yedi ʿot ʿAkko* "congratulating" Mohamed Shaʿaban on his selection as adviser to the mayor for

Arab affairs. Ben Shoshan noted that two of Shaʿaban's brothers, his son, and a nephew were employed by the municipality — and that his family consisted of 317 voters. The Likud Party had contested the election, but a recount confirmed De Castro's victory.

The first council meeting in early April was explosive. After an initial round of yelling, De Castro brought forward his candidates for deputy mayor for approval. The opposition (the Likud members, the Shas representative, and Ben Shoshan's two representatives) abstained from voting, so the candidates were approved unanimously. A new round of yelling broke out, which culminated in Bar Lev jumping onto the table, striding to the front, where De Castro was seated, pulling out a package, and announcing, "I found it proper to give you this, since you're obliged to Arabs." He pulled a red and white *kûfîya* (traditional Arab headdress for men) from the package, threw it on De Castro's head, and walked back across the table. As he returned to his seat, he said, "He prevented me from speaking. I will liquidate him; I'll be mayor in any event."[53]

A pattern of harassment ensued from this meeting onward. Arab members of the council were particularly subject to jeers and insults. Expressions such as "Arabs out of Acre" or "Arabs to Jordan" were common. The opposition council members disrupted every meeting possible. They also continued publishing notices to try to hurt De Castro. Thus, on 2 June Ben Shoshan again attacked De Castro, this time for giving a job to the daughter of Hasan Sarwan as a "repayment." On 14 July, the representatives of Shas, the Likud, and For a Jewish Acre published a "municipal report," in which they listed the "achievements" of the coalition opposite the "claims and demands" of the opposition. Their achievements included the investment of money to develop the Old City, a decision to postpone Jewish requests for aid so that Arab residents could be assisted, the closing of a MATNAS in the eastern part of town and the opening of a center in the Old City, and so on. Their claims and demands? They wanted the municipality to invest an equal amount in every part of the town, to grant all requests for aid (including one from a crippled soldier), to reopen the MATNAS, and so on. They concluded, "It's no wonder that De Castro says on radio that the Jews in the city are losing their majority status and in another five years there'll be an Arab mayor."[54] On 28 July, the governing coalition responded to the opposition with an advertisement of their own, "The Public in Acre Needs to Know," in which they provided answers to questions concerning what actions the municipal council had been taking. One of the questions asked who suffers from the atmosphere of racism and tension in the city, and their answer was the residents, especially the Jewish ones, some of whom were leaving due to the problem. Their solution? "Arab and Jewish life in

Acre — it's a fact like in Israel generally. We need to foster relations of friendship and peace and to prevent fanatics from both sides. In such a situation, Jews will want to come to Acre and its residents won't abandon her (also for other reasons)."[55]

Some residents, tired of the tension in the council, formed a group, the Forum, which demanded that the coalition and opposition cease their fighting and work together to solve the city's problems.[56] The major problem that members of the Forum saw facing the city was the out-migration of Jewish residents to nearby cities such as Nahariyya. In the months after the election, they claimed that 250 families had left. The Forum received support from the Jewish shopkeepers of the city, who joined together in their own organization, the Parliament of Acre, to demand that the municipality do something to stop the worsening social and economic situation. In late July, members of the local council united to call on residents to prevent emigration from the city. They also called on the appropriate government officials to raise Acre's status to that of the surrounding Jewish cities. Residents were asked to see remaining in Acre as part of their "Zionist destiny" and to contribute to fortifying the city.[57] At a meeting with the Parliament, De Castro called Jews who were leaving the city "traitors to the Jewish people" and blamed the out-migration on the "lists and parties that let the racist genie from the bottle: 'Jewish Acre,' 'transfer,' and so on."[58]

The effects of the local election also reverberated throughout Acre's residential areas. In Shkhūnāt Wolfson, many Jewish residents saw it as having a significant effect on Jewish-Arab relationships in the neighborhood. A Mizraḥi woman explained, "In the elections, they [the Arabs] got security. Now they're getting lots of help from the mayor; he really helps them, he even promised them a mosque here!" Another Mizraḥi woman insisted that the mayor was to blame for the situation in the city. "He worries about votes for himself. A man without conscience. The Arabs raised him to the leadership of the city and he took out the Jewish deputies, and there a man *'Am Ha'Aretz* [of the people of the land] is Arab instead of Jewish." The theme that De Castro's election had brought security to the Arabs of Wolfson was repeated by many Jewish residents. Others reported that they no longer felt safe going to the Old City. In July, a young Jewish man told me of an alleged incident in which a young Arab man walked over to a Jewish woman he knew and grabbed her breast. The youth would get off, he explained, because his father was a strong supporter of De Castro, the "Arab" mayor. This Jewish man had already moved his family to Nahariyya because he was afraid of what would happen to his three-year-old daughter if she grew up in Acre in contact with Arabs, especially Arab boys.

Not all Arab residents of the city shared their Jewish neighbors'

assessment of the election's outcome in terms of increased "security."
While there was an increase in "incidents," usually involving young men
who threw stones at passersby or harassed Jewish people touring the Old
City, many Arab residents were uneasy about the continued attacks of
the opposition faction on the Arab sector of Acre. A number of people
reported increased tension and more confrontations. One young woman
noted that in these confrontations Jews would say things like "I'll do
terror" or "I'll make an *intifada* here" as well as swearing and using
insulting epithets such as "whore." Another woman said, "The *intifada*
has become the readiest word on their lips during fights. . . . 'What are
you doing here? An *intifada?* Go and make an *intifada* in the Strip, not
here!'" An Arab man added, "Every person who has a quarrel is told
'we'll throw you out.' "

The municipal election campaign stirred up a great deal of anger
and fear in both Arab and Jewish residents. On the afternoon of 9 May
1989, the day Israelis were remembering their fallen soldiers, this atmosphere, in combination with increased tensions nationally, contributed
to the stabbing death in Acre's municipal market of Jerais Ben Awad, a
fourteen-year-old Arab boy from Makr. After the memorial services the
previous evening, a group of Jewish youths had rampaged through a
mixed Acre neighborhood yelling, "Arabs are dirty sons of bitches,"
and, "Arabs get out." Rumors had circulated on the streets earlier that
day about an alleged stabbing of a Golani Brigade soldier by a local
Arab on the main street.[59] There were also reports of Arab youths who
refused to stand respectfully during the sounding of the siren on Remembrance Day. Greengrocers who witnessed the attack on the boy said that
some people in the market had incited the Jewish man guilty of the
stabbing to go to the stall of the Arab boy.[60]

The opposition's disruptive behavior at municipal council meetings
did not stop, however. At a meeting in May 1990, opposition members
attacked the Arabs on the council because they did not attend the Remembrance Day ceremony for Israeli soldiers. One member of the For
Jewish Acre list asked Deputy Mayor Ḥilmi Shafʿī if the reason he did
not attend was because he was afraid of the shock committees (committees in the territories that are believed to control the *intifada*) or the
intifada commanders. Morris Ben Shoshan was even more caustic: "You
said you came to Holocaust Day, sure you came. We'll soon be coming
to your Holocaust Day."[61]

By 1992, De Castro had cemented his control over the council. He
brought one of the Likud members, Aharon Lahiani, into his governing
coalition by giving him the education portfolio. The oppositional stance
that the Likud members had assumed toward the council had continued,
but instead of bringing about De Castro's downfall it had caused an

internal crisis in the party itself. Likud unity dissolved into factional fights. With Labor's victory in the national elections in 1992, De Castro's position was further strengthened. The demographic battle over the city's future also appeared to have been decided. Eight thousand Russian and three thousand Ethiopian immigrants were settled in or near Acre between 1990 and 1992. The new immigrants brought with them funding from the Jewish Agency, programs to help with their absorption, and an injection of new capital into the community. Since they account for almost one-quarter of the city's population, there is no longer any question about whether Acre will remain a Jewish city.

CHAPTER 6

Revisiting Coexistence

Israeli Jews and Palestinians who live in Acre continue to confront the realities of living in a border zone, where the boundaries of identities and social relations do not neatly mesh. Consider the following incident one of my informants related in 1988–89: Basma and Ahmed went to visit their good friends, Yossi and Shula, for the evening. While their children played quietly in another room of the apartment, the adults turned on the television to watch *Mabat,* the nightly Israeli news program. A visitor walking through their neighborhood would probably have heard the announcer's voice echoing from apartment to apartment. Watching the news is a nightly ritual for most Israelis. On the program, the female announcer reported that a lone Arab terrorist had attacked and killed three Jewish residents of Jerusalem: a young female soldier, a middle-aged man, and an elderly male academic. Yossi exploded and began to curse. "We should just kill all the Arabs!" he raged. In the moment of quiet that followed his outburst, Basma calmly picked up the fruit knife from the bowl in front of her, handed it to him, spread her arms, and said, "Go ahead. Here I am."

That evening, Yossi's outburst was probably repeated in many homes in Tel Aviv, Jerusalem, Haifa, Afula, Rehovot, and Rishon L'Tzion. In those homes, there was no Basma present to challenge the characterization of all Arabs as terrorists, worthy of death. No Basma to disrupt and say, "Wait, what about me, your friend? Will you kill me as well? Are your categories absolute?"

Identities and Action in Acre

In this work, I have argued that while the residents of Acre may create their own local understandings of other people through their daily experiences, the Israeli state exercises considerable control over how identity (and thus social relations) are constructed in the local arena. Neighborly relations, lessons in school, and local political struggles do conform at times to the national logic. Acre's residents, however, have been constructing, modifying, and rejecting various components of the categories as they reflect on their local histories and life experiences, so that the content of the categories has not remained static.

That Israel is both a democratic and a Jewish state is the fundamental contradiction in the lives of all Israelis. These two terms — *democratic* and *Jewish* — underlie opposite ways of understanding the relations between individuals, identity, and the state. Israel as a democratic state implies that individuals, regardless of what other identities they may possess, are directly and uniformly linked to the state. This conception entails ideals of freedom and equality and suggests a community of individuals who express their political will at the ballot box. Here the state is the "organic community of free citizens as a whole" (Worsley 1984, 257). Israel as a Jewish state implies that only particular individuals, namely, those who are born or properly become Jewish, are directly and uniformly linked to the state. Those who are not Jewish (or not properly Jewish) have an inferior relation as objects, not subjects, of the state. This conception entails ideals of preferential treatment and suggests a community of individuals whose political will is the joint product of historical traditions, adherence to a common belief system, and birth. Here the state is the fullest expression of the genius of the Jewish people.

The tension between these two political ideas can be seen at work in each of the preceding chapters. In fact, Acre's residents manipulate this tension as they seek to reduce the ambiguities they experience living in a pluralistic environment. Thus, some Jewish residents of Shkhūnāt Wolfson vent their frustrations over living in a less than desirable neighborhood by scapegoating the Arab residents and asserting that things would be better if only Jews lived in the neighborhood. This allows them to mask their own low-class status within Acre. Many Mizraḥi residents get angry at the "democratic" treatment offered to their Arab neighbors. In critiquing the Israel as democracy frame in this way, they don't call into question their own discriminatory treatment by Israel as a Jewish state. To admit to themselves that the hardships and suffering they have endured as Israelis have not had some higher purpose (to help build Eretz Israel) would be psychologically devastating. At the same time, their privileging of Israel as a Jewish state is an indication that national prescriptions and identities have infiltrated local discourse. While local Mizraḥi residents manipulate the two frames to serve their own needs and interests, in doing so they also serve the state's interests — state accountability for Mizraḥi mistreatment is displaced onto the Palestinians. For the Palestinian residents, the democracy frame provides them with the ability to critique the discriminatory treatment they receive. Many of them believe that the Jewish residents must have been taught to be racist, rather than seeing their racism as an essential quality of Judaism. They explicitly link this racism to actions by state officials and to the notion that Israel is a Jewish state. Memories of violence serve as boundary markers. Jewish violence and intolerance reinforces Palestinian residents' beliefs that they are in the right and that Israel must become a democratic state. Palestinian violence and intolerance reinforce Jewish residents' fears and further strengthen their belief that Israel must remain a Jewish state.

Some residents of Wolfson have chosen to make a more complex, ambiguous construction of their categories so they can see their neighbors as human beings. They value the neighborhood's pluralistic nature because of the possibility that all sides will learn from each other and begin to create a social reality different from the one in which they are trapped. Coexistence offers the promise of a future when Palestinian and Jew can live together in peace and respect. For some of these people, the most important element in their relations with other residents is to be treated with respect. While "all Israel is one," some Jewish residents pragmatically note that they are treated with more honor and are cared for better by their Arab neighbors than their Jewish ones. Family honor notwithstanding, some Arab residents receive more assistance and support from Jewish neighbors than from their own family members. People make distinctions between the actions and relations they create due to "reality" and the ideal sets of relations suggested by broader categories of identity. They will still be galvanized into action on behalf of Arab or Jewish honor if they feel threatened.

The outcomes of the "Educating for Democracy" programs in Acre highlight outside efforts to control identity and some local resistance to these attempts. The Hebrew educational system teaches Jewish children that Israel is a Jewish state, that they have a historical and legitimate right to the land, and that they are a chosen people, a "light unto the nations." However, Mizraḥi children in Acre also internalize negative self-images of themselves as slow learners, needy, and "not quite human." They learn to resist by blocking out much of what they learn, but they retain the nationalist messages. The democracy programs attempt in a few short lessons and planned encounters to reverse the predominant messages present in the rest of the educational curriculum. Local Jewish students perceived the democracy programs as Ashkenazi impositions coming from outsiders with no real knowledge about what life is like in a mixed city. These students resisted the state's attempt to impose a "democratic" frame on them. Arab children expressed more willingness to participate because they are struggling to find some way to deal with the contradictions inherent in being an Israeli citizen and a Palestinian. Jewish teachers reject the programs because they call into question some of the knowledge they have been imparting to their students. Arab teachers reject the programs because they do not provide adequate knowledge for their students about the reality of life in Israel.

In the events surrounding the mixed *ganim,* Arab parents were will-ing to accept arguments for Jewish exclusivity because it meant that they would acquire new educational resources for their own children. Some Arab parents wanted their children to be exposed to a different culture and set of values at an early age so they could begin to learn about the Jews. They perceived this knowledge about Jewish culture as crucial to their child's future well-being and ability to successfully advance in Israeli society. Some Jewish parents did not want their children to be exposed to Arab culture. In this, they are aspiring to be like upper-class Israelis, people who can afford to live in areas where Arab families are unlikely to be found. Some Jewish parents were not bothered about the Arab chil-dren in the *ganim* because for them all children are the same.

The municipal election campaign most clearly illustrated the contra-dictions in the "democratic, but Jewish" formula for statehood. Faced with the threat of Jewish exclusivity, Acre's Palestinians threw their support behind a Zionist candidate who offered a more democratic (but still Jewish) vision of future life in the city. While many of Acre's Jewish residents initially supported Bar Lev's call for Judaizing Acre, they be-gan to tire of his ongoing battle when the city's economic condition did not improve. Bar Lev's cry of wolf marked Acre's Jewish residents as somehow second class, the occupants of a marginal area. De Castro was able to mobilize a new rhetoric after the close election campaign in which those Jews who remained in Acre were heroes, while any Jew who left the city was labeled a traitor. By casting the decision to remain in Acre as supporting coexistence (democratic values) and fulfilling the Zionist imperative of settlement (Jewish values), De Castro successfully, for the moment, resolved the contradictions inherent in the Israeli na-tional identity.

Anzaldua (1987) has focused our attention on borderlands and bor-der culture. The border zone is an area of partially realized identities, manifest contradictions, and deliberate ambiguity. Acre, since its incor-poration within the state of Israel, has been just such an ambiguous border zone. From its beginnings as part of Israel, it has been a mixed city, with all the contradictions that status entails. Preserving ambiva-lence, however, has provided the space for local residents to build lives and come to their own decisions about how to interact. Such zones present problems for the project of nationalism, which craves timeless-ness, unity, and homogeneity. When national concerns or issues have intruded on local life, shattering its ambiguity and replacing it with clear-cut agendas for action, local residents have had to deal with increased tensions and violence as different groups of residents find themselves polarized on one side or another of an issue. Peace has been preserved in Acre by working to recover ambiguity as quickly as possible. It appears that Arabs and Jews will continue to live together in Acre as long as they can do so in an indeterminate fashion. But can they continue in this fashion indefinitely?

Acre a Decade Later

In 1998, I returned to Acre after an absence of eight years, seeking answers to that question. During those intervening years, Israelis witnessed a number of national political events that had repercussions for their personal lives. During the Persian Gulf conflict of 1990–91, both Israeli Jews and Israeli Palestinians, armed with gas masks, were confined to sealed rooms in their homes, as Scud missiles launched by Iraq landed in various parts of Israel.[1] When Israeli Jewish men had to sit helpless in the face of the possible gas attacks, it damaged their image of themselves as invincible Israeli soldiers; shelters and crisis centers reported that male violence against women and children increased during and after the conflict (Sharoni 1995, 126).[2]

In the aftermath of the Gulf War, international attention once again focused on trying to achieve a peaceful solution to the Israeli-Palestinian conflict in the Middle East. The process begun in November 1991 at the Madrid conference culminated several years later in the Oslo Peace Accords and the signing of the *Declaration of Principles* by then Israeli Prime Minister Yitzhak Rabin and PLO Chairman Yasir Arafat in September 1993. As flawed as this process has been, it has still brought about important transitions in the ways in which Israeli Jews view Palestinians and Palestinian Israelis envision their futures as Israeli citizens.

One final event that occurred during this period was the November 1995 assassination of Prime Minister Rabin at a peace rally in a public plaza in Tel Aviv. He was killed by a young Jewish man who belonged to the nationalist-religious camp that opposed the peace process with the Palestinians. This event shattered Israeli society. As Peri noted in his analysis of it, the "assassination of Rabin — the prime minister who represents political stability and the minister of defence who is the symbol of security more than anyone else in Israel — produced a palpable sense of insecurity, a fear of social disintegration and apprehension of what the future held: subversion of the public order, the crumbling of the normative system, civil war, even war with foreign powers. If the personification of security was murdered, anything could happen" (1997, 444).

In the aftermath of Rabin's murder, Shimon Peres became prime minister. In 1996, he led the Israeli army into another disastrous Lebanese engagement — Operation Grapes of Wrath. Not only did the operation not achieve its goal, but on 18 April 1996 Israeli army units shelled a UN outpost near Qana, Lebanon, which was sheltering a civilian population at the time. Their direct hits killed more than a hundred men, women, and children. Peres himself felt the repercussions of Qana about a month later when he lost the national election and Benjamin Netanyahu became the prime minister at the head of a Likud-Gesher-Tsomet alliance. In the aftermath of the election (which many again saw as a vote over Israel's future), political analysts highlighted the cleavages it revealed in Israeli society. One commentator noted that "the place of the melting pot was taken over by social pluralism, by a recognition of the fact that we Jews will never become one homogeneous society. Rather, we are composed of at least four societies: the religious-traditional one . . . , the world of the so-called 'granny glasses' . . . , the mainstream, striving to combine Zionist values with a bourgeois lifestyle based on the values of the Western civilization; and the Arab public."[3] Another commentator wrote, "Israel has really become a binational state. Starting from this morning we are two nations: Jews A and Jews B. The Kingdom of Israel and the Kingdom of Judea."[4] Netanyahu consolidated his control over the Knesset by bringing the religious parties of Shas (ten seats), the NRP (nine seats), and United Torah Judaism (four seats) into his government.[5] The increased power of religious parties within the government has in turn increased the tensions between religious and secular Israeli Jews — not all Israelis want to live in a "religiously" Jewish state — and between religious Jews and Israeli Palestinians.[6]

The Israel I returned to had a much different feel. Everywhere I looked I saw new freeways and American-style strip malls, home to McDonald's, Burger King, Kentucky Fried Chicken, Office Depot, and Ace Hardware. The landscape was dotted with the marks of new construction as buildings, shopping centers, and homes went up. There has been so much building that, paradoxically, the country now feels larger, more impersonal. Gone was the noisy central bus station of Tel Aviv, which sprawled over several city streets, where one could eat lunch, shop at the open-air stalls for cassette tapes and toiletries, and then continue one's trip to Jerusalem or Haifa. In its place, a modern high-rise station now serves as the transportation hub of the city; its architecture encourages one to move through it as quickly as possible. The physical changes in the country had their analogues in people's lives. The previous eight years had been a difficult time financially for many of the people I knew in Israel. When I returned, I was struck by how focused people were on achieving a certain valued lifestyle, the materialism of which I had read so much. More importantly, however, people seemed to have withdrawn into their own lives and were focusing only on the things that mattered to them and their families. They were divided between those who believed the peace negotiations would usher in a new era of prosperity and cooperation and those who saw Israel as headed toward internal civil war and external conflict with the surrounding Arab countries. Sometimes people believed both at the same time.

Acre is no different than the rest of the country. A new north-south road now bypasses the city east of Shkhūnāt Ben-Gurion. Traffic has been rerouted, and the city as a whole is now more integrated. Part of the main shopping street in the Mandate City is now a pedestrian mall. Gone are the trees that had once lined the street; in their place is a concrete walkway along which modern art constructions meant to emulate a ship's sails are strung about. While at first glance the effect seems to be a revived commercial space, numerous trips along this mall during the heat of the day made me realize that the loss of shade probably discouraged pedestrian traffic. Other additions included new library and court buildings, both of which were located in the Mandate City. Some shoppers have probably been lost to the mini-mall south of the Acre-Safed highway near the entrance to Shkhūnāt Ben-Gurion. The new center boasts a Home Center (an Ace Hardware affiliate) as well as a McDonald's fast-food restaurant. American suburban mall culture is fast making headway in Israel.

Residents of the Old City have also seen some improvements since 1989. UNESCO has declared Acre one of the hundred sites that best preserves the world's medieval heritage.[7] In the mid-1990s, the Old Acre Development Company took over the management of projects in the Old City. Under a new director and with support from the Ministry of Tourism, considerable sums of money ($100 million over five years) are being invested in basic infrastructural improvements as well as ongoing excavations and antiquities work. The open-air market was roofed. Two-thirds of the work has been completed to provide underground electrical, telephone, television, and cable television lines as well as water, sewer, and drainage connections throughout the Old City. Streets have been paved and new lighting added.[8] The national government built two new kindergartens (rather than installing portable classroom structures as they had in the past). The excavations of Crusader buildings employ local men as workers. Residents of the Old City are now allowed to repair and renovate the interiors of their apartments, although external renovations have become more difficult because of the requirement that the historical facade of the building must be preserved (similar to the requirements of historical districts in the United States). At the same time, the loss of the regional courthouse in the Old City has harmed the business of the merchants in the markets surrounding the old building. People who come to town on court business now take their shopping to merchants in the New City.

Getting around in Acre is easier. In addition to the ubiquitous Egged buses, taxi service is readily available. From my apartment in the north, I could catch a *sherut* (service taxi) to the center of the city, the bus station, the eastern neighborhoods, or even Haifa for less than what a comparable bus ride would cost. Many of the drivers (and owners) of these vehicles were Palestinians from nearby villages.

One of the more distressing changes is the decline of the physical condition of the city. While Acre had an unkempt appearance eight years earlier, in 1998 it was downright filthy. Broken glass, plastic containers, paper, and food litter lined the beaches, parks, and walkways in every neighborhood. I was afraid to let my three-year-old daughter walk outside for fear that she would fall and cut herself on the broken glass that carpeted the sidewalks. Matters were even worse in the Old City, where many of the pathways along the walls (favorites of visiting tourists) were choked with garbage. Residents explained the mess as the fault of the mayor and the local council. Because sanitation workers had not been paid for the previous two to three months, they had simply stopped working. In fact, matters were so bad that the city was not allowed to open its public beaches for swimming that summer due to the hazards to potential bathers. For a city that has chosen tourism as one of its development strategies, it made little sense to let the physical condition of the city deteriorate to this degree.

As elsewhere in Israel, the influx of the new immigrants from the former Soviet Union beginning in 1990 altered the dynamics of the local housing market. Almost overnight, landlords were able to double their rents because the new immigrants, subsidized by the Jewish Agency and the Israeli government, could pay more. In Acre, this drove many young Arab couples who had been renting privately back to their parents' homes elsewhere in the city or to the nearby Arab villages. Empty Amidar apartments in various locations throughout the city were given to the new immigrants. In 1989, $65,000 bought a five-room, nicely appointed apartment in the center of the city. For $20,000 to $28,000, you could purchase a three- or four-room apartment in the newer Ben-Gurion neighborhood in the east. By 1998, a family or young couple would spend $156,000 for a five-room apartment in the center of the city, while three- or four-room apartments in Ben-Gurion were selling for $80,000 to $98,000. New housing developments have mushroomed in the northern parts of the city, from west to east. Bolos-Gad, the largest local construction company (and, ironically, Palestinian owned), has three developments in progress — 'Akko L'Yad Ha'Yam, Tamar Ha''Ir, and Tsameret 'Akko. Units range in price from $120,000 (for three rooms) and $158,000 (four rooms) to $248,000 (penthouses). Ceramic floors, electric blinds, underground parking, stone facings, private storage facilities, lobbies, and elevators are featured amenities.

The new immigrants settled in Acre have brought its population to a total of 45,000, 75 percent Jewish and 25 percent Palestinian. However, from 1989 to 1998 established Jewish families continued to flee Acre by moving to neighboring towns, especially Nahariyya and Karmi'el. By 1997, this out-migration included a total of four thousand families. Thus, Acre's Jewish population is now actually lower as a percentage of total population than it was in 1987–89 when I did my initial research. The living standards of its residents remain below those of Karmi'el and Nahariyya, as well as national averages (table 10). For example, 17 percent of Acre's residents own a personal computer, compared to 26 percent of Nahariyya's, 30 percent of Karmi'el's, and a national average of 27 percent. Fifty percent of homes in Nahariyya are air-conditioned, compared to 36 percent in Karmi'el and 29 percent in Acre. The educational levels of Acre's residents are lower, with 66 percent having less than a matriculation degree (compared to 50 percent in Nahariyya, 34 percent in Karmi'el, and a 51 percent national average). As noted earlier, Acre's residents still rely heavily on industrial

TABLE 10.   Socioeconomic Characteristics of Acre Compared to National Averages and the Neighboring Cities of Nahariyya and Karmi'el, 1995 (percentages)

	Acre	Karmi'el	Nahariyya	Israel
Own personal computer	17.1	30.0	26.1	27.0
Home air-conditioned	29.2	35.5	50.2	40.1
Own car	39.5	53.2	52.8	56.1
Own home	68.6	65.1	73.7	73.0
Average household size	3.4	3.2	2.9	3.3
Education				
Academic degree	10.3	26.3	15.0	20.1
Matriculation+	34.0	65.7	49.6	48.9
Less than matriculation	66.0	34.3	50.4	51.1
Occupation				
Skilled industrial	34.7	31.3	25.6	25.4
Sales and services	19.0	14.8	17.4	17.2
Clerical	14.9	14.7	17.6	18.9
Academic, professional, technician	15.1	25.8	24.8	24.4

Source: Israel, Central Bureau of Statistics 1998 (from Census of Population and Housing, 1995, table 27.1 and 27.2 [Households by Selected Housing Characteristics] and table 27.3 and 27.4 [Population Aged 15 and Over Employed in Annual Civilian Labour Force by Selected Labour Characteristics and Education], <http://www.cbs.gov.il> [July 1999].

employment (34.7 percent), followed by sales and services (19 percent). Academic/professional employment accounts for only 15.1 percent of Acre's employment, compared to a national average of 24.4 percent and averages of 25.8 percent for Karmi'el and 24.8 percent for Nahariyya.

Schools

What has happened in Acre's schools? Nationally, the Labor/Meretz government (1992–96) adopted a new five-year plan to correct inequality in the allocation of resources to Arab and Jewish schools. Then Minister of Education Amnon Rubinstein (1993–96) gave Arab schools better plans for books, clerical staff, and teachers as well as increased budgets. Lavy (1998) documents the disparities that exist in the school systems and the effects of those disparities on student achievement. For example, in medium-sized towns in 1990–91, the government was spending on average 1,435 shekels per Jewish student, compared to 572 per Arab student.[9] Lavy demonstrates that increasing expenditures per student, hours of instruction per student, and the percentage of certified teachers in the schools can help eliminate more than half the gap between Arab and Jewish students in terms of performance on standardized tests (1998, 189–90). However, with the change in government in 1996, these policies were reversed.

While the national government made an effort for a few years to improve conditions in the Arab schools, in Acre over this same time period the schools have deteriorated even further. The elementary school in the Old City was closed, and all Arab elementary students in Acre now attend one school, situated on five dunams (1.25 acres) of land. This school, which was built several years before to serve 400 to 500 students, now has a student population of 1,600. Average class size is 40 students. To handle the overflow of students, the municipality brought in caravans (mobile homes used in transit camps and new settlements as temporary housing) to use as classrooms. There is no auditorium and no yard to serve as a playground; therefore, there are no sports activities. One principal supervises seventy-six teachers in a physical space that encompasses four floors of a building and numerous caravans. As one informant noted, sometimes the principal is unaware that teachers have not reported for work until he sees their students running loose in the hallways. There is no computer room (the computers are in a bomb shelter) and no library. A member of the Parents' Committee for the Arab schools indicated that 80 percent of the elementary teachers are not Acre residents. When tested recently by the Ministry of Education and

Culture in reading and comprehension, only 40 percent of the students achieved a passing score.

When the new elementary building was constructed, the old one (Amal) was taken over. A new floor was added, and it became part of the junior-senior high school. Because of the addition of the new building, there is now a principal for the junior high school and a principal for the senior high school, which together enroll six hundred students. Neither principal resides in Acre. Parents and students went on strike for three months beginning in September 1997 to protest physical conditions in the schools. Broken doors and windows, no working copy machine, no paper, and no materials for the technical and professional studies are just a sampling of the problems in the junior-senior high school. In recent years, only ten to twelve students from Acre have taken the *bagrut* exam. The system has witnessed an increase in the flight of good students to nearby schools. In addition to Haifa, parents send their children to schools in Ibillin, Makr/Judeidah, and even Nazareth. I was told that during the 1998–99 school year, one hundred students from Acre intended to begin their ninth-grade studies in Ibillin.[10] Given such a mass exodus, the municipality has asked the Ministry of Education and Culture to intervene and prevent the students from leaving. When I left, the school in Ibillin had announced it would not accept the students. The parents in Acre, however, did not see the battle as over.

The situation in the nursery schools is not much better. For ages three to four, there are now eleven *ganim,* three in the Old City, three in Wolfson, and another five in the Mandate City. For ages four to five, there are only eight *ganim,* and they are concentrated in one area of the city, with three in the Old City and five near the elementary school in caravans. The five caravan facilities have only a small yard where the children can play. Each caravan enrolls thirty-five students. The deputy mayor in charge of education, Aharon Lahiani, has adopted an informal policy of not allowing more than five Arab children in any one municipal nursery facility. The municipality closed four nursery schools and transferred two others to the local religious system. What this has meant in practice is that Arab children who live elsewhere in the city are often denied space in their neighborhood nursery school. Parents who live in the north may be told that they can enroll their children in a school in the east. With private facilities often costing six hundred shekels a month, parents have little choice but to enroll their children in inadequate facilities. Ironically, the municipality also will not enroll more than five children of new immigrants in any one municipal *gan,* which means that the parents of these children often must seek options elsewhere. Children from the Ethiopian immigrant camp north of the city were refused entry into any municipal *gan.*

Shkhūnāt Wolfson

What of developments in Wolfson? As mentioned in chapter 4, neighborhood residents who had been active in frameworks initially established by Project Van Leer formed their own association in 1990 and began to lobby to take over management of the soon-to-be-completed neighborhood community center. They maintained the dual Arab-Jewish leadership structure that Van Leer had pioneered in creating their management team. One of the first steps they took as a neighborhood group was to lobby the Ministry of Absorption and Amidar to settle new Soviet immigrants in the many empty Amidar apartments in the neighborhood. In their appeal, they noted that they wanted to maintain Wolfson as a mixed neighborhood. Empty apartments attracted prostitutes, drug users, and vandals. Amidar settled immigrants in twenty apartments. An additional sixty to seventy people were accommodated through private rentals or outright purchases. These new immigrants are younger than the other Jewish residents of Wolfson, and they have young children. Their interest in the neighborhood has meant that housing in Wolfson is currently more expensive per square meter than similar apartments in other areas of the city. Demand for this housing issues from both Arab residents and the new Jewish immigrants.

When I asked how relations were between Arab and Jewish residents of the neighborhood, I heard a variety of anecdotes about how they were assisting each other. These ranged from respecting mutual holidays (Yom Kippur and Ramadan) to mutual assistance during the tense period of the Gulf War. Some immigrants who arrived during this period needed help acquiring gas masks and the proper materials for sealing their windows. JACA made arrangements for elderly residents who were alone as well as new immigrants. Often younger Arab neighbors helped purchase materials and came over to make sure they were properly installed. As one person put it, "It was as if we could unite to face a common enemy."

With the opening of the neighborhood community center in 1992, all of the resources of JACA went into making the center a success. The municipality built a new children's playground in proximity to the new center (fig. 9). The center continued some of the educational enrichment programs that had been offered through Project Van Leer. Classes in music, computers, ballet, and theater were available for a minimal charge. When the center first offered these courses, it had no trouble attracting Arab students because there were no other frameworks available to them in the city. Jewish children, however, were slow to come. In this context, the children of the new immigrants were essential to maintaining the mixed character of the center's activities. Immigrant parents

FIG. 9.   Neighborhood children in Wolfson (1998). (Photo by author.)

were only too pleased to make use of JACA's programs. The center facilitated their integration by offering services that catered to the needs of the new immigrants (such as flexible language programs). The older immigrants in the neighborhood wasted no time in staking their claim to the facility — for them, it has become a cultural center, a place where they can meet to hear lectures, talk, sing, and see performances. In addition to the early childhood program that the center ran for Arab children in the neighborhood, it opened a nursery program for the children of new immigrants. The center has also been a locus for the development of a joint Palestinian-Jewish women's leadership group. When I visited, these women were in the process of establishing a domestic-violence hotline for women in Acre and surrounding areas.

When demand for property in the neighborhood began to increase, some Jewish residents of Wolfson were able to sell their apartments and move elsewhere. A small minority remains of people who were the original residents of the neighborhood as well as a small group of Moroccans who were settled there in later years. They have been joined by two groups of new immigrants — White Russians and Jews from Azerbaijan. The new immigrants are characterized by activists in the neighborhood as being less racist; as one Jewish informant put it, "They don't drink it from their mother's milk." A Palestinian informant explained relations in the neighborhood in a different way. It is easier, he said, for the new immigrants to live with Arabs because the established Jewish residents of Acre don't treat them well. The older residents resent the assistance the immigrants are receiving and claim that they are taking over their jobs and professions and getting things from the government for free. In this context, the Arabs of Wolfson serve as mediators between the senior Jewish residents and the new arrivals.

One other change in the neighborhood concerns its incorporation within the framework of Project Renewal. Project Renewal paid to construct new pathways and garden areas in Wolfson. In addition, it helped facilitate plans to allow residents to expand their apartments by building two-room additions. Six of the buildings were in various stages of this process, while in another three initial organizing was beginning to convince residents to get involved in the project. The management team for JACA admitted that it had not been paying much attention to the physical condition of the neighborhood, which had deteriorated following the exit of Project Van Leer in 1993. In 1999, they intended to focus their attention on the building additions, garden and yard upkeep, and the overall cleanliness of the neighborhood. While I was there, they elected a new Management Committee for JACA. Out of the fourteen members, half are Arab and half are Jewish. Other forms of diversity are represented as well: six of the members are women, several are new immigrants, some are young residents in their twenties, several are in their thirties, and several are pensioners.

Project Van Leer left an additional legacy in Acre — the Association for Community Development and the Association for Community Advocacy, both formed by Harry Frey, one of the former directors of Project Van Leer. When Van Leer's citywide project formally came to an end in 1994, these associations really began to develop. They took over some Van Leer programs that JACA did not continue such as citywide efforts in early childhood education. In addition, they developed women's leadership training and community advocacy programs. In 1996, they expanded their operations into the caravan site established to house new immigrants in Acre (once again, at Tel Napoleon). They have also continued some of the efforts begun by Project Van Leer in the Old City. The community advocacy program trains local residents to function as paralegals under the direction of trained lawyers who donate their services. The community advocates then assist local residents with a variety of legal issues ranging from problems with immigrant rights and rental contracts to medical claims and property rights. The associations operate out of offices in the municipal market as well as facilities in the Old City. While they are no longer focused on offering joint (i.e., mixed) services, in fact Frey continues to assist both the Arab and Jewish residents of the city. His most recent effort, if successful, will provide an experiment in citizen control of development policy. Using a model that has been implemented in Germany and England, he is seeking funding to establish a citizen's jury, which will research and prepare a new master development plan for the Old City.

Local Politics

In November 1993, the local elections were again hotly contested. The national context had shifted considerably since the contentious election campaign of 1989. Only two months earlier, the historic handshake between Prime Minister Rabin and Chairman Arafat had signaled the beginning of a new era in Israeli-Palestinian relations. In Acre, major power struggles occurred in both the Labor and the Likud primaries over choosing their candidates for the position of mayor. Eli De Castro defeated Yehoshua Katz in the Labor contest, while David Bar Lev again prevailed, this time over Aharon Lahiani, who was the candidate of the Likud establishment. Bar Lev's victory split the Likud, and Lahiani left to form his own local list. Five other candidates entered the race for the mayor's seat, including Lahiani, Yossi Fitosi, Arik Brami, and Mohamed Houbeishe. Brami, a newcomer to the political scene in

Acre, was a former army officer who received support from new immigrants and from the merchants of the municipal market. In the elections for council seats, thirteen lists fielded candidates. These included the established parties (Labor, Likud, Meretz, Shas, Rakah, and Mafdal) as well as a number of independent lists led by local notables (Aharon Lahiani, Morris Ben Shoshan, and Arik Brami from the Jewish community and Ḥilmi Shafʿī and Mousa Ziad from the Palestinian community). Notable new entrants in this election were the Islamic Party and a Likud-affiliated Arab list.

In the first round of the mayoral contest, no candidate received enough votes to be declared the winner. A runoff election was held two weeks later between the two candidates who had garnered the highest percentages of the initial vote — De Castro (37 percent) and Bar Lev (35 percent). De Castro made arrangements before this election with Lahiani, Ziad, Ben Shoshan, and Shafʿī to gain the support of their followers for his campaign. Bar Lev received support from Meretz, Mafdal, the Islamic Party, and Yossi Fitosi's Ometz. He courted the Arab vote this time by encouraging the creation of a Likud-affiliated Arab party and by making a surplus votes agreement with the Islamic Party. Many local Palestinian residents, however, remembered the 1989 campaign and viewed his change of heart with great suspicion.

De Castro was elected mayor by 668 votes. His support came from the Old City and the Mandate City as well as the Wolfson area. Bar Lev's strongholds in the east and north were not enough to give him the victory. De Castro rewarded his supporters by giving deputy mayor portfolios to Aharon Lahiani (education), Israel LaLevy (from Ben Shoshan's party, engineering), and Ḥilmi Shafʿī (Arab affairs). On the local council, Labor held four seats; Likud four; Ben Shoshan three; Lahiani, Shafʿī, and the Islamic Party two each; and Brami and Shas one each. In terms of votes, the Islamic Party received more than the independent list headed by Shafʿī. However, because they had signed an agreement with the Likud, their surplus votes helped to ensure another seat for its list. For the first time, the Mafdal (the local branch of the NRP) was not represented on the council.

The Struggle to Rescue the City:
Coexistence Realized?

In April 1997, the national government announced to municipal officials that it intended to cut 4.5 million shekels from Acre's school budget.[11] The ORT Hebrew high school network would lose 1 million shekels, the Arab high school 1.3 million, and the religious high school 1.5 million.

This money had been provided to Acre by the previous Labor/Metz government in an effort to help the city improve living standards. The funds were used to provide extra hours of classroom instruction to benefit both weak and strong students in the system. Acre's residents had seen the fruits of this financial investment as they witnessed a higher percentage of their children passing the matriculation exams than the national average.

The national government had given money to Acre before, only to later revoke its largesse. This time, however, several people decided that they would not give in without a fight. Led by Shmaryahu Biran, principal of the ORT secondary-school complex, they formed a group, Mateh L'Hatsālāh Hinūkh B ʿAkko (Staff to Rescue Education in Acre; *mateh* is used to refer to the army's general staff or headquarters) and published a call for members in *Yediʿot ʿAkko,* the local news sheet. They held their first meeting in early May and witnessed a large turnout (overall attendance at their meetings averaged seventy to eighty people). As people began discussing the issue at that meeting, it became clear that the problem was much more complex than simple concern about the schools. People felt there was no culture in Acre, no cleanliness, no city management. They asked why Acre had always been denied the status of a border-town development area (the A+ status discussed in chapter 5), when Karmi'el (about twenty kilometers to the southeast) had always had this status. People knew that their friends or their children's friends had moved from Acre to towns like Nahariyya, Karmi'el, Maʿalot, or the Qrayot. By the end of this meeting, it had become clear that a broader effort was needed, and the Mateh L'Hatsālāh Ha ʿĪr ʿAkko (Staff to Rescue the City of Acre) was born.

As with earlier scares about the city's future, the opportunity was available for the members of this group to approach the government for assistance by arguing that without such aid Acre would become an Arab city. Over a two-year period, Acre had lost thousands of its Jewish citizens (especially from the middle and upper classes) to nearby communities (although middle-class Palestinian families were also leaving). Local residents and officials knew that raising the specter of an Arab city had always worked to their benefit in the past. This time, however, there was a remarkable shift in the discourse about Acre's future. Founding members of the Mateh recognized the economic incentives that impelled many people to leave, particularly the 15 to 17 percent discount in income taxes that was available to the residents of Jewish communities in the region. They determined that they were going to wage their campaign as a joint Jewish-Arab battle for the well-being of the city. To that end, they created a coalition of Arabs and Jews of all social classes who worked together for the first time to achieve a common goal. While some local residents who got involved in the Mateh's efforts did try to argue that Acre was becoming an Arab city, such rhetoric was heavily censured by the organizers of the struggle. They clearly saw Acre's problems as the result of economic factors that were under the direct control of the national government. In this battle, the alliances were not Acre's Jewish citizens and the national government against its Arab residents; instead, Acre's Arab and Jewish residents were uniting to demand equal treatment from the national government.

As the base for their operations, the Mateh used the Parents' Committees of the three high schools (ORT, Arab, and religious). These committees gave them a solid organizational basis from which to work. For example, the members of the Parents' Committee at the ORT high school had worked hard to develop it as a strong, autonomous unit. With a budget of four million shekels, the committee had made sure the school had a new library, Internet connections, and new computers. Now these same committees were asked to invest in the struggle to save the schools. Their money provided the funds needed for signs, ads, publicity, and the chartering of buses for protests in Jerusalem, and their members provided the volunteer labor needed to organize them.

Their first demonstration was at the local municipality, where the Parents' Committees and high school students (10 percent from each school) turned out to protest. This demonstration of about a thousand people received good local media coverage. More importantly, the mayor and municipal council, which had previously appeared to oppose the group's efforts, now publicly supported their cause. In June of 1997, they staged a larger demonstration by sealing off the city of Acre to all incoming and outgoing traffic. By demonstrating at all the major road junctions and blocking the rail lines, they were able to stop the north-south traffic flow long enough to gain the attention of the national press. With this success behind them, they took ten busloads of residents to Jerusalem to demonstrate outside the offices of the prime minister, who received their delegation and discussed the issue with them. In Acre, they continued to put pressure on the system. The committees went out on strike and said they would not allow the schools to open for the next year because there was no money. They used every avenue at their disposal to wage the fight. Individual members of the Mateh wrote letter after letter to members of the Knesset protesting the treatment that Acre was receiving at the hands of the national government. A Web site on the Internet was used to encourage the involvement of young people and solicit the support of people outside Acre. Delegations from the Mateh met with Knesset members, many of whom supported the struggle and indicated that they would recommend that Acre also be granted A+ development status. One Palestinian member of the committee remembers the opportunity he had to directly confront members of the government about the discrimination that Acre suffered. He told them, "We all know you don't help Acre because Arabs live there."

One of the messages members of the delegation received in their contacts with national officials was the need to take control of their own city and elect new leadership. If Acre is in trouble, they were told, why does your mayor continue to tell us everything is fine? Campaigning for the primary for the coming year's local elections was due to begin in November and December 1997. Members of the Mateh were faced with the decision of whether to get involved in local politics. When Shmaryahu Biran eventually decided to run in the Labor Party's primary for the position of mayor of Acre, the Mateh was forced to suspend its activities. Part of its success had been the public perception that it was apolitical. It had succeeded in getting the national government to revoke its decision to cut the school budget for the coming year. It also had won Acre A+ development status in the areas of housing, education, and industrial development (high technology only), although the city was not granted a discounted income tax rate.[12] As one member told me, it was a good point at which to suspend activities pending the outcome of the local elections.

When I returned to Acre in May of 1998, I arrived just as the primaries for the next round of local elections (scheduled for December) were coming to a close. De Castro had effectively ended his tenure as mayor because he did not run in the Labor primary. Two other candidates, Yehoshua Katz and Biran, entered the race, and people who might have supported De Castro threw their support behind the others. Biran went on to win the primary, garnering 80 percent of the vote to Katz's 17 percent. De Castro held out the possibility of running for mayor as an independent, but he officially announced on 3 July that he would not stand for another term.

Even more interesting was the primary contest within the Likud. Arik Brami ran against David Bar Lev (as well as a third candidate). Brami, a relative newcomer, had already managed to defeat Bar Lev in the election for the position of head of the local party branch. As a member of the municipal Market Committee, he had the support of those merchants in his campaign. Brami promised "to restore the honor of the Likud."[13] In his campaign literature, he attacked Bar Lev as someone who had failed to advance the interests of the Likud in Acre. Bar Lev, now sixty-four years old, was presented as a failed old man who, refusing to step aside, was preventing young and vibrant "natural" leaders (like Brami, who was forty-six) from restoring the honor of the party. Bar Lev struck back by publicizing Brami's business failures.

How, he asked, could someone who failed at small things be expected to succeed at larger ones?[14]

In the end, Bar Lev once again prevailed. How he prevailed, however, is where the true irony lies. He was elected by a tiny margin (fifty-eight votes) over Brami.[15] Privately, many people noted that the votes that gave him the victory were those of the Arab members of the party who had been recruited in the intervening years.[16] People reported to me that on the evening of the primary, when it became clear that Bar Lev had won, cars circled in the Old City honking their horns in celebration. Bar Lev now found himself in the same position he had placed De Castro in nine years earlier — Brami and his supporters labeled him the "Arab candidate" and claimed that the Jewish members of the Likud had preferred another. Unlike the events of 1989, however, Brami's "Arab" label was passed by word of mouth. It was not the focus of either the campaign or Brami's subsequent attempt to have the primary voided and a new round of elections held.

The outcomes of the local elections were by no means a foregone conclusion. During the Likud primaries, I heard many Acre residents say that they doubted Biran could successfully manage the city. His image as an intellectual of the Ashkenazi elite led some residents to believe that he would not be strong enough to deal with Acre's problems. They preferred someone like Arik Brami — a former military officer who impressed people with his take-charge manner. In the local elections in December, however, Biran was elected mayor with 56 percent of the vote, defeating Bar Lev, who received 44 percent, a decisive victory given the close results of the previous two campaigns. Biran's support came from his own Labor Party as well as Rakah, Mafdal, the united Islamic-Shaf'ī list, and the new immigrants list. Bar Lev was supported by the Likud and its affiliated Arab list, Ben Shoshan, Lahiani, and Shas. For the local council, the Labor Party and the new immigrants list each won three seats. Shas, Likud, Lahiani, Ben Shoshan, and a combined Islamic-Shaf'ī list each won two. Rakah, Mafdal, and the Likud-affiliated Arab list each won one.

What can we make of the outcome of this election? Biran, the political outsider catapulted to local fame through his leadership of the successful campaign to save the schools, ran as a candidate who now intended to save the city in a new way. By highlighting the economic aspects of Acre's plight, he united a broad coalition of citizens in the Mateh to demand from the national government treatment equal to that given nearby cities. He now faces the challenge of uniting a more diverse local council to continue the battles begun by the Mateh. Clearly, politics as usual will go on in Acre, as evidenced by the continued strength of local lists headed by Ben Shoshan, Shaf'ī, and Lahiani. But there are new actors on the political scene (the immigrants list as well as the Likud–affiliated Arab list) as well as returning actors (Rakah and Mafdal), and they account for almost one-third of the seats on the local council.

It is tempting to see the struggle over the schools and the subsequent election of Biran as mayor as what Daniel (1996) calls an *agentive moment.* As he notes, humans are creatures of habit, but, most importantly, we are capable of habit change. Agentive moments are times when interruptions of habit are not easily resolved. They represent breaches in the order of things such that prevailing habits are not capable of soothing the resultant shock or providing new frames for understanding (Daniel 1996, 191). Daniel was looking at the breach in national habits created by outbreaks of violence in Sri Lanka. While nothing this horrific has happened in Acre, the shape of coexistence hinted at in the Mateh's successful coalition efforts represents a radical break with the dominant definitions of Jewish-Palestinian coexistence in Israel. As Daniel reminds us, whether familiar habits will yield to new configurations is a question that can be answered only in retrospect, when the effects of the moment are fully realized.

Writing in January 1999, after the collapse of the Netanyahu government, Edward Said again raised questions about the peace process begun in Oslo in 1993.[17] He noted that the problem with the current process is that it is based on a principle of separation for both Israeli Jews and Palestinians yet this separation flies in the face of the reality on the ground — "short of ethnic cleansing or mass transfer as in 1948 there is no way for Israel to get rid of the Palestinians or for Palestinians to wish Israelis away." Said called instead for a radical new vision of coexistence: "The beginning is to develop something entirely missing from both Israeli and Palestinian realities today: the idea and practice of citizenship, not of ethnic or racial community, as the main vehicle for coexistence." This vision of citizenship would be based on equality of rights, privileges, and access to resources.

In Acre, the efforts of grassroots organizations such as Project Van Leer, JACA, the Association for Community Development, the Association for Community Advocacy, and most recently the Mateh L'Hatsālāh Ha 'Īr 'Akko have laid a foundation for the new conception of citizenship that Said advocates. These organizations have worked to bring the residents of Acre to an awareness of their common situation and the need for cooperation to improve their lives, in the process replacing a narrowly focused vision or habit framed by separation and notions of rights as vested in ethnic communities. Ambiguous boundaries as Arab and Jew may be reworked into more inclusive identities as fellow citizens. The question remains as to whether local residents will have the will to follow an uncertain path. Events at the national level may still intrude on local life and return Acre's residents to established habits of separation and rigid boundaries. Only time will tell.

'Im tīrtsū, 'ēyn zōt agādāh.

[If you will it, it is no fairy tale.]

— Theodore Herzl

Notes

Introduction

1. Romann and Weingrod (1991) followed a similar procedure in their study of Arab and Jewish interactions in Jerusalem. Romann, a geographer, analyzed at a macrolevel how the two previously separate city systems became integrated in economic and spatial terms after 1967. Weingrod, an anthropologist, analyzed at a microlevel four specific contexts within which Arabs and Jews engaged in regular contacts—two residential border neighborhoods where Arabs and Jews live in close proximity, a large factory, and a major hospital.

2. Many Israeli investigators don't even question whether their research with Arab respondents is valid. Smooha's discussion of this issue is one exception (1992, 287–88). See also Rabinowitz 1997, 20–23: "The anthropologist as comrade, secret agent, interlocutor."

Chapter 1

1. Remarks made to the class "Jews and Palestinians on Both Sides of the Green Line," University of Haifa, 13 June 1988.

2. The mixed cities include Ramla, Lod, Tel Aviv–Jaffa, Haifa, Acre, Jerusalem, Upper Nazareth, and Maʿalot-Tarshīha. Jerusalem is a special case because of the resident-only status of East Jerusalem Palestinians. Maʿalot and Tarshīha are separate communities divided by a distance of two kilometers that share a single local council. Upper Nazareth was built to overlook the Arab city of Nazareth; originally intended as an all-Jewish community, it has attracted Arabs who are driven to live there by Nazareth's tight housing market.

3. I use the English name *Acre* rather than the Hebrew ʿ*Akko* or Arabic ʿ*Akka* in order to prevent confusion. In addition, much of the construction of difference in Israel revolves around the opposition of Arab to Jew. I use the terms *Arab* and *Israeli Palestinian* interchangeably to describe the residents of Acre.

4. Statistics compiled by the Associated Press, reported in the *St. Louis Post Dispatch* on 9 December 1989.

5. Ferguson (1993) chooses the term *mobile* over the more common formulation *multiple* in order to avoid any notion of stability in the framing of identities. She sees identities not as stable points that an individual moves between but as particular positionalizations that are concrete and historical. As she notes, these positionalizations "are both the products and producers of discursive

and institutional practices, both the outcomes of the operations of power and the starting points for the practices of resistance" (159).

6. See Avineri 1981; Avishai 1985; Cohen 1992; and Weinstock 1989.

7. See Shapira 1992; Miller 1985; Stein 1984; Horowitz and Lissak 1978; Khalidi 1997; Farsoun and Zacharia 1997; and Hadawi 1989.

8. I am using here Sider's (1987) insights into the process of domination as he developed them based on consideration of the encounters between early European explorers in the New World and Native Americans.

9. Haidar 1991; Kretzmer 1990; Al-Haj and Rosenfeld 1988.

10. Elazar, for example, argues that *Mizrahi* and *Oriental* are "loaded terms to advance a convenient Ashkenazic myth in a situation where to be 'Western' is often synonymous with being 'modern' " and advocates use of the term *Sephardi* instead (1989, 24).

11. Lewis calls the category oriental Jew "a phantom, a figment of collective Israeli imagination, a symbolic vehicle by which cultural differences capable of masking socioeconomic inequality are explained" (1985, 150). This phantom, however, is part of the Israeli discourse on difference. This process of labeling and unlabeling is reminiscent of similar battles in the United States over American Indian identity.

12. The Sephardi chief rabbi carries the title *rishon l'tzion* (first in Zion). Until the 1920s, only the Sephardi chief rabbinate existed in what was then Palestine. An increased Ashkenazi population necessitated the creation of the Ashkenazi chief rabbinate. With the establishment of the state in 1948, Ashkenazi religious ritual and practice became dominant. One current expression of this anomaly can be seen in the numbers of Orthodox religious Mizrahi men who must learn Yiddish to study in the *yeshivot* (religious schools) and who have adopted standard Orthodox Eastern European forms of dress.

13. See the discussions in Dominguez 1989, 169–73, and Smooha 1978, 26–27.

14. See also Anzaldua 1987, 1990; hooks 1990; and Trinh 1989.

15. Bernstein notes that this question, and the other concerns that spring from it, are at the heart of the work of Gadamer, Habermas, Ricouer, Foucault, Derrida, Levinas, and Lyotard among others. Add to this works in cultural studies, the subaltern studies group, feminist psychoanalytical theorists like Jessica Benjamin, educational theorists like Henry Giroux, and feminists of color like Trinh T. Minh-ha, bell hooks, and Gloria Anzaldua. It is important to remember, however, that otherness takes on different faces across these varied debates.

16. Uchendu (1975) notes how the individual may be characterized by different attributes as the frame of reference shifts from family to locale, region, or nation-state. Rosen (1984) used the metaphor of negotiating to describe how Moroccans privilege occupation, religion, class, family, or tribal origin in creating dyadic relations for economic, political, or social interchanges.

17. Consider but a few examples: soldiers who are willing to die or kill others for their country, blacks in the American South who were lynched because of their racial identity, and the thousands of women who are abused by men acting out their patriarchal gender identity.

18. Anthony Smith's *Theories of Nationalism* (1971) sets forth in a chapter on "typologies" the various taxonomies that have been developed to characterize forms of nationalism. These include Hans Kohn's distinction between Eastern and Western nationalisms; Handman's scheme of irredentism, oppression, precaution, and prestige; Louis Wirth's typology of hegemonic, particularist (secession), marginal (frontier), and minority nationalisms; and Worsley's categories of unitary, new state (what Smith terms heterogeneous), and "pan" movements. He presents two pages of tables of types of nationalisms (228–29), with examples, and notes that a given case may be classified under more than one heading. So much for conceptual clarity.

19. Smooha and Cohen are exceptions here, and each in their work notes how the identities of Arab and Jew include other identities (Muslim, Christian, Mizrahi, and so on) and that these identities are often important in understanding why people act as they do in particular circumstances.

20. See, for example, Enloe 1989; Phillips 1991; Pateman 1988; Sharoni 1995; Maynard and Purvis 1996; and Yuval-Davis and Anthias 1989.

21. In fact, nationalism and racism are so intertwined in the modern world that it is almost impossible to speak of one without the other. In racialized discourse, skinheads and neo-Nazis talk about white nationalism and the need to protect and retain the purity of the white (or Aryan) nation. Racist discrimination in the United States spawned an oppositional black nationalism — Elijah Muhammad and the Nation of Islam, Marcus Garvey's call for repatriation to Africa. From 1928 to 1957, the Communist Party of the United States took the official position that blacks in the "black belt" of the southern states were an oppressed nation whose liberation required self-determination and national independence. On white nationalism, see, for example, Frederickson 1971, 1981; and Saxton 1990. On black nationalism, see, for example, Bracey et al. 1970; Stuckey 1970; and Pinkney 1976.

22. I would like to thank Art Wirth for pointing out that Reeves's definition does not highlight the negative connotations of racial ideologies; in fact, it allows for consideration of possible positive connotations. Given that such ideologies are products of power relations, and that power itself both creates and negates (as noted by Foucault), it would behoove us to document both the negative features of racial practices (segregation, discrimination, and domination) and the ways in which such ideologies produce things and discourses, induce pleasure, and create knowledge. One such attempt is Crapanzano's 1985 study of whites in South Africa, which details the effects of a racial ideology on the dominant class.

23. In particular, Moroccan immigrants to Israel have been stereotyped as violent and uncontrollable; in the 1950s, they were labeled *morocco sakīn* (literally, "Morocco knife"). Several studies examined violence in Moroccan communities in Israel (Bar Yosef 1959; Marx 1976; Palgi 1966; Shokeid 1982), while Elam (1978) compared levels of violence in the Moroccan and Georgian Jewish communities. I am not aware of any studies of violence within the Ashkenazi Jewish communities in Israel.

24. See Ben-Ari 1998, 106–17, for a discussion of the links among military service, masculinity, and the consequences for civilian life.

25. See Sharoni 1995 and Emmett 1996 for penetrating discussions of the ways in which women's lives are affected by the particular formations of militarized masculinity that frame Israeli national identity.

26. The Holocaust trope is used in discourses that challenge the cultural supremacy of European Jews in Israel. Eisenstadt (1985, 530) noted that graffiti reading "AshkeNazi" appeared in affluent, Ashkenazi, North Tel Aviv after police demolished an illegally built home in the poor Hatikvah quarter of Tel Aviv in the early 1980s (see also Chafets 1986, 137; and Shipler 1986, 346). These same expressions of anger and challenge — AshkeNazis — can be found today in many *shikūnōt* (neighborhoods, ghettos that are home to the Mizraḥim) (Hamburg 1992, 891). Palestinians (both inside and outside Israel) use Holocaust analogies in making their claims that the Israeli state is racist. Holocaust imagery is even powerfully present in gender dynamics — what Israeli women call Holocaust pornography, in which women are posed next to light fixtures that look like shower heads or blazing ovens or a man is pouring gasoline into a woman's face (Dworkin 1990).

27. Collectivizing private grief did not cease with Holocaust survivors. Weiss (1997) examines how bereavement in contemporary Israeli society is "appropriated by the collectivity and reproduced in public life so as to sustain collective boundaries, an ethos of sacrifice, and a standardization of commemorative practices" (91).

28. Zuckermann argues that it is not possible to "remember the Holocaust as a reality, as the concrete perceptible objectification of an ideologically-planned, industrially-organized and bureaucratically-realized systematic extermination of people. . . . It is impossible to remember Auschwitz as an everyday routine." He goes on, however, to say that people confronted with the Holocaust are faced with "the fundamental and inescapable dichotomous matrix of their own identity. They must decide between the identity of murderer and murdered. Because of its far-reaching consequences, this is the hardest and most extreme moral decision" (1988–89, 52–53).

29. There is a link between Zionism and anti-Semitism: anti-Semitism, in that it encourages Jewish immigration to Israel, is seen as an important ally for the Zionist cause. Boʿaz ʿEvron, in the 4 April 1991 *Yediʿot Aharonot,* had this to say: "So it is that each spark of anti-semitism fills the hearts of Zionists with hope."

30. Shohat (1989) notes that juxtaposing the Holocaust and nazism with the Israeli-Arab conflict (associating Arabs with nazis) is a staple of Zionist rhetoric; what is ignored is that Arab animosity toward Israelis stems from an actual process of Arab victimization. ʿEvron sees equating Palestinians with Nazis as producing hysterical responses rather than sound policy; the ahistorical world thus created prevents leaders from understanding the real historical processes through which the Israeli state is unfolding (1981, 26).

31. This displacement of nazi identity to Palestinians and other Arabs is not solely an Israeli obsession. Consider the Gulf War, when both President Bush and the American media labeled Saddam Hussein another Hitler. One news magazine went so far as to doctor Hussein's moustache to make the resemblance more striking.

32. Even Israeli Jews recognized the parallels. Ya'ir Kotler's (1986) biography of Kahane is entitled *Heil Kahane.*

33. See, for example, Smooha 1978, 231–32, and Israeli reporter Yosef Goell's comments in Dominguez 1989, 92–93.

34. *Yedi'ot Aharonot,* 14 February 1988.

35. Omi and Winant 1986 details the workings of this process in U.S. society.

36. Yigal Sarna, "He Is Our Israeli Hero," *Yedi'ot Aharonot,* 25 May 1990.

37. See Jiryis 1976; Zureik 1979; Lustick 1980; Smooha 1978; and Eisenstadt 1985.

38. Emile Habiby and Anton Shammas chose to analyze this disjuncture through the writing of fiction, Habiby's (1985) *The Secret Life of Saeed, the Pessoptimist* and Shammas's (1986) *Arabesques.* Fouzi El-Asmar's (1975) *To Be an Arab in Israel* uses autobiographical narrative to describe the Palestinian plight.

39. See Amir 1987 for a fictional (partly autobiographical) description of such a kibbutz setting. At least 342 children disappeared from the camps, most of them from Yemen and the rest from other Arab countries. In some cases, their families were told they had died and been buried. Yet twenty years later their parents received draft notices for these same children. A Knesset committee was appointed to investigate the matter. In March 1968, the committee produced 316 death certificates, fewer burial certificates, and four living children. There were procedural problems with the investigation (e.g., bodies were not exhumed to verify identity), but eventually the matter was dropped (Segev 1986).

40. See Swirski 1989, 26–28, for a discussion of the prevalence of these ideas in Israeli society.

41. The criteria for determining which children need special care are (1) father's country of origin, (2) father's level of education, and (3) family size. These criteria are more typical of Mizrahim than Ashkenazim (Swirski 1989, 36). Project Renewal, an urban development project that pairs American Jewish communities (and their monies) with distressed Israeli neighborhoods, included 160 Israeli locations in its original design, most of which were Mizrahi neighborhoods (ibid., 23).

42. Avi Temkin and Shlomo Maoz, "It's Better to Be an Ashkenazi," *Jerusalem Post,* 22 January 1989.

43. Linn writes, "It refers basically to the idea of keeping the weapon 'pure' by preserving its use for definite cases of self-defense" (1996, 142–43). Linn goes on to say that this moral code is translated into practice in two ways: (1) soldiers are taught not to blindly obey orders they find morally suspect, and (2) officers are expected to adopt a "follow me" policy, that is, to fulfill their moral responsibility toward their troops.

44. Claims of moral superiority may be just that—claims and not any reality. See, for example, the reactions of the Israeli soldiers who fired on the UN outpost at Qana in Lebanon, in the process killing over one hundred men, women, and children, as reported by Gil Riva in "The Soldiers Who Fired at Kufr Kanna Did Not Care about the Massacre," *Kol Ha'ir,* 10 May 1996, as translated in *From the Hebrew Press* 8 (6), June 1996.

45. See James Diamond's (1986) study of Yonatan Ratosh and the Canaanite movement. As he notes at the end, "The Jews have survived not because of political power but because of the religious tradition they created, transmitted, and developed, . . . it is this alone that would again validate their existence, not as a nation-state that confuses itself with this tradition and, what is more, confuses the world about the Jews and Judaism" (132).

Chapter 2

1. See appendix A, "Selected Chronology Influencing the History of Acre," in Rubin 1974.

2. From a series of articles appearing in the newspaper *Hēd Ha'Mizrāh,* 21 September 1945, 7 (in Hebrew).

3. See the intriguing discussion about exodus and conquest in Schwartz 1997. As she notes, "In this sequence of events, the Exodus [of Israel from Egypt] serves as the best of all moral justifications for the Conquest. With the captivity in Egypt and the Exodus from it positioned first, Israel is a victim before she is an aggressor. The Hebrews are a powerless group of people preyed upon by an evil mighty empire, and their deity offers them a homeland as a refuge from the terrors of history" (56). One could extrapolate from this to the modern founding of the Israeli state — where the evil empire is Nazi Germany and the Zionists are returning to their earlier promised land as a refuge from the terrors of extermination.

4. Israel 1990, 18, table 1.1.

5. Farah and Khoury 1936, 23.

6. Yehieli n.d., 104 (in Hebrew).

7. Morris 1987, 107.

8. For further information on the events of 1948–49 and their repercussions for both Palestinians and Israeli Jews, see Morris 1987; Nazzal 1978; Hadawi 1989; Segev 1986; and Palumbo 1987.

9. See, for example, the account of Hussain Khalil ʿAwad in Nazzal 1978, 53. He moved his family to Acre from Es Sumeiriya. After the village fell, he went to Acre and took his family to the neighboring village of El Ghabisiya. When it, too, fell, they fled to ʿAmqa. From ʿAmqa, they continued to Abu Sinan, and when it surrendered they moved to Tarshiha. With the capture of Tarshiha, they left for Lebanon, never to return.

10. Kamen 1988, 99.

11. Yehieli n.d., 114 (in Hebrew).

12. Ibid.

13. Israel 1990, 69, table 2.16.

14. See Morris 1986; 1987, 155–96.

15. Morris 1987, 161.

16. Kibbutz Meuhad Archives — Aharon Zisling Papers 9/9/1, IDF General Staff (Zvi Ayalon) to OCs (commanding officers) of brigades, battalions, districts, corps, the military police and branches, 6 July 1948, cited in Morris 1987, 163.

17. The details of the proposal are provided by both Morris (1987, 110) and Kamen (1987, 485) both of whom reconstructed the incident from files in the Israel State Archives, Ministry of Minorities, Box 307, File 10: Shimoni to Shitrit, 13 July 1948; Minority Affairs Minister to Shimoni, 19 July 1948.

18. Quoted in Kamen 1987, 485, from Israel State Archives, Ministry of Minorities, Box 307g, File 49.

19. The report is available at the United Nations Archive, file DAG-13/3.3.1: 8, Central Truce Supervision Board, and file DAG-13/3.3.1: 13, Refugees.

20. See Morris 1987, 113–15, 205–6, 222–23, 227–34; and Palumbo 1987, 47–57, 163–74, on Israeli atrocities during the fighting.

21. Acre Municipality 1978, 13.

22. Personal interview, 31 August 1988.

23. Personal interview, 21 November 1988.

24. Details are provided in Morris 1987, 192, from documents in the Israel State Archives, Foreign Ministry Papers, 2564/11, protocol of the meeting of the Military Government Committee, 9 September 1948; and 2564/13, protocol of the meeting of the Ministerial Committee for Abandoned Property, 10 September 1948.

25. As recorded in Ben-Gurion's personal diary, entries for 18 September and 22 November 1948, cited in Morris 1987, 192.

26. Personal interview with Yosef Katran, 13 October 1988.

27. Acre Municipal Archives, Sōkhnūt [Jewish Agency] File 15/11/49, Memo 23/KL/224, 2 August 1949, to Mr. Kalman Levin, Manager, Absorption Department, Jewish Agency, Haifa, from B. Noy (in Hebrew).

28. These properties are usually referred to in both journalistic and scholarly accounts of the period as abandoned houses. *Abandoned* in English carries the connotation of having been forsaken or deserted or of having surrendered one's claim to something. Many properties in Acre were taken from their still-resident owners under the provisions of the Absentee Property Regulations of 1948. It is therefore more accurate to describe these properties as uninhabited, not abandoned. In many cases, Israeli Palestinians have continued to press legal claims for the return of properties and land seized from them in 1948–49.

29. Acre Municipal Archives, Sōkhnūt File 15/11/49, Memo 1143 י/13צ/9411/9032, 29 August 1949, to the Municipal Committee, Acre, from D. Goldstein, Absorption Department, Tel Aviv, the Sōkhnūt (in Hebrew).

30. Palmon became the prime minister's adviser on Arab affairs after he and others instigated the dissolution of the Ministry for the Minorities (Segev 1986, 67).

31. Acre Municipal Archives, Old City Housing 1949/50, File 8/11, Memo 575/למרי/90, 19 August 1949, B. Noy to Yehoshua Palmon, Prime Minister's Office (in Hebrew).

32. Acre Municipal Archives, Old City Housing 1949/50, File 8/11, Memo 89/16868, 23 August 1949, Yehoshua Palmon, Prime Minister's Office to Military Governor's Headquarters (in Hebrew).

33. Acre Municipal Archives, Old City Housing 1949/50, File 8/11, Memo 417/קל/91, 26 August 1949, B. Noy to Kalman Levin and M. Sirutah, the Jewish Agency, Haifa (in Hebrew).

34. Acre Municipal Archives, Old City Housing 1949/50, File 8/11, Protocol of a meeting on 27 October 1949 between B. Noy, Mr. Kobber, the Superintendent of Absentee Property in Acre, Mr. Sirutah, Mr. Winer, and Mr. Mostovsky from the Jewish Agency, and Mr. Adler and Mr. Segal from the Soldier's Settlement Committee in Haifa (in Hebrew).

35. Acre Municipal Archives, Old City Housing 1949/50, File 8/11, Memo 1625/54/1, 25 December 1949, Baruch Noy to the Supervisor of Absentee Property, Acre (in Hebrew).

36. Acre Municipal Archives, Sōkhnūt File 15/11/49, Memo 14/ר2w/4157, 8 August 1949, Absorption Department, Northern District, to Absorption Department, Tel Aviv (in Hebrew).

37. Acre Municipal Archives, Sōkhnūt File 15/11/49, Memo 95/מ/502, 5 September 1949, Baruch Noy to Commander, Israeli Police, Acre (in Hebrew).

38. Acre Municipal Archives, Sōkhnūt File 15/11/49, Memo 95/מ/933, 1 November 1949, Baruch Noy to the Police Chief, Acre (in Hebrew).

39. Personal interview, 16 October 1988.

40. Acre Municipal Archives, Old City Housing 1949/50, File 8/11, Memo 661/ט/91, 22 September 1949, B. Noy to Kalman Levin, the Jewish Agency, Haifa (in Hebrew).

41. Acre Municipal Archives, Military Governor, Western Galilee, File 2/6, Memo 22, n.d., Zaher Yacoub Faddoul to the Military Governor (in English).

42. Such individuals were designated as "present absentees" to distinguish them from absentees who were no longer resident on Israeli-held territory. Present absentees are Israeli citizens, but they are not entitled to reclaim their personal property or landholdings. Approximately seventy-five thousand individuals fall into this classification (Kretzmer 1990, 57).

43. Acre Municipal Archives, Military Governor, Western Galilee, File 2/6, Memos 33–36, 38–39, for example (in Arabic).

44. Cited in Karmen 1987, 475, from Government of Israel, Ministry of Minorities, *Activities, May, 1948–January, 1949* (Jerusalem, 1949), 24.

45. Acre Municipal Archives, Military Governor, Western Galilee, File 2/6, item 72. I found only two letters referring to the release from this camp of prisoners who were being returned to their families in Acre. Only one of the letters included the voucher stipulating how long the prisoner had been held in the camp.

46. See Kamen's discussion on refugees from Haifa and the conditions set for their return (1987, 490; 1988, 69–77).

47. Kamen 1988, 82, from Israel State Archives, Ministry of Minorities, Box 301, File 81.

48. Acre Municipal Archives, Military Governor, Western Galilee, File 2/6, Memo 94/מע/952, 2 November 1949, Baruch Noy to Lieutenant Colonel ʿAmnoel Markovsky, Military Government Headquarters in the Occupied Territories (in Hebrew).

49. Acre Municipal Archives, Military Governor, Western Galilee, File 2/6, Memo 243/2566, 25 November 1949, Rehavʿam ʿAmir, Major, Military Governor, Western Galilee and Villages of Haifa District, to Chairman, Municipal Committee, Acre (in Hebrew).

50. A census was carried out in November 1948, and all Arabs resident in the country at that time were registered and issued identity cards.

51. See Morris 1987, 237–53, for a more complete discussion of the process of clearing the borders.

52. Acre Municipal Archives, Military Governor, Western Galilee, File 2/6, Memo 1935/113, 24 September 1949, Sheikh Muhammad Younis to the Military Governor of Western Galilee, Acre (in English).

53. Segev 1986, 64. Fouzi El-Asmar tells of his aunt's return after three years under this program (1978, 11).

54. Acre Municipal Archives, List of Arabs Returned to Acre, 14/18-אר (in Arabic and French).

55. Acre Municipal Archives, Military Governor, Western Galilee, File 2/6, Memo of 17 June 1949, Tabari to Town Commander; Memo 21/מט/75, 21 June 1949, Baruch Noy to Police Commander, Acre station; Memo 24/49, 28 June 1949, Acre Police Commander to Municipal Committee, Acre; Memo 44/מצר/94, 28 June 1949, Baruch Noy, representative of the Military Government in Acre to Military Governor, Western Galilee (in Hebrew).

56. Cited in Segev 1986, 71, from files in the Israel State Archives, Prime Minister's Office, Custodian, 5440/C. 210/05.

57. Acre Municipal Archives, Military Governor, Western Galilee, File 2/6, Memo 8245/1/1, 5 February 1951, Mayor Baruch Noy to Ministry of the Interior, Local Rule Branch, Jerusalem (in Hebrew).

58. Acre Municipality 1978, 14 (in Hebrew).

59. The first round of elections actually took place on 26 June 1951. According to Ramzi Ḥouri, the envelopes that were used for the ballots were transparent. Anyone who voted for the Communist Party was recorded on a list as he or she handed in the ballot. When the votes were counted, the Communists had won two seats. The local military governor asked the courts to void the results because the election had not been secret. The courts complied, and a second round was scheduled for two months later. Individuals who had voted for the Communists were approached privately and urged to change their political allegiance. In the second round of elections, the Communists received only one seat.

60. Acre Municipal Archives, Municipal Elections Committee File 1/8, Protocol, Municipal Elections Committee, 19 March 1951 (in Hebrew).

61. Acre Municipal Archives, Municipal Elections Committee File 1/8 (in Hebrew).

62. Acre Municipal Archives, File 14/8, Investigation of Baruch Noy, Letter to Acre Affairs Sub-Committee, Internal Affairs Committee of the Knesset, from J. L. A. Watson, municipal engineer, Acre, 17 September 1952.

63. See Rubin 1974, 25. There is also a file on this matter in the Acre Municipal Archives. The scandal destroyed Noy politically. He resigned and eventually went to live overseas, where he died.

64. Acre Municipal Archives, Sōkhnūt File 15/11/49, Memos 14/5346 and 14/5344, 1 October 1950, Absorption Department, Northern District, to Central Labor Office, Tel Aviv, and to the Office of Kupat Holim, Western Galilee Branch, Haifa (in Hebrew).

65. See Bernstein 1981 for a description of conditions in such camps. She notes that by the end of 1963, at least 12,750 people were still living in these "temporary" quarters.

66. Personal interview, 4 September 1989.

67. Acre Municipal Archives, Sōkhnūt File 15/11/49, Memo 1/46/2380, 20 February 1950, Mayor Noy to Kalman Levin, Absorption Department, the Jewish Agency, Haifa (in Hebrew).

68. Acre Municipal Archives, Sōkhnūt File, 15/11/49, Memo 11/7/4732, 21 December 1956, Y. Gadish, Mayor, to Y. Sarid, Jewish Agency, Haifa (in Hebrew).

69. Acre Municipal Archives, Welfare File 1950/51, Memo 348/סק‏·טס, 26 January 1951; Memo 8239/100/1, 5 February 1951; Memo 1372/5/ט/ם, 7 February 1951; Memo 8455/100/1, 13 February 1951; Memo from social worker to Mayor Noy, 14 February 1951; Memo 8571/7/1, 19 February 1951; Memo 07179/13/0, n.d.; Memo 8602/100/1, 20 February 1951; Memo 8603/100/1, 20 February 1951; Memo 19944/13/2, 15 April 1951 (in Hebrew).

70. Acre Municipal Archives, Military Governor, Western Galilee, File 2/6, Memo 10.603/100/1, 28 March 1951, Old City residents to Mayor Noy (in Arabic).

71. 'Igeret L'Tōshāv (Note to Resident), Acre Municipality, Independence Day, 1959, 4 (in Hebrew).

72. Acre Municipal Archives, File 14/5, Employment and Housing for Arab Refugees in Acre (in Hebrew).

73. Acre Municipal Archives, File 12/1, Manager, Branch Office for Emigration (in Hebrew).

74. Acre Municipal Archives, File 14/5, Employment and Housing for the Arab Refugees in Acre, Memo 1072/208/1, 21 May 1953, Y. Gadish, Mayor, and S. Mamluk, Deputy Mayor for Arabs, to Mr. Houbeishe, Manager, Minorities Department, Labor Office, Haifa (in Hebrew).

75. "Acre Renovating Old Quarter," *Jerusalem Post,* 21 September 1961.

76. George Leonof, "Putting Acre on the Tourist Map," *Jerusalem Post,* 15 October 1965.

77. *Jerusalem Post,* 22 September 1961.

78. *Jerusalem Post,* 26 September 1961.

79. The final blow to the movement came when three members were convicted in 1967 of harboring Palestinian guerrillas. The group's leadership was broken up, and at least four key members left Israel in the early 1970s (Zureik 1979, 174).

80. *Jerusalem Post,* 19 August 1964.

81. Gideon Weigert, "Pillar of Acre," *Jerusalem Post,* 21 November 1965.

82. Dov Goldstein, "Acre: Together in Peace," *Ma'ariv,* 15 November 1968.

83. "Suspected Link between the Fatah and the Deputy Mayor of Acre under Investigation" *Ma'ariv,* 23 November 1968. Also reported in "Ex-Deputy Mayor of Acre Sues 'Ma'ariv' for Libel," *Jerusalem Post,* 31 January 1969.

84. "Most of Acre's Arabs See It as an Arab City—Like the Partition

Plan," *Ha'Aretz,* 3 December 1968; "Houbeishe Returns to His Suggestion to Found a Bi-National State," *Davar,* 3 December 1968; "Acre's Deputy Mayor Denies Connections with Fatah," *Al Ha'Mishmar,* 3 December 1968; "Demand to Return to Partition Borders and Unite Acre to the Autonomous Arab Territory," *Ha'Tzofah,* 3 December 1968. *Davar* is the paper of the Histadrut, and it is known as moderate. *Ha'Aretz* is Israel's equivalent of the *New York Times,* and it is moderate and dovish. *Al Ha'Mishmar* is the paper of the Mapam Party. *Ha'Tzofah* is the paper of the National Religious Party. *Ma'ariv* is a right-wing independent evening paper.

85. "Acre Deputy Mayor Resigns over Partition Statement," *Jerusalem Post,* 6 December 1968.

86. "Dismissal Sought of Acre Deputy Town Clerk," *Jerusalem Post,* 8 December 1968.

87. "Five Terrorist Groups Smashed," *Jerusalem Post,* 21 November 1969.

88. "Police Disperse Jewish Hotheads in Acre Rally," *Jerusalem Post,* 23 November 1969.

89. "Acre, Nazareth Arabs Denounce Terror Actions," *Jerusalem Post,* 23 November 1969.

90. Joel Dar, "Seven Hurt in Acre Riot after Car Is Blown Up," *Jerusalem Post,* 24 November 1969.

91. Ibid.

92. Quoted in Zureik 1979, 146, from "The Test Hour of the Israeli Arabs," *Yedi'ot Aharonot,* 28 November 1969.

93. Yoel Dar, "Confidential Reports Says Acre 'in Trouble,' " *Jerusalem Post,* 17 July 1970.

94. "About the Deprivation of Old Acre," *Zo Ha'Dereh,* 5 May 1970; "Arabs in Acre Complain about the Neglect of Their Housing Problems," *Ha'Aretz,* 5 May 1970; "Acre Councillors Complain of Slums," *Jerusalem Post,* 1 May 1970.

95. M. Rahat, "Density in Old Acre: Hothouse of Hostile Activity," *Ma'Ariv,* 9 March 1971.

96. *Jerusalem Post,* 21 January 1974.

97. *Jerusalem Post,* 24 December 1976.

98. *Jerusalem Post,* 15 August 1973, 5 and 20 September 1973, 19 February 1974, 11–12 and 14–16 July 1974.

99. Ya'acov Ardon, "Acre Ma'bara Residents Protest 'Intolerable' Squalor," *Jerusalem Post,* 7 July 1975.

100. *Jerusalem Post,* 15 and 26 September 1977, 4 January 1978, 23 April 1978.

101. From the Wolfson survey conducted by the researcher in 1989.

102. *Jerusalem Post,* 15 and 21 September 1982.

103. *Jerusalem Post,* 27 October 1983.

104. *Jerusalem Post,* 19 September 1984.

105. Karlos Lomovsky, adviser to the mayor on planning, prepared the report and presented it on 19 April 1984. The report covered housing, industry, employment, tourism, education, and the Arab sector.

106. *Jerusalem Post,* 28 October 1985.

107. David Rudge, "Arab Gang Attacks Acre Police," *Jerusalem Post,* 8 September 1986.

108. David Rudge, *Jerusalem Post,* 21 October 1986.

109. David Rudge, "Vandals Visit Acre Church," *Jerusalem Post,* 16 April 1987.

110. David Rudge, "New Stamp Honours Moslem Community," *Jerusalem Post* (international edition), 17 May 1986.

111. Acre is divided into twelve statistical areas for census purposes. East Acre comprises areas 1–3 and 10, North Acre 4–8, Mandate Acre 9–11, and the Old City 12.

112. In terms of absolute numbers, Jerusalem's Arab population is far greater (120,000 in 1983), but in terms of percentages (Jerusalem, 29 percent; Acre, 23 percent) there is only a small difference (figures for Jerusalem are from Romann and Weingrod 1991, 117–18).

113. There are neighborhoods in other cities, such as Abu Tor in Jerusalem or the Halissa quarter in Haifa, where Arabs and Jews live together. See, for example, ibid., 63–98, for a discussion of Jerusalem. In Acre, no neighborhood is without an Arab presence today (Haifa and Galilee Research Institute 1989, 9).

114. This geographic version was made available to me through the Data Archive of the Faculty of Social Sciences at Hebrew University in Jerusalem. The file contains data drawn from the general census for a sample of families in each of the statistical areas of Acre except for areas 5 and 6.

115. Cohen 1973, 8.

116. David Rudge, "In Acre—the Walls Tumble Down," *Jerusalem Post,* 20 November 1986.

117. Prices of houses and apartments for sale or rent in Israel are always given in American dollars. See Dominguez 1990 for a discussion of the "dollarizing" of Israel's economy.

Chapter 3

1. For further details, see Tibawi 1956 and Marʿi 1978.

2. These schools were eventually nationalized and placed under strict government supervision so that no antigovernment components could enter the curriculum. By 1914, there were almost four hundred Muslim schools in Palestine (Tibawi 1956).

3. This information is drawn from articles in *Hēd Ha'Mizrāh* written by H. Dromi on the history of Jewish settlement in Acre.

4. Emile Habiby's fictional character Saeed attended secondary school in Acre, which "was still academically superior to the one in Haifa" and to which he commuted daily by train, along with Yuaad, his first love, who attended the girls' school there (1985, 17).

5. *Mizraḥi* here refers to the separate religious Zionist Party within the World Zionist Organization (composed of Ashkenazim) and should not be

confused with *Mizrahi* as the racial-political term that refers to a segment of Israel's Jewish population. Mizrahi merged with Ha'po'el Ha'Mizrahi in 1956 to form the National Religious Party (NRP), one of the largest of the religious parties and an important coalition partner in most Israel governments since 1948.

6. The *heder* (Hebrew: "room") was the traditional form of Jewish schooling. One teacher would take in twenty to thirty boys aged four to thirteen for the purpose of religious instruction — in the *Tanakh,* Talmud, and commentaries. At the age of thirteen, the best students would transfer to the yeshiva, where they would continue with their religious instruction but at a more advanced level. "Roughly speaking, one may regard the Heder as the elementary school, compulsory for all (boys), the 'Yeshiva' as a secondary school for the *élite*" (Bentwich, 1965, 7).

7. Gofer's story was part of an introductory section in Acre Municipality 1978.

8. See Bentwich 1965 and Kleinberger 1969 for more comprehensive discussions of the structure of the educational system in Israel.

9. Mar'i (1978) reported that in 1978 more than 40 percent of Arab teachers remained unqualified, compared to a negligible number of Jewish teachers — a difference he believed was due to the fact that there were sufficient Jewish training institutions to fill the demand for qualified teachers.

10. "Jockeying for position in order to get a hold on the electorate of the day-after-tomorrow," as one education correspondent put it (Gerda Luft, "Politics and Education," *Jerusalem Post,* 12 March 1950).

11. This "reform" has been slow to occur in the educational system. When Arnold Lewis studied the schools of Sharonia in 1975–76, they were still operating under the old structure. A number of elite schools (e.g., the Reali School in Haifa and the Herzlia Gymnasia) continue to follow the model of eight years of elementary and four years of high school.

12. The medium of instruction in the Arab system is Arabic, although students also learn both Hebrew and English. Students who plan to attend a university must master Hebrew and English, since there are no Israeli Arabic-language universities. Arab students at all levels have units on Arabic language and literature and Arab history in addition to Jewish/Israeli studies.

13. See the discussion of the Wadi Salib riots in Smooha 1978, 209, 211–12; and Swirski 1989.

14. Kleinberger has this to say about the gifted boarding schools: "They [a small, handpicked number of exceptionally talented new immigrants] attend selective secondary schools with an academic or vocational bias, where they rub shoulders with the 'normal' Western middle-class population of such institutions" (1969, 302–3).

15. Stein 1985, 211; Swirski 1989, 27; Smooha 1978, 161–63, 191.

16. *Jerusalem Post,* 25 June 1968.

17. Compare this to Willis 1977, in which the "lads" also rejected the school's ideology and actively resisted the values and knowledge imposed upon them.

18. Avi Temkin and Shlomo Maoz, "It's Better to Be an Ashkenazi," *Jerusalem Post,* 22 January 1989.

19. The Pedagogical Center in Acre had many of these materials about ethnic communities in Israel. I found a series of materials by Avraham Stahl, published through the Education Department of Hebrew University in 1987 or 1988, *Sources for the Study of Mizrahi Jewish Culture,* that covered topics such as education, children, marriage, husband, and wife. The center also had a copy of his two-volume *'Edōt Israel* (Israeli ethnic communities) as well as materials from another program, *'Am Israel u'Tfūtsotāv* (The people of Israel and their diaspora). Teachers can borrow these materials for use in preparing lectures or for classroom exercises, but most (according to the center's director) do not.

20. Personal interview, 13 March 1989.

21. The document took the name of Deputy Minister of Education Aharon Yadlin, who headed a committee established to define goals for Arab education in Israel.

22. Chaim Nachman Bialik (1873–1934) is known as the national poet of Israel. He wrote poetry that extolled Palestine and exhorted Jews to return to the land.

23. Acre Municipal Archives, Budget Reports, 1949/50 to 1952/53.

24. Acre Municipal Archives, File 15/11/49, Letter 11/7/1955.

25. Lewis (1979, 40) notes that in 1975–76 secondary-school tuition was several thousand Israeli pounds per year per child. He also notes that to obtain a skilled working-class job (not to mention any sort of white-collar employment), ten to twelve years of formal education were required. This trend has intensified. Currently, about half a million jobs in Israel require successful completion of the *bagrūt* examination as one of the minimum qualifications; this is approximately one-third of the Israeli job market (Shlomo Swirski, personal communication).

26. Students attend elementary and junior high schools based on their place of residence. For high school, however, parents can (and often do) send their children to schools in other locations. The major limiting factor is the cost of transporting the child to and from school each day. Thus, some students from Acre, for example, travel to Haifa every day.

27. *Ha'Aretz,* 31 July 1970.

28. Lewis (1979) reported the same pattern for Sharonia — many teachers lived in the nearby community of Seaview and commuted to school each morning.

29. Although Terra Sancta is a Catholic school, about 85 percent of its students are Muslims. It is located in the heart of the Old City, near the port.

30. Amal and the upper-grade school are located one block from the central police station, near the sea.

31. Obshestwo Propostranienia Truda (the Society for Handicrafts and Agricultural Work, which eventually came to be known by its Russian acronym, ORT) was founded in 1880 by wealthy Jews in St. Petersburg to develop Jewish trade schools, to facilitate migration of artisans between cities, and to support Jewish agricultural colonies, farms, and agricultural schools. Today it is a global, nonprofit organization, meeting the education and training needs of contemporary societies around the world. The ORT network extends to more than fifty

countries, and the number of students enrolled this year is in excess of 200,000, with a staff of 10,000 educators, engineers, instructors, and administrative personnel. ORT runs its own junior, junior high, and comprehensive schools, technical high schools, and colleges, covering an age range of seven to eighteen, as well as offering postsecondary training toward practical engineering degrees and B.Sc. degrees for technical teachers within its own Teacher Training Institutes.

32. Project Renewal is an urban renewal program launched by the Begin government in 1977. Most of the 160 neighborhoods chosen for the program are Mizraḥi. Funding for the program comes from the national government and Jewish communities in the United States. American Jewish communities are often paired with an Israeli neighborhood, and delegations of Americans from the donor cities frequently visit to see how "their" neighborhoods are managing.

33. Ha'Torah and Eyal are the Agudah schools, while Maftan is a special youth-employment program. It is well known that Agudah schools receive state support, even though they are supposedly in the "unofficial, recognized" category and therefore are not state supported.

34. *Jerusalem Post,* 27 January 1987. The Amal elementary school was in a building that had formerly housed the Hebrew Weitzman school. Weitzman had been moved to more modern quarters in a building constructed near Town Hall.

35. *Kol Ha'Tsafon,* 8 January 1988.

36. See reports in *Tsafon 1,* 9, 16, and 23 September 1988; and *Kol Ha'Tsafon,* 16 September 1988.

37. *Tsafon 1,* 6 January 1989.

38. He also noted that conditions had deteriorated during the last five years. It was well known where certain people stood on giving assistance to the Arab schools.

39. See Resh 1998 for a discussion of how tracking works in Israel. One of the findings from her study was that, while ability and academic performance were strong predictors of track placement, placement was also affected by the student's socioeconomic status, ethnic origin, and gender.

40. Scores are computed using a composite of elementary school grades; scores from standardized tests of English, Hebrew, and mathematics; and the recommendation of the elementary school staff.

41. The non-*bagrūt* track is further divided into different levels: the *masmat* track (a high-level vocational track that emphasizes electronics), the *masmar* track (an ordinary vocational track), and the *masmam* track (a lower-level vocational track).

42. *Hēd Ha'Tsafon,* 18 August 1989.

43. One teacher did indicate that she had been told there would be a change the following year and that Israeli geography would be included in the junior high school curriculum.

44. One teacher told me that Arabs carry a different map around in their heads — all the Arabic names of the places that have been Hebraized.

45. The Israeli army still has forces located in Lebanon in an area called the Security Zone. Israeli soldiers there remain major targets of Palestinian and Shiʿite paramilitary forces operating in the area.

46. For three days and two nights, Lebanese Special Units (Christian Phlange forces) systematically massacred the Palestinian residents (men, women, and children) of the Sabra and Shatila refugee camps. The Lebanese units were allowed into the camp by IDF forces that had surrounded the camps. The Israeli forces controlled the perimeter and prevented escape from the camps, blocked the main exits, and set off flares to light up the alleys at night (Sayigh 1994, 118). Estimates of the number of people killed range from 700 to 3,000; an accurate count was never made. It is commonly estimated that 400,000 Israelis turned out for the Peace Now demonstration in Tel Aviv, where the organization demanded that the government launch a full inquiry into the Israeli role in the massacre (Hall-Cathala 1990, 50, 59; Lehman-Wilzig 1990, 41; Shindler 1991, 101).

47. Peace Now is the mainstream peace movement in Israel. As an organization, it opposes continued Israeli rule over the West Bank and Gaza Strip, supports territorial compromise, and affirms the democratic *and* Jewish character of the Israeli state. With the outbreak of the *intifada* in the West Bank and Gaza Strip, Peace Now was pushed to adopt a more radical stance as new peace groups that espoused more progressive visions of an Israeli future started to draw off its energies and membership.

48. After Kahane's election, new antiracist groups, such as Citizens against Racism, formed spontaneously in Jerusalem, Tel Aviv, Acre, Haifa, and many of Israel's smaller towns. Many of these groups later united under the auspices of the United Kibbutz Movement to form an umbrella organization, Ma'aneh (Answer) (Hall-Cathala 1990, 67–68).

49. See Tsemah and Tsin 1984. In 1985, a poll conducted at the Bnei 'Akiva Nehalim yeshiva, the "flagship" of the National Religious Party's *yeshivot*, disclosed that 62 percent of the one hundred sixteen-year-old students surveyed supported Kahane's views of Arabs (*Jerusalem Post*, 27 June 1985). In a 1989 follow-up study to the 1984 poll, 40 percent of Israeli Jewish high school students said that they hate all or almost all Arabs (Dan Izenberg, "Poll Shows Widespread Hatred for Arabs among Israeli Youths," *Jerusalem Post*, 8 August 1989).

50. Even the army became involved in fighting racism by "teaching democracy" to new conscripts (Hall-Cathala 1990, 68).

51. *Jerusalem Post*, 14 July 1962.

52. This is Israel's equivalent of Princeton's Institute for Advanced Study.

53. While the education ministry promoted meetings between Jewish and Palestinian students, the Chief Rabbinical Council and the head of the education ministry's Religious Schools Division issued directives that forbade such meetings due to fears of *kashrut* violations and intermarriage (*Jerusalem Post*, 8 August 1985). Both the chief rabbis and the division head agreed to permit meetings under the condition that they be segregated by sex (Shipler 1986, 521).

54. See, for example, Amir 1969, 1976; and Amir et al. 1981.

55. Daniel Bar-Tal has gone on to conduct research on how the Israeli-Arab conflict is reflected in textbooks (Or Kashti, "Research on School Textbooks: All Arabs Are Presented as 'Murderers, Pogromists, and Robbers,'" *Ha'Aretz*, 17 November 1996). Bar-Tal found that textbooks emphasize the

security issue and endorse beliefs that "refer mainly to the praise of heroic deeds of Jewish history. Jews are presented as a minority which always has justice on its side, struggling against many enemies stronger than they are."

56. In reporting on action research conducted within the School for Peace, Eady (1988) mentions that sometimes participants felt that "one people was being used to change the other."

57. *Kol Ha'Tsafon,* 25 March 1988.

58. Yossi Bar Moha, " 'Interns for Peace' Withers," *Tsafon 1,* 9 September 1988.

59. Ibid.

60. Ibid.

61. I was not able to make a comparison with the Arabic workbook or determine whether the content of books is exactly the same.

62. This atmosphere was an outgrowth of the bitter fight waged over local elections held in February 1989. See chapter 5 for a more complete discussion of the election battle and its repercussions.

63. *Kol Ha'Tsafon,* 5 May 1989.

64. *Hed Ha'Tsafon,* 30 June 1989.

65. The history of land purchases in Palestine by Zionist organizations is much more complex than this simple rendering of events indicates. See Stein 1984; Lehn and Davis 1988.

66. This holds true for Israeli Jews and foreign academics who choose to study Israel as well. Both Shohat (1988, 32) and Dominguez (1989, 158–66) address what happens to those who seek to represent the reality of Israeli life in terms that oppose the dominant discourse. Those who cannot be "persuaded" to return to the accepted images are ostracized as anti-Semitic (non-Jews) or self-hating (Jews).

67. At the School for Peace, for example, I was told they "also work with Mizraḥi youth."

68. East for Peace, a movement of Mizraḥi intellectuals, was formed to counter the stereotypes of Mizraḥim as Arab-haters that proliferated in the aftermath of peace activist Emil Grunzweig's death from a hand grenade thrown by a presumed Mizraḥi counterdemonstrator during a Peace Now antiwar demonstration. East for Peace is largely made up of Moroccan intellectuals who were brought to Israel to study in the early 1960s (the Oden Programme) in the hope they would remain and become leaders of the North African community there (Hall-Cathala 1990, 105). Hall-Cathala notes that its popular image as intellectual has hampered the group's ability to cross the class divide and gain membership from the majority, working-class, Mizraḥi community.

69. Israel 1990, 614, table 22.11.

70. One Arab child, after enduring abuse from his Jewish classmates for a time, climbed to the roof of his *gan* and jumped. Landing in the grass, he was unhurt, but he informed his mother that if he had to return to that school, he would continue jumping off the roof until she stopped sending him. Her desperation provided the impetus to start the new *gan;* by 1988, it was enrolling about one hundred children in two sections. In addition, the Women's Association has

developed a Pedagogical Center that yearly enrolls and trains about fifty Palestinian women as early childhood (ages zero to four) educators. The women are also working to develop curriculum and instructional materials that focus on Arab culture and daily life and educate children about their Arab identity.

71. *Kol Ha'Tsafon,* 18 August 1989.

72. Yossi Bar Moha, "To Separate Them When They're Still Small," *Tsafon 1,* 11 May 1990.

73. Ibid.

74. Yoel Dar, "Yossi Fitosi: Separation of the *Gans* is a Failure of Coexistence in the City of Acre," *Kol Ha'Tsafon,* 11 May 1990.

75. *Tsafon 1,* 11 May 1990.

76. Harry Frey, personal communication, 10 August 1992. Frey was one of the directors of the Van Leer joint Arab-Jewish social action project, which operated in the Wolfson quarter from 1986 to 1993. The project was active in providing new educational services to the neighborhood. It also attempted to develop a more integrated educational framework in the mixed day-care centers but was only successful in placing Arab teacher's aides in such facilities.

77. See Virginia Dominguez's discussion of how Israelis appropriate the other, "using what they see in the other for the sake of self-objectification" (1989, 179). The other is not simply the opposite of the self—the self can internalize, embody, and appropriate the other.

78. As quoted in Yoel Kotzer, "Sixty-Eight Percent of Israelis Are for Denying Those Who Support the Establishment of a Palestinian State the Right to Vote," *Hadashot,* 5 June 1990.

Chapter 4

1. The term *development town* refers officially to twenty-seven settlements: Eilat, Ofakim, Beersheba, Beth Shean, Beth Shemesh, Dimona, Hatzor Ha'Galilit, Tiberias, Yokneam Illit, Yeruham, Karmi'el, Migdal Ha'Emek, Metulla, Menahemia, Ma'alot, Mitzpe Ramon, Upper Nazareth, Netivot, Acre, Afula, Arad, Safed, Qiryāt Gat, Qiryāt Malachi, Qiryāt Shemona, Shderot, and Shelomi (Swirski and Shoushan 1986, 11). These towns were an integral part of the national plan of economic development, but they were also intended to provide the framework for the development of their inhabitants, immigrants from underdeveloped countries (mostly Mizraḥim). As Swirski and Shoushan note, the term *underdevelopment towns* would be a more accurate description (1986, 6).

2. Israel 1998, table 2.14, Population in Localities Numbering above 5,000 Inhabitants on 31 XII 1997(1), web version.

3. *Jerusalem Post,* 19 April 1963.

4. *Jerusalem Post,* 20 April 1966.

5. Ibid.

6. *Yedi'ot 'Iriyat 'Akko,* April 1966 (in Hebrew).

7. *Yedi'ot 'Iriyat 'Akko,* May 1965 (in Hebrew).

8. Housing conditions in the Old City have remained a matter of great concern. On 2 February 1988, *Mabat Shenī,* Israel TV's news program, did a special report on these housing problems — buildings falling apart, walls and roofs collapsing, overcrowding, and people living below ground or in rooms open to the elements.

9. Rubin 1974, 114. The Kesten Report of 1963 noted that 36 percent of the buildings in the Old City were not in good condition and only 8 percent were bad. However, when Waterman surveyed the same area in 1967 he noted that he would have classified most of the buildings in the Old City as in bad condition (1969, 60–61). He credits the discrepancy to differences in the criteria used to determine the quality of buildings in the two surveys.

10. This comment and those that follow are from the survey conducted in the neighborhood during 1989. Comments by Jewish residents were in Hebrew, and I have provided the English translations. The comments by Arab residents, in Arabic, were translated into English by Elektra Spathopoulos.

11. *Jerusalem Post,* 12 September 1974.

12. *Jerusalem Post,* 5 September 1973.

13. *Jerusalem Post,* 24 December 1976.

14. See Deutsch and Avitsour 1982; Deutsch 1985 and Deutsch 1988 are shorter summaries of the survey and its results.

15. Their survey of sixty-two questions was divided into three parts: personal data (such as age, country of origin, education, occupation, and so on); questions about Arab-Jewish contacts and daily life; and more general questions on economic life, education, politics, and so on. While they do not provide data on the gender of respondents, the use of masculine forms in the questions asked and the characterization of respondents as "family heads" tend to suggest that the respondents were all men.

16. Ironically, they interviewed the segment of the population that probably had the least contact — the men, who were absent from the neighborhood at work for large parts of the day. It is interesting to speculate how their results might have varied had they interviewed the women and children, whose lives were more confined to the neighborhood and who probably interacted on a more intensive, regular basis.

17. These figures are taken from the tables that appear as an appendix in Deutsch 1988, which is an English translation of Deutsch and Avitsour 1982, with the addition of a postscript.

18. Deutsch (1988, 68), in fact, described them as sharing a common cultural background with the Arab respondents, although he notes that this is not the same as a common cultural identity.

19. See, for example, Smooha's surveys (1992, 148).

20. See Frey and Assadi 1986.

21. Mayor Doron publicly criticized the Israel Lands Administration because it had not allocated land for constructing better-quality flats in Acre. The more affluent residents of the town were therefore purchasing homes in other areas and leaving Acre (*Jerusalem Post,* 23 April 1978).

22. Amidar owned and still owns 36 percent of the housing stock in

Wolfson. Its apartments are rented to new immigrants or veteran Israelis who cannot afford to purchase housing. Two-thirds of the Jewish families still living in Wolfson in 1989 who were renting from Amidar moved into the neighborhood during 1965–69 and had five or more children. Jewish residents who are renting from Amidar find it difficult, if not impossible, to transfer to apartments in other parts of the city.

23. In many cases, the housing stock belonged to Amidar (which received it from the Custodian for Absentee Property); Amidar neglected these properties, putting its efforts instead into housing stock in the Jewish sector.

24. Some researchers (Goering 1978; Grodzins 1957) use the notion of the "tipping point" to designate a certain percentage of minority residents that triggers flight from a neighborhood. Other studies (Wolf 1963; Pryor 1971) find no evidence for the existence of such a psychological stage.

25. Some residents reported finding used hypodermic needles littering the stairways in their buildings. The police were called to the neighborhood in one instance to close down a brothel that was operating in one of the apartment blocks.

26. For a more extensive discussion of the activities of the project in the Wolfson neighborhood, see the two evaluation reports prepared for the Bernard Van Leer Foundation: Rechman 1990 and Rhodes and Spathopoulos 1994.

27. This section is based on an extensive survey of neighborhood residents that I conducted in 1989 in cooperation with Oren Rechman, the evaluator of Project Van Leer. The interviews were mainly conducted by a team of Jewish and Arab residents of Acre, almost all women and students at Haifa University or the Teacher Training College. Arab residents were interviewed in Arabic by an Arab member of the team, while Jewish residents were interviewed in Hebrew by myself or a Jewish member of the team. I trained all the interviewers and supervised the Jewish group. The Arab interviewers were supervised by Elektra Spathopoulos. Each interview took approximately one and a half hours. As part of the interview, residents were asked to describe in their own words how Arab-Jewish relations have developed in the neighborhood.

28. All of the blocks were four-story buildings. Two (nos. 5 and 46) were single-entrance buildings with four apartments on each floor (for a total of sixteen units). Blocks 8 and 6 had two entrances with four apartments on each floor except the ground floor, which had only two apartments (twenty-eight units). Block 36 was the same except that it had three entrances (forty-two apartments). Blocks 4 and 7 had five entrances with two apartments on each floor (forty units). Blocks 40, 44, and 57 each had six entrances with two apartments on each floor (forty-eight units). Block 3 had five entrances with two apartments on each floor and one entrance with four apartments on each floor (fifty-six units). Block 55 had seven entrances with two apartments on each floor (fifty-six units).

29. Rechman, who wrote the evaluation report on Project Van Leer's work in the neighborhood, states that the development comprises eleven apartment blocks with 467 housing units. However, several residents had expanded their homes by purchasing an adjacent apartment and knocking out walls to increase

the living space. In other cases, very large families were often assigned two adjacent apartments. This accounts for the discrepancy between Rechman's figure of 467 units and mine of 459. When a family occupied more than one flat, I counted it as a single dwelling unit.

30. The largest apartments are the result of a project funded by the Ministry of Housing that allowed residents to add onto their apartments. In a multiunit building, residents must cooperate in order for expansion to occur. A number of residents were anxiously waiting to see if the ministry would expand on the project to all blocks in the neighborhood. For some residents, that would determine whether they would remain in Wolfson or not.

31. A Project Van Leer worker who was also a resident of Wolfson put together a unit-by-unit map of the neighborhood, giving each apartment's location and noting whether its residents were Jewish, Arab, or a mixed couple or whether it was empty. By the time we began to interview neighborhood residents three months later, the map was invalid for a number of buildings. Corrections were made by the interviewers as necessary, but the map should still be viewed as valid only for that period in 1989 when it was initially composed.

32. The households were randomly selected within each block roughly in proportion to the total number of Arab and Jewish families that lived in the block. If a block had twenty Jewish and ten Arab households, we selected ten Jewish and five Arab households to interview.

33. Smooha found in his 1988 survey that 13 percent of Jewish respondents, 16.5 percent of Christians, 25 percent of Druze, and 35.5 percent of Muslims considered themselves to be religious or very religious (1992, 42–43). He found a decline in the proportion of the religious from 1980 to 1988 for all four religious groups, although he notes that Muslims are the least secular and least secularizing.

34. These statistics are from the Haifa and Galilee Research Institute 1989, 37, table 2.

35. See table 2 in ibid.

36. The immigration wave in 1951–55 was mostly from Morocco, while that in 1961–65 was from Morocco and Romania.

37. Immigration from the Soviet Union had not yet begun in earnest at the time I left Acre in 1989. As the numbers of arrivals increased over the next year, Acre once again began to receive new Jewish arrivals. As of August 1992, approximately eight thousand Soviet immigrants had been given housing accommodations in Acre. An additional three thousand Ethiopians were living in a nearby youth camp (Harry Frey, personal communication, 10 August 1992).

38. The Khan al Umdan is one of the Old City's major historical landmarks. Today it stands empty most of the year. It comes alive only during the Alternative Theatre Festival and other special events.

39. I was told by several Palestinian informants that they would deliberately refrain from speaking in Arabic when riding on the public transportation system because they feared negative reactions from Israeli Jewish passengers on the bus.

40. For a more detailed exposition of the stereotypes that Arabs and Jews have of each other, see part 2, "Images," in Shipler 1986, 181–352.

41. For religious Jews, it is forbidden to make a fire (which includes using electricity) on Shabbat and holidays, days that are meant for rest and contemplation. However, most Israeli Jews are not religious and do not refrain from using electrical power or going on cookouts on these days.

42. Arabs (except for Druze and Bedouins) do not serve in the military because they have been exempted from army service by the defense ministry. Christian and Muslim Arabs who try to volunteer for service are almost always refused. Army service carries many benefits, and Palestinian residents of Israel feel the discrimination that springs from their nonservice.

43. Israeli employers use army discharge papers as part of the job application process; they serve as a character reference of sorts for prospective employees. This prevents many Arabs from obtaining lucrative positions; others are refused for security reasons.

44. *Hamūlōt* represents a linguistic appropriation from Arabic to Hebrew: Arabic *hamula* (clan), plural *hamayil,* to the Hebrew plural form *hamūlōt*. It could be translated as "clannishness," an accusation often leveled at Jews in Europe.

45. Consider, for example, the common argument that Arabs have twenty-two countries and Jews only one. Why should Jews be required to give away part of their country? Let the Palestinians move to one of the other Arab countries. After all, Jews from Arab countries moved to Israel to fulfill their aspirations for a state. This line of argument denies Palestinians recognition as a separate and autonomous group, apart from that of Arabs, and ignores the real social, cultural, and political distinctions to be found in the various Arab states. It also ignores the failure within Israel of the Jewish melting-pot ideology.

46. See Swirski 1989, 121.

47. See, for example, Joan Peters, *From Time Immemorial: The Origins of the Arab-Jewish Conflict over Palestine* (1984), in which she purports to present scholarly evidence of massive Arab in-migration to Palestine during the period 1922–44. Norman Finkelstein, in his (1988) review of her work, found extensive irregularities that largely discredited her conclusions.

48. Amalek is the enemy tribe that the Jewish people must fight eternally and destroy: "First of the peoples was Amalek, but his end is to perish forever" (Num. 24:20). Amalek as an archetype stands for all who would destroy the Jewish people.

49. Yehuda Elkana, "A Plea for Forgetting," *Ha'aretz,* 2 March 1988, 13.

50. Shohat (1989) critically analyzes these dichotomies in her study of Israeli film as representation.

51. In fact, many Mizraḥim would have been content to remain in their countries of origin. The tensions that developed between the new state of Israel and other Arab countries, however, foreclosed that possibility. The common assertion that Mizraḥi Jews had to flee for their lives because of Arab hatred of Jews is myth. In fact, in Iraq it was Israeli agents who planted bombs in Jewish synagogues to provoke fear in the Jewish community and promote emigration (see the discussion of this in Shohat 1988).

52. Ammiel Alcalay, "Reorienting: Sephardim in the Middle East," paper presented at the conference "The Easterners and Peace: Research, Action, and Politics," Hebrew University, Jerusalem, 26 January 1988.

53. Consider depictions, since Israel's Lebanon campaign, of Israeli soldiers in theater and song as "shooting and crying," soldiers who follow orders while in uniform only to join Peace Now war protest marches while on leave. Si Hyman's protest song "Shooting and Crying" crystallizes this dilemma for the current generation of Israeli soldiers policing the *intifada*.

Shooting and crying, burning and laughing
When did we ever learn to bury people alive?
Shooting and crying, burning and laughing
When did we ever forget that our children too have been killed?

The Arabs' view of this? "A hunter went killing sparrows one cold day. As he carried on the slaughter, his eyes were streaming. Said one bird to another: Look at the man crying. Said the other: Never mind his tears, watch his hands" (Howarth and Shukrallah 1944, 24).

Chapter 5

1. Regina Schwartz traces the futility of linking land and identity: land can never really be owned, so a people that vests its identity in the possession of land is always in danger of losing both (1997, 39–76).

2. Estimates of the number of destroyed villages range from 369 (Morris 1987) to 472 (Saleh and Mustafa 1987). The most comprehensive source on these villages to date is the work edited by Walid Khalidi, *All That Remains: The Palestinian Villages Occupied and Depopulated by Israel in 1948* (1992).

3. See Swedenburg 1995, 38–43, for a discussion of how the Palestinian presence was literally whitewashed from the walls of the Museum of Heroism.

4. These entries may be found in the Acre Municipal Archives, File 83/8, 1950/62.

5. George Leonof, "Putting Acre on the Tourist Map," *Jerusalem Post,* 15 October 1965.

6. Yaacov Ardon, "Acre," *Jerusalem Post,* 17 August 1979.

7. While the Declaration of Independence promises equality of rights to all Israeli citizens irrespective of race, religion, or sex, Israel lacks a constitution or bill of rights that would provide mechanisms for implementing that promise. The special status accorded the Jewish Agency and the World Zionist Organization in national legislation fosters discrimination against non-Jewish citizens. See Tekiner 1987 and Kretzmer 1990 on the inequalities of Israel citizenship.

8. The Biltmore Program was a resolution approved by the Zionist General Council that called for unlimited Jewish immigration into Palestine. It also demanded that immigration be placed under the control of the Jewish commonwealth.

9. Morris 1987 provides a detailed discussion of the events leading to the

"refugee problem." He prefers to present the causes as complex and insists that they were not due to any detailed plan or instructions by Israel's new leaders. Orders were issued, however, that hostile villages could be "removed," and the actions of Yosef Weitz's Transfer Committee were not curtailed until considerable opposition appeared within the government. Ben-Gurion was said to have ordered the expulsion of the Arab population of Lydda and Ramla. There seems little doubt that unofficially Israel's leaders approved of expulsion because it solved their "Arab problem."

10. Moledet sent three members to the Thirteenth Knesset and held two seats in the Fourteenth (1996–99). They did not participate in elections for the Fifteenth Knesset.

11. The program was discontinued in 1959 because it was widely believed that most of the winners of the awards were Arab women (Portugese 1998, 93).

12. Palestinian nationalists consciously pursue pro-natalist policies for the same purposes. They are also fighting a war on the baby front. The best contribution that a woman can make to the cause is to bear sons for the movement.

13. The name refers to the practice of immediately setting up a fence and guard tower to protect a new settlement from nighttime attacks.

14. Amnon Dankner, "I Have No Sister," *Ha'Aretz*, 18 February 1983.

15. Program for the Elections, 1988, Tehiya (in English).

16. Arab villages in the north were also excluded from the special development areas.

17. Yossi Lebowitz, "Yehoshua Katz: Israel Is Likely to Lose the Jewish Population of Acre," *Kol Ha'Tsafon*, 5 August 1988.

18. Judy Maltz, "Koor Bases Working Plan on Slow Economy," *Jerusalem Post*, 9 November 1988.

19. Moshe Tov El and Yossi Lebowitz, "Increase of 30% in Unemployment Rate in Western Galilee," *Kol Ha'Tsafon*, 11 November 1988.

20. Yossi Lebowitz and Moshe Tov El, "1023 Seeking Work Registered in November in Acre," *Kol Ha'Tsafon*, 9 December 1988.

21. Yossi Lebowitz, "Acre Laid Off and Striking," *Kol Ha'Tsafon*, 6 January 1988.

22. Moshe Tov El, "Problems of Acre in Demonstration in Jerusalem," *Kol Ha'Tsafon*, 27 January 1989.

23. Rahel Nehama Abdi, "The PLO Is Financing Arab Organizations in Acre," *Tsafon 1*, 2 September 1988.

24. Arieh Kizel, Sharga Eshel, and Yoram Hamizraḥi, "Acre's Arabs Threaten a General Strike Today," *Yedi'ot Aharonot*, 8 September 1988; David Rudge, "Acre's Old Quarter Market Paralysed by Arab Strike," *Jerusalem Post*, 9 September 1988.

25. Zoheir Andrus, "Why Are They Making This a Story? Overall, a Quarrel between Seller and Buyers," *Tsafon 1*, 9 September 1988; Moti Ophir, "Pure Hooliganism That Was Given a National Meaning by Interested Parties," *Hēd Ha'Tsafon*, 9 September 1988.

26. David Rudge, "Acre Jews Find Feces and Eggs Smeared on Shop Windows," *Jerusalem Post*, 16 September 1988; Yossi Lebowitz, "Other Jewish Shops Destroyed in the Old City," *Kol Ha'Tsafon*, 16 September 1988.

27. Rahel Nehama Abdi, "The Kahanists' Tour Ended at the Police Station," *Tsafon 1,* 23 September 1988; Yossi Lebowitz, "Kach Members Visited to Demonstrate in the Old City, Interfering Police Unit Stopped Them," *Kol Ha'Tsafon,* 23 September 1988.

28. *Yedi'ot 'Akko* is published weekly by a local firm. It is comprised of one or more large (13 × 19 in.) sheets of white paper, printed on both sides. It usually consists of announcements by the municipality regarding payment of taxes, school registration, information for residents, announcements about movies and cultural events, advertisements by local shops, and personal ads placed by residents to send birthday greetings and congratulations on weddings and special occasions and to commemorate deaths. During the local election campaign, it became a forum for the Labor and Likud Parties as they battled for votes.

29. Rahel Nehama Abdi, "De Castro: 'City of Coexistence,' " *Tsafon 1,* 9 December 1988; Toviel Leibowitz, "They Open Shops on Shabbat Next to Synagogues and Chase Away Jewish Girls," *Kol Ha'Tsafon,* 9 December 1988; Moti Ophir, " 'Positive Transfer' — Cynical Use of a Sickening Idea That Is Not Accepted Even by the Likud Leadership," *Hēd Ha'Tsafon,* 9 December 1988.

30. Moti Ophir, *Hēd Ha'Tsafon,* 9 December 1988 (see previous note).

31. Rahel Nehama Abdi, "Morris Ben Shoshan Is Running on an Independent List," *Tsafon 1,* 25 November 1988. The word *transfer* in Hebrew, טרנספר, is the English word spelled in Hebrew letters. It begins with the letter *tet.*

32. Rahel Nehama Abdi, "Ben Shoshan: 'They Stole My Idea,' " *Tsafon 1,* 9 December 1988.

33. Rahel Nehama Abdi, "Bar Lev: 'The Seat Is Not Important to Me,' " *Tsafon 1,* 9 December 1988. Similarly, at the national level Likud-led governments are often blamed for increased Israeli Jewish settlement in the West Bank and Gaza Strip, when in fact the settlements were first implemented and tolerated under Labor governments, which have been successful at hiding their collusion in such activities.

34. In Hebrew. "J'Accuse" (I accuse) is the title of Emile Zola's article defending Alfred Dreyfus, which accused the French general staff of a miscarriage of justice and shielding the true spy. It appeared on 13 January 1898 in *L'Aurore.* Anti-Semitic riots broke out in French and Algerian towns in reaction to the article.

35. Esther Hen Barzili, "3.2 Million Shekels for Developing Tourism in Acre," *Kol Ha'Tsafon,* 6 January 1989.

36. "Project Renewal in Acre Will Include All Parts of the City," *Hēd Ha'Tsafon,* 27 January 1989.

37. Moshe Tov El, "Families from France and South America — to Acre," *Kol Ha'Tsafon,* 10 February 1989.

38. Moti Ophir, "I'll Recognize Acre as an Exclusive National Model for Purposes of Incentives and Development," *Hēd Ha'Tsafon,* 24 February 1989.

39. Rahel Nehama Abdi, "New List Established in Acre," *Tsafon 1,* 20 January 1989.

40. *Yedi'ot 'Akko,* 30 December 1988.

41. Rahel Nehama Abdi, "Yosef Iluz: 'No Matter What Election Outcome, I Will Not Sit with Shaʿfī in a Coalition,'" *Tsafon 1,* 6 January 1989.

42. Eddie Gal, "The Likud Leads in Acre, Labor in the Old City," *Hadashot,* 1 March 1989.

43. Rahel Nehama Abdi, "The Quiet after the Storm," *Tsafon 1,* 3 March 1989.

44. My analysis of the election data from Acre is based on a printout of the results (per polling station) that was provided to the local Labor Party by the Elections Committee.

45. See Wasserfall n.d. regarding women's roles as gatekeepers of the collective.

46. I found evidence of only six mixed couples in the neighborhood. When Erik Cohen studied the phenomenon of intermarriage in Acre in 1966, he was able to identify only a dozen mixed marriages. He noted that Mizraḥi Jewish informants spoke of such marriages in highly emotional terms; they saw a Jewish girl having sexual relations with an Arab as shameful and dishonorable (1969, 50). Life for mixed couples in the villages and Jewish towns is always somewhat tense. The integrated environment of Wolfson is probably an easier environment for such a couple.

47. See Wasserfall 1990 on mistrust between Mizraḥi (Moroccan) husbands and wives. On the *moshav* (agricultural settlement) she studied, relations between the sexes were characterized by suspicion. Men feared that if their wives worked outside the home they would become involved in adulterous relationships with their male coworkers; women feared that their husbands were involved in adulterous relations with their female coworkers.

48. While I am by no means arguing that diplomats as a group are "feminine," I do find it intriguing that the most successful acts of diplomacy in the Israeli case (Begin and the peace with Egypt, Rabin and the Palestinian peace accords) were those carried out by men who were first and foremost seen as hardliners and soldiers.

49. David Rudge, "Israel's Arabs, the PLO, and the Polls," *Jerusalem Post,* 14 October 1988.

50. Moshe Tov El, "Acre: They Called Me Mahmoud De Castro," *Kol Ha'Tsafon,* 3 March 1989.

51. *Yediʿot ʿAkko,* 10 March 1989, 2.

52. Rahel Nehama Abdi, "Quick Coalition in Acre," *Tsafon 1,* 10 March 1989.

53. Moshe Tov El, "In a Stormy Council Meeting, Bar Lev 'Granted' a Kûfîya to Eli De Castro," *Kol Ha'Tsafon,* 14 April 1989.

54. *Yediʿot ʿAkko,* 14 July 1989, 3.

55. *Yediʿot ʿAkko,* 28 July 1989, 2.

56. Rahel Nehama Abdi, "The 'Forum' of Acre: To Rescue Acre from Catastrophe," *Tsafon 1,* 14 July 1989; "Establishment of Acreite Forum to Benefit Acre," *Hēd Ha'Tsafon,* 14 July 1989; Hen-Barzili Lebowitz, "Special Forum Established in Acre to Ease the Tension in the City Council," *Kol Ha'Tsafon,* 14 July 1989.

57. Rahel Nehama Abdi, "The Acre Municipal Council Calls on Residents Not to Leave," *Tsafon 1,* 21 July 1989.

58. "De Castro: 'The Jew Who Leaves Acre — Traitor to His People,' *Hed Ha'Tsafon,* 6 October 1989.

59. The Golani Brigade is one of the elite units of the IDF. It's a mark of status for a new recruit to make it into its ranks.

60. Sharga Eshel, "The Arab Youth Refused the Beggar — and Was Stabbed to Death," *Yedi'ot Aharonot,* 11 May 1989.

61. Yossi Bar Moha, "To Separate between Them When They're Still Small," *Tsafon 1,* 11 May 1990.

Chapter 6

1. Palestinians in the occupied territories during this period were held under a twenty-four-hour curfew that lasted a month and a half. They had no sirens to warn them of impending missile attacks and no gas masks (Sharoni 1995, 82–83).

2. Here is one case in which use of the term *Israeli* serves to obscure important information. Did levels of violence increase only in Israeli Jewish homes? Or did Israeli Palestinian women and children also experience them?

3. Lapid 1996. "Granny glasses" is a popular nickname for Meretz supporters. Meretz is a bloc composed of members of the Zionist left, supporters of Peace Now, and other left-leaning factions.

4. Miberg 1996.

5. The gains for the religious parties, particularly Shas and the NRP, are striking. In the two previous elections to the Knesset, Shas had six seats in each, while the NRP won five in the Twelfth and six in the Thirteenth Knesset. In the elections for the Fourteenth Knesset, each party gained four additional seats.

6. In 1996, Rabbi Ya'akov Ariel, at the time Ashkenazi rabbi of Ramat Gan and a senior adviser to the NRP, called for legislation in the Knesset to prevent Arab members from voting on issues, such as peace agreements, that could decide the fate of Israel and to prohibit them from being named as government ministers. He explained his demands by saying that Israel is "the state of the Jewish people and not a state of all its citizens" Ilan 1996.

7. Esther Hecht, "A Sinking City," *Jerusalem Post,* 31 October 1997.

8. Ibid.

9. Lavy 1998, 177, table 2, "Ethnic Disparities in Educational Resources."

10. One parent explained to me that in the schools in Ibillin most of the teachers hold doctorates. They offer fourteen years of schooling so that students who want advanced technical or professional training can get it. It is said that the first Arab university in Israel will be built there.

11. The following account was constructed from interviews with one of the organizers of the association, Albert Levy, as well as several other Acre residents who joined the struggle.

12. While I was in Israel in the summer of 1998, people told me that the

government would like to get rid of the discounted tax rates. However, it faced opposition from people living in those communities and so nothing had yet been decided.

13. *Yedi'ot 'Akko,* 3 June 1998, 1.

14. Ibid.

15. *Kōl Ha'Tsafon,* 26 June 1998.

16. One informant told me that Arab members of the party numbered about seven hundred and that they had been recruited to join by a Bar Lev associate at his direction.

17. Said 1999.

Bibliography

Abu El-Haj, Nadia
 1998 Translating Truths: Nationalism, the Practice of Archaeology, and the Remaking of Past and Present in Contemporary Jerusalem. *American Ethnologist* 25 (2): 166–88.
Acre Municipality
 1978 *Acre, Thirty Years: Telephone Directory for Acre.* Acre: Acre Municipality.
Adler, Chaim
 1984 School Integration in the Context of the Development of Israel's Educational System. In *School Desegregation: Cross-Cultural Perspectives,* ed. Yehuda Amir and Shlomo Sharan, 21–45. Hillsdale, N.J.: Lawrence Erlbaum Associates.
Akenson, Donald H.
 1992 *God's Peoples: Covenant and Land in South Africa, Israel, and Ulster.* Ithaca: Cornell University Press.
Al-Haj, Majid
 1987 *Social Change and Family Processes: Arab Communities in Shefar-'Am.* Boulder: Westview.
Al-Haj, Majid, and Henry Rosenfeld
 1988 *Arab Local Government in Israel.* Tel Aviv: International Center for Peace in the Middle East.
Amir, Eli
 1987 *Scapegoat.* Trans. Dalia Bilu. London: Weidenfeld and Nicolson.
Amir, Y.
 1969 Contact Hypothesis in Ethnic Relations. *Psychological Bulletins* 71 (5): 319–42.
 1976 The Role of Intergroup Contact in Change of Prejudice and Ethnic Relations. In *Towards the Elimination of Racism,* ed. P. Katz, 245–308. New York: Pergamon.
Amir, Y., M. Rivner, A. Bizman, and R. Ben-Ari
 1981 Contact between Israelis and West-Bank Arabs and Its Effects: A Theoretical and Empirical Evaluation. *Megamot* 26 (2): 179–92.
Anderson, Benedict
 1991 *Imagined Communities: Reflections on the Origins and Spread of Nationalism.* Rev. ed. London: Verso.
Anzaldua, Gloria
 1987 *Borderlands La Frontera: The New Mestiza.* San Francisco: Aunt Lute.

1990   *Making Face, Making Soul Haciendo Caras: Creative and Critical Perspectives by Feminists of Color.* San Francisco: Aunt Lute.

Arian, Asher, Ilan Talmud, and Tamar Hermann
1988   *National Security and Public Opinion in Israel.* Jaffee Center for Strategic Studies. Boulder: Westview.

Avineri, Shlomo
1981   *The Making of Modern Zionism: The Intellectual Origins of the Jewish State.* New York: Basic Books.

Avishai, Bernard
1985   *The Tragedy of Zionism: Revolution and Democracy in the Land of Israel.* New York: Farrar, Straus, and Giroux.

Bairey, Ariela
1988–89a   School for Peace — Foci of Educational Activities with Special Emphasis on the Context of the Intifada. The Neve Shalom/Wahat Al-Salam School for Peace.
1988–89b   School for Peace — Aims and Planned Activities, 1988/89. The Neve Shalom/Wahat Al-Salam School for Peace.

Balandier, Georges
1986   An Anthropology of Violence and War. *International Social Science Journal* 110:499–511.

Barth, Fredrik
1969   Introduction to *Ethnic Groups and Boundaries,* ed. Fredrik Barth, 9–38. Boston: Little, Brown.

Bar-Yosef, R.
1959   The Moroccans: The Background of a Problem. *Molad* 17:247–51.

Ben-Ari, Eyal
1998   *Mastering Soldiers: Conflict, Emotions, and the Enemy in an Israeli Military Unit.* New York: Berghahn.

Ben-Gal, Talia, and Daniel Bar-Tal
1989   Training Teachers for Jewish-Arab Coexistence in Israel. Paper presented at the International Society of Political Psychology annual meeting, Tel Aviv.

Ben-Gurion, David
1954   *Netsah Israel.* Jerusalem: Shnaton Hamemshala.
1982   *Yoman Hamilhama, 1948–1949* [The war diary, 1948–1949]. Ed. Gershon Rivlin and Elhannan Orren. 3 vols. Tel Aviv: Israel Defense Ministry Press.

Benjamin, Jessica
1988   *The Bonds of Love: Psychoanalysis, Feminism, and the Problem of Domination.* New York: Pantheon.

Ben-Rafael, Eliezer
1982   *The Emergence of Ethnicity: Cultural Groups and Social Conflict in Israel.* Westport, Conn.: Greenwood.

Ben-Rafael, Eliezer, and Stephen Sharot
1987   Ethnic Pluralism and Religious Congregations: A Comparison of Neighborhoods in Israel. *Ethnic Groups* 7 (1): 65–83.

1991   *Ethnicity, Religion, and Class in Israeli Society.* Cambridge: Cambridge University Press.

Ben-Sasson, H. H., ed.
1976   *A History of the Jewish People.* Cambridge: Harvard University Press.

Bentley, G. Carter
1987   Ethnicity and Practice. *Comparative Studies in Society and History* 29 (1): 24–55.

Bentwich, Joseph S.
1965   *Education in Israel.* Philadelphia: Jewish Publication Society of America.

Ben Yitzhak, Yehuda
1981   *Social Services in the Arab Sector.* Jerusalem: Misrad Ha'Avodah V'Ha'Revaha, Ha'Agaf L'Mekhar, Tikhnun V'Hakhshara, Maklehet Mekhkar.

Bernblum, A.
n.d   *Acre at the Time of Transition.* Acre: Acre Municipality.

Bernstein, Deborah
1980   Immigrants and Society: A Critical View of the Dominant School of Israeli Sociology. *British Journal of Sociology* 31 (2): 246–64.
1981   Immigrant Transit Camps: The Formation of Dependent Relations in Israeli Society. *Ethnic and Racial Studies* 4 (1): 26–43.

Bernstein, Richard J.
1992   Reconciliation and Rupture: The Challenge and Threat of Otherness. In *Discourse and Practice,* ed. Frank Reynolds and David Tracy, 295–314. Albany: State University of New York Press.

Bhabha, Homi, ed.
1990   *Nation and Narration.* London: Routledge.

Blass, Nachum, and Benyamin Amir
1984   Integration in Education: The Development of a Policy. In *School Desegregation: Cross-Cultural Perspectives,* ed. Yehuda Amir and Shlomo Sharan, 63–98. Hillsdale, N.J.: Lawrence Erlbaum Associates.

Bonacich, Edna
1972   Theory of Ethnic Antagonism: The Split Labor Market. *American Sociological Review* 37 (5): 547–59.
1979   The Past, Present, and Future of Split Labor Market Theory. *Research in Race and Ethnic Relations* 1:17–64.

Bonné-Tamir, Batsheva
1980   A New Look at Jewish Genetics. *Mada* 24 (4–5): 181–86.

Boyarin, Jonathan
1992   *Storm from Paradise: The Politics of Jewish Memory.* Minneapolis: University of Minnesota Press.

Bracey, John, Jr., August Meier, and Elliott Rudwick
1970   *Black Nationalism in America.* Indianapolis: Bobbs-Merrill.

Brandt, Godfrey L.
1986   *The Realization of Anti-racist Teaching.* London: Falmer Press.

Calhoun, Craig
    1991   Indirect Relationships and Imagined Communities: Large-Scale Social Integration and the Transformation of Everyday Life. In *Social Theory for a Changing Society,* ed. Pierre Bourdieu and James S. Coleman, 95–121. Boulder: Westview.

Canfield, Robert
    1988   Afghanistan's Social Identities in Conflict. In *Le Fait Ethnique en Iran et en Afghanistan: Colloques internationaux,* ed. Jean-Pierre Digard, 185–99. Paris: Editions du CNRS.

Caplan, Gerald, with Ruth B. Caplan
    1980   *Arab and Jew in Jerusalem: Explorations in Community Mental Health.* Cambridge: Harvard University Press.

Carnoy, Martin
    1989   Education, State, and Culture in American Society. In *Critical Pedagogy, the State, and Cultural Struggle,* ed. Henry A. Giroux and Peter McLaren, 3–23. Albany: State University of New York Press.

Chafets, Ze'ev
    1986   *Heroes and Hustlers, Hard Hats and Holy Men: Inside the New Israel.* New York: William Morrow.

Chetrit, Sami
    1992   New State, Old Land: The East and the Easterners in the Jewish State of Theodor Herzl. Paper presented at the American Anthropological Association annual meeting, San Francisco, Calif.

Cohen, Abner
    1969   *Custom and Politics in Urban Africa: Hausa Migrants in Yoruba Towns.* Berkeley: University of California Press.

Cohen, Erik
    1969   Mixed Marriage in an Israeli Town. *Jewish Journal of Sociology* 11 (1): 41–50.
    1971   Arab Boys and Tourist Girls in a Mixed Jewish-Arab Community. *International Journal of Comparative Sociology* 12 (4): 217–37.
    1973   *Integration vs. Separation in the Planning of a Mixed Jewish-Arab City in Israel.* Jerusalem: Levi Eshkol Institute for Economic, Social, and Political Research.

Cohen, Mitchell
    1992   *Zion and State: Nation, Class, and the Shaping of Modern Israel.* Morningside ed. New York: Columbia University Press.

Connerton, Paul
    1989   *How Societies Remember.* Cambridge: Cambridge University Press.

Connolly, William E.
    1991   *Identity/Difference: Democratic Negotiations of Political Paradox.* Ithaca: Cornell University Press.

Crapanzano, Vincent
    1985   *Waiting: The Whites of South Africa.* New York: Vintage.

Daniel, E. Valentine
    1996   *Charred Lullabies: Chapters in an Anthropography of Violence.* Princeton: Princeton University Press.

Davis, Uri
   1977   *Israel: Utopia Incorporated.* London: Zed.

Despres, Leo
   1967   *Cultural Pluralism and Nationalist Politics in British Guiana.* Chicago: Rand McNally.

Deutsch, Akiva
   1985   Social Contacts and Social Relationships between Jews and Arabs Living in a Mixed Neighborhood in an Israeli Town. *International Journal of Comparative Sociology* 26 (3–4): 220–25.
   1988   Social Contacts and Social Relationships between Jews and Arabs Living in a Mixed Neighborhood in an Israeli Town. In *Social and Cultural Integration in Israel,* ed. A. Deutsch and G. Tulea, 65–93. Ramat Gan: Sociological Institute for Community Studies, Bar Ilan University.

Deutsch, Akiva, and Mordecai Avitsour (with Dov Kelat)
   1982   The Impact of Daily Contacts between Arabs and Jews Living in a Mixed Neighbourhood in an Israeli Town on Their Attitudes and Social Relationships. Sociological Institute for Community Studies, Bar Ilan University. Research Report.

De Vos, George
   1975   *Ethnic Pluralism: Conflict and Accommodation.* In *Ethnic Identity,* ed. G. De Vos and L. Romanucci-Ross, 363–90. Palo Alto: Mayfield.

Diamond, James S.
   1986   *Homeland or Holy Land: The "Canaanite" Critique of Israel.* Bloomington: Indiana University Press.

Doleve-Gandelman, Tsili
   1987   The Symbolic Inscription of Zionist Ideology in the Space of Eretz Israel: Why the Native Israeli Is Called Tsabar. In *Judaism Viewed from Within and from Without: Anthropological Studies,* ed. Harvey E. Goldberg, 257–84. Albany: State University of New York Press.

Dominguez, Virginia
   1986   *White by Definition: Social Classification in Creole Louisiana.* New Brunswick, N.J.: Rutgers University Press.
   1989   *People as Subject, People as Object: Selfhood and Peoplehood in Contemporary Israel.* Madison: University of Wisconsin Press.
   1990   On the Politics of Invoking Culture. Paper Presented at the American Anthropological Association annual meeting, New Orleans, La.

Dworkin, Andrea
   1990   Israel: Whose Country Is It Anyway? *Ms.* 1 (2): 69–79.

Dwyer, Kevin
   1982   *Moroccan Dialogues: Anthropology in Question.* Baltimore: Johns Hopkins University Press.

Eady, Elias
   1988   The Contribution of Ongoing Action Research to the School for Peace, 1985–88. Neve Shalom/Wahat Al-Salam School for Peace.

Efrat, Elisha
    1984   *Urbanization in Israel.* London: Croom Helm.
Eisenstadt, S. N.
    1985   *The Transformation of Israeli Society.* Boulder: Westview.
Elam, Y.
    1978   Use of Force among Moroccan and Georgian Immigrants (in He-
            brew). *Megamot* 24:169–85. In Hebrew.
El-Asmar, Fouzi
    1978   *To Be an Arab in Israel.* 2d ed. Beirut: Institute for Palestine Studies.
Elazar, Daniel J.
    1989   *The Other Jews: The Sephardim Today.* New York: Basic Books.
Elon, Amos
    1971   *The Israelis: Founders and Sons.* New York: Penguin.
Emmett, Ayala
    1996   *Our Sisters' Promised Land: Women, Politics, and Israeli-Palestinian
            Coexistence.* Ann Arbor: University of Michigan Press.
Enloe, Cynthia
    1989   *Bananas, Beaches, and Bases: Making Feminist Sense of Interna-
            tional Politics.* Berkeley: University of California Press.
Epstein, A. L.
    1978   *Ethos and Identity: Three Studies in Ethnicity.* London: Tavistock.
'Evron, Bo'az
    1981   The Holocaust: Learning the Wrong Lessons. *Journal of Palestine
            Studies* 10 (3): 16–26.
Ezrahi, Sidra Dekoven
    1985–86 Revisioning the Past: The Changing Legacy of the Holocaust in
            Hebrew Literature. *Salmagundi* 68–69: 245–70.
Farah, Saleem R., and M. N. Khoury
    1936   *The History of Acre.* Acre: National Press.
Farsoun, Samih K., with Christina E. Zacharia
    1997   *Palestine and the Palestinians.* Boulder: Westview.
Feldman, Alan
    1991   *Formations of Violence: The Narrative of the Body and Political Ter-
            ror in Northern Ireland.* Chicago: University of Chicago Press.
Ferguson, Kathy E.
    1993   *The Man Question: Visions of Subjectivity in Feminist Theory.* Berke-
            ley: University of California Press.
Finkelstein, Norman G.
    1988   Disinformation and the Palestine Question: The Not-So-Strange
            Case of Joan Peters's *From Time Immemorial.* In *Blaming the Vic-
            tims: Spurious Scholarship and the Palestinian Question,* ed. Edward
            Said and Christopher Hitchens, 33–69. London: Verso.
Flapan, Simha
    1987   *The Birth of Israel: Myths and Realities.* New York: Pantheon.
Foucault, Michel
    1980   *Power/Knowledge: Selected Writings and Other Interviews, 1972–*

1977. Ed. Colin Gordon, trans. Colin Gordon, Leo Marshal, John Mepham, and Kate Soper. New York: Pantheon.

Franks, Lynne R.
  1987   *Israel and the Occupied Territories: A Study of the Educational Systems of Israel and the Occupied Territories and a Guide to the Academic Placement of Students in Educational Institutions of the United States.* Washington, D.C.: American Association of Collegiate Registrars and Admissions Officers.

Frederickson, George
  1971   *The Black Image in the White Mind.* New York: Harper.
  1981   *White Supremacy: A Comparative Study in American and South African History.* New York: Oxford University Press.

Freire, Paulo
  1970   *Pedagogy of the Oppressed.* Trans. Myra Bergman Ramos. New York: Seabury.

Frey, Harry, and Mohammed Assadi
  1986   *The Van Leer Project, Acre: The Kiryat Wolfson Neighborhood.* Acre: Project Van Leer.

Friedl, Erika
  1997   *Children of Deh Koh: Young Life in an Iranian Village.* Syracuse: Syracuse University Press.

Geertz, Clifford
  1963   The Integrative Revolution: Primordial Sentiments and Civil Politics in the New States. In *Old Societies and New States,* ed. Clifford Geertz, 105–57. New York: Free Press.
  1983   *Local Knowledge: Further Essays in Interpretive Anthropology.* New York: Basic Books.

Gilroy, Paul
  1987   *"There Ain't No Black in the Union Jack": The Cultural Politics of Race and Nation.* London: Hutchinson.

Giroux, Henry
  1989   *Schooling for Democracy: Critical Pedagogy in the Modern Age.* New York: Routledge.
  1992   *Border Crossings: Cultural Workers and the Politics of Education.* New York: Routledge.

Goering, J. M.
  1978   Neighborhood Tipping and Racial Transition: A Review of Social Science Evidence. *Journal of the American Institute of Planners* 44:68–78.

Gordon, David
  1984   *The Myths of School Self-Renewal.* New York: Teachers College Press.

Grodzins, M.
  1957   Metropolitan Segregation. *Scientific American* 197:33–41.

Grossman, David
  1993   *Sleeping on a Wire: Conversations with Palestinians in Israel.* Trans. Haim Watzman. New York: Farrar, Straus, and Giroux.

Haberer, Rose
  1985   Status, Power, and Influence of Women in an Arab Village in
         Israel. Ph.D. diss., Department of Anthropology, Purdue Uni-
         versity.
Habiby, Emile
  1985   *The Secret Life of Saeed, the Pessoptimist.* Trans. Salma Khadra
         Jayyusi and Trevor LeGassick. London: Zed.
Hadawi, Sami
  1989   *Bitter Harvest: A Modern History of Palestine.* New York: Olive
         Branch.
Haidar, Aziz
  1991   *Social Welfare Services for Israel's Arab Population.* Boulder: West-
         view.
Haifa and Galilee Research Institute
  1989   *Acre: Policy Guidelines for Renewal and Development.* Haifa: Uni-
         versity of Haifa.
Haley, Alex, and Malcolm X
  1965   *The Autobiography of Malcolm X.* New York: Ballantine.
Hall-Cathala, David
  1990   *The Peace Movement in Israel, 1967–1987.* New York: St. Mar-
         tin's.
Halper, Jeff, Moshe Shokeid, and Alex Weingrod
  1984   Communities, Schools, and Integration. In *School Desegregation:
         Cross-Cultural Perspectives,* ed. Yehuda Amir and Shlomo Sharan,
         47–62. Hillsdale, N.J.: Lawrence Erlbaum Associates.
Hamburg, Jill E.
  1992   Who Speaks for the Sephardim? *Nation* 254 (25): 891–92.
Hechter, Michael
  1975   *Internal Colonialism: The Celtic Fringe in British National Develop-
         ment.* Berkeley: University of California Press.
Hertz-Lazarowitz, Rachel, Taha Ashkar, and Hani Elfar
  1989   Youth Meetings between Jews and Arabs: Beit Hagefen Project.
         Paper presented at the International Society of Political Psychology
         annual meeting, Tel Aviv.
Hobsbawm, E. J.
  1990   *Nations and Nationalism since 1780: Programme, Myth, Reality.* Cam-
         bridge: Cambridge University Press.
Hofman, John E., and N. Rouhana
  1976   Young Arabs in Israel: Some Aspects of a Conflicted Social Identity.
         Journal of Social Psychology 99:75–86.
hooks, bell
  1990   *Yearning: Race, Gender, and Cultural Politics.* Boston: South End.
Horowitz, Dan, and Moshe Lissak
  1978   *Origins of the Israeli Policy: Palestine under the Mandate.* Chicago:
         University of Chicago Press.
Howarth, Herbert, and Ibrahim Shukrallah
  1944   *Images from the Arab World.* London: Pilot Press.

Ilan, Shahar
    1996   The Racist Proposal of Rabbi Ya'akov Ariel to Prohibit Arab MKs from Participating on Decisive Issues. *Ha'Aretz,* 10 May, trans. in *From the Hebrew Press* 8 (7): 12–13.

Isaacs, Harold P.
    1975   *Idols of the Tribe: Group Identity and Political Change.* New York: Harper and Row.

Israel, Central Bureau of Statistics
    1988   *Statistical Abstract of Israel.* Jerusalem: Central Bureau of Statistics.
    1990   *Statistical Abstract of Israel.* Jerusalem: Central Bureau of Statistics.
    1998   *Statistical Abstract of Israel.* Jerusalem: Central Bureau of Statistics.

Israel, Ministry of Education and Culture
    1975   *Report of the Committee on Arab Education for the Eighties.* Jerusalem: Ministry of Education and Culture.

Israel, Ministry of Education and Culture, Planning Department
    1981   *The Socioeconomic Situation of the Elementary School System in Local Authorities and Regional Councils.* Jerusalem: Ministry of Education and Culture.

Jiryis, Sabri
    1976   *The Arabs in Israel.* Trans. Inea Bushnaq. New York: Monthly Review Press.

Kamen, Charles
    1987   After the Catastrophe I: The Arabs in Israel, 1948–51. *Middle Eastern Studies* 23 (4): 453–95.
    1988   After the Catastrophe II: The Arabs in Israel, 1948–51. *Middle Eastern Studies* 24 (1): 68–109.

Kaniuk, Yoram
    1988   The Vultures (a Story). Trans. Dalya Bilu and Barbara Harshav. *Tel Aviv Review* 1:27–49.

Kapferer, Bruce
    1988   *Legends of People, Myths of State: Violence, Intolerance, and Political Culture in Sri Lanka and Australia.* Washington, D.C.: Smithsonian Institution Press.

Katznelson, Kalman
    1964   *The Ashkenazi Revolution.* Tel Aviv: Hanach.

Kesten, Alex
    1963   *Acre, the Old City: Survey and Planning.* Jerusalem: Government of Israel.

Khalidi, Rashid
    1997   *Palestinian Identity: The Construction of Modern National Consciousness.* New York: Columbia University Press.

Khalidi, Walid, ed.
    1992   *All That Remains: The Palestinian Villages Occupied and Depopulated by Israel in 1948.* Washington, D.C.: Institute for Palestine Studies.

Kimmerling, Baruch
    1985   Between the Primordial and the Civil Definitions of the Collective

Identity: Eretz Israel or the State of Israel? In *Comparative Social Dynamics,* ed. E. Cohen, M. Lissak, and U. Almagor, 262–83. Boulder: Westview.

Klein, Zev, and Yohanan Eshel
1980   *Integrating Jerusalem Schools.* New York: Academic.

Kleinberger, Aharon F.
1969   *Society, Schools, and Progress in Israel.* Oxford: Pergamon.

Kotler, Ya'ir
1986   *Heil Kahane.* New York: Adama Books.

Kretzmer, David
1990   *The Legal Status of the Arabs in Israel.* Boulder: Westview.

Laclau, Ernesto, and Chantal Mouffe
1985   *Hegemony and Socialist Strategy: Towards a Radical Democratic Politics.* Trans. Winston Moore and Paul Cammack. London: Verso.

Lapid, Yosef
1996   A Social Upset. *Ma'ariv,* 2 June, trans. in *From the Hebrew Press* 8 (7): 13–14.

Laqueur, Walter, and Barry Rubin, eds.
1984   *The Israel-Arab Reader: A Documentary History of the Middle East Conflict.* 4th ed. New York: Penguin.

Lavie, Smadar
1990   *The Poetics of Military Occupation: Mzeina Allegories of Bedouin Identity under Israeli and Egyptian Rule.* Berkeley: University of California Press.
1991   Arrival of the New Cultured Tenants: Soviet Immigrants to Israel and the Displacing of the Sephardi Jews. *Times Literary Supplement,* 14 June, 11.
1992   Blow-Ups in the Borderzones: Third World Israeli Authors' Gropings for Home. *New Formations* 18 (winter): 84–106.

Lavy, Victor
1998   Disparities between Arabs and Jews in School Resources and Student Achievement in Israel. *Economic Development and Cultural Change* 47 (1): 175–92.

Lehman-Wilzig, Sam
1990   *Stiff-Necked People, Bottle-Necked System: The Evolution and Roots of Israeli Public Protest, 1949–1986.* Bloomington: Indiana University Press.

Lehn, Walter, and Uri Davis
1988   *The Jewish National Fund.* London: Kegan Paul.

Lemish, Peter
1993   Politics of Difference: Educators as Enlightened Oppressors. Paper presented at the American Educational Research Association annual meeting, Atlanta, Ga.

Lewis, Arnold
1979   *Power, Poverty, and Education.* Ramat Gan: Turtledove.
1985   Phantom Ethnicity: "Oriental Jews" in Israeli Society. In *Studies in*

Israeli Ethnicity: After the Ingathering, ed. Alex Weingrod, 133–57. New York: Gordon and Breach Science Publishers.

Liebman, Charles, and Eliezer Don-Yehiya
  1983 *Civil Religion in Israel: Traditional Judaism and Political Culture in the Jewish State.* Berkeley: University of California Press.

Liebman, Charles S., and Steven M. Cohen
  1990 *Two Worlds of Judaism: The Israeli and American Experiences.* New Haven: Yale University Press.

Linn, Ruth
  1996 *Conscience at War: The Israeli Soldier as a Moral Critic.* Albany: State University of New York Press.

Lustick, Ian
  1980 *Arabs in the Jewish State: Israel's Control of a National Minority.* Austin: University of Texas Press.

Makhouly, N., and C. N. Johns
  1946 *Guide to Acre.* 2d ed., rev. Jerusalem: Government of Palestine, Department of Antiquities.

Mar'i, Sami Khalil
  1978 *Arab Education in Israel.* Syracuse: Syracuse University Press.

Marx, Emanuel
  1976 *The Social Context of Violent Behavior: A Social Anthropological Study in an Israeli Immigrant Town.* New York: Routledge.

Masalha, Nur
  1992 *Expulsion of the Palestinians: The Concept of "Transfer" in Zionist Political Thought, 1882–1948.* Washington, D.C.: Institute for Palestine Studies.

Maynard, Mary, and June Purvis, eds.
  1996 *New Frontiers in Women's Studies: Knowledge, Identity, and Nationalism.* London: Taylor and Francis.

Me'ari, Mahmood
  1975 A Comparative Survey of School Curricula in the Arab Sector in Israel. Supplementary report to the final report of the Committee for the Planning of Arab Education for the 1980s. Jerusalem.

Miberg, Ron
  1996 The Election Reveals the Deep Division of the Israeli Jewish Nation. *Ma'ariv,* 31 May, trans. in *From the Hebrew Press* 8 (7): 14–15.

Miller, N., and M. Brewer, eds.
  1984 *Groups in Contact: The Psychology of Desegregation.* New York: Academic.

Miller, Ylana
  1985 *Government and Society in Rural Palestine, 1920–1948.* Austin: University of Texas Press.

Minkowich, Avram, Dan Davis, Joseph Bashi, and Research Team
  1982 *Success and Failure in Israeli Elementary Education: An Evaluation Study with Special Emphasis on Disadvantaged Pupils.* New Brunswick: Transaction.

Morris, Benny
    1986   Yosef Weitz and the Transfer Committees, 1948–49. *Middle Eastern Studies* 22 (4): 522–61.
    1987   *The Birth of the Palestinian Refugee Problem, 1947–1949.* Cambridge: Cambridge University Press.

Moughrabi, Fouad, and Elia Zureik
    1988   *Different Scales of Justice: Arabs and Jews in Israel, Results of a National Survey.* Occasional Papers, no. 11. Kingston, Ontario: Near East Cultural and Educational Foundation of Canada.

Muslih, Muhammad Y.
    1988   *The Origins of Palestinian Nationalism.* New York: Columbia University Press.

Nazzal, Nafez
    1978   *The Palestinian Exodus from Galilee, 1948.* Beirut: Institute for Palestine Studies.

Olzak, Susan, and Joanne Nagel
    1986   *Competitive Ethnic Relations.* New York: Academic.

Omi, Michael, and Howard Winant
    1986   *Racial Formation in the United States from the 1960s to the 1980s.* New York: Routledge and Kegan Paul.

Palgi, P.
    1966   Cultural Components of Immigrants' Adjustment. In *Migration, Mental Health, and Community Services,* ed. H. P. David, 71–82. Geneva: American Joint Distribution Committee.

Palumbo, Michael
    1987   *The Palestinian Catastrophe: The 1948 Expulsion of a People from Their Homeland.* London: Quartet.

Pateman, Carole
    1988   *The Sexual Contract.* Stanford: Stanford University Press.

Peres, Yohanan
    1970   *Patterns of Urbanization: A Comparative Study of Three Development Towns.* Jerusalem: Chamul Press.
    1990   Tolerance: Two Years Later. *Israeli Democracy* (winter): 16–18.

Peres, Yohanan, and Nira Yuval-Davis
    1969   Some Observations on the National Identity of the Israeli Arab. *Human Relations* 22 (3): 219–33.

Peretz, Don
    1958   *Israel and the Palestine Arabs.* Washington, D.C.: Middle East Institute.

Peri, Yoram
    1997   The Rabin Myth and the Press: Reconstruction of the Israeli Collective Identity. *European Journal of Communication* 12 (4): 435–58.

Peters, Joan
    1984   *From Time Immemorial: The Origins of the Arab-Jewish Conflict over Palestine.* New York: Harper and Row.

Phillips, Anne
  1991   *Engendering Democracy.* University Park: Pennsylvania State University Press.
Pinkney, Alphonso
  1976   *Red, Black, and Green: Black Nationalism in the United States.* New York: Cambridge University Press.
Plotkin, Sidney
  1991   Community and Alienation: Enclave Consciousness and Urban Movements. In *Breaking Chains: Social Movements and Collective Action,* ed. Michael Peter Smith, 5–25. New Brunswick: Transaction.
Portugese, Jacqueline
  1998   *Fertility Policy in Israel: The Politics of Religion, Gender, and Nation.* Westport, Conn.: Praeger.
Pryor, F. L.
  1971   An Empirical Note on the Tipping Point. *Land Economics* 47:413–17.
Quandt, William, Fuad Jabber, and Ann Mosley Lesch
  1973   *The Politics of Palestinian Nationalism.* Berkeley: University of California Press.
Rabinovich, Abraham
  n.d   *Palphot's Pictorial Guide and Souvenir: Acre, St. Jean D'Acre.* Tel Aviv: Palphot.
Rabinowitz, Dan
  1990   Relations between Arabs and Jews in the Mixed Town of Natzerat Illit, Northern Israel. Ph.D. diss., Department of Social Anthropology, Cambridge University.
  1997   *Overlooking Nazareth: The Ethnography of Exclusion in Galilee.* Cambridge: Cambridge University Press.
Rechman, Oren
  1990   *Final Summary Evaluation Report of the Jewish-Arab Community and Education Project, Acre: Education and Community Work Programmes, 1986–1989.* Acre: Project Van Leer.
Reeves, Frank
  1983   *British Racial Discourse.* Cambridge: Cambridge University Press.
Resh, Nura
  1998   Track Placement: How the "Sorting Machine" Works in Israel. *American Journal of Education* 106 (3): 416–38.
Rhodes, Harry, and Elektra Spathopoulos
  1994   *Can We Change Our Children's City? Summative Evaluation Report.* Acre: Acre Association for Community Development.
Romann, Michael, and Alex Weingrod
  1991   *Living Together Separately: Arabs and Jews in Contemporary Jerusalem.* Princeton: Princeton University Press.
Rose, Dan
  1989   *Patterns of American Culture: Ethnography and Estrangement.* Philadelphia: University of Pennsylvania Press.

Rosen, Lawrence
    1984   *Bargaining for Reality: The Construction of Social Relations in a Muslim Community.* Chicago: University of Chicago Press.

Rouhana, Nadim
    1988   The Civic and National Subidentities of the Arabs in Israel: A Psychopolitical Approach. In *Arab-Jewish Relations in Israel,* ed. J. Hofman. Bristol, Ind.: Wyndham Hall.
    1991   Palestinization among the Arabs in Israel: The Accentuated Identity. Paper presented at the conference "Arab Minority in Israel: Dilemmas of Political Orientation and Social Change," Dayan Center, Tel Aviv University, Tel Aviv.

Rubin, Morton
    1974   *The Walls of Acre: Intergroup Relations and Urban Development in Israel.* New York: Holt, Rinehart and Winston.

Said, Edward
    1979   *The Question of Palestine.* New York: Vintage.
    1985   *After the Last Sky: Palestinian Lives.* Jean Mohr, photographer. New York: Pantheon.
    1990   Zionism from the Standpoint of Its Victims. In *Anatomy of Racism,* ed. David Theo Goldberg, 210–46. Minneapolis: University of Minnesota Press.
    1999   Truth and Reconciliation. *Al-Ahram Weekly* 412 (January): 14–20, <http://www.ahram.org.eg/weekly>.

Saleh, Abdul Jawad, and Walid Mustafa
    1987   *Palestine: The Collective Destruction of Palestinian Villages and Zionist Colonization, 1882–1982.* Amman: Jerusalem Center for Development Studies.

Saxton, Alexander
    1990   *The Rise and Fall of the White Republic.* New York: Verso.

Sayigh, Rosemary
    1979   *Palestinians: From Peasants to Revolutionaries.* London: Zed.
    1994   *Too Many Enemies: The Palestinian Experience in Lebanon.* London: Zed.

Schölch, Alexander
    1981   The Economic Development of Palestine, 1856–1882. *Journal of Palestine Studies* 10 (3): 35–58.

Schwartz, Regina M.
    1997   *The Curse of Cain: The Violent Legacy of Monotheism.* Chicago: University of Chicago Press.

Scott, James
    1985   *Weapons of the Weak: Everyday Forms of Peasant Resistance.* New Haven: Yale University Press.
    1990   *Domination and the Arts of Resistance: Hidden Transcripts.* New Haven: Yale University Press.

See, Katherine O'Sullivan
    1986   *First World Nationalisms: Class and Ethnic Politics in Northern Ireland and Quebec.* Chicago: University of Chicago Press.

Segev, Tom
1986 *1949: The First Israelis.* New York: Free Press.
Shama, Avraham, and Mark Iris
1977 *Immigration without Integration: Third World Jews in Israel.* Cambridge, Mass.: Schenkman.
Shamgar-Handelman, Leah, and Don Handelman
1986 Holiday Celebrations in Israeli Kindergartens: Relationships between Representatives of Collectivity and Family in the Nation-State. In *The Frailty of Authority,* ed. M. J. Aronoff, 71–103. New Brunswick, N.J.: Transaction.
Shammas, Anton
1986 *Arabesques.* Translated by Vivian Eden. New York: Harper and Row.
Shapira, Anita
1992 *Land and Power: The Zionist Resort to Force, 1881–1948.* New York: Oxford University Press.
Sharkansky, Ira
1991 *Ancient and Modern Israel: An Exploration of Political Parallels.* Albany: State University of New York Press.
Sharoni, Simona
1995 *Gender and the Israeli-Palestinian Conflict: The Politics of Women's Resistance.* Syracuse: Syracuse University Press.
Shehadeh, Raja
1982 *The Third Way: A Journal of Life in the West Bank.* London: Quartet.
Shindler, Colin
1991 *Ploughshares into Swords? Israelis and Jews in the Shadow of the Intifada.* London: I. B. Tauris.
Shipler, David K.
1986 *Arabs and Jews: Wounded Spirits in a Promised Land.* New York: Penguin.
Shohat, Ella
1988 Sephardim in Israel: Zionism from the Standpoint of Its Jewish Victims. *Social Text* 19–20 (fall): 1–35.
1989 *Israeli Cinema: East/West and the Politics of Representation.* Austin: University of Texas Press.
1992 Staging the Quincentenary: Beyond Sephardi Exotica. Paper presented at the American Anthropological Association annual meeting, San Francisco.
Shokeid, Moshe
1982 The Regulation of Aggression in Daily Life: Aggressive Relationships among Moroccan Immigrants in Israel. *Ethnology* 21 (3): 271–81.
Shtal, Abraham, Tamar Agmon, and Matathia Mar-Haim
1976 Teachers' Attitudes towards the Culturally Disadvantaged. *Eyonim Bahinukh* 11:45–58.
Shumsky, Abraham
1955 *The Clash of Cultures in Israel: A Problem for Education.* New York: Teachers College Press.

Sider, Gerald
   1987   When Parrots Learn to Talk and Why They Can't: Domination,
          Deception, and Self-Deception in Indian-White Relations. *Compara-
          tive Studies in Society and History* 29 (1): 3–23.
Silk, Dennis
   1988   On the Situation. *Tel Aviv Review* 1:155–65.
Smith, Anthony D.
   1971   *Theories of Nationalism.* London: Duckworth.
   1981   *The Ethnic Revival.* Cambridge: Cambridge University Press.
Smooha, Sammy
   1978   *Israel: Pluralism and Conflict.* Berkeley: University of California
          Press.
   1989   *Arabs and Jews in Israel.* Vol. 1, *Conflicting and Shared Attitudes in a
          Divided Society.* Boulder: Westview.
   1992   *Arabs and Jews in Israel.* Vol. 2, *Change and Continuity in Mutual
          Intolerance.* Boulder: Westview.
Stein, Colman Brez, Jr.
   1985   Israeli Policy toward Sephardi Schooling. *Comparative Education
          Review* 29 (2): 204–15.
Stein, Kenneth
   1984   *The Land Question in Palestine, 1917–1939.* Chapel Hill: University
          of North Carolina Press.
Stuckey, Sterling
   1970   *The Ideological Origins of Black Nationalism.* Boston: Beacon.
Swedenburg, Ted
   1995   *Memories of Revolt: The 1936–1939 Rebellion and the Palestinian
          Past.* Minneapolis: University of Minnesota Press.
Swirski, Shlomo
   1989   *Israel the Oriental Majority.* London: Zed.
Swirski, Shlomo, and Menachem Shoushan
   1986   *The Development Towns of Israel: Towards a Brighter Tomorrow.*
          Haifa: Breirot.
Taguieff, Pierre-Andre
   1990   The New Cultural Racism in France. *Telos* (83): 109–22.
Taussig, Michael
   1987   *Shamanism, Colonialism, and the Wild Man: A Study in Terror and
          Healing.* Chicago: University of Chicago Press.
Tekiner, Roselle
   1987   On the Inequality of Israeli Citizens. *Without Prejudice: The EA-
          FORD International Review of Racial Discrimination* 1 (1): 48–57.
   1991   Race and the Issue of National Identity in Israel. *International Jour-
          nal of Middle East Studies* 23 (1): 39–55.
Tibawi, A.
   1956   *Arab Education in Mandatory Palestine.* London: Luzac.
Timerman, Jacobo
   1982   *The Longest War: Israel in Lebanon.* Trans. Miguel Acoca. New
          York: Knopf.

Trinh, T. Minh-Ha
    1989   *Woman, Native, Other: Writing Postcoloniality and Feminism.* Bloomington: Indiana University Press.
    1991   *When the Moon Waxes Red: Representation, Gender, and Cultural Politics.* New York: Routledge.

Tsemah, Mina, and Ruth Tsin
    1984   *The Attitudes of Youth toward Democratic Values.* Jerusalem: Van Leer Jerusalem Foundation.

Uchendu, Victor
    1975   The Dilemma of Ethnicity and Polity Primacy in Black Africa. In *Ethnic Identity,* ed. G. DeVos and L. Romanucci-Ross, 265–75. Palo Alto: Mayfield.

Va'ad Hapo'el Hatzioni
    1949   *Meetings of the General Council of the Zionist Movement, 1949.* Jerusalem: Zionist Executive.

Verdery, Katherine
    1983   *Transylvanian Villagers: Three Centuries of Political, Economic, and Ethnic Change.* Berkeley: University of California Press.

Wasserfall, Rahel
    1990   Bargaining for Gender Identity: Love, Sex, and Money in an Israeli Moshav. *Ethnology* 29 (4): 327–40.
    n.d   Israeli Jewish Women and the Representative of the Collective. Typescript.

Waterman, Stanley
    1969   Some Aspects of the Urban Geography of Acre, Israel. Ph.D. diss., Trinity College, University of Dublin.
    1980   Alternative Images in an Israeli Town. *Geoforum* 11:277–87.

Weil, Shalva
    1986   The Language and Ritual of Socialisation: Birthday Parties in a Kindergarten Context. *Man* 21 (2): 329–41.

Weingrod, Alex
    1979   Recent Trends in Israeli Ethnicity. *Ethnic and Racial Studies* 2 (1): 55–65.

Weingrod, Alex, and Michael Gurevitch
    1977   Who Are the Israeli Elites? *Jewish Journal of Sociology* 19 (1): 67–77.

Weinstock, Nathan
    1989   *Zionism: False Messiah.* Ed. and trans. Alan Adler. 2d ed. London: Pluto.

Weiss, Meira
    1997   Bereavement, Commemoration, and Collective Identity in Contemporary Israeli Society. *Anthropological Quarterly* 70 (2): 91–101.

West, Cornel
    1992   A Matter of Life and Death. *October* 61 (summer): 20–23.

Willis, Paul
    1977   *Learning to Labour.* Westmead: Saxon House.

Winter, Percy H.
      1944   *Survey and Report: Preservation and Reconstruction of Acre.* Jerusa-
              lem: Government of Palestine, Public Works Department.
Wolf, Eleanor P.
      1963   The Tipping Point in Racially Changing Neighborhoods. *Journal of
              the American Institute of Planners* 29 (3): 217–22.
Worsley, Peter
      1984   *The Three Worlds: Culture and World Development.* Chicago: Univer-
              sity of Chicago Press.
Xenos, Nicholas
      1989   Intifadah. *Grand Street* 9 (1): 229–36.
Yashar, Rabbi Baruch
      1953   *Birurim* [Clarifications]. Tel Aviv: Heritage.
Yehieli, M.
      n.d   *V'eleh Toldot 'Akko* [This is Acre's history]. Acre: Abu Dahmon.
Young, Crawford
      1983   The Temple of Ethnicity. *World Politics* 35 (4): 652–62.
Young, James E.
      1988   *Writing and Rewriting the Holocaust: Narrative and the Consequences
              of Interpretation.* Bloomington: Indiana University Press.
Yuval-Davis, Nira
      1987   The Jewish Collectivity. In *Women in the Middle East,* ed. Khamsin
              Collective, 60–93. London: Zed.
      1989   National Reproduction and "the Demographic Race" in Israel. In
              Woman-Nation-State, ed. Nira Yuval-Davis and Floya Anthias, 92–
              109. New York: St. Martin's.
Yuval-Davis, Nira, and Floya Anthias, eds.
      1989   *Woman-Nation-State.* New York: St. Martin's Press.
Zanbank-Wilf, Aliza
      1958   Hagan K'markiv B'yetzirat Avirat Khag B'Bayit [The kindergarten
              as a component in creating a holiday atmosphere at home]. In
              Khagim U'moadim B'hinuch [*Holidays and Festivals in Education*],
              57–59.
Zuckermann, Mosche
      1988–89 The Curse of Forgetting: Israel and the Holocaust. Trans.
              Nanette Funk. *Telos* 78:43–54.
Zulaika, Joseba
      1988   *Basque Violence: Metaphor and Sacrament.* Reno: University of Ne-
              vada Press.
Zureik, Elia T.
      1979   *The Palestinians in Israel.* London: Routledge and Kegan Paul.

Index